BEGINNING
SHAREPOINT® 2013 DEVELOPN

MW00994983

BEGINNING

SharePoint® 2013 Development

BEGINNING

SharePoint® 2013 Development

Steve Fox
Chris Johnson
Donovan Follette

WILEY

John Wiley & Sons, Inc.

Beginning SharePoint® 2013 Development

Published by
John Wiley & Sons, Inc.
10475 Crosspoint Boulevard
Indianapolis, IN 46256
www.wiley.com

Copyright © 2013 by John Wiley & Sons, Inc., Indianapolis, Indiana

Published simultaneously in Canada

ISBN: 978-1-118-49584-1
ISBN: 978-1-118-49586-5 (ebk)
ISBN: 978-1-118-65477-4 (ebk)
ISBN: 978-1-118-65487-3 (ebk)

Manufactured in the United States of America

10 9 8 7 6 5 4 3 2 1

For general information on our other products and services please contact our Customer Care Department within the United States at (877) 762-2974, outside the United States at (317) 572-3993 or fax (317) 572-4002.

Wiley publishes in a variety of print and electronic formats and by print-on-demand. Some material included with standard print versions of this book may not be included in e-books or in print-on-demand. If this book refers to media such as a CD or DVD that is not included in the version you purchased, you may download this material at http://booksupport.wiley.com. For more information about Wiley products, visit www.wiley.com.

Library of Congress Control Number: 2012955721

ABOUT THE AUTHORS

 STEVE FOX is a Director in MCS for Microsoft with more than 17 years of IT experience ranging from natural language to Office and SharePoint and most recently to Windows Azure development. His current focus is enabling the cloud for enterprise organizations.

 DONOVAN FOLLETTE is a Sr. Technical Evangelist for Microsoft with more than 25 years of experience designing and building enterprise business applications. His current focus is on developers and helping them wrap their mind around the all-new cloud app model for Office and SharePoint 2013.

 **CHRIS JOHNSON** is an avid developer and a speaker. He is the General Manager of Provoke Solutions, Inc. and a Microsoft Gold Partner in Seattle, Washington, that is one of the world's most renowned and sought-after online experience consultancies. Provoke Solutions specializes in software solutions for SharePoint and the Microsoft technology stack (http://www.provokesolutions.com). In November 2011, Chris left Microsoft Corporation after nine and a half years where he most recently was a Senior Technical Product Manager for the SharePoint product group in Redmond, Washington, managing SharePoint's professional developer audience technical marketing programs. Chris moved to Redmond in 2007 to work on the software engineering team on the SharePoint 2010 release after working for Microsoft New Zealand. In New Zealand he consulted for customers across the Asia Pacific region on designing and implementing Content Management Server and SharePoint deployments. Chris's background is in Microsoft software development and he enjoys all things technical. He is a speaker at numerous conferences around the world such as Tech.Ed, SharePoint Best Practices Conference, SharePoint Connections, and the worldwide SharePoint Conference. Chris holds a Bachelor of Computer Science and enjoys throwing himself out of perfectly good airplanes from time to time. Contact Chris on his blog at www.looselytyped.net.

ABOUT THE TECHNICAL EDITOR

 **ANDREW CONNELL** is a developer, author, instructor, and co-founder of Critical Path Training, a SharePoint education–focused company. He has a background in content management solutions and Web development that spans back to his time as a student at the University of Florida in the late 1990s managing class sites. He has consistently focused on the challenges facing business today to maintain a current and dynamic online presence without having to rely constantly on Web developers or have a proficiency in Web technologies.

Andrew is an eight-time recipient of Microsoft's Most Valuable Professional (MVP) award (2005–2012) for Microsoft Content Management Server (MCMS) and Microsoft SharePoint Server. He has authored and contributed to numerous MCMS and SharePoint books over the years, *including Professional SharePoint 2007 Web Content Management Development* (Wrox, 2008), *Inside Microsoft SharePoint 2010* (MSPress, 2011) and (Wrox, 2010), and *Real World SharePoint 2010* (Wrox), among others, and is the author of numerous articles both for the Microsoft Developer Network (MSDN) and for various magazines.

Andrew has presented at numerous conferences in the United States, Europe, and Australia. You can find Andrew on his blog (`www.andrewconnell.com/blog`) or follow him on Twitter @andrewconnell.

CREDITS

Acquisitions Editor
Mary James

Project Editor
Victoria Swider

Technical Editor
Andrew Connell

Production Editor
Christine Mugnolo

Copy Editor
Paula Lowell

Editorial Manager
Mary Beth Wakefield

Freelancer Editorial Manager
Rosemarie Graham

Associate Director of Marketing
David Mayhew

Marketing Manager
Ashley Zurcher

Business Manager
Amy Knies

Production Manager
Tim Tate

Vice President and Executive Group Publisher
Richard Swadley

Vice President and Executive Publisher
Neil Edde

Associate Publisher
Jim Minatel

Project Coordinator, Cover
Katie Crocker

Proofreader
Sarah Kaikini, Word One New York

Indexer
Robert Swanson

Cover Designer
Elizabeth Brooks

Cover Image
© Stefano Borsani / iStockphoto

ACKNOWLEDGMENTS

FIRST, thanks to the acquisitions and editorial staff at Wiley. It's great to continue to work with such a good crew of people. Next, thanks to Andrew Connell for helping steer us in the right direction through technical editing. Also, thanks to Victoria Swider who tirelessly moved us through the editing and production process. Additionally, thanks to the many Microsoft folks who gave their time for technical questions and conversations. And last, thanks to you, the developer community. Without you, this book would not even be possible.

—STEVE FOX

THANKS to Andrew Connell, technical editor, for providing his technical expertise and insight and Victoria Swider, project editor, for her patience as the authors juggled busy travel and conference schedules to find time-slices for writing. I would also like to acknowledge my Microsoft colleagues whom I learned much from as Office and SharePoint 2013 were taking shape: Mauricio Ordonez, Rob Howard, Mike Ammerlaan, Rolando Jimenez Salgado, Gareth Pinto, Stephen Oliver, and Brady Gaster. You are all a pleasure to work with and greatly respected. And thanks to you, the reader, My hope is that this book will introduce you to the opportunity for developing a new class of productivity solutions in the form of Apps for Office and SharePoint, and that your solutions, whether built and provided behind the firewall or installed from Office.com, will find their way into the hands of the all-important end users, whose day will be a bit better because they are using your software. Enjoy!

—DONOVAN FOLLETTE

THANKS must go out to our wonderful editors and staff at Wiley for ushering me through my first technical book project. Their patience and flexibility were invaluable given the authors' hectic day jobs, speaking engagements, and travel schedules. I know at times it was like herding cats! A huge debt of gratitude to the one and only Andrew Connell who provided the elite technical air cover and expertise to keep us all on the straight and narrow and accurate! Thanks to Nick Swan and the team at Lightning Tools for their insights into real-world SharePoint application metrics. Finally, to all the folks at Microsoft who assisted with answering questions, providing support, and generally being really helpful as I wrote this book — Thank you all.

—CHRIS JOHNSON

CONTENTS

PART II: FUNDAMENTAL SHAREPOINT 2013 DEVELOPMENT BUILDING BLOCKS

CHAPTER 6: DEVELOPING, INTEGRATING, AND BUILDING APPLICATIONS IN SHAREPOINT 2013

CHAPTER 7: PACKAGING AND DEPLOYING SHAREPOINT 2013 APPS

INTRODUCTION

SHAREPOINT IS AN AMAZINGLY BROAD collaborative platform; it is used by many people for a range of collaborative activities such as content management, project management, social networking, information governance, and so on. In SharePoint 2013 you will find some significant and evolutionary leaps — specifically the movement toward a cloud-based approach to building and deploying SharePoint apps. For those of you who are new to SharePoint, this won't seem like such a radical evolution — especially those of you who are Web developers today. However, for those of you who are returning SharePoint enthusiasts, SharePoint 2013 is quite an evolution for how you build and develop SharePoint applications.

What you'll learn in this book is that SharePoint 2013 has a lot to offer the developer. You can move from the small-scale development project where you're building custom apps such as Web Parts, to the larger, enterprise-grade solution that leverages cloud-hosted apps and services, and integrates with other Microsoft and non-Microsoft technologies. This is the incredible part about SharePoint — it is a platform with huge potential in multiple directions. If you're a beginning SharePoint developer, you should strap yourself in, because you're in for a great ride.

WHO THIS BOOK IS FOR

Simply put, this book is aimed at the developer who is new to SharePoint. The book assumes that you have some programming experience and a passion to learn how to develop for SharePoint, but this book does not assume that you've programmed against SharePoint before.

With regard to your general development background, the two assumptions in this book are that you have some familiarity with Web development, and you have an understanding of .NET programming. With regard to Web development, this book assumes that you understand HTML, and you might have an understanding of Cascading Style Sheets (CSS), Extensible Markup Language/Extensible Stylesheet Language (XML/XSL), and dynamic languages such as JavaScript. You might also have a light understanding of ASP.NET and are looking to better understand how to leverage these skills with SharePoint. In any case, you have some understanding of the fundamentals of Web and .NET development, and are looking to apply that knowledge to the SharePoint space.

As you work throughout this book, your knowledge will certainly grow in the previously mentioned areas. The authors recommend that you take some time to ensure you're up to speed on the HTML5 standards and how you can leverage JavaScript as well as the many JQuery libraries that are becoming increasingly important in Web development. Understanding the design concepts behind cloud computing is also beneficial.

If you are already familiar with SharePoint, then you're starting from a point of advantage. For example, you'll recognize SharePoint artifacts such as lists, document libraries, and of course you'll see familiar APIs in the Server Object Model and Client-Side Object Model. However, don't expect everything to be exactly the same in SharePoint 2013 as it was in SharePoint 2010. For example, there is a broader array of SharePoint services available; you'll need to start thinking about the new cloud-hosted app model, as well as treating core artifacts within SharePoint as "apps," and so on.

Irrespective of whether you're new to SharePoint or a returning developer from SharePoint 2010, you're going to get something out of this book. For the new SharePoint developer, think of this book as a new journey for you where we'll lay out the fundamentals to get you going. For the returning SharePoint developer, think of this book as a refresher and guide to what's new.

WHAT THIS BOOK COVERS

Just like SharePoint 2010 was, SharePoint 2013 is a significant leap forward from its previous release, and you will find a ton of features built into the platform for you to leverage in your solution development. Because SharePoint is a broad platform that covers so much, this book also covers quite a bit of ground. As a Wrox Beginning book, though, the goal of the book is to get you started with many of the fundamentals to provide adequate knowledge for entry-level SharePoint programming and to provide preparation for advanced programming in the future.

In this book you can expect to see coverage of the following:

- ➤ Getting started with development for SharePoint 2013
- ➤ Becoming familiar with tools that you will use to develop for SharePoint
- ➤ Becoming familiar with common SharePoint development tasks
- ➤ Understanding "the cloud"
- ➤ Programming against lists and developing custom Web Parts
- ➤ Integrating line-of-business (LOB) data with SharePoint and Microsoft Office
- ➤ Building and deploying apps to the Office Store
- ➤ Creating service-oriented solutions for SharePoint
- ➤ Leveraging many of the out-of-the-box features in your SharePoint development
- ➤ Integrating SharePoint and Microsoft Office
- ➤ Implementing OAuth and security in SharePoint

This book does not cover earlier versions of SharePoint per se (you might find references to how features have changed), but does cover areas that span SharePoint Foundation 2013, SharePoint Server 2013, and Office 365, given the importance of cloud-hosted apps in this version of SharePoint. You can also expect to find references to other resources as you work through the book — resources such as blogs, Microsoft Developer Network (MSDN) articles, C9 training modules, and source code — all the things that you need to get started developing for SharePoint.

HOW THIS BOOK IS STRUCTURED

The goal is to quickly take you from the basics of SharePoint to creating a new instance of SharePoint and setting up your development environment, and then into how you can develop for SharePoint. The book is heavy on coding exercises, but tries to stick to a common set of .NET patterns to ensure you walk away understanding the different ways in which you can code for SharePoint. Moving from beginning to advanced means that you can expect the walk-throughs and chapters to become increasingly more complex as you move deeper into the book. The walk-throughs have been created to be concise and walk you through all the steps you must accomplish to complete a coding task.

The structure of the book mimics the development ramp-up cycle for SharePoint. That is, you must first understand the breadth of the SharePoint platform. You then install it and the development environment, and begin to code — the tasks are simple at first, but grow increasingly more complex. You will find that when coding against SharePoint, you might do certain development tasks more than others (such as programming against lists and creating custom Web Parts). As such, Part II covers these topics. Also, you might find that as you advance in your SharePoint development, you will need to incorporate either HTML5, Windows Azure, or Web services in your SharePoint solutions. Part III covers advanced topics such as workflow and leveraging BCS because you might need to begin to integrate different concepts into one solution, such as Web services and content types to build an external list programmatically.

This book is structured in three parts. The reason for this three-way split was to help ramp you up gradually to the different areas of SharePoint development.

Part I: Getting Started with SharePoint 2013 — Part I is about the fundamentals, and as such, covers the following areas:

Chapter 1: Introduction to SharePoint 2013 — This chapter introduces you to the fundamental concepts and areas in SharePoint.

Chapter 2: Overview of SharePoint 2013 App Model — This chapter provides an overview of the new way in which you build SharePoint apps using the SharePoint-hosted and Cloud-hosted app model.

Chapter 3: Developer Tooling for SharePoint 2013 — This chapter walks through the primary developer tools you use when building and deploying SharePoint applications.

Chapter 4: Understanding Your Development Options — This chapter discusses the different options available to a developer such as SharePoint solutions vs. apps and which APIs to use when developing your SharePoint applications.

Chapter 5: Overview of Windows Azure for SharePoint — This chapter provides an introduction to Windows Azure, a critical ingredient in cloud-hosted apps.

Part II: Fundamental SharePoint 2013 Development Building Blocks — Part II dives a little deeper into the SharePoint platform to begin discussing some of the more common areas you'll come across, and as such, covers the following:

Chapter 6: Developing, Integrating, and Building Applications in SharePoint 2013 — This chapter focuses on some of the more common developer tasks that you'll need to understand.

Chapter 7: Packaging and Deploying SharePoint 2013 Apps — This chapter discusses how you can use the developer tools to build and deploy SharePoint applications.

Chapter 8: Distributing SharePoint 2013 Apps — This chapter walks through the ways in which you distribute a SharePoint application, such as through the Office Store.

Chapter 9: Overview of the Client-Side Object Model and REST APIs — This chapter discusses how you can use the Client-Side Object Model in your SharePoint-hosted or cloud-hosted apps.

Chapter 10: Overview of OAuth in SharePoint 2013 — This chapter discusses the ways in which you need to build OAuth into your SharePoint apps to ensure your cloud-hosted apps and app events are able to integrate seamlessly with SharePoint.

Part III: Advanced Developer Topics in SharePoint 2013 — The final part of the book, Part III, covers more advanced topics, some of which you may not use until you've mastered the basics of SharePoint. The areas covered in this part are as follows:

Chapter 11: Developing Integrated Apps for Office and SharePoint Solutions — This chapter discusses the different types of integration that you can achieve by using the new Apps for Office model in your SharePoint apps.

Chapter 12: Remote Event Receivers in SharePoint 2013 — This chapter provides an in-depth view of how to develop and deploy event receivers in SharePoint.

Chapter 13: Building Line-of-Business Solutions Using Business Connectivity Services (BCS) — This chapter discusses how to integrate external systems, also known as line-of-business systems, into your SharePoint site.

Chapter 14: Developing Applications Using Office Services — This chapter explores some of the newer Office Services and walks through ways in which you can build compelling applications through services such as Excel Services or Access Services.

Chapter 15: Developing Workflow Applications for SharePoint 2013 — This chapter discusses how you can integrate custom workflow into your application to manage business processes.

By the time you finish this book, you will have a well-grounded view of SharePoint 2013 and be able to actively develop and deploy applications to SharePoint. For the new SharePoint developer, you may want to tackle the chapters in order; the book was designed to take you from least to most complex. If you're an experienced SharePoint developer, then you may find yourself jumping ahead. Either way, the goal is to collectively ensure you get something out of this book that helps you in your SharePoint journey.

WHAT YOU NEED TO USE THIS BOOK

To use this book, at a minimum you'll need to have the following:

➤ An instance (or access to an instance) of SharePoint set-up. This could be Office 365, SharePoint Foundation, or SharePoint Server. You might find for specific sections of the book you need one or more of these types of SharePoint.

➤ Visual Studio 2012 Professional or above

➤ Microsoft Office 2013 Professional

➤ SharePoint Designer 2013

➤ Windows Azure SDK and Windows Azure Tools for Visual Studio

➤ Windows Azure Subscription

Any other special requirements (for example, an Office Store account) are discussed in the individual chapter.

CONVENTIONS

To help you get the most from the text and keep track of what's happening, we've used a number of conventions throughout the book.

TRY IT OUT

The *Try It Out* is an exercise you should work through, following the text in the book.

1. They usually consist of a set of steps.

2. Each step has a number.

3. Follow the steps through with your copy of the database.

How It Works

After each *Try It Out*, the code you've typed is explained in detail.

> **WARNING** *Boxes like this one hold important, not-to-be forgotten information that is directly relevant to the surrounding text.*

> **NOTE** *Notes, tips, hints, tricks, or asides to the current discussion are offset and placed in italics like this.*

As for styles in the text:

➤ We *highlight* new terms and important words when we introduce them.

➤ We show keyboard strokes like this: Ctrl+A.

➤ We show filenames, URLs, and code within the text like so: `persistence.properties`.

➤ We present code in two different ways:

```
We use a monofont type with no highlighting for most code examples.
We use bold to emphasize code that's particularly important in the present context.
```

SOURCE CODE

As you work through the examples in this book, you may choose either to type in all the code manually or to use the source code files that accompany the book. All the source code used in this book is available for download at `http://www.wrox.com`. After you're at the site, simply locate the book's title (either by using the Search box or by using one of the title lists) and click the Download Code link on the book's detail page to obtain all the source code for the book.

> **NOTE** *Because many books have similar titles, you may find it easiest to search by ISBN; this book's ISBN is 978-1-118-49584-1.*

After you download the code, just decompress it with your favorite compression tool. Alternatively, you can go to the main Wrox code download page at `http://www.wrox.com/dynamic/books/download.aspx` to see the code available for this book and all other Wrox books.

ERRATA

We make every effort to ensure that there are no errors in the text or in the code. However, no one is perfect, and mistakes do occur. If you find an error in one of our books, like a spelling mistake or faulty piece of code, we would be very grateful for your feedback. By sending in errata you may save another reader hours of frustration and at the same time you will be helping us provide even higher quality information.

To find the errata page for this book, go to `http://www.wrox.com` and locate the title using the Search box or one of the title lists. Then, on the book details page, click the Book Errata link. On this page you can view all errata that has been submitted for this book and posted by Wrox editors. A complete book list including links to each book's errata is also available at `www.wrox.com/misc-pages/booklist.shtml`.

If you don't spot "your" error on the Book Errata page, go to www.wrox.com/contact/techsupport.shtml and complete the form there to send us the error you have found. We'll check the information and, if appropriate, post a message to the book's errata page and fix the problem in subsequent editions of the book.

P2P.WROX.COM

For author and peer discussion, join the P2P forums at p2p.wrox.com. The forums are a Web-based system for you to post messages relating to Wrox books and related technologies and interact with other readers and technology users. The forums offer a subscription feature to e-mail you topics of interest of your choosing when new posts are made to the forums. Wrox authors, editors, other industry experts, and your fellow readers are present on these forums.

At http://p2p.wrox.com you can find a number of different forums that can help you not only as you read this book, but also as you develop your own applications. To join the forums, just follow these steps:

1. Go to p2p.wrox.com and click the Register link.
2. Read the terms of use and click Agree.
3. Complete the required information to join as well as any optional information you want to provide and click Submit.

You will receive an e-mail with information describing how to verify your account and complete the joining process.

> **NOTE** You can read messages in the forums without joining P2P but to post your own messages, you must join.

After you join, you can post new messages and respond to messages other users post. You can read messages at any time on the Web. If you want to have new messages from a particular forum e-mailed to you, click the Subscribe to this Forum icon by the forum name in the forum listing.

For more information about how to use the Wrox P2P, be sure to read the P2P FAQs for answers to questions about how the forum software works as well as many common questions specific to P2P and Wrox books. To read the FAQs, click the FAQ link on any P2P page.

PART I
Getting Started with SharePoint 2013

Introduction to SharePoint 2013

WHAT YOU WILL LEARN IN THIS CHAPTER:

- ➤ Understanding what SharePoint is
- ➤ Learning about the high-level feature areas and functionality of SharePoint 2013
- ➤ Understanding the relevance of these feature areas and functionality to the developer

SharePoint 2010 launched a major evolution in the product's life — it was a first-class platform that enabled you to not only leverage a wide array of out-of-the-box features to manage collaboration, but it also provided a rich development platform. This made developing solutions powerful and relatively straightforward. With SharePoint 2013 arrives a new paradigm shift, one much more closely aligned to Microsoft's overall shift to the cloud. For those of you who have been on the SharePoint train for some time, this means thinking in a slightly different way about how you develop applications for SharePoint. For those who are new to SharePoint, welcome. You're in for one heck of a ride!

SharePoint is an exciting Web-based technology. In its fifth version, SharePoint has undergone quite a transformation from the initial releases, and the types of things you can do with SharePoint run far and wide. Those who have had the chance to see the product grow up will be surprised and happy with many of the changes that are now built into the platform. In fact, existing SharePoint developers will witness what arguably is a sea-of-change in the features and functionality that SharePoint provides, as well as an evolution in the tools supported and the developer community that rallies around the technology. Aspiring SharePoint developers will realize quite a bit of power exists in the platform and should have the capability to put it into practice by the end of this book.

SharePoint is maturing into a *cloud-centric* platform that will enable you to build and deploy a wide array of solutions, as well as take advantage of the build-and-publish model that SharePoint users and developers have come to enjoy. It has also evolved into a platform that is much more open by design. This means that developers are moving beyond what was predominantly an ASP.NET- or JavaScript-based development approach. In SharePoint 2013, you have the ability to bring your own hosted Web applications and technologies to the table and use OAuth authentication and registration hooks that are built into SharePoint to integrate those apps into the SharePoint experience. This is a significant evolution, and one not to be undersold.

Similar to SharePoint 2010, SharePoint 2013 offers such a wide array of features that claiming to be an expert across all the workloads will be challenging for any one person. You will need to dedicate some time to become an expert, but the journey will be worth it.

With that in mind, this chapter introduces you to what SharePoint is and walks through some of the high-level areas for the developer. This chapter also answers the question of what capabilities make SharePoint a platform that is interesting and compelling for you, the developer, to learn. It also helps you understand why SharePoint 2013 is evolving to the cloud.

Specific topics include discussion around programmability, new app models, platform services, and the ways in which you can build and deploy a SharePoint solution.

GETTING TO KNOW SHAREPOINT

Simply put, SharePoint 2013 (also referred to as SharePoint after this point) is a platform to support collaboration — a central Web-based portal for you to manage your own and your colleague's documents, social activities, data, and information. This definition is pretty broad, but try framing it within a scenario: you manage projects on a daily basis and must also manage teams of people across those projects. Within the project, people are having meetings, creating documents, exchanging ideas, managing schedules, and so on. Without a central place to manage these activities and documents, you're using file shares on servers; you're exchanging documents via mail; and you're using one or more different types of management software to help keep a common view of activities. Within this one scenario, you should be able to see the problem. A file share can go down anytime, so what's the backup? Documents aren't versioned. Context is lost around a project as elements are spread out across different technologies. And security around those documents is difficult to manage and control in an effective in an effective and efficient way.

Project management is but one scenario that paints a picture of collaboration. Many others exist, and this is why SharePoint has seen such broad adoption. Often companies see great advantages with SharePoint through simple document management; that is, being able to store, version, create, and manage documents in one central place. However, what these companies soon discover is that many more features are built into SharePoint such that its use goes beyond simple document management. Users soon begin to see Business Intelligence (BI) features, discoverability benefits (that is, search functions), social features, and governance abilities, among the many other areas of which they can take advantage.

Defining SharePoint by Function

To provide you with an idea of the types of things that you can do with SharePoint, Figure 1-1 breaks SharePoint out into three separate areas:

➤ **Collaboration** — As you read through this book, you'll see the notion of *collaboration* as a very strong theme for SharePoint. This is because SharePoint is about bringing people together through different types of collaboration, such as enterprise content management (ECM), Web content management (WCM), social-computing through the use of newsfeeds, discoverability of people and their skills, creating dashboards to fulfill your BI needs, and so on. Given the new app model in SharePoint 2013, collaboration is managed through apps. Developers can extend, customize, or build their own Apps for SharePoint as well manage collaboration on SharePoint.

➤ **Interoperability** — SharePoint is also about bringing this collaboration together through *interoperability*. This means Office and Web-based document integration, and the capability to build and deploy secure and custom solutions that integrate line-of-business (LOB) data with SharePoint and Office, integrating with wider Web technologies, or deploying applications to the cloud.

➤ **Platform** — As you'll see, SharePoint is a *platform* that supports not only interoperability and collaboration but also extensibility, through a rich object model, a solid set of developer tools, and a growing developer community. One of the key paradigm shifts here, though, is the notion of the cloud in SharePoint. The cloud introduces new app models: new ways of developing, deploying, and hosting SharePoint applications; new forms of authentication through OAuth; and new ways of data interoperability using OData (and REST).

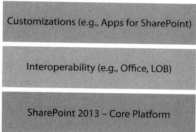

FIGURE 1-1

These are three key themes that you will find crop up throughout most discussions of SharePoint and implicitly through many of the capabilities you'll get to explore throughout this book.

So, at its essence, SharePoint is a Web-based platform that provides the following:

➤ A set of native, out-of-the-box capabilities to support productivity and collaboration

➤ An open and extensible set of APIs and services that you can use to build light apps or cloud-based apps using your own hosting technology

➤ Infrastructure to manage security and permissions against the various artifacts (for example, documents and list items)

➤ A management and configuration engine that provides deep administrative abilities, both for the cloud-hosted version of SharePoint and the on-premises SharePoint server.

Defining SharePoint by User

Depending on the role of the person who is using SharePoint, the stated definition might take on a slightly different hue.

For example, for the end user, SharePoint enhances productivity by providing a core set of connected applications that essentially act as the Web-based application platform. The applications enable people to connect using wiki sites, workspaces, lists, document libraries, and integration with Microsoft Office applications such as Outlook, Excel, and Word 2010.

From an organizational point of view, the unified infrastructure enables the organization to rally around a central point of collaboration — be it through an organizational portal, a team site, or a personal My Site. It also enables organizations to integrate LOB systems, such as SAP, Siebel, PeopleSoft, and Microsoft Dynamics, into the information worker experience through SharePoint. Furthermore, it enables you to tap into your growing cloud services and data that you might be developing and deploying.

From a developer's perspective, you can take advantage of a wide platform (arguably the widest historically for the platform) to build and deploy many different types of applications. These range from simple HTML and JavaScript applications to managed code and .NET cloud apps that are deployed to Windows Azure.

The response to business needs arrives through the capability to use SharePoint as a toolset in the everyday work lives of an organization's employees — for example, routing documents through managed processes, providing social newsfeeds and updates, or managing and tracking project documents. In essence, SharePoint represents a platform that offers the organization a lot of functionality to do many different things, with collaboration lying at the heart of them.

Introducing the User Interface

Taking a look at the SharePoint user interface at this point might be helpful for you. Although you can create sites from many different templates, Figure 1-2 shows a Team Site and calls out some of the areas of the page:

➤ Area 1 is where you can access other areas of Office 365 such as Outlook or the Site Settings.

➤ Area 2 provides a search box for you to enter queries and search the site collection.

➤ Area 3 contains some quick launch tiles that can help you get started with your site (note you can click the Remove This link to hide them).

➤ Area 4 provides a place for you to upload and view documents.

➤ Area 5 shows quick links to other areas of your Team Site.

You'll find a common set of options in many sites (such as the link bar at the top of the site). Depending on the type of site that you create, you'll find a different set of default options available. For example, some have more BI functions or governance workflow or social features built into them. This all depends on the type of site.

If you're a developer reading this book, you might be happy to know that many parts of the SharePoint development experience are customizable. For example, in Figure 1-2 you could programmatically add data from external LOB systems into your site, you could integrate a Web app from Windows Azure, or you could create a light HTML and JavaScript and deploy to your Team site. You could also customize the branding of the site. For example, Figure 1-3 shows a sample SharePoint site that has more branding. This example uses some of the native SharePoint capabilities to configure the look and feel, but you could create a much more elaborate, branded, and custom look-and-feel for any of your SharePoint sites.

FIGURE 1-2

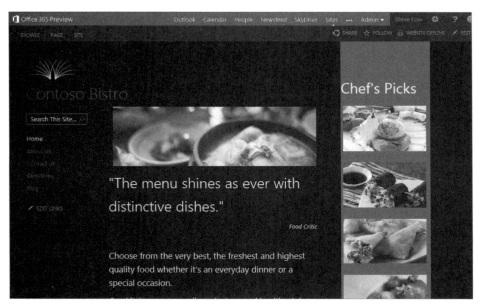

FIGURE 1-3

Thus, the Web-based experience that SharePoint provides out-of-the-box integrates core (as well as external) applications and functionality that end users can employ during their daily work lives.

In Figure 1-4, note that the default view has changed. This is because the site is now in Edit mode, which enables you to customize the SharePoint site. In this view, you can add Web parts, HTML or JavaScript apps, integrate external applications, and so on. The fact that you can quickly put a site into Edit mode, make some changes, and then save those changes back to the server is one of the great advantages of SharePoint.

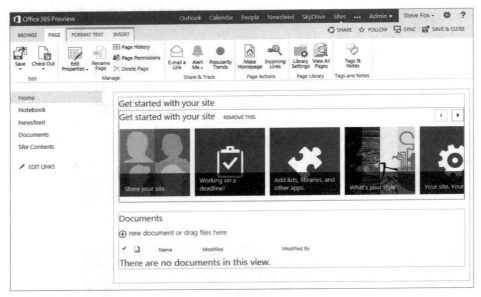

FIGURE 1-4

Introducing the Structure

The structural taxonomy of SharePoint comprises multiple levels. On the first level you have a site that is made of a template. As mentioned earlier, you have a variety of templates that you can use for a given site — either out of the box or custom. Within a site, you can create more subsites — using the same set of site templates. So it's essentially a parent site, or site collection, with subsites. Within a specific site, you then add (or create and deploy to the sites) *apps*. Now for those of you who have been around SharePoint for a while, this will feel a little weird: *Everything is now an app.* That is, lists, document libraries, form libraries, and so on are all apps — just different types of apps. For those who are new to SharePoint, this idea won't seem so jarring; thinking about a site comprising apps is a pretty natural way to think about Web platforms today. Also, as you start building apps for a marketplace, then the concept of an app (as opposed to differentiating across lists, document libraries, and so on) begins to make even more sense. Figure 1-5 shows you a small set of apps that are available to you by default within your SharePoint site.

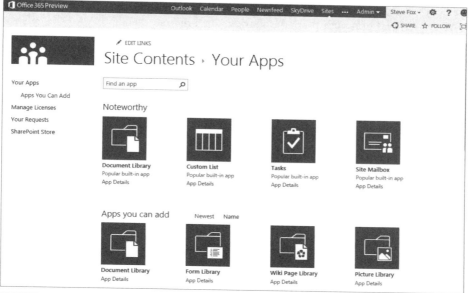

FIGURE 1-5

For organizations, SharePoint provides a one-stop shop for leveraging the SharePoint infrastructure not only for internal sites to manage your day-to-day project needs and as a business process work-flow, but also activities and infrastructure to manage your publicly facing sites. The key point is that SharePoint provides the infrastructure for many types of sites and for site and app development.

As you'll see throughout this book, the native SharePoint experience is, in many ways, customizable. Given the breadth of integration possibilities with SharePoint 2013, there's an adjunct set of tech-nologies including Windows Azure, PHP, and other Web technologies that might factor into your SharePoint development experience.

ADDRESSING THE NEEDS OF THE DEVELOPER

At its essence, SharePoint is a platform. And to see how SharePoint can help you as a developer, you must understand those platform capabilities. When you explore and learn the range of functionality that make up the platform, you'll begin to see some interesting and compelling opportunities emerge for the developer.

Take a look at a practical example. As you have seen, a business productivity platform implies having a platform for end users to make them more collaborative and productive in their day-to-day work lives — and SharePoint can certainly do that. In short order, it can be used as an application for end users. For example, a Human Resources (HR) department might use SharePoint to manage employee reviews, or a sales team might use it to manage a monthly sales-forecasting dashboard for BI.

In all of these scenarios, SharePoint first represents an end user collaboration platform, and second represents a base that skilled developers can augment or extend. So, when your sales manager comes to you (the developer) and asks you to design a SharePoint site collection that integrates daily sales data from an SAP system and plot high-potential markets on a map in the SharePoint site — so salespeople can see current sales pipeline versus opportunity areas — you wonder in what ways this type of app would manifest in SharePoint.

Let's look at this task from two perspectives:

➤ **End users** want a site they can open, manage their sales documents and spreadsheets, filter and pivot data in, and then get a quick view on the map to see where they should be targeting. They want ease of use and actionable apps.

➤ **Developers** want to craft an experience that is easy to use and intuitive — but also efficient to manage.

As a developer, you'll want to keep both perspectives in mind when performing the task. In doing so, implementing a solution for each task will likely require leveraging a combination of native features — such as document libraries and lists — and core services, capabilities, and APIs built into the platform to get you to the next level from a development perspective. You can also integrate either third-party or your own custom cloud-based services to round out the development experience.

For this particular example with your sales manager, you could use a combination of Business Connectivity Services (BCS), which is a set of services within SharePoint that enables you to connect to LOB systems and Excel Services, so you can create "pivotable" spreadsheets for salespeople. The end result of using BCS is a dynamically generated list app to contain the sales data and a document library app where you would house the spreadsheets. Therefore, you need to create two types of apps — a document library that leverages Excel Services and an external list app that loads the external LOB data. You could then integrate an HTML or JavaScript-based app that uses a cloud-deployed service to create a Bing map, and then overlay pushpins that are color-coded green for high potential, and red for low potential (or saturated) markets. This app would be the third one needed — but behind it sits a service you're plugging into (such as the Bing Maps service) and your own custom service that has the logic to create the pushpins based on some set of business rules or information. You can accomplish the development and deployment of these three apps either using apps that are deployed to an existing Team site, or by creating your own custom site with the Sales department branding.

The key takeaway from this example is that depending on what your audience requires, you can use SharePoint to create interesting experiences. You should be thinking about all these options as you design and build your SharePoint experience.

Extending SharePoint 2013

Although SharePoint represents a set of connected apps and functionality, it still has a vast array of opportunities for developers to extend and enrich the end-user experience at multiple levels. This experience is obviously important when you think about SharePoint in the context of the enterprise developer. However, when independent software vendors (ISVs) think about the custom experience they want to deploy to their customers, having a reliable platform beneath their feet that they can deploy to and use to customize their SharePoint solutions becomes vital. Furthermore, they require a place to monetize; that is, a marketplace that provides not only a place for deployment and advertising, but also a place for in-product or catalog integration. Their business depends on platform stability, predictability, accessibility, and discoverability. So what does it mean to extend SharePoint 2013?

With the entry and integration of broader cloud-hosted models, extending and building on SharePoint means a wider array of Web development partners, customers, and ISVs can participate in the SharePoint phenomenon. Some of these forms of participation include the following:

➤ Building "light" apps (for example, HTML and JavaScript apps) for SharePoint

➤ Leveraging the new cloud-hosted app models to either build Windows Azure–based apps or use technologies from a broader set of Web standards and technologies

To further understand this extensibility in a paper available through Forester Research (`www.for rester.com/rb/Research/now_is_time_to_determine_sharepoints_place/q/id/45560/t/2`) entitled, "Now Is the Time to Determine SharePoint's Place in Your Application Development Strategy," John R. Rymer and Rob Koplowitz reinforce a model of SharePoint 2013 that is composed of different layers. The two authors propose that SharePoint has an *application layer*, where end users integrate with the out-of-the-box collaboration and productivity applications; a *customization layer*, where either power users or developers can begin to customize the SharePoint experience for the end user; and a third layer, which is the *application development layer*.

This application development layer is where things get very interesting for developers. At this layer you'll mostly find the solution developer who builds and deploys (or integrates through existing SharePoint artifacts such as Web parts or event receivers) applications or business solutions. What's also interesting is how this application development layer has evolved. Figure 1-6 illustrates how SharePoint 2013 has evolved from earlier application development paradigms.

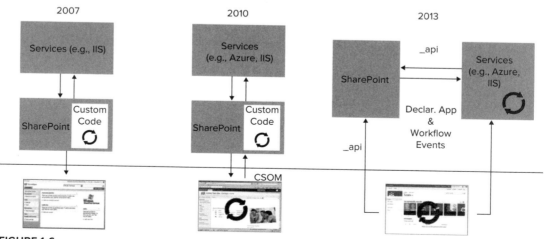

FIGURE 1-6

Figure 1-6 shows that SharePoint 2007 ran custom code or services from IIS or other servers. The custom code for the most part ran within an application pool using IIS resources. In 2010, SharePoint supported running on IIS (or other servers) and also introduced sandboxed solutions and the Client-side Object Model (CSOM), which then enabled contained solutions and client-side code to run. This version also brought the introduction of a Windows Azure that was more integrated with the SharePoint development paradigm — both on the server and on the client. In 2013, this development paradigm takes Windows Azure integration to the next level — in some cases natively using Windows Azure as the deployment, storage, and computing mechanism. Figure 1-6 illustrates workflow running in Windows Azure and hooking into SharePoint through a refactored REST API (_api). Thus, at the application development layer quite an evolution has occurred within SharePoint 2013.

> **NOTE** *If you're not familiar with Windows Azure yet, don't worry. Read Chapter 5, "Overview of Windows Azure for SharePoint"; you'll also see lots of examples throughout the book that introduce you to this new cloud technology from Microsoft.*

In light of these different layers, extending SharePoint means something slightly different in SharePoint 2013 than in past versions, including:

➤ A more open approach to development

➤ A broader integration with the cloud

➤ Support for open source and non-Microsoft technologies

➤ Bringing your own hosted apps to the SharePoint experience (Think of the Facebook app model: Facebook is a rich social platform that enables you to run apps, but those apps don't run within Facebook; they just consume parts of Facebook.)

Breaking It Down for Developers

As you might have gathered by now, SharePoint development can mean a number of things. For example, if you want to simply add an app to a page, you might consider yourself a developer. If you customize the branding of a SharePoint site, you might only have to interact with page layouts or master pages (that is, the way in which you structure content in SharePoint) but you still may be a developer. Finally, if you do deeper-level solution development, you might be creating HTML5 and JavaScript applications that interact with SharePoint through native APIs, or use .NET and the cloud-hosted app model with Windows Azure. This type of development would mean you're a developer who uses Visual Basic or C# along with potentially leveraging different application programming methods such as Model, View, and Controller (MVC) apps and REST services. As you delve more into the managed-code side of the house to build your SharePoint apps, you will, of course, enter into a more complex development paradigm.

> **NOTE** *This book doesn't get into a lot of non-Microsoft Web technologies that you could use with SharePoint. However, you can use many different types of open-source, third-party, or non-Microsoft technologies to build Web applications that you could then integrate back with SharePoint.*

Exploring the Different Levels of SharePoint Development

The point is that there are different levels of "development" in regards to SharePoint, and each level serves the *end user* of the SharePoint site in some way. One way of looking at it is to think of development as cutting across a spectrum with the following areas:

➤ **Power user:** Someone who has advanced privileges on a SharePoint site, administers permissions, manages administration of a SharePoint site, manages apps on the site, and might even create lightly customized sites for consumption.

➤ **Designer:** Someone who is largely in charge of branding and master page customizations, designing the user experience, designs graphics for the site, implements CSS or other style sheets, and so on.

➤ **Website developer:** Someone who develops managed code, mark-up code, or unmanaged/client-side code solutions for SharePoint sites. This is you!

Although those of you who have a SharePoint background might split this spectrum even further, development in general can fall within the preceding three areas. You might argue that the people performing both tasks of site-branding and app development are equally identified as developers on the SharePoint platform, but the fact is that actual development can range from using HTML5 and JavaScript to .NET and service-based technologies (that is, REST or WCF) to non-Microsoft Web technologies. This spectrum is not only symptomatic of SharePoint being a broad platform but also a symptom of the different standards, applications, and interoperability that SharePoint must support as a good citizen of the Web. Web interoperability is even more important with the 2013 release given the focus on cloud-hosted apps.

If you break down these levels of development and use across Rymer and Rob Koplowitz's different layers of SharePoint, you'll find that the largest population of SharePoint consumers interacts with the applications layer. These consumers are the end users, and they represent your core audience for building and deploying your custom applications to SharePoint. Power users of SharePoint might operate at the customization layer because they possess a high degree of SharePoint knowledge.

Then there is the Web (or SharePoint) developer. You are, in many cases, the person who develops those custom applications for SharePoint or the next killer app in the ISV ecosystem. You are also the one for whom this book was written. In some cases, you as the developer might collaborate with the power users or designers, and in others you will work independently of one another.

As a power user, designer, or Web developer, you have a number of development tools at your disposal. They range from in-browser tools, for example, Napa, to designer tools such as SharePoint Designer, to more traditional development IDEs, including Visual Studio 2012, that support managed, unmanaged, and client-side code; debugging; ALM; and so on.

With regard to developer productivity, this means that you can use either Visual Studio 2012 or SharePoint Designer (SPD) as your core set of developer tools. As a professional Web developer, you'll likely use Visual Studio as your core toolset — especially if you're a .NET programmer looking to get into the SharePoint space. As for SPD, you're more than likely going to use it to edit master pages and page layouts, as well as to build noncomplex workflows using a Visual Rules approach (for example, using Visio 2013 and SPD). As a complement to these tools, you might also use Expression Blend either as a way to build more advanced and interactive UIs (through Expression Blend) or through Expression Web for baseline Websites.

> **NOTE** *Chapter 3, "Developer Tooling for SharePoint 2013," explores developer tools in more detail.*

In terms of rich platform services, SharePoint 2013 offers the developer a wide array of methods for getting, managing, and updating objects and data within a SharePoint site. With this version of SharePoint you'll see increased investments in REST and OData, app authentication through OAuth, and, of course, a host of client-side APIs using the client-side object model to enable many different types of application programming and solution development. In this book, you'll discover new application programming interfaces (APIs), new investments in the developer, and new services that will enable you to build many different types of apps, and you'll also learn about how to enable LOB system integration to bring external data into your SharePoint applications.

> **NOTE** *This book is divided into three parts, each of which covers these new areas in increasingly greater detail and at increasingly advanced levels.*

Deploying Your Application

After you build your application, you need to deploy it. In SharePoint 2013, you can deploy two primary types of apps: Apps for SharePoint and SharePoint Solutions.

Those who have been around SharePoint before might recognize Solutions: they are the Windows SharePoint Services Solution Packages (WSPs) that represent small- to large-scale packages that are used to customize or augment SharePoint sites in some way. SharePoint Solutions are typically run as full-trust solutions and require a farm-level deployment. In SharePoint 2010, you could also run Solutions (.WSP) in a partial-trust sandboxed environment, and although this sandboxed environment still exists in 2013, it will be deprecated in the future.

> **NOTE** *Because SharePoint deployments typically comprise Web front-end servers, application servers, and database servers, the deployment and configuration of these servers is called a SharePoint farm. WSPs run at the farm level, meaning you can install and manage them across the entire SharePoint farm. Sandboxed solutions run in a special partial-trust environment that has its own measures and quota to ensure the application is isolated.*

Apps for SharePoint (.APP) are new to SharePoint 2013 and are standalone applications that provide specific configuration information and functional components to a SharePoint site. Apps for SharePoint are easy to install, use, manage, upgrade, and delete. You can add Apps for SharePoint from a corporate catalog or the Marketplace. You can also leverage two different hosting models: one that is a lighter app and is hosted within SharePoint (think HTML and JavaScript apps) and one that is hosted within the cloud-hosted model (think Windows Azure–hosted apps).

Within these different types of SharePoint deployment techniques, you can do the following:

➤ Import a standard Windows SharePoint Services Solution Package (WSP) into your SharePoint farm.

➤ Build and deploy a solution to a SharePoint instance within the corporate firewall.

➤ Build and deploy solutions to a SharePoint site hosted on the wider Internet.

➤ Package and deploy the .APP to the cloud, but configure and register it to load in SharePoint.

As you think about SharePoint 2013 development, keep the following things in mind:

➤ SharePoint's new direction is more cloud-centric. You should be thinking about this from design to deployment.

➤ SharePoint has a rich object model, as well as a set of services and APIs that you can leverage when developing custom solutions.

➤ Visual Studio 2012 has a mature, out-of-the-box experience for building and deploying SharePoint solutions.

➤ You can build and debug SharePoint sites remotely.

➤ A number of ways are available to interact with SharePoint data (for example, the client-side object model).

➤ You can leverage BCS to build rich LOB apps.

➤ Multiple integration points exist across other Microsoft and third-party applications (such as Office 2010, SAP, PeopleSoft, Microsoft Dynamics, Microsoft Silverlight, and so on).

➤ A cloud-based deployment methodology now exists for SharePoint 2013 that is defined using the .APP deployment.

➤ You can deploy SharePoint 2010 solutions on premises or to the cloud (that is, SharePoint Online). However, the future is deployment to the cloud.

These points represent just a sampling of what you can do with SharePoint, and the goal of this book is to show you how you can get started with all of these tasks and more. Keep in mind that when SharePoint references business productivity, it not only means for the applications that you'll be building and customizing for your end users, but also for the developers as you build apps that deploy into this platform for business productivity.

SHAREPOINT 2013: THE PLATFORM

SharePoint maintains a high-level architecture that is made up of a number of components (see Figure 1-7). You first install the core software on Windows so you can create SharePoint farms. A SharePoint farm is, in essence, one or more servers that make up your SharePoint instance. As a developer you should understand the three-tiered structure and roles of the SharePoint farm architecture, which includes a Web server role (a fast, load-balanced, lightweight server that responds to user requests and loads Web pages), Application server role (which provides the service features for SharePoint such as Excel Services), and Database server role (which stores content and service data). Your apps may interact with any one or all of these server roles.

You can have a standalone server acting as the entire farm (for example, all the components listed in Figure 1-7 installed or working on one machine). For testing and light workloads, this configuration might be adequate, depending on the hardware specifications. For larger organizational deployments, inclusive of failover and redundancy, a one-server farm is not adequate. However, the Windows operating system is your underlying install base — specifically, Windows Server 2008, 2008 R2, and Windows Server 2012. SharePoint heavily leverages SQL Server as its underlying content database and ASP.NET/IIS as the application service server. You can then install either SharePoint Foundation (the free version) or SharePoint Server (which is loaded with enterprise-grade features),

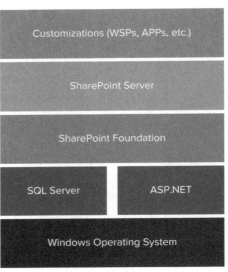

FIGURE 1-7

on top of which you would build and install your customizations. Or, as an alternative to installing SharePoint Foundation or SharePoint Server, you can sign up for Office 365, which provisions and manages the underlying infrastructure for you but still gives you the power of programmability.

SharePoint Installation Types

When you install SharePoint, you can choose different types of deployments and installation types. There are three main ways to install and use SharePoint.

SharePoint Foundation

SharePoint Foundation ships as a free, downloadable install and represents the foundational parts of SharePoint. It includes a number of features such as security and administration, user and Team site collaboration, and a number of apps (such as document libraries and lists). In essence, it provides a baseline set of features that enable you to get started with both using and developing for SharePoint.

Although the functionality that ships in SharePoint Foundation is less broad than that which ships in SharePoint Server, downloading and installing SharePoint Foundation costs you nothing. You can get up and running very quickly with this version and begin your development work using it. In SharePoint 2013, though, you also have the ability to create SharePoint Online sites very quickly — and have a rich development model there as well.

SharePoint Server

SharePoint Server offers a wealth of features that extend upon those offered in SharePoint Foundation. These features include additional app types, Office server-side services such as Word and Excel Services, enhanced search versions, enhanced BI, and much more.

> **NOTE** You can get more information from an IT pro perspective on topics such as what's new in SharePoint 2013, installation methods, farm architecture, and more from the following TechNet article: http://technet.microsoft.com/en-us/sharepoint/fp142366.aspx.

The following list provides a sampling of some of the services available in SharePoint Server:

> ➤ **Access Services:** Allows creation of new Access service applications using the Access 2013 Preview client. View, edit, and interact with Access Services databases in a browser.

> ➤ **Access Services 2010:** Allows continued maintenance of SharePoint 2010 Access service applications by using Access 2010 clients and Access 2013 Preview clients. Does not allow users to create new applications.

> ➤ **App Management Service:** Allows you to install apps from the internal app catalog or the public SharePoint store.

> ➤ **Business Data Connectivity:** Access line-of-business data systems.

> ➤ **Excel Services:** View and interact with Excel files in a browser.

> ➤ **Machine Translation Service:** Performs automated machine translation.

> ➤ **Managed Metadata Service:** Access managed taxonomy hierarchies, keywords, and social tagging infrastructure as well as content type publishing across site collections.

> ➤ **PerformancePoint:** Provides the capabilities of PerformancePoint Services.

> ➤ **PowerPoint Conversion:** Converts PowerPoint presentations to various formats.

> ➤ **Search:** Crawls and indexes content and serves search queries.

> ➤ **Secure Store Service:** Provides single sign-on authentication to access multiple applications or services.

> ➤ **State Service:** Provides temporary storage of user session data for SharePoint Server components.

> ➤ **Usage and Health Data Collection:** Collects farm-wide usage and health data and provides the ability to view various usage and health reports.

> ➤ **User Profile:** Adds support for My Sites, profile pages, social tagging, and other social computing features.

> ➤ **Visio Graphics Service:** Views and refreshes published Microsoft Visio diagrams in a Web browser.

> ➤ **Word Automation Services:** Performs automated bulk document conversions.

> ➤ **Work Management:** Provides task aggregation across work management systems, including Microsoft SharePoint Products, Microsoft Exchange Server, and Microsoft Project Server.

> ➤ **Microsoft SharePoint Foundation Subscription Settings Service:** Tracks subscription IDs and settings for services that are deployed in partitioned mode. Windows PowerShell only.

You can also choose to purchase the Internet-specific edition, SharePoint for Internet Sites, which provides rich publishing templates and workflow that you can use to create and deploy SharePoint sites to the wider Web (for example, building a scalable SharePoint site for public, anonymous access).

Office 365

Office 365 has emerged as a third, fully cloud-hosted model for SharePoint — as opposed to hosting your own farm in your own on-premises Data Center. It has also become a great place where you can develop rich applications (both as SharePoint-hosted and cloud-hosted apps) and scale without the cost of managing the on-premises infrastructure. It doesn't have all the same services and features as SharePoint Server, but does carry with it some great development capabilities.

As a developer, you have the capability to customize any of the SharePoint editions, whether it's SharePoint Foundation, Server, or Office 365. For example, beyond thematic or branding customizations, you can also develop and deploy custom solutions to each of these SharePoint versions. There are .NET applications that you build using C# or Visual Basic and then deploy into SharePoint as .WSPs or .APPs, or there are lighter-weight apps such as HTML5 and JavaScript apps that you can also deploy. What's important to understand is how that customization opportunity varies across the different versions; you'll explore this throughout the book to understand how to choose across these options.

SharePoint 2013 Capabilities

A default set of capabilities (or features) is built into SharePoint that enables you to take advantage of the platform without doing any development. You can also use or extend these core capabilities when building your apps. Microsoft has historically referred to these capabilities as *workloads*. These workloads provide a way to talk about the different capabilities of SharePoint coming together, and you should see these workloads as not only representing a core set of related applications but also as opportunities for your application development.

For those who are experienced SharePoint developers, you'll remember that Microsoft described the core capabilities for the SharePoint through workloads (seen in many 100-level presentations on SharePoint). In SharePoint 2010, these workloads were:

- ➤ **Sites:** Representing the different types of sites available for use and the features within these sites
- ➤ **Communities:** Representing the community and social features such as blogs and wikis
- ➤ **Content:** Representing core enterprise content management features
- ➤ **Search:** Representing the search-driven features
- ➤ **Insights:** Representing business intelligence features such as KPIs
- ➤ **Composites:** Representing the ability to integrate external applications by using, for example, Business Connectivity Services

These previous workloads have not gone away in SharePoint 2013; moreover, Microsoft has extended them to add more features and provide tighter integration.

Table 1-1 lists a sampling of the core capabilities for SharePoint 2013. Those of you who are experienced developers will see a lot of familiar areas because a lot of what you had in SharePoint 2010 is still available in SharePoint 2013, with a number of added areas. For example, note from the services listed previously in the "SharePoint Installation Types" section that Machine Translation Service, Access Services, App Management Service, and Work Management Service are new to SharePoint 2013. Furthermore, rather than Office Web Apps being a service, it is now a separate server product — which for IT pros will impact the design of your SharePoint farm topology. Also, what was FAST search in 2010 as a separate server product has been subsumed within SharePoint 2013 — which is fantastic because it improves the search experience immensely in this release. The whole movement to the cloud in general is a major shift in the way of thinking about SharePoint development; it is simultaneously exciting and challenging as developers need to think about app design and deployment in different ways than before.

Each of the example capabilities in Table 1-1 offers many different development opportunities.

TABLE 1-1: Sample SharePoint Capabilities

CAPABILITY	NATIVE FEATURES	EXAMPLE EXTENSIBILITY
Sites	Sites is where you'll predominantly find the collaborative aspects of SharePoint. Sites contain an abundance of features, including the capability to create, store, and retrieve data, and manage, tag, and search for content, documents, and information. You also have connectivity into the Microsoft Office 2013 client applications through the list and document library.	Sites, site templates, Apps for SharePoint, workflow, master pages, site pages
Social	Provides social and social networking capabilities, newsfeeds, and profile searching and tagging, along with the capability to search, locate, and interact with people through their skills, organizational location, relationships, and rating of content.	Search customization, rating and tagging capabilities, blogs, wikis, metadata tags
Content	Contains the capability to explore, search, and manage content using Web pages, apps, workflow, or content types.	Apps for SharePoint, workflows, Word or Excel Services
Search	The ability to search content inside and outside of SharePoint in a rich and dynamic way with real-time document views through Office Web Apps. Also, the integration of information in structured database systems and on-premises or cloud-based LOB systems such as SAP, Siebel, and Microsoft Dynamics.	SharePoint Search, Search customization, Business Data Connectivity (BDC)

continues

TABLE 1-1 *(continued)*

CAPABILITY	NATIVE FEATURES	EXAMPLE EXTENSIBILITY
Insights	Predominantly about BI and support, for example, the capability to integrate Microsoft Access into SharePoint; leverage Excel and SQL Server to access and display data on a Web page; enable the use of dashboards and key performance indicators (KPIs) to transform raw data into actionable information.	Excel Services, Access Services, dashboards, BDC, PerformancePoint Services
Interoperability	Ranges from LOB integration to Office integration through the new Apps for Office application model (think HTML and JavaScript-fueled custom task panes that link to cloud services instead of VSTO managed code add-ins) to custom solution development.	BDC, Apps for Office, custom development
Branding	Changing the look and feel of your site through built-in template changes or more detailed and organizationally driven branding.	Out-of-the-box configuration (for look and feel), master pages and customized Apps for SharePoint

You will discover many more ways to develop for SharePoint as your journey deepens and you become more familiar with all the different facets of the SharePoint capabilities. For a complete list of updates for SharePoint 2013, visit: `http://technet.microsoft.com/en-us/library/ff607742(v=office.15)`.

Site Collections and Sites

The site is the core artifact to SharePoint and represents the starting point for developers; that is, you can't start developing until you have created a site collection. A variety of site templates are available for you to use. Figure 1-8 shows a selection of default templates from which you can choose when creating a new site collection. This example includes some of the choices available for creating a new site collection within an Office 365 instance, but a similar set of templates are available within SharePoint Foundation and Server. The ones in Figure 1-8 are only a subset of those available. To view the other ones, when creating a new site collection in the new site collection dialog click the Meetings, Enterprise, Publishing, or Custom tabs to see more. Each of these tabs contains specific templates that you can use for those purposes — for example, managing meetings, blogs, short-term document workspaces, longer-term projects, and, of course, building custom templates.

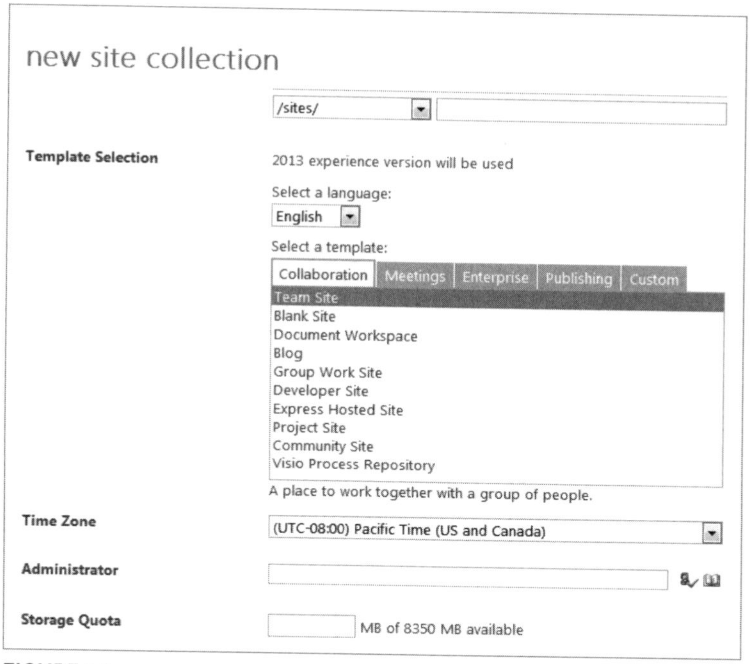

new site collection
/sites/
Template Selection
2013 experience version will be used
Select a language:
English
Select a template:
Collaboration
Meetings
Enterprise
Publishing
Custom
Team Site
Blank Site
Document Workspace
Blog
Group Work Site
Developer Site
Express Hosted Site
Project Site
Community Site
Visio Process Repository
A place to work together with a group of people.
Time Zone
(UTC-08:00) Pacific Time (US and Canada)
Administrator
Storage Quota
MB of 8350 MB available

FIGURE 1-8

Because you need a SharePoint site as a starting point, let's first go ahead and create a SharePoint site. This exercise assumes you have an Office 365 tenancy up and running. At the time of writing, you could go to: `http://www.microsoft.com/office/preview/en` and click the Try button, and then under the Enterprise category click Try. You'll then be guided through a short wizard to provision an Office 365 instance.

TRY IT OUT Creating Your First SharePoint Site

To create a simple Team site within your Office 365 instance:

1. Navigate to the administration portal of your Office 365 portal: `https://portal.microsoftonline.com/admin/default.aspx`. Enter your Office 365 user ID (for example, `superme@mydomain.onmicrosoft.com`) and a password.
2. Click the Admin drop-down list and select SharePoint, which opens the SharePoint Administrator Center, (see Figure 1-9).

Outlook
Calendar
People
Newsfeed
SkyDrive
Sites
Admin
Steve Fox
Office 365 Preview
Exchange
Lync
SharePoint

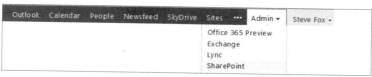

FIGURE 1-9

3. In the SharePoint Administration Center, click Site Collections — located on the left side of the screen.

4. Under the Site Collections tab, select New and then click Private Site Collection as shown in Figure 1-10.

FIGURE 1-10

5. In the new site collection dialog (shown in Figure 1-11), provide a Title and a Public Website Address, select a Template (for this example choose the Developer Site under the Collaboration tab), leave the Time Zone to the default setting, add yourself as the Administrator, and provide a Storage Quota and Server Resource Quota.

6. Click OK.

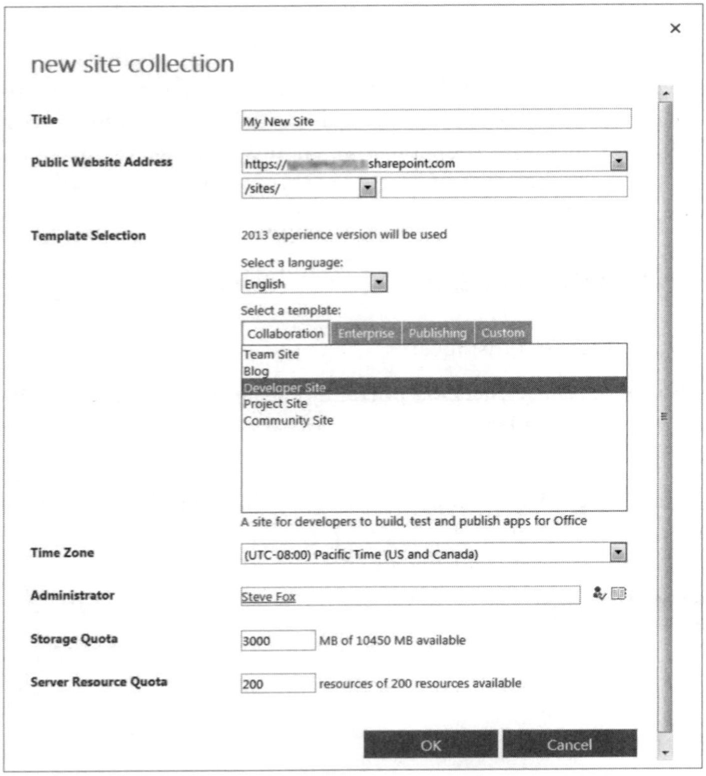

FIGURE 1-11

7. Wait a couple of minutes while Office 365 provisions the new site using the Developer Site template. When it's done, click the link to your new site, shown in Figure 1-12: `https://mydomain.sharepoint.com/sites/dev`.

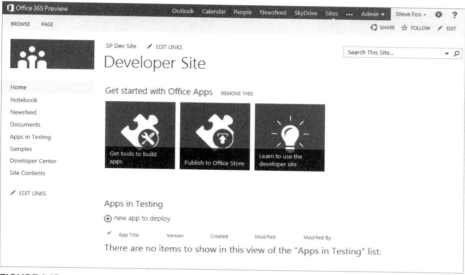

FIGURE 1-12

The new site should look similar to Figure 1-12. Go ahead and explore the site. You can click the live tiles at the top of the site, click the links on the left-hand side of the site, add subsites to this site collection, and so on.

How It Works

The baseline artifact that you created here was a site collection. The site collection in this case was a developer-specific site and represents the uppermost root site that you'll work from within SharePoint. You can now add default apps (such as lists or document libraries), create and deploy Apps for SharePoint, configure the look and feel of the site, and so on.

The site collection is a site that you can customize and interact with. You grow your SharePoint site collection by adding additional Websites to it. Any site you create underneath the site collection is called a *subsite*. This might seem confusing, but just think of the site collection being the *parent* and the sites within that collection being the *children*. This is important because by default children sites inherit the parent site's properties (such as permissions).

Creating the site collection is the most fundamental development task within SharePoint; once you've completed this, you're ready to begin building apps. To do so, it helps to understand the types of APIs that are available to you.

SharePoint 2013 APIs

After you create a new site collection, you now have the fundamental parent object in place to begin coding against. As a developer, you'll want to understand what you can do with this site now that it's created. This requires a baseline understanding of the available APIs and services. You'll want to be most familiar with two sets of object model levels: the server object model and the client-side object model.

Server Object Model

The server object model is reserved for full-instance SharePoint Foundation or SharePoint Server installations. You essentially have *carte blanche* access to the server when you install and host it yourself. It is also the broadest of the available APIs within the managed SharePoint classes. You can build many different types of applications using the server object model for tasks such as document library or list creation or manipulation, retrieving user information, site administration, backup, taxonomy and metadata management, and so on. The bulk of the server object model classes are available in the `Microsoft.SharePoint` namespace.

The server object model is available through a set of assemblies that are deployed to the global assembly cache (GAC), so you must deploy apps on the server for them to use these classes and libraries. However, you can do quite a lot with them. For example, the following code snippet sets the title and description for a list called Tasks and then calls the `Update` method to update the changes:

```
SPList myTaskList = mySPTaskSite.Lists["Tasks"];
myTaskList.Title="Sales Task List";
myTaskList.Description="A list of sales tasks.";
myTaskList.Update();
```

Client-side Object Model

The client-side object model is also available for your use in remote or client-side applications. These applications could be .NET, Silverlight, or one of the new additions to SharePoint 2013, the mobile API. This is significant because it provides you with the ability to create and deploy apps that are not necessarily dependent on server-side resources. For example, the following code snippet shows a sampling of SharePoint client-side code. You can see right away that the client-side object model looks somewhat different; in this snippet, you're setting the context for your SharePoint site, loading it, and then calling the `ExecuteQuery()` method — which executes everything that has been set before that line of code (think of a more optimized, batch processing approach). The final line of code sets the `Text` property of the `lblSPLabel` object (a label) to be the title of the SharePoint site.

```
ClientContext context = new ClientContext("http://MySharePointSite");
Web web = context.Web;
context.Load(web);
context.ExecuteQuery();
lblSPLabel.Text = web.Title;
```

JavaScript Object Model

SharePoint 2013 also has a JavaScript object model. This is an extension to what is available in the client-side object model and provides an opportunity for you to build a broad variety of SharePoint-hosted apps that can further integrate with HTML5, JQuery, and other Web technologies.

Moving Beyond the Models

Beyond the server object model and client-side object model, many other ways exist that you can build applications and solutions for SharePoint. For example, you can use a rich set of OData and REST (Representational State Transfer) services to interact with SharePoint data. Note also that the client-side object model has many REST counterparts to ensure you have multiple ways to build your Web apps. The REST services within SharePoint support both Atom and JSON formats.

Within each SharePoint site that you create, you're going to find many different opportunities to create and program against data. In the world of SharePoint, *data* can mean many different things, such as:

➤ Integrating with Access Services

➤ Interacting with SQL Server data

➤ Interacting with service endpoints through BDC to integrate with LOB and non-Microsoft systems

➤ Leveraging SQL Server Reporting Services or PerformancePoint Server to bring enhanced BI into your solutions

➤ Coding against data that might come from a SharePoint list where users manually enter the list data, and you programmatically code against it

To help with data programmability, you can use both the server- and client-side object models, but WCF Data Services are also supported within SharePoint. This enables you to interact with data through a LINQ provider and use LINQ syntax in .NET or Silverlight applications. For example, you can target both `listdata.svc` for list data or `client.svc` for accessing SharePoint entities beyond list data.

The preceding APIs represent a core set of ways in which you can program against SharePoint — from the fully self-hosted server instance to the cloud-hosted Office 365. Beyond these core APIs and services, you'll find you can programmatically interact with many of the services that ship with SharePoint Foundation or Server. You'll also find that you can build and deploy cloud-hosted apps (whether to Windows Azure or to other domains or Web technologies).

Many of you who will develop for SharePoint may also administer certain aspects of your SharePoint site. This might mean that you have to install and configure SharePoint, understand how to upgrade some of your solutions from SharePoint 2010 to 2013, or even create new Web applications or sites using the Central Administration site functions. Because cases may occur where you want to leverage the capabilities built into SharePoint Central Administration, the following section provides an overview of interacting with SharePoint 2013 in this manner.

SHAREPOINT CENTRAL ADMINISTRATION

Although this book is not on administration, it is worth having a high-level introduction to the topic. After you install SharePoint 2013 (Foundation or Server), a separate site collection is created for your use for performing the different administrative functions that you might do on a daily basis. This site collection is called the Central Administration site. This site collection is run as its own Web application in IIS and is separate from the site collections you create, but it is still the central point of administration for your SharePoint site. All farm server administrators can access this site, and, much like your regular SharePoint sites, you can edit and customize the Central Administration site. Figure 1-13 shows the SharePoint Central Administration site.

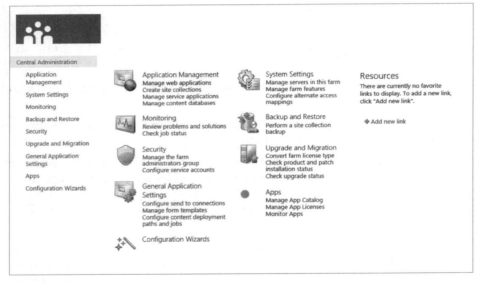

FIGURE 1-13

If you sign up for an Office 365 instance, you also have an administration site that you will certainly use. You saw this already in the exercise you walked through earlier, and in Figure 1-14 you can see a variety of site collection administration features — including BCS content type management, profile management, term store management, and search management, among others.

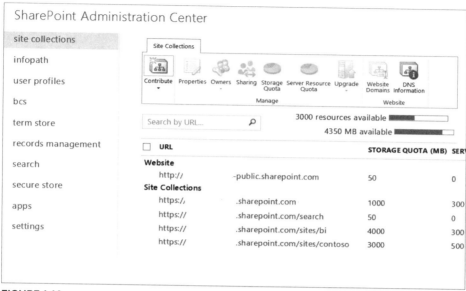

FIGURE 1-14

Within these administrative features you can manage a number of activities, which are broken out into the following nine areas:

- ➤ Application management
- ➤ Monitoring
- ➤ Security
- ➤ General application settings
- ➤ System settings
- ➤ Backup and restore
- ➤ Upgrade and migration
- ➤ Configuration wizard
- ➤ Apps

The following sections explain how to use the Central Administration site to manage activities across all of these nine areas.

Application Management

Application Management is the place where you can accomplish tasks such as create new Web applications and site collections, and, more generally, manage the services that are installed on your SharePoint site (for example, Excel Services or BCS) and manage your content database. Using the application management options, you can accomplish tasks such as modify the properties of the content database, activate features, create new site collections, and so on.

> **NOTE** *The content database is a SQL Server that stores SharePoint data, and is the reason why SharePoint takes a dependency on SQL Server upon installation.*

Monitoring

Monitoring is the central place within Central Administration to manage reporting, monitoring, and the status of your SharePoint site. The Monitoring site contains three areas:

➤ **Health status:** Health status provides a place for you to see the status of different services on your SharePoint Server (such as Visio services or farm-level services). You can see which services are failing, for example, through reports you access in this area. Health status also enables you to define rules (such as the scheduling of application pool recycles).

➤ **Timer jobs:** Timer jobs enable you to define specific jobs to run and when to run them (such as search crawl log cleanup or audit log trimming jobs).

➤ **Reporting:** Reporting provides you with a set of tools that enables you to create and manage reports, run diagnostic logging, and view reports on various server-side activities.

Security

Security covers a number of areas, including the management of administrator accounts, the configuration and management of service accounts, the management of password change settings and policies, and the specifications of authentication providers, trusted identity providers, antivirus settings, blocked file types, self-service security, and secure token services. The security settings in this area supplement the security in the main browser UI, where users and site administrators can assess specific permissions that relate to users for their sites.

General Application Settings

The General Application Settings site is where you configure a number of general options for your SharePoint site collections and sites. For example, you'll often find that you want to have the capability for your SharePoint site to send mail to users. You configure these options from within this part of the site.

Also, in the context of WCM, you might want to manage a number of deployment and approval options (such as content deployment location and approvers of that content). You also manage that type of activity from within the General Application Settings.

In general, think of this site as the generic settings for your SharePoint sites.

System Settings

Converse to using the SharePoint site settings, you might also want to configure more server-centric settings such as farm-level or access features, or even manage the services (for example, Excel Services) that are available to users of the site collection. You manage these types of settings from within the System Settings site.

Backup and Restore

At some point, you might find that you must back up and restore your SharePoint site. The backup and restore features within Central Administration enable you to create and schedule regular back-ups for your SharePoint, perform ad hoc backups, restore from a previously backed-up SharePoint site, and so on. Essentially, this is your point of entry if you want to ensure that you have a failover plan for backing up a site.

Although you might think you'll never need to use the backup and restore features, sometimes heightened permissions sets converge with mistakes, which often result in new users deleting parts of a site by accident — which might include something you've created as a developer.

Upgrade and Migration

At some point, you might find yourself wanting to upgrade from one version of SharePoint to another — for example, moving from SharePoint Standard to SharePoint Enterprise. This requires a license and some facility to upgrade the server.

You can do this type of action from within the Upgrade and Migration part of the Central Administration site. Note that you can also install service patches and check on installation and upgrade progress from within this part of the administration toolset.

Configuration Wizard

The Configuration Wizard is simply a step-by-step wizard that configures your SharePoint server for you. You should have seen this wizard when you first installed SharePoint. However, if you want to run it again after installation to change some of the configurations on your SharePoint server, you can do so.

Apps

Apps is a new category within the Central Administration site that enables you to manage different facets of the apps that are installed on your SharePoint instance. For example, you can use Apps to manage the licenses, ensure that apps are running and performing in an error-free way, and also manage the App Catalog.

SUMMARY

This chapter provides a first look at SharePoint — both for those who have never seen it and for those who are experienced SharePoint developers.

In this chapter, SharePoint is broadly defined as a business productivity platform for the enterprise and the Internet. More specifically, for the developer (and in the context of this book), you should see SharePoint as a platform that supports developer productivity, has extensive platform services, and can support multiple deployment options. With SharePoint you can leverage an abundance of APIs, a rich server and client-side object model, and a powerful set of services to create some very compelling applications. A great set of tools is also available that will support your efforts at evolving or improving your SharePoint development skills.

EXERCISES

Answers to Exercises can be found in Appendix A.

1. Define what SharePoint is for both the end user and the developer.

2. What are the different types of applications you can build for SharePoint 2013?

3. What are some of the key services in SharePoint 2013?

4. What are the two different types of object models in SharePoint, and how might you use them?

5. Create a new SharePoint site using the Team site template. Add a new list and document library. Add list items to the list and add documents to the document library.

▶ **WHAT YOU LEARNED IN THIS CHAPTER**

ITEM	DESCRIPTION
SharePoint	Collaborative platform for many different types of organizations.
SharePoint for the Developer	SharePoint is about developer productivity, the availability of rich platform services, and the capability to manage and deploy your applications with maximum flexibility.
SharePoint Foundation	Core edition for SharePoint. It ships as a free download.
SharePoint Server	The Enterprise edition of SharePoint (full-featured) referred to as SharePoint throughout the book.
Office 365	Cloud-hosted version of Office and SharePoint that provides you with a rich version of SharePoint both for collaboration and development.
SharePoint Central Administration	The site collection that you use to administer your SharePoint site.
SharePoint Administration Center	The administration site for Office 365.

RECOMMENDED READING

SharePoint 2013 Developer Overview — `http://msdn.microsoft.com/en-us/library/jj164084(v=office.15).aspx`

TechNet article on API updates — `http://technet.microsoft.com/en-us/library/ff607742(v=office.15)`

Overview of the SharePoint 2013 App Model

WHAT YOU WILL LEARN IN THIS CHAPTER:

➤ Understanding what Apps for Office and Apps for SharePoint are

➤ Introducing the three new Apps for SharePoint deployment models

WROX.COM DOWNLOADS FOR THIS CHAPTER

The wrox.com code downloads for this chapter are found at
`http://www.wrox.com/WileyCDA/WroxTitle/productCd-1118495845.html` on the
Download Code tab. The code for this chapter is divided into the following major examples:

➤ AutohostedEmployeeList.zip

➤ SPHostedApp_SimpleDateApp.zip

The first chapter of this book covered what SharePoint 2013 is and why you should care.
It also walked you through some of the basic architectural concepts and showed you some
screenshots to get you familiar with the look and feel of a SharePoint site — both the
SharePoint site you would interact with on a daily basis and the Administration site.

This chapter dives deeper into the new SharePoint 2013 app model, building on the discussion
from Chapter 1. This chapter also walks you through a couple of how-to examples, showing
you some basic development examples against the new app models.

SHAREPOINT 2013 APP MODEL

You can install SharePoint in two primary ways. As with SharePoint 2010, you can install
the full version of SharePoint Server and have all of your assets and content running in an
on-premises environment. Alternatively, you can provision an instance of Office 365 (O365)

and then take advantage of SharePoint Online (or a cloud-hosted version of SharePoint). You saw some examples of SharePoint Online in Chapter 1, "Introduction to SharePoint 2013," and you'll see more in this chapter. Irrespective of how you deploy your SharePoint instance, the new app model for SharePoint holds true for both on-premises versions of SharePoint (SharePoint Server) and cloud-hosted versions (O365).

Although you have the ability to manually create SharePoint 2013 site collections and configure and brand those sites to your business needs, this book is about development. One of the key evolutionary areas in SharePoint 2013 is the new app model. You implement the new cloud model, broadly speaking, through the creation and deployment of either Apps for SharePoint or Apps for Office.

Apps for Office

Apps for Office are a new breed of Office 2013 applications that use a nonmanaged code approach to building in-context document and mail apps (think Excel, Word, and Outlook add-ins). These apps enable you to use HTML, CSS, or JavaScript to build lightweight apps that integrate with cloud-based apps. The cool thing here is that you can use a rich JavaScript object model to integrate with parts of the document or mail item. Apps for Office consist of a web page plus an XML-based configuration file called a *manifest* file, which configures items such as links to an external website, permissions, and so on. You can think of Apps for Office as web apps.

Although Apps for Office primarily target Office, you can integrate them with Office 365, documents, and mail items — artifacts that might in some way integrate with SharePoint. Figure 2-1 shows an example of an App for Office. In this example, the App for Office is integrated with the mail and it displays data from a Windows Azure SQL database within the mail item: Related Requests from Chris Johnson.

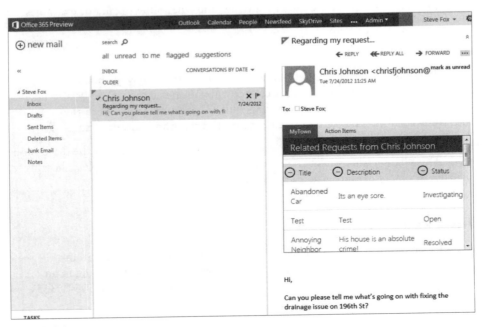

FIGURE 2-1

Apps for SharePoint

Apps for SharePoint (or SharePoint App) is the official name for apps you build and deploy to SharePoint. For those familiar with SharePoint, think of the SharePoint App as the evolution of the SharePoint Solution (that is, WSP). As mentioned in Chapter 1, the SharePoint App uses the .APP extension (whereas the SharePoint Solution uses .WSP).

The SharePoint App is a move toward a more cloud-centric development model — one where the code does not reside on the same server as SharePoint. This is a result of a greater migration of code to the cloud and a need to architect a platform to support smother updates and code that is loosely coupled to SharePoint and deployed to the cloud, as well as to mitigate the growing problems that server-side code typically presents (for example, performance and site-loading issues if the code is not properly written, deployed, or tested). Figure 2-2 shows an example of an app for SharePoint that integrates Windows Azure data — in fact, the same data that is being consumed in the app in Figure 2-1 is likewise integrated with SharePoint in Figure 2-2.

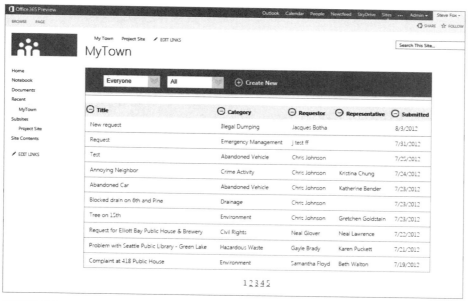

FIGURE 2-2

As mentioned earlier, when you build an app for SharePoint, you are building an .APP file. In reality, the .APP file is a "package" of files similar to a CAB file. Within the .APP package are a number of key files that are primarily made up of configuration files and libraries. For example, Figure 2-3 illustrates an .APP file that is created when you build and publish an app for SharePoint (you will walk through this later in this chapter). If you change the .APP extension to .ZIP you can see that the .APP consists of a number of files and another ZIP file. The zipped files represent the web portions of your SharePoint application, whereas the XML files represent more detailed configuration information for your app.

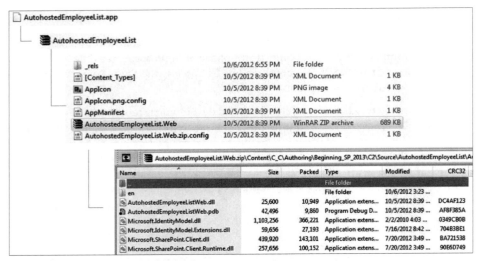

FIGURE 2-3

One of the key XML configuration files that you'll see in both Apps for SharePoint and Apps for Office is the `AppManifest.xml` file. In this configuration manifest you'll find key elements such as app meta data, app permissions and scope for those permissions, GUIDs for Web apps, and so on. The following code snippet shows a simple example of an `AppManifest.xml` file.

```xml
<?xml version="1.0" encoding="utf-8" ?>
<App xmlns="http://schemas.microsoft.com/sharepoint/2012/app/manifest"
     Name="AutohostedEmployeeList"
     ProductID="{125f9ba3-5efc-414a-ac53-023919ac2142}"
     Version="1.0.0.0"
     SharePointMinVersion="15.0.0.0"
>
  <Properties>
    <Title>AutohostedEmployeeList</Title>
    <StartPage>~remoteAppUrl/Pages/Default.aspx?{StandardTokens}
    </StartPage>
  </Properties>

  <AppPrincipal>
    <AutoDeployedWebApplication/>
  </AppPrincipal>

  <AppPrerequisites>
    <AppPrerequisite Type="AutoProvisioning" ID="RemoteWebHost" />
  </AppPrerequisites>
<AppPermissionRequests><AppPermissionRequest
Scope="http://sharepoint/content/sitecollection/web"
Right="Write" /></AppPermissionRequests></App>
```

> **NOTE** You can edit the `AppManifest.xml` file using either the Visual Studio 2012 IDE (visual designer), or you can right-click the `AppManifest.xml` file and select View Code to directly work with the XML.

MOVING TO THE CLOUD

The .APP structure enables you to configure and deploy apps to SharePoint while also building, packaging, and referencing libraries that are deployed to the cloud. Although the new app model is very "cloud-centric," you're not always forced to deploy code into the cloud. Alternatively, you could deploy your cloud data to an on-premises IIS server. In this deployment scenario, the code does not live on the SharePoint server, but you're still using the cloud-app model to deploy it to IIS. In this *non-cloud* application, you're using IIS — which could be an entirely on-premises installed and deployed app (which might be the case if you've installed the full SharePoint Server version on-premises). In the cloud app, the Windows Azure domain is off-premises (for example, in the public cloud data centers that Microsoft manages). However, both types of apps have two components: the configuration file (.APP), and the assemblies that execute your code, which are deployed into a separate server domain. Thus, you're either running these new SharePoint Apps in your or your customer's premises or the Internet.

The point is that the method for deploying a cloud app in each architecture is similar; the difference lies in where each app is hosted. Figure 2-4 illustrates two potential application architectures, reflecting on code that is deployed to Windows Azure or code that is deployed to IIS. In the non-cloud application, you're using IIS — which could be an entirely on-premises installed and deployed app (which might be the case if you've installed the full SharePoint Server version on-premises). In the cloud app, the Windows Azure domain is off-premises (for example, in the public cloud data centers that Microsoft manages). However, both types of apps have two components: the configuration file (.APP), and the assemblies that execute your code, which are deployed into a separate server domain. Thus, you're either running these new SharePoint Apps in your or your customer's premises or the Internet.

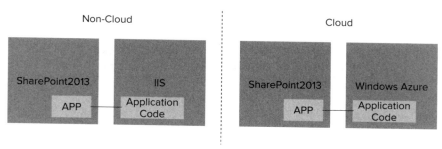

FIGURE 2-4

One of the major shifts away from previous SharePoint App models has been a new design goal to move code off of the server. The term *design goal* refers to the fact that backward compatibility is still possible with SharePoint 2013, but because of where SharePoint is heading, continuing to use these server-intensive development/deployment models is not recommended. Microsoft will be de-emphasizing a lot of these non-cloud areas moving forward (and in some cases deprecating support; for example, the future deprecation of support for Sandboxed Solutions). Microsoft just can't stop the support for these across one release though given the amount of apps that were written and are supported by SharePoint.

As you consider the development story for SharePoint 2013, keep the following facts in mind:

➤ A key future direction is in the cloud, so you should get engaged with this new app model now.

➤ Microsoft will continue to support some older capabilities in 2013, but not necessarily pervasively talk about them due to a strategy to drive deployment to the cloud.

➤ Some platform capabilities will be deprecated more quickly at some to-be-determined future date, therefore you should begin to cease use of them today (for example, Sandboxed Solutions).

In short, heed the evolution to the cloud and design apps appropriately. The implication of this evolution towards the cloud is no server-side code. SharePoint 2013 offers new options centered on a growing set of client-side APIs and programmability. This means leveraging HTML, CSS, and JavaScript more. It also means getting used to managing and authenticating cross-domain calls using OAuth and interacting with SharePoint data using an expanded set of REST and OData capabilities.

This chapter specifically discusses the Apps for SharePoint — Chapter 11 discusses Apps for Office in greater detail. The App for SharePoint deployment model has three different flavors, as discussed in the next section.

UNDERSTANDING THE THREE APPS FOR SHAREPOINT DEPLOYMENT MODELS

Because SharePoint 2013 is moving in the direction of the cloud, there are three new types of deployment models available to help you achieve this goal for the Apps for SharePoint:

➤ SharePoint-hosted

➤ Autohosted

➤ Provider-hosted

Each one of these types of deployment models possesses characteristics that make it ideal for different types of app development. The following sections examine the deployment models in greater detail.

SharePoint-Hosted

The SharePoint-hosted deployment type represents a way to deploy client-side, lightweight apps to SharePoint 2013. The easiest way to think about the SharePoint-hosted app is as an application that has no server-side code. It is an application made up of static application files or pages that reside on your SharePoint tenancy or instance. Think of HTML and JavaScript files that enable client-side coding. When users access the SharePoint-hosted app, they are redirected to the page that contains your application. The SharePoint-hosted deployment type is good for lighter-weight apps such as branded list views, media apps, or weather apps.

If you decide to leverage the SharePoint-hosted deployment model, then you are limited to code that does not run on the server. However, also know that client-side applications can be quite powerful. For example, you can still use Silverlight with SharePoint 2013, and as mentioned, you also can take advantage of HTML (more specifically the newer HTML5 standards) along with JavaScript. You can use these in tandem with the client-side object model to interact with SharePoint data (for example, list data).

To help illustrate how you build a SharePoint-hosted app, let's go ahead and create a simple SharePoint-hosted app using the following steps.

TRY IT OUT   Creating a SharePoint-Hosted App (SPHostedApp_SimpleDateApp.zip)

To complete this exercise, ensure you have the following:

➤ Visual Studio 2012 downloaded and installed

➤ SharePoint Developer Tools installed

➤ An Office 365 trial site set up for your use

You can reference the following TechNet article to walk through the process to set up your development environment: http://msdn.microsoft.com/zh-cn/library/sharepoint/ee554869%28v=office.15%29.

After you have your environment set up and ready, you can begin to create your first SharePoint-Hosted app:

1. Open Visual Studio, and click File ➪ New Project. Navigate to Office/SharePoint ➪ Apps, and then select App for SharePoint 2013.

2. Provide a name for the app (**SPHostedApp_SimpleDateApp**), select a location for the project, and click OK, as shown in Figure 2-5.

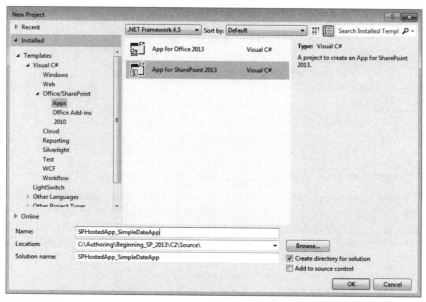

FIGURE 2-5

3. In the New App for SharePoint wizard, add the SharePoint site URL that you want to debug and then select the SharePoint-hosted model as the way you want to host your app for SharePoint (see Figure 2-6).

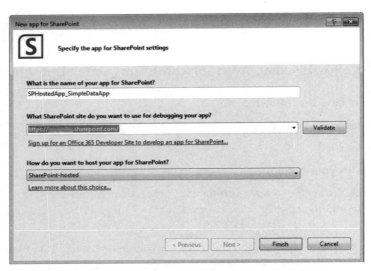

FIGURE 2-6

4. Click Finish.

5. After Visual Studio generates the project, double click the AppManifest.xml file, which is located within the SharePoint project.

6. In the Scope drop-down list, select Web, which is the scope of permissions that you're configuring. See Figure 2-7.

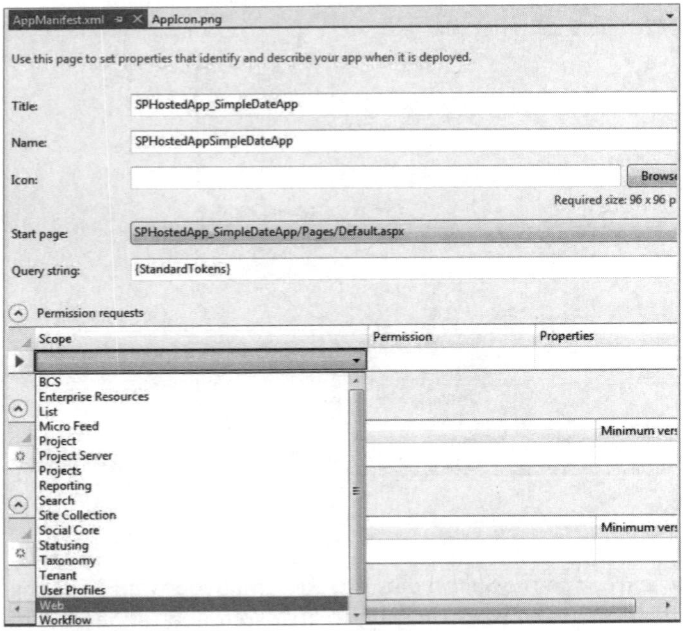

FIGURE 2-7

7. In the Permission drop-down list, select Read, which is the type of permission you're configuring. See Figure 2-8.

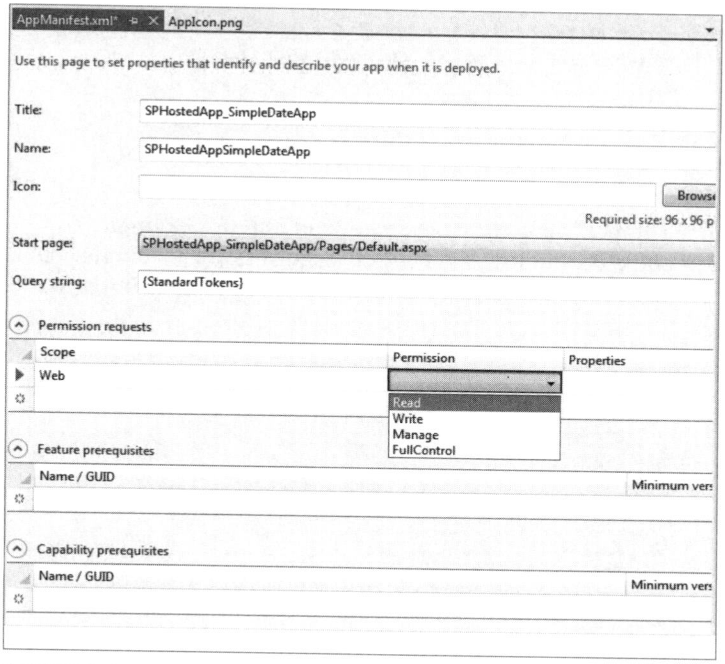

FIGURE 2-8

8. Double-click the `Default.aspx` file and replace `PlaceHolderAdditionalPageHead` and `PlaceHolderMain` with the following bolded code.

```
<%@ Page Inherits="Microsoft.SharePoint.WebPartPages.WebPartPage,
Microsoft.SharePoint, Version=15.0.0.0, Culture=neutral, PublicKeyToken=71e9bce111e9429c"
MasterPageFile="~masterurl/default.master" language="C#" %>
<%@ Register Tagprefix="SharePoint"
Namespace="Microsoft.SharePoint.WebControls"
Assembly="Microsoft.SharePoint, Version=15.0.0.0,
Culture=neutral, PublicKeyToken=71e9bce111e9429c" %>
<%@ Register Tagprefix="Utilities" Namespace="Microsoft.SharePoint.Utilities"
Assembly="Microsoft.SharePoint, Version=15.0.0.0,
Culture=neutral, PublicKeyToken=71e9bce111e9429c" %>
<%@ Register Tagprefix="WebPartPages" Namespace="Microsoft.SharePoint.WebPartPages"
Assembly="Microsoft.SharePoint,
Version=15.0.0.0, Culture=neutral, PublicKeyToken=71e9bce111e9429c" %>

<asp:Content ID="Content1" ContentPlaceHolderId="PlaceHolderAdditionalPageHead"
runat="server">
    <script type="text/javascript" src="../Scripts/jquery-1.6.2.min.js"></script>

    <link rel="Stylesheet" type="text/css" href="../Content/App.css" />
    <script type="text/javascript" src="../Scripts/App.js"></script>
```

```
</asp:Content>

<asp:Content ID="Content2" ContentPlaceHolderId="PlaceHolderMain" runat="server">
    <script type="text/javascript">
        function hello() {
            var currentTime = new Date();
            $get("timeDiv").innerHTML = currentTime.toDateString();
        }
    </script>
    <div id="timeDiv"></div>
    <input  type="button" value="Push me!" onclick="hello();"/>
</asp:Content>
```

9. After you finish adding the code snippet, right-click the SharePoint app (for example, SPHostedApp_SimpleDateApp) and click Publish, as shown in Figure 2-9. This builds your SharePoint-hosted app (that is, the .APP package discussed earlier) and prepares it for you for deployment to your SharePoint site.

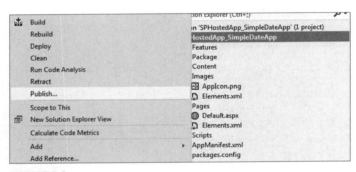

FIGURE 2-9

10. When prompted, click Finish to complete the build process.

11. Windows Explorer automatically opens when the app is built, so copy the Windows Explorer folder path to the clipboard (see Figure 2-10). You'll use this folder path when uploading the .APP package to SharePoint.

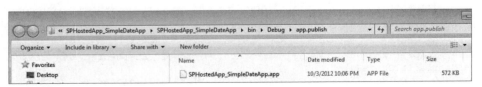

FIGURE 2-10

12. Navigate to your SharePoint Online site, and then click the New App to Deploy link.

13. In the Deploy App dialog, click the Upload link.

14. Click Browse, and then paste the folder path you copied to the clipboard in the Choose File to Upload dialog. Click Open.

15. Click OK, and then click Deploy.

16. When prompted to trust the app, click Trust It (see Figure 2-11).

17. When the app has been deployed, click the Site Contents link. You should now see your app listed on the page.

18. Click the app tile to load your SharePoint-hosted app (see Figure 2-12). Click the Push me! button.

FIGURE 2-11

How It Works

The SharePoint-hosted app is a lightweight application, and in this example you created and deployed a simple app that displayed the current time when you clicked a button object. To accomplish this, you can see in the following code that you added the `hello` function,

FIGURE 2-12

created a new `var` object called `currentTime`, and then set the inner HTML of the `timeDiv` DIV object to be the string representation of the current `Date`.

```
...
<asp:Content ID="Content2" ContentPlaceHolderId="PlaceHolderMain" runat="server">
    <script type="text/javascript">
        function hello() {
            var currentTime = new Date();
            $get("timeDiv").innerHTML = currentTime.toDateString();
        }
    </script>
    <div id="timeDiv"></div>
    <input type="button" value="Push me!" onclick="hello();"/>
</asp:Content>
...
```

You then deployed the App for SharePoint using the Publish feature in Visual Studio 2012. You also explicitly set the permissions level of the app before you deployed it, so when you clicked the Trust It button, this level of permission was enabled by SharePoint for your application. Setting permissions is a common task that you'll do across many different SharePoint apps.

The benefits here are that you can not only get code off of the server, but you're now leveraging JavaScript to bring your app to life on the client. The SharePoint-hosted deployment technique is lightweight, but you will find yourself doing a lot of client-side coding such as JavaScript or HTML, so make sure if you're not up to speed on either of these two technologies you spend a little time learning them. If you want to move beyond the client and build cloud-based apps, you can use the Autohosted deployment model.

Autohosted

The Autohosted deployment model is a significant departure from previous SharePoint applications. In this model you build Apps for SharePoint, but the code is seamlessly deployed to Windows Azure in the background — so SharePoint automatically creates the cloud-hosted app for you. Thus, for all intents and purposes code looks like it's running on SharePoint, when in fact in the background it's deployed to a special Office 365 Windows Azure instance (so in effect a different domain) and registered as an authenticated and authorized app with SharePoint.

You don't have complete access to the entire platform capabilities of the Windows Azure platform with the Autohosted deployment model; however, you do have enough of the platform to build some interesting applications. (You'll learn more about Windows Azure in Chapter 5.) In essence, you can leverage Windows Azure Web Sites and Windows Azure SQL Database in the Autohosted model. To help illustrate the Autohosted deployment model, take a look at the following example.

TRY IT OUT   Creating an Autohosted App (AutohostedEmployeeList.zip)

To create an Autohosted app, follow these steps:

1. Open Visual Studio 2012 and click File ⇨ New Project.

2. Navigate to the Office/SharePoint option, select Apps, and then click App for SharePoint 2013.

3. Provide a name for the app (`AutohostedEmployeeList`) and a location, and then click OK (see Figure 2-13).

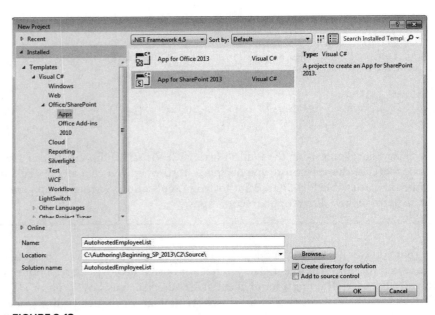

FIGURE 2-13

4. In the New App for SharePoint wizard, add your O365 SharePoint developer site URL. Click Validate and enter your O365 credentials to cache the developer site credentials with your project.

5. Select Autohosted from the How do you want to host your app for SharePoint? drop-down list (see Figure 2-14).

6. Click Finish.

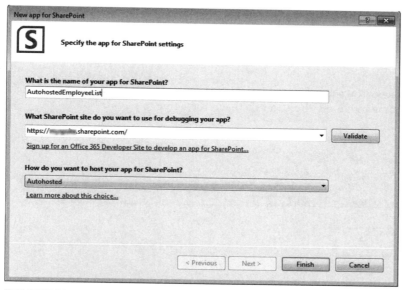

FIGURE 2-14

7. Double-click the `Default.aspx` page and click the Source tab at the bottom of the Visual Studio IDE.

8. Replace the code in the `Default.aspx` page with the following bolded code:

```
<%@ Page Language="C#" AutoEventWireup="true" CodeBehind="Default.aspx.cs"
Inherits="AutohostedEmployeeListWeb.Pages.Default" %>
<!DOCTYPE html PUBLIC "-//W3C//DTD XHTML 1.0
Transitional//EN" "http://www.w3.org/TR/xhtml1/DTD/xhtml1-transitional.dtd">
<html xmlns="http://www.w3.org/1999/xhtml">
<head runat="server">
    <title>Employee List</title>
</head>
<body>
    <form id="form1" runat="server">
    <div>Employee List</div>
        <table>
            <tr><td><asp:Label ID="lblName" runat="server" Text="Name:"
```

```
Font-Names="Calibri"></asp:Label></td>
            <td><asp:TextBox ID="txtbxName" runat="server" Width="205px">
</asp:TextBox></td></tr>
            <tr><td><asp:LinkButton ID="lnkbtnAddEmployee"
runat="server" Font-Names="Calibri"
OnClick="lnkbtnAddEmployee_Click">Add Employee</asp:LinkButton></td>
            <td></td></tr>
            <tr><td></td><td><asp:ListBox ID="lstbxEmployee"
runat="server" Width="212px" Font-Names="Calibri"></asp:ListBox></td>
            </tr>
            <tr><td><asp:Label ID="lblErrorMsg" runat="server" Text=""
Font-Names="Calibri"></asp:Label></td></tr>
        </table>
    </form>
</body>
</html>
```

9. Switch to the Design view. You should see something similar to Figure 2-15. The user interface enables you to add a name into a text box and then add the name to the list box.

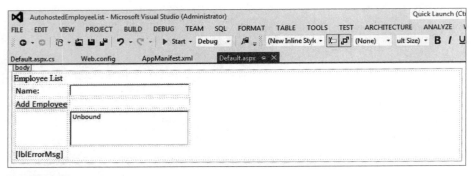

FIGURE 2-15

10. Right-click the `Default.aspx` page in Solution Explorer and select View Code. The C# code-behind for the ASP.NET page opens.

11. Replace the code in the `Default.aspx.cs` page with the following bolded code:

```
using System;
using System.Collections.Generic;
using System.Linq;
using System.Web;
using System.Web.UI;
using System.Web.UI.WebControls;

namespace AutohostedEmployeeListWeb.Pages
{
    public partial class Default : System.Web.UI.Page
    {
        string strEmployeeName = "";
```

```
        SharePointContextToken contextToken;
        string accessToken;
        Uri sharepointUrl;

        protected void Page_Load(object sender, EventArgs e)
        {
            TokenHelper.TrustAllCertificates();
            TokenHelper.TrustAllCertificates();
            string contextTokenString = TokenHelper.GetContextTokenFromRequest(Request);

            if (contextTokenString != null)
            {
                contextToken = TokenHelper.ReadAndValidateContextToken(contextTokenString,
Request.Url.Authority);
                sharepointUrl = new Uri(Request.QueryString["SPHostUrl"]);
                accessToken = TokenHelper.GetAccessToken(contextToken,
sharepointUrl.Authority).AccessToken;
                lnkbtnAddEmployee.CommandArgument = accessToken;
            }

        }

        protected void lnkbtnAddEmployee_Click(object sender, EventArgs e)
        {
            string accessToken = ((LinkButton)sender).CommandArgument;

            if (IsPostBack)
            {
                sharepointUrl = new Uri(Request.QueryString["SPHostUrl"]);
            }

            strEmployeeName = txtbxName.Text;

            if (txtbxName.Text != "")
            {
                lstbxEmployee.Items.Add(new ListItem(strEmployeeName));
            }
            else
            {
                lblErrorMsg.Text = "Please enter a valid name.";
            }
        }
    }
  }
}
```

12. Right-click the top-level SharePoint project and select Publish. This builds your project and creates the .APP package. At this point, you can follow the exact same process you did earlier in "Creating a SharePoint-Hosted App," using steps 9–16 to upload, deploy, and explicitly trust the SharePoint app.

13. When you're done, click the Site Contents link, and click the tile for the newly added App for SharePoint. Your Autohosted app loads.

14. Add some names into the Name field, and then click the Add Employee link to add the names to the list box. Your app should look similar to Figure 2-16.

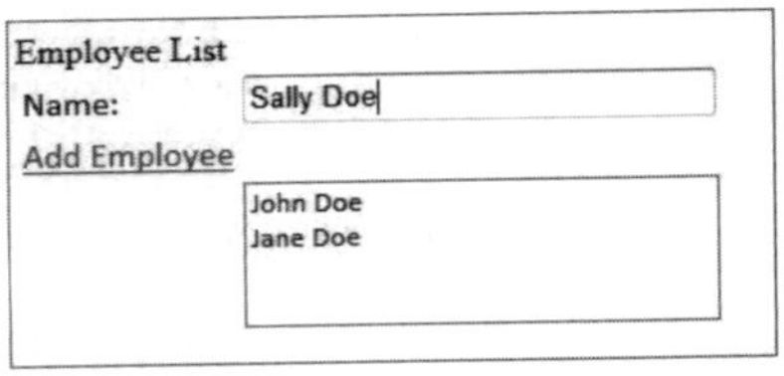

How It Works

The Autohosted app is a lightweight cloud-hosted application that auto-deploys code into Windows Azure and then surfaces this code within SharePoint 2013. In this example, you created a simple employee list app that enables the user to enter and add some names to a list box. In the code, you used a set of class-level objects to store key variables such as the name of the employee (strEmployeeName), security token data (contextToken and accessToken), and SharePoint URI (sharepointUri). The key event method (lnkbtnAddEmployee_Click) was triggered by the link button.

A couple things worth noting: With the new hosted models, the question of how you authenticate your app is an important one. SharePoint 2013 introduces a new authorization model that leverages OAuth to register apps and events within that app with SharePoint. At a high level, a SharePoint App requests permissions when it is installed — you explicitly trust the app that you're installing into your SharePoint instance. If you do not trust the app, it will not be installed. To facilitate trusting the app, you set the security token using the TokenHelper class, but then you needed to ensure that token was tied to the object sending the request (LinkButton object). Also, within the lnkbtnAddEmployee_Click event, you're configuring the security against the SharePoint URI as well. Setting trust and security context for the app are two critical aspects of the new world of cloud apps.

Beyond the security elements, the following code that you used in the exercise is fairly straightforward: you're assigning the strEmployeeName string variable with the text the user enters into the Name field. Then, assuming the text field is not null, you're adding it to the list box.

```
...
        protected void lnkbtnAddEmployee_Click(object sender, EventArgs e)

            string accessToken = ((LinkButton)sender).CommandArgument;

            if (IsPostBack)
            {
                sharepointUrl = new Uri(Request.QueryString["SPHostUrl"]);
            }

            strEmployeeName = txtbxName.Text;

            if (txtbxName.Text != "")
            {
                lstbxEmployee.Items.Add(new ListItem(strEmployeeName));
            }
            else
            {
                lblErrorMsg.Text = "Please enter a valid name.";
            }

        }
...
```

Employee List
Name: Sally Doe
Add Employee

John Doe
Jane Doe

FIGURE 2-16

You might have noticed the new URL for your Autohosted app; it probably looks something like the following:

```
https://a9d21e97-5c8d-4f75-9804-b548b8df8d21.o365apps.net/Pages/Default.aspx?SPHostUrl=
https%3a%2f%myspsite.sharepoint.com%2fsites%2fspdev&SPLanguage=en-US
```

From this URL, you can begin to see how the new cloud-hosted app model leverages a GUID specific to your app, deploys it to Windows Azure (using the O365apps.net domain), and then appends a set of standard tokens to ensure the application integrates and maps to your SharePoint site. This is built from the following element within the `AppManifest.xml` file.

```
<StartPage>~remoteAppUrl/Pages/Default.aspx?{StandardTokens}</StartPage>
```

Of course, many other configuration options are available to you within the `AppManifest.xml` file, and you can build many interesting apps using the Autohosted deployment model.

The Autohosted model is one of two cloud-hosted app models that are new to SharePoint 2013. Autohosted provides the automated deployment and management of your cloud-hosted app, but it does come with some restrictions. For example, you have limited surface area for leveraging Windows Azure, database size limits of the SQL Database, and no direct connection string access to the SQL Database. The other cloud-hosted model, the Provider-hosted app, gives you much more flexibility and allows you to draw on all of the Windows Azure features.

Provider-Hosted

The Provider-hosted deployment model is a richer and more flexible version of the Autohosted deployment model. In this model, your code runs in a different domain — often framed in the context of cloud deployment. For example, you can deploy your code to Windows Azure and then register it to authenticate and integrate with SharePoint 2013.

> **NOTE** You can also deploy an application to IIS and it could be considered Provider-hosted.

When users access a cloud-hosted application deployed using the Provider-hosted app model, they are redirected to a web page that resides in an external domain or server — where the application code resides. One of the key reasons this is relevant is that the external server doesn't necessarily need to be a Windows Server–based application; you could be running a PHP app on a Linux/Apache server and still have that web application integrated with SharePoint.

For example, Figure 2-17 illustrates an ASP.NET MVC4 web app that is deployed to Windows Azure. It uses jQuery, MVC, HTML5, and other modern web development techniques to create rich web applications. It is possible to integrate this app with SharePoint 2013 — and more. The bigger question is, "How does it work?"

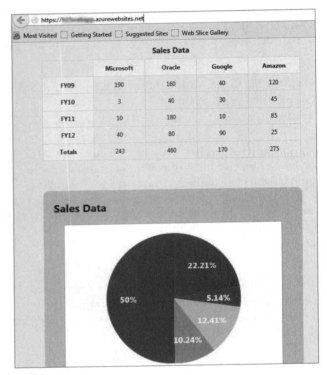

FIGURE 2-17

Similar to the Autohosted model, a special Visual Studio project template is available for you to use to create, integrate, and deploy a web application that is married and registered to SharePoint 2013. The process is fairly exhaustive to describe in this chapter; however, later chapters cover it in greater detail (see also the Recommended Reading for a link to a walk-through). At a high level, though, you need to ensure you have registered the application such that SharePoint is aware of the app. You do this through the creation of a client ID (that is, a GUID), which is included in the web.config of the web app and the AppManifest.xml file. To follow is an example of a Provider-hosted AppManifest.xml file.

```
<?xml version="1.0" encoding="utf-8" ?>
<App xmlns="http://schemas.microsoft.com/sharepoint/2012/app/manifest"
     Name="MyFirstProviderHostedApp"
     ProductID="{4b640267-b19a-4555-8af4-80a67ecf6f88}"
     Version="1.0.0.0"
     SharePointMinVersion="15.0.0.0">
```

```
<Properties>
  <Title>MyFirstProviderHostedApp</Title>
  <StartPage>http://mysalesdataapp.azurewebsites.net/?{StandardTokens}
  </StartPage>
</Properties>

<AppPrincipal>
  <RemoteWebApplication ClientId="9F579786-BD34-4736-8E30-97D6AF648E7B" />
</AppPrincipal>
<AppPermissionRequests><AppPermissionRequest
Scope="http://sharepoint/content/sitecollection/web" Right="Read" /></
AppPermissionRequests></App>
```

You also need to ensure that the application is registered and secured using the `TokenHelper` class, much like you did with the Autohosted app. You might also need to register and associate a certificate with the app and your developer site given that SharePoint Online is HTTPS. After you've created and are hosting the Windows Azure (or another type of Web app) in your hosted domain, you can then integrate it with SharePoint. For example, securing and deploying the Windows Azure app that was represented at the high-level architecture in Figure 2-4 looks similar to Figure 2-18 when deployed to SharePoint. The Windows Azure application is now fully integrated and loading from a separate domain — but looks and feels like a SharePoint app and is registered with SharePoint.

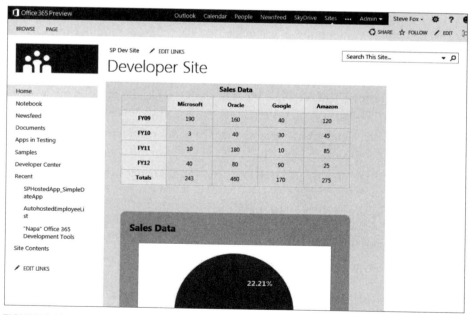

FIGURE 2-18

The Provider-hosted model is the most flexible of the three new types of deployment models. The key item to remember with the Provider-hosted deployment model is that you own the management of that code in a separate domain — this would include managing the billing of apps, data, or services deployed to Windows Azure in a Provider-hosted app. (The Autohosted model is managed automatically by SharePoint with one bill through your Online Services subscription.) This also means you own updating, testing, integrating, and so on for this separately hosted application. With that management overhead, though, comes quite a bit of power to integrate an array of different types of web applications and technologies, making it necessary to have all three options available from which to choose.

SUMMARY

The three new deployment models for Apps for SharePoint are the SharePoint-hosted, Autohosted, and Provider-hosted app models.

The SharePoint-hosted app model should be used for lightweight, smaller apps where you don't need server-side code. You can build them using the client-side object model, HTML and JavaScript. The scope for a SharePoint-hosted app is the site collection.

The Autohosted app model is also used for lightweight apps, but the code for this app is automatically deployed to Windows Azure. You can tap into the power of Windows Azure Web Sites and SQL Database to build data-driven apps. The scope for Autohosted apps is at the site or tenancy level.

The Provider-hosted app model is about power and flexibility. The code does not live in SharePoint, but lives in a separate domain. This could be Windows Azure — in which case you can take full advantage of all of the features of the Windows Azure platform, or it could be IIS (by leveraging the Provider-hosted template in Visual Studio), or even a completely separate PHP app that lives in your own domain-hosted environment. There is quite a bit of flexibility built into this app model, but what comes with it is the need to manage your own code that lives in this separate domain.

These new models are a paradigm shift from previous versions of SharePoint and will surely change the way in which you think about, design, and deploy your apps.

The next chapter explores the SharePoint 2013 developer tooling in greater detail.

EXERCISES

Answers to Exercises can be found in Appendix A.

1. What are the different deployment model types for Apps for SharePoint?

2. What key Web technologies can you use with the Provider-hosted deployment model?

3. Build a Provider-hosted app that uses IIS on your local server instead of using Windows Azure.

▶ **WHAT YOU LEARNED IN THIS CHAPTER**

ITEM	DESCRIPTION
App for Office	A new type of app to integrate Web apps or services with Office or SharePoint.
App for SharePoint	The new way of deploying apps to SharePoint 2013.
SharePoint-hosted App	A lightweight, client-side app. The scope is the site collection and code must be client-side (e.g., HTML and JavaScript).
Autohosted App	A cloud-hosted app that auto-deploys code to Windows Azure and automatically registers apps with SharePoint. It can be scoped to site collection or tenancy, and app permissions are managed through OAuth.
Provider-hosted App	A cloud-hosted app that can leverage Windows Azure or other web technologies. It is the most flexible of cloud-hosted apps and can be scoped to site collection or tenancy. App permissions are managed through OAuth.

RECOMMENDED READING

SharePoint 2013 Development Environment Setup — `http://msdn.microsoft.com/zh-cn/library/sharepoint/ee554869%28v=office.15%29`

SharePoint 2013 Developer Resources — `http://msdn.microsoft.com/en-us/office/apps/fp160950.aspx`

Creating a Basic Provider-Hosted App — `http://msdn.microsoft.com/en-us/library/office/apps/fp142381%28v=office.15%29.aspx`

3

Developer Tooling for SharePoint 2013

WHAT YOU WILL LEARN IN THIS CHAPTER:

➤ Understanding the different tooling options for SharePoint 2013

➤ Choosing to use one tool over another

WROX.COM DOWNLOADS FOR THIS CHAPTER

The wrox.com code downloads for this chapter are found at `http://www.wrox.com/WileyCDA/WroxTitle/productCd-1118495845.html` on the Download Code tab. The code for this chapter is divided into the following major examples:

➤ SP_Hosted_Custom_List.zip

At this stage in the book, you've now been introduced to what SharePoint is, you've learned about the new app model, and you've even written a couple of applications for SharePoint 2013. From here on out, you're going to dive deeper into the developer world.

This chapter covers the different tools that you as a developer will want to have in your toolkit. You may have or use more or fewer tools than what this chapter discusses, but ultimately this chapter is about the core developer tools you should either use or need to be aware of when embarking on your SharePoint development projects.

With that in mind, this chapter covers three main developer tools: Web-based development using the new Napa development app, SharePoint Designer 2013, and Visual Studio 2012. Depending on your skills and design goals, you might use these environments or tools in different ways, and so the goal of this chapter is to not only introduce you to these different possibilities but to also walk you through some practical examples.

SHAREPOINT DEVELOPMENT ACROSS DEVELOPER SEGMENTS

Chapter 1, "Introduction to SharePoint 2013," discussed the spectrum of SharePoint developers and the different ways in which they use SharePoint. As a reminder, you can divide this spectrum into the following:

➤ *End users:* who use the platform as an application platform

➤ *Power users:* who create and administer (and maybe brand) sites

➤ *Designers:* who brand the site and build the user experience

➤ *Developers:* who build and deploy apps

Thinking about a life cycle around each of these personas, you can imagine ways in which these people might work together or act independently on something that was created for or by them. For example, the end user is the ultimate consumer of what exists out of the box. Meanwhile, the developer builds apps and the designer brands and builds the user experience for the SharePoint sites that the power user configures, thus the end users are downstream from the development process. Further upstream, you have the developer and the designer who might work together (and in some cases are the same person) to deliver both the code and the user experience, branded or otherwise, to the power user and ultimately to the end user. The point is that a range of people interact with SharePoint — from the developer all the way downstream to the end user — you can see a representation of this in Figure 3-1.

FIGURE 3-1

Keeping in mind these various types of developers, this chapter is all about the different tools that you can use to develop for SharePoint and the types of apps that you would build or tasks that you would accomplish with these tools. Figure 3-2 provides an interesting way to divide up the tasks and apps that have traditionally been associated with SharePoint development tasks. On the Design side, you can see apps and tasks that would require a more lightweight toolset (for example, SharePoint Designer and Napa), and on the Develop side you see apps that require a more managed code approach

- Lightweight apps (HTML, JS)

- Create sites, lists, doc libraries, etc.

- Branding/themes

- ...

Design

- Custom artifacts (Web parts, lists, content types)

- Cloud-based apps/services

- Workflow

- ...

Develop

FIGURE 3-2

(for example, Visual Studio). Each of these tools will be discussed in this chapter within the context of these developer tasks and a broader set of developer experiences.

On the Design side of Figure 3-2, you might be creating apps such as custom lists, HTML apps, master pages, and the like. You could also get into some coding activities, and more than likely that code experience will center on HTML, XML, ASP.NET, JavaScript, and other client-side languages. You might also get into some integration with Silverlight.

On the Develop side of Figure 3-2, development centers on C# or VB.NET (managed code) and possibly scripted languages as well. Using Visual Studio, you'll also find that development efforts might be managed as a part of an application life cycle, which is more broadly called application life-cycle management (ALM), where source code is checked into team folders (in Team Foundation Server, for example), and you can add SharePoint development projects to those folders and manage them centrally. You'll also find custom solutions that leverage other parts of the .NET Framework such as Windows Workflow (WF)–based solutions or REST-based services built and leveraged in other SharePoint apps. Using the .NET Framework is especially useful for when you build out your cloud-hosted apps using Windows Azure.

What this development paradigm results in for you, though, is ultimately choice. Depending on what you're trying to develop for SharePoint, each of these tools offers varying degrees of usefulness for your task at hand.

The following sections walk through each of these development experiences so you can get a better sense for how you might leverage each of them in different ways.

WEB-BASED DEVELOPMENT IN SHAREPOINT

As mentioned earlier, one can define SharePoint development in a number of ways. As a power user you might leverage more of the native SharePoint features to do development through the Web-based environment. Power users typically have escalated permissions on a SharePoint site and are able to accomplish tasks such as the following:

➤ Creating and managing site collections and site permissions

➤ Configuring a new theme to the site

➤ Adding a new app to the site

➤ Creating and deploying multimedia for site-wide consumption

➤ Configuring and customizing searches

➤ Creating external data lists

Although some might argue that these are merely *tasks* that a power user or IT pro might perform, one thing about SharePoint is that the lines are sometimes blurred where one user persona starts and another ends. For example, with many of the Web-based functions that you can perform when developing for SharePoint a direct relationship exists to a development task. That is, you might see the SharePoint Web interface as an *endpoint* to the development experience. For example, if you create a custom app you will need to add it from an organizational-wide gallery (for example, a corporate catalog). If you're working with a designer to create a new master page, you'll need to associate that new master page with a specific site through the site settings of that SharePoint site. The types of Web-based tasks that you can perform go on and on (and you'll likely evolve from the more Web-based tasks to the more difficult coding tasks as you get deeper into SharePoint development).

To some people these Web-based tasks are more centric to power-user features, and to others they are inclusive within the development process. However, the main takeaway is that a developer will interact with the Web-based features with SharePoint as well as potentially leverage other tools discussed in this chapter. A power user might also leverage these same Web-based features. In either case you require escalated privileges on the SharePoint site, and a connection exists to the development process (that is, a power user creates a site to which a developer drops his custom app). Thus, SharePoint development comprises a broad spectrum of activities and tools.

SITE SETTINGS

One of the main parts of SharePoint you should become familiar with (if you haven't already) is the Site Settings. You can access the Site Settings page by clicking the gear icon in the right-hand corner of the SharePoint site and then selecting Site Settings. You'll find most of the configurations for your site on this page, so it's a good place to start when trying to understand where you can, for example, change the theme of your site, activate features, manage permissions, and so on. Figure 3-3 shows the Site Settings page. Note that the core features of the Site Settings page are split out into major categories. For example, most of your security settings are available to you in the Users and Permissions category, theming in Web Designer Galleries, and so on.

FIGURE 3-3

As you can see from Figure 3-3, you can manage many functions through Site Settings. One of the key tasks you'll do as a developer or site administrator, for example, is to view the permissions of an app. Permissions are core to SharePoint and allow you to control who has access to specific areas and apps within your site and also to provision augmented permissions for, say, people you want to have editing capabilities on your site. With regard to app permissions, you saw in Chapter 2, "Overview of SharePoint 2013 App Model," how you could configure permissions through Visual Studio 2012 (using the `AppManifest.xml`), but you also have a way to view app permissions from the Site Settings. To view the app permissions, click Site App Permissions under Site Settings. Figure 3-4 shows this page. Specifically, you can see that a number of apps are deployed to this SharePoint site, each with a specific identifier used for permissions.

FIGURE 3-4

For those of you familiar with SharePoint 2007 or 2010, you also know that you can build "features," which are a special type of SharePoint solution that you can deploy. After you deploy them, you can activate or deactivate features through a configuration page within Site Settings. To see the Feature Gallery, click Manage site features under Site Actions. Note that a number of features are either activated or deactivated in this gallery. Site administrators (and those who have full control over the site) can also use the Site Features page as a place to manage the features in your SharePoint farm. Figure 3-5 shows the Site Features page.

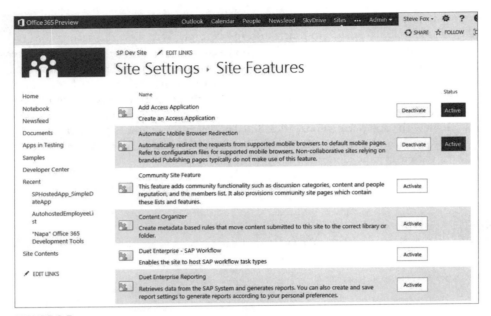

FIGURE 3-5

It you have some extra time, it is a good idea to explore the different areas of the Site Settings page to become familiar with all the configuration settings you can manage in SharePoint.

Although you can use Site Settings to configure elements of your SharePoint site, you can also directly edit your SharePoint site. Editing a site enables you to accomplish many different tasks, such as adding a Web part, adding HTML content to your page, configuring apps, and so on. If you return to the home site of your SharePoint site, click Site Actions ➪ Edit Page. The functions available to you at this point range from inserting apps to editing to custom list generation. If you click inside the top-level Web part to expose the in-context ribbon, you'll see that you can now edit the page using the ribbon controls. Thus, although the Site Settings provide you with configurable settings for the applications that you deploy to SharePoint (or for changing the configuration of the site that hosts your applications such as themes or master pages), the Edit mode enables those with elevated permissions to contribute to the development of content on the site — see Figure 3-6.

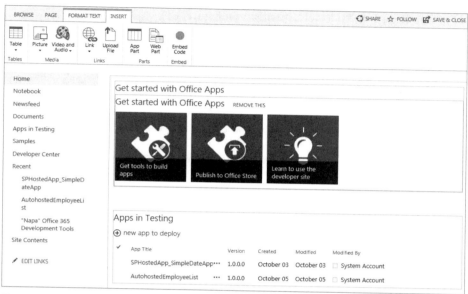

FIGURE 3-6

The editing experience ranges from formatting text to adding images or multimedia. For example, suppose you've created a training video and you now want to embed that video in a Web part on a page. You can use the Edit menu to add the video to the Web page, where SharePoint will then provide you with the necessary controls to play the video. Although this type of task might not constitute hard-core, managed code development, you are still advancing the content of your site, so in a sense you are technically "developing" your site.

You can get a little more into the code by embedding HTML directly within your SharePoint site when it's in Edit mode. This task feels a little more like development, so give it a try in the following activity.

TRY IT OUT Embedding HTML

To embed HTML into your SharePoint site, follow these steps:

1. Open your SharePoint site and navigate to the home page of the site.

2. Click the Page tab, and then click Edit ⇨ Insert.

3. Position your cursor on the page, and click Embed Code, as shown in Figure 3-7.

FIGURE 3-7

4. Add some HTML code into the code field, as shown in Figure 3-8.

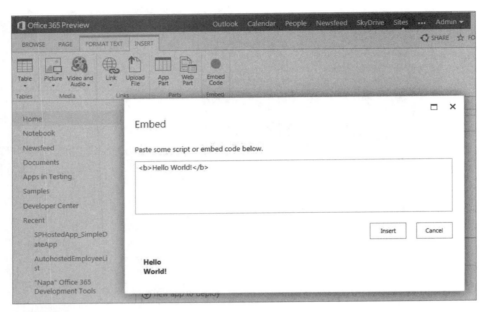

FIGURE 3-8

5. Click Insert. The result will be similar to what's shown in Figure 3-9.

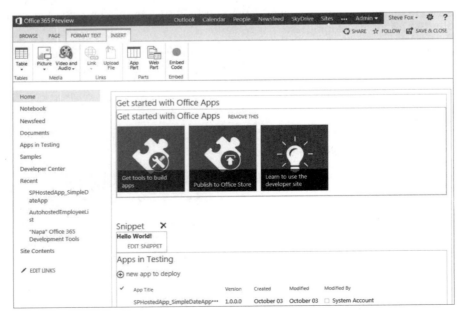

FIGURE 3-9

6. Click Page ⇨ Save. This saves the HTML you entered to the SharePoint site as in Figure 3-10 — see the "Hello World!" text added inline.

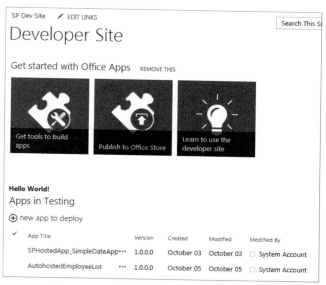

FIGURE 3-10

How It Works

This exercise is a very simple example to illustrate the ease with which you can enter HTML into your SharePoint site and pages. You add code, and behind the scenes SharePoint uses a special "container" that renders your HTML on the SharePoint page.

The HTML container (or App part) represents a way for you to add HTML source to the page. When the site loads, the source is treated as a part of the page and is then rendered.

Note that you're not limited to only HTML when embedding code on the page; you can add code such as JavaScript that will also run when the page loads.

Let's move on to something a little different and add a video to a SharePoint site. This exercise serves to contrast the more Web-based use of SharePoint with adding markup.

TRY IT OUT   Adding a Media Player App

To add a Media Player app to your SharePoint site:

1. Open your SharePoint site and navigate to the home page of the site.

2. Click the Page tab, and then click Edit ⇨ Insert.

3. Position your cursor on the page, and click Insert.

4. Click Web Part ⇨ Media Web Part, and then click Add. The result should look like Figure 3-11.

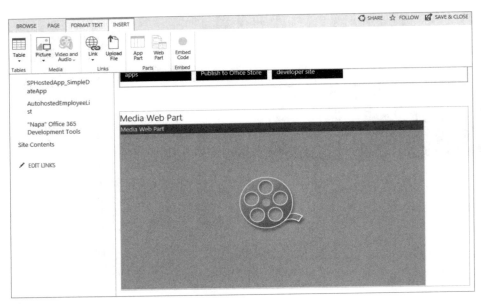

FIGURE 3-11

How It Works

SharePoint natively supports multimedia as well as Silverlight, which you can use to create and deploy rich media applications to SharePoint. Two main out-of-the-box Web parts are available that are media-centric. The first is the generic Silverlight Web part, which represents a "host container" for Silverlight applications. The second is the Multimedia Web part, which is in essence a Silverlight Web part that supports and serves the multimedia that is associated with the Web part. So, in this exercise you "mapped" a video with the Multimedia Web part, which further enabled you to view the video when you clicked the play button. The generic Multimedia control is nice in that it provides a set of controls to play, pause, and stop the video as well as increase the volume or toggle between thumbnail and full-screen views. The mapping of the video essentially represents a source property that is being set behind the scenes so that the `mediaelement` object, a native part of the Silverlight video-playing capabilities, understands where to find and play the video.

The two preceding Try It Outs reinforce the point that development for SharePoint can start out in relatively simple ways. As you'll see throughout this book though, developing apps will evolve to an exercise that is more complex and one that accesses and uses resources from other domains.

DEVELOPING SHAREPOINT APPLICATIONS USING SHAREPOINT DESIGNER

A lot of developers say they prefer not to use SharePoint Designer as a tool for developing against SharePoint. However, you might be remiss if you didn't include SharePoint Designer within your toolkit, because you're going to find that SharePoint Designer can make some development tasks easier.

SharePoint Designer has evolved from FrontPage (an earlier Web designer tool) to SharePoint Designer (a SharePoint-centric designer tool that was rolled out with SharePoint 2010). SharePoint Designer can be used for a variety of designer functions for SharePoint, including creating and editing sites, pages, lists, and content types. Also, SharePoint Designer is useful for creating rules-based, declarative workflow that can then be imported in Visual Studio for deeper-level customization.

When you first open SharePoint Designer, you need to provide it with the URL for your SharePoint site and authenticate as an elevated user — or else you won't be able to make any changes to the site. SharePoint Designer inherits standard SharePoint permissions.

After you open your site in SharePoint Designer, a number of navigable options and some information about your site appear, such as site metadata, permissions, subsites, and so on, as shown in Figure 3-12.

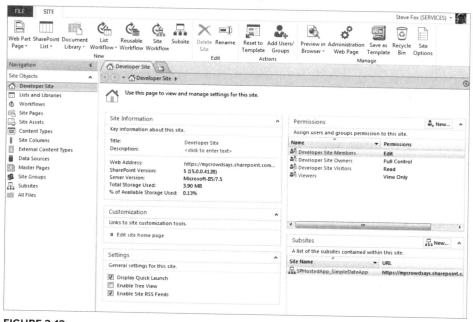

FIGURE 3-12

The Navigation pane on the left in Figure 3-12 provides a way for you to navigate across the major functional areas of SharePoint Designer to quickly get to the things that you need to do. The Navigation pane provides links to the following functionality:

- ➤ **Lists and Libraries:** Allows you to create, edit, and manage lists and libraries.
- ➤ **Workflows:** Facilitates the creation of rules-based workflow (that you can import into Visual Studio and extend).
- ➤ **Site Pages:** Provides the ability to create and edit site-level Web pages.
- ➤ **Site Assets:** Different assets such as content, files and folders within a SharePoint site.
- ➤ **Content Types:** Provides the ability to create, edit, and manage content types.
- ➤ **Site Columns:** Supports the creation, editing, and management of site columns.
- ➤ **External Content Types:** Enables you to create ADO.NET or Web service–based external content types for deployment to the Business Connectivity Services.
- ➤ **Data Sources:** Create and manage data source connections to a SharePoint site.
- ➤ **Master Pages:** Create, edit, and manage the master pages mapped to a specific SharePoint site.
- ➤ **Site Groups:** Displays the groups of sites within your SharePoint site.
- ➤ **Subsites:** Shows the subsites within the site collection.
- ➤ **All Files:** Displays all files in the SharePoint site.

Depending on your level of permission to a given site, some of these features might be hidden to you from within the SharePoint Designer IDE. For example, without administrator privileges, you can't see the Master Pages link in the Navigation pane, so you will not be able to build and deploy master pages to that SharePoint site.

SharePoint Designer offers some very useful features and to cover them all would take a separate book. However, this book covers a few to get you at least started and familiar with SharePoint Designer. For example, in this chapter you'll use SharePoint Designer to create site pages and master pages. In later chapters in the book, you'll also use SharePoint Designer for creating external content types and workflow.

To get you started, use the following steps to create a list using SharePoint Designer.

TRY IT OUT   Creating a List Using SharePoint Designer

To create a list in SharePoint using SharePoint Designer, perform the following steps:

1. Open SharePoint Designer 2013.

2. On the left-hand navigation, click Lists and Libraries. The default options appear for Lists and Libraries.

3. Click SharePoint Lists in the ribbon and select Tasks, as shown in Figure 3-13.

4. Provide a name for the Tasks List (such as **My To Do List**), as shown in Figure 3-14, and click OK.

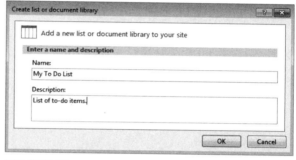

FIGURE 3-14

FIGURE 3-13

5. Click the Save button.

6. After you've saved the Tasks list, return to your SharePoint site. You should now see your new My To Do List there, as shown in Figure 3-15.

FIGURE 3-15

7. Return to SharePoint Designer and click the InfoPath Forms button in the ribbon. The InfoPath Designer opens, which enables you to customize a list form for your new To Do list (see Figure 3-16).

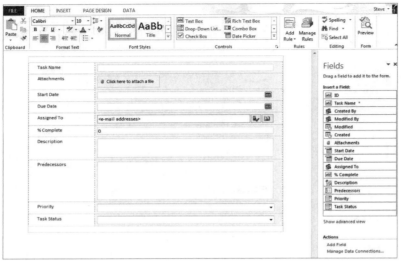

FIGURE 3-16

8. You can explore the UI and controls if you want; otherwise, simply click the File tab and then Save to save a version of the InfoPath template locally, and then click the Quick Publish button to publish the list form to your SharePoint site. (Note that while not visible in the Figure 3-16, you'll find a small set of shortcut icons above the File tab in the InfoPath UI, such as Save, Quick Publish, Redo, etc.)

9. Navigate to your SharePoint site to view the new To Do list form, shown in Figure 3-17.

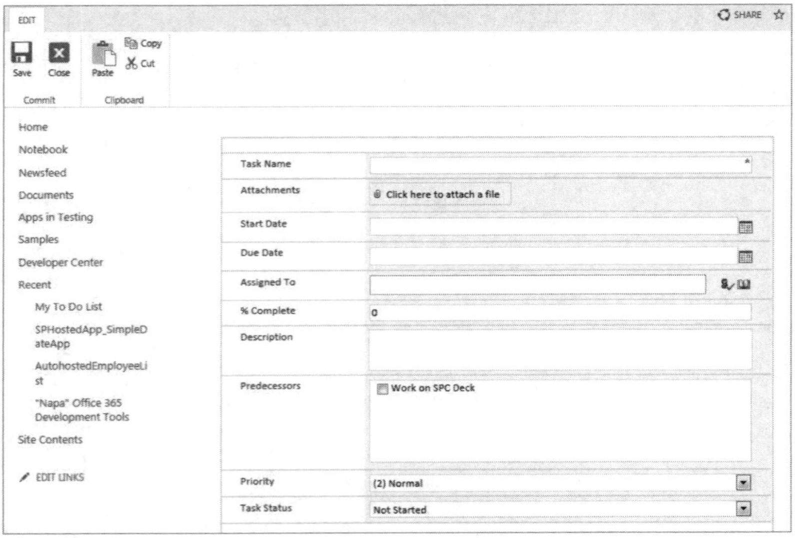

FIGURE 3-17

10. Use the form to enter new list items, and then click Save when complete.

How It Works

SharePoint Designer provides you with a way to design and customize your SharePoint site. In this example, SharePoint Designer uses the client-side SharePoint APIs and permissions to create artifacts in SharePoint on your behalf. It also uses InfoPath, which is a forms tool, to create a very simple custom form for your SharePoint list.

Although the preceding exercise showed you a relatively simple task, you can create some interesting and rich customizations with SharePoint Designer. Furthermore, SharePoint Designer is but one of a few tools you can use. A newer addition to SharePoint (and Office) development is Napa, a browser-based development tool.

DEVELOPING SHAREPOINT APPLICATIONS USING NAPA

For those of you who are not new to SharePoint development, you know that getting your development environment set up can take a little time. In SharePoint 2010, you had to locally install a number of software applications, such as SharePoint, SQL Server, Visual Studio, and so on, and configure your environment for use. You were then relegated to debug on your locally installed SharePoint instance. Fast-forward to SharePoint 2013, and the development story has evolved quite a bit. For example, you can set up a cloud-based version of SharePoint (Office 365) and develop remotely against that instance; you can have a locally installed version of SharePoint and have your tools locally installed; and you also have browser-based options for quicker, lightweight application development — which you can export to Visual Studio. Enter Napa.

Napa enables you to very quickly build and deploy solutions into SharePoint using a rich browser-based approach. It allows developers to get started quickly developing for SharePoint, and if you desire, to migrate the code you write in Napa to run and debug in Visual Studio as well.

As you've seen, SharePoint 2013 has evolved towards the "App" model. Interestingly, Napa is really just another rich app that you can use to develop for SharePoint. So, you install it and use it just like any other app; start at the developer site and proceed from there. Figure 3-18 illustrates the live tiles that are by default available to you when you first create your SharePoint developer site. You can see the "Get tools to build apps" link in the first tile on the left.

Clicking this link redirects you to the install location for Napa, where you can follow the instructions to download and trust the Napa app within your Office 365 tenancy. (Installing the Napa development tools app is similar to installing other apps.)

After you install Napa, you can then go ahead and launch it and use it to build apps for

FIGURE 3-18

SharePoint 2013. For example, in Figure 3-19 you can see the default Napa experience. The main window offers the code view. This is where you add your client-side code. Note to the left of the main window the folders (for example, Content, Images, Pages, and Scripts) with files within them. You can navigate and use these different folders to add your code to build out your app. The left-hand portion of the screen contains another set of important options for running the project, removing the app, viewing the properties of the app, opening the app in Visual Studio, and sharing the project.

FIGURE 3-19

Napa doesn't have all the features of Visual Studio; however, you can get started very quickly with your coding efforts and, of course, open the project in Visual Studio to leverage all the options within a fully featured development IDE.

Use the following steps to go ahead and build a simple app using Napa.

TRY IT OUT   **Building a Simple JavaScript App Using Napa**

To create a SharePoint-hosted app using Napa:

1. Open your SharePoint site.

2. Click Get tools to build apps in the live tiles on your home page.

3. If you haven't installed the tools, you will be prompted to install at this point. If you have installed the tools already, click Add New Project.

4. As shown in Figure 3-20, click App for SharePoint, provide a name for the app (such as `MyFirstNapaApp`), and click Create.

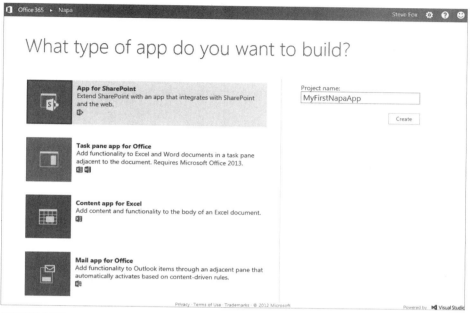

FIGURE 3-20

5. On the left side of the page that appears, click Pages, and then click Default.aspx.

6. Within `PlaceHolderMain`, add the following highlighted code.

```
<%-- The markup and script in the following Content element will be placed in
the <body> of the page --%>
<asp:Content ContentPlaceHolderId="PlaceHolderMain" runat="server">

    <div>
        <p id="message">
            <!-- The following content will be replaced with the user name
when you run the app - see App.js -->
            initializing...
        </p>
    </div>

  <div>
    <select id='dropdiv' onchange="getBookInfo(this)">
      <option value='1'>Beginning SharePoint 2013 Development</option>
      <option value='2'>Beginning ASP.NET 4.0</option>
      <option value='3'>Professional SharePoint Development using Silverlight</option>
    </select>
  </div>

</asp:Content>
```

7. Note the `onchange` event in the HTML that you added. You need to add this event code as JavaScript. You could add inline, or to conform to JavaScript-coding best practices, you could add to the `Apps.js` file in the Scripts folder. Click the `Apps.js` file and then add the following JavaScript code at the bottom of the file:

```javascript
// This function is executed if one of the choices is selected in the table.
function getBookInfo(object)
  {
      var selected = object.options[object.selectedIndex].value;
      var ISBN;
      var Price;
      var Message;
        if (selected == '1')
          {
            ISBN = "091283900129";
            Price = "$39.99";
            Message = "Book Info: " + ISBN + " | " + Price;
            alert(Message);
          }
            else if (selected == '2')
            {
              ISBN = "298734689102";
              Price = "$42.99";
              Message = "Book Info: " + ISBN + " | " + Price;
              alert(Message);
            }
    else if (selected == '3')
              {
                ISBN = "948302381002";
                Price = "$36.99";
                Message = "Book Info: " + ISBN + " | " + Price;
                alert(Message);
              }
  }
```

8. You can now click Run Project (as shown in Figure 3-21) using the options in the bottom-left tray to debug the project in SharePoint. Your project will package, upload, and deploy, and you'll be prompted to trust it. The dialog shown in Figure 3-22 appears as the project is being packaged and deployed, and you'll be prompted to trust it when it is deployed to SharePoint.

9. To test out the SharePoint-hosted app (which in this case is a drop-down list with options), open the app. You should see a message on the page that says "hello" to whoever is logged into the Office 365 session. When you click one of the options in the drop-down list, the app prompts you with some additional information about that option, as shown in Figure 3-23.

FIGURE 3-21

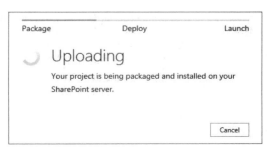

FIGURE 3-22

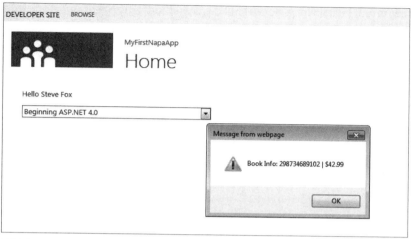

FIGURE 3-23

How It Works

A couple of things are going on in this code. For example, the simple message that is displayed is default code that is included within every app for SharePoint you build using Napa. You can remove it and add your own code. In this exercise, you added the Select HTML object that provides you with a type of HTML drop-down box with three options — different books that have been added as selections. Also, a JavaScript function called getBookInfo() is called every time you change your selection in the drop-down box.

JavaScript is a dynamic language that runs on the client. What that means is when the client loads the browser and subsequently the page, it runs the script that you've embedded within the page within your Napa app. However, one of the key things you need to be aware of when using JavaScript to develop for SharePoint is that it doesn't maintain state, so you have to incorporate it into the design of your applications.

As you can see from the code in the preceding Try it Out, JavaScript events are encapsulated within the script tag and live in the page within which they are called. This is not the only way to call JavaScript code — you can also store the code in a separate file (for example, foo.js) that is further stored within SharePoint as a site asset. If you were to store the JavaScript separately, you would not encapsulate the script in script tags — you would merely add the methods and any helper functions to that .JS (.js) file so they execute when called from the page.

```
<script language="javascript" type="text/javascript">
function foo()
{
...

}
 </script>
```

With the example using inline JavaScript, the `getBookInfo` method call triggers when the user changes her selection within the list box. You can see in the following code that the event that triggers is the `onChange` event.

```
<select id='dropdiv' onchange="getBookInfo(this)">
 <option value='1'>
Professional SharePoint 2007 Development
 </option>
 <option value='2'>
Beginning ASP.NET 3.5
 </option>
 <option value='3'>
Professional SharePoint Development using Silverlight
 </option>
</select>
```

Depending on what the user selects, you can see that the object (that is, the selected item) is passed with the call to `getBookInfo`. The variable called `selected` then gets the value of the selected item, which further enables the code to run a conditional check against the selected item. So, if the selected item is the first item, other variables are set and then subsequently concatenated and pushed out in an `alert` event to the user.

As you can see, Napa is an exciting evolution in the SharePoint development story. Lightweight apps can be simple to build and easy to deploy. However, in some cases you might require a more rigorous and powerful set of capabilities such as those offered by IntelliSense, ALM options, rich debugging, and so on. For these types of features, you'll likely want to use Visual Studio, covered next.

DEVELOPING SHAREPOINT APPLICATIONS USING VISUAL STUDIO 2012

Visual Studio 2012 ships with a standard set of project-level and item-level templates that make SharePoint development much easier and more powerful than in previous versions. With SharePoint 2010, you could leverage Visual Studio 2010 to do a lot of your development, and with Visual Studio 2012 you now have many new features and options.

To help with your development efforts, Microsoft ships a standard set of project templates out of the box with an additional set of project item templates. For example, you can create a SharePoint 2013 Project and then add any number of SharePoint project items to that project using the template options. (You do require a local instance of SharePoint to be installed to use these options.) Figure 3-24 illustrates the different project-level options for you.

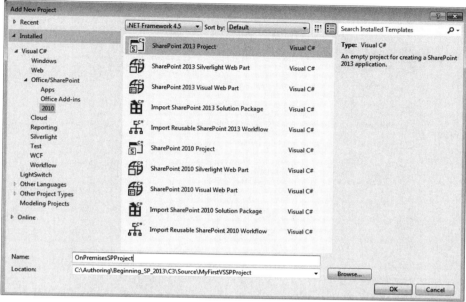

FIGURE 3-24

The following project-level templates are available by default in a Visual Studio project:

➤ **SharePoint 2010 Project/SharePoint 2013 Project:** An empty SharePoint project that enables you to add one or more item-level templates to build out a solution

➤ **SharePoint 2010 Silverlight Web Part/SharePoint 2013 Silverlight Web Part:** Rich media Web part that uses Silverlight as the rendering engine

➤ **SharePoint 2010 Visual Web Part/SharePoint 2013 Visual Web Part:** Web part that provides designer capabilities so you can drag and drop ASP.NET UI controls and then add code-behind

➤ **Import SharePoint 2010 Solution Package/Import SharePoint 2013 Solution Package:** Template that enables you to import and then redistribute packaged solutions to your SharePoint farm

➤ **Import Reusable SharePoint 2010 Workflow/Import Reusable SharePoint 2013 Workflow:** Template that enables you to import and then redistribute and deploy existing workflow solutions to your SharePoint farm

These project-level templates provide a wide array of functionality, ranging from an empty SharePoint project to different types of Web parts to workflow applications, or the importation of legacy applications that you want to run in SharePoint 2013.

In addition to project-level templates, a set of options is available for the item level. An item is something you add to a project, such as a list or event receiver (see Figure 3-25).

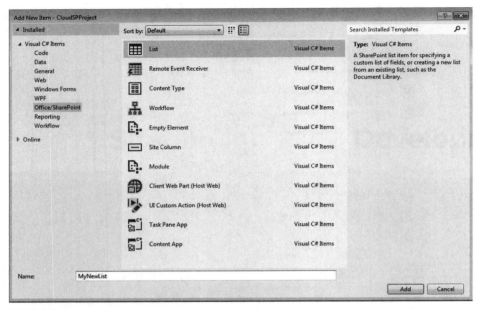

FIGURE 3-25

The item-level templates available in Visual Studio are as follows:

➤ **List:** Provides a list designer experience for you to quickly design, build, and deploy lists to SharePoint.

➤ **Remote Event Receiver:** Enables you to build event-driven applications (for example, an event fires when a new list item is added to a list) that respond to specific user or site actions.

➤ **Content Type:** Enables you to create custom content types that derive from existing SharePoint content types such as documents, announcements lists, columns, fields, and so on, that can be reused across your SharePoint site.

➤ **Workflow:** Supports application code that manages activities defined within a business process (for example, multi-tiered approval process).

➤ **Empty Element:** Provides a way for you to leverage Visual Studio to build SharePoint artifacts that don't have project- or item-level templates associated with them.

➤ **Site Column:** A column that can be reused across your SharePoint site.

➤ **Module:** Container that you can use to deploy files or dependency assets (for example, JavaScript source) to your SharePoint site.

➤ **Client Web Part (Host Web):** Type of Web part that is a container that loads external assets or apps (could be external to the SharePoint site such as a Bing map or an asset or Web page within the SharePoint site).

➤ **UI Custom Action (Host Web):** Represents a method to host buttons, links, or menus that support a customized path for the user.

➤ **Task Pane App:** A new type of App for Office artifact that can surface HTML/CSS/JavaScript apps within parts of SharePoint (for example, a task pane within Outlook in O365).

➤ **Content App:** A new type of App for Office that is surfaced within the doc itself (for example, a floating app that links Excel Web access data to Bing maps).

You'll come across other templates as you leverage the Visual Studio tools — and as you engage with the SharePoint community that built a number of Visual Studio add-ins for SharePoint. The goal for these project- and item-level templates is to make the tasks of building, debugging, and deploying a range of application types and artifacts to SharePoint easy. In SharePoint 2013, a range of new features exist that have been added to Visual Studio 2012. The following are a sampling of these new feature areas:

➤ Designers for lists and content types

➤ Ability to create site columns

➤ Silverlight Web part options

➤ Ability to publish SharePoint solutions to remote SharePoint servers

➤ Test SharePoint performance by using profiling tools

➤ Create sandboxed Visual Web parts

➤ Improved support for sandboxed solutions

➤ Support for JavaScript debugging and IntelliSense for JavaScript

Each of the preceding is important in different ways. For example, if you look at the underlying structure of lists, you're into heavy XML structures, so having a designer experience is a much more efficient way to lay out, build, and deploy custom list templates to SharePoint. Further, remote development and debugging is a huge leap forward. In SharePoint 2010, you were relegated to debugging against your local instance. This is especially important when trying to discover ill-performing code artifacts, and the profiling tools help you to identify those performance sore spots such that code on your SharePoint site doesn't slow down overall use and load times. You could package and deploy remotely, but debugging was limited. Also, with the increased focus on JavaScript, having the right tools to debug and leverage IntelliSense is important to increase your developer productivity.

Beyond the wealth of available templates, Visual Studio supports even more great features. For example, the Server Explorer provides you with the capability to visualize the key artifacts within your SharePoint site such as lists, list items, workflows, and so on. Visual Studio also has standard ways to build, package, and publish applications using right-click menu options, as shown in Figure 3-26. Using these menu options, you can build and deploy through the Build menu and then right-click your project to Retract it; Visual Studio does all the cleanup for you — exactly what you would expect when cleaning your solutions and apps from the SharePoint instances.

FIGURE 3-26

Given the different types of available templates, the developer now has more options than ever to structure and deploy an application to SharePoint in a more productive and manageable way.

Whether you're building a SharePoint solution (that is, .WSP) or a new App for SharePoint (that is, .APP), you have the right options for your development needs.

Another work item that returns in Visual Studio 2012 is source-code control (often discussed within the context of application life-cycle management or ALM). With the ALM features built into Team Foundation Server (TFS), you have ample opportunity to manage your source code in a streamlined way. For example, when you create a new project you can right-click the project in Solution Explorer, select Add Solution to Source Control (see Figure 3-27), and then configure a TFS server for your application code.

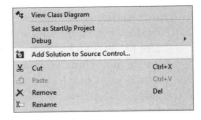

FIGURE 3-27

Because there are so many features Visual Studio offers to help develop applications in SharePoint, it is helpful to familiarize yourself with them in greater detail. Use the steps in the following Try It Out to explore some of the Visual Studio 2012 features through the creation of a SharePoint-hosted app.

TRY IT OUT   Building a SharePoint-Hosted App Using Visual Studio 2012

To create a SharePoint-hosted app:

1. Open Visual Studio 2012, and click File ⇨ New ⇨ Project.
2. Navigate to the Office/SharePoint template folder and then click Apps. Select Apps for SharePoint 2013.
3. Provide a name for the app (`SP_Hosted_Custom_List`), and click OK.
4. When prompted, select SharePoint-hosted and click Finish, as shown in Figure 3-28.

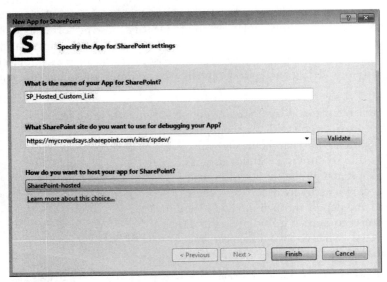

FIGURE 3-28

5. When Visual Studio creates the project, right-click the project in Solution Explorer, and then select Add ➪ New Item.

6. Select the List item and then provide a name (`Employees`) and click Add, as shown in Figure 3-29.

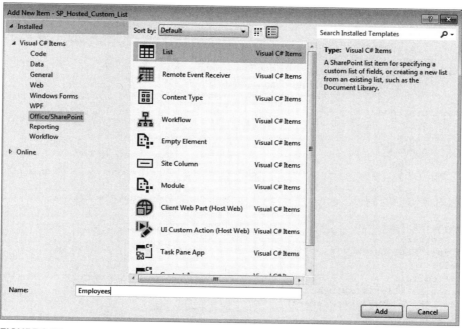

FIGURE 3-29

7. After you add, you'll be prompted to select the type of list you want. Leave the default choice, which is Default (Blank), and click Finish.

8. Visual Studio loads the default view into the main IDE window. Select additional columns to add to your custom list as shown in Figure 3-30. You can select as many as you like or type in your own column name and select a Type.

9. When you've finished adding columns, double-click the `AppManifest.xml` file and amend the Scope to be Web and the Permission to be Read.

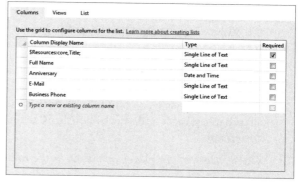

FIGURE 3-30

10. Double-click the `Default.aspx` page and add the bolded code from the following snippet.

```
<asp:Content ContentPlaceHolderId="PlaceHolderAdditionalPageHead"
runat="server">
    <script type="text/javascript" src="../Scripts/jquery-1.6.2.min.js">
</script>

    <link rel="Stylesheet" type="text/css" href="../Content/App.css" />

    <script type="text/javascript" src="../Scripts/App.js"></script>

    <script type="text/javascript">
        $(document).ready(function () {
            SP.SOD.executeFunc('sp.js', 'SP.ClientContext', function ()
{ sharePointReady(); });
            });
    </script>
</asp:Content>

<%-- The markup and script in the following Content element will be placed in
the <body> of the page --%>
<asp:Content ContentPlaceHolderId="PlaceHolderMain" runat="server">

<WebPartPages:WebPartZone
    runat="server"
    FrameType="TitleBarOnly"
    ID="full"
    Title="loc:full" >
<WebPartPages:XsltListViewWebPart
    ID="XsltListViewEmployeeWebPart"
    runat="server"
    ListUrl="Lists/Employees"
    IsIncluded="True"
    NoDefaultStyle="TRUE"
    Title="Employees"
    PageType="PAGE_NORMALVIEW"
    Default="False"
    ViewContentTypeId="0x">
</WebPartPages:XsltListViewWebPart>
</WebPartPages:WebPartZone>

</asp:Content>
```

11. When done, press F6 to build the project. When the project builds successfully, right-click the SharePoint project and select Publish. When prompted, click Finish to prepare the SharePoint-hosted app.

12. When Windows Explorer opens, copy the folder path of the .APP file.

13. Navigate to your SharePoint site, and click New App to Deploy.

14. In the Deploy App dialog, click the Upload link, browse to your .APP by clicking the browse button (here's where you can paste in your folder path), and click OK.

15. Click Deploy, and when prompted, click the Trust It button.

16. After your app successfully deploys, click the Site Contents link and then click the newly deployed SharePoint-hosted app. Your newly deployed SharePoint-hosted app loads.

17. Add a couple of new list items to your Web part view of the Employees custom list — see Figure 3-31.

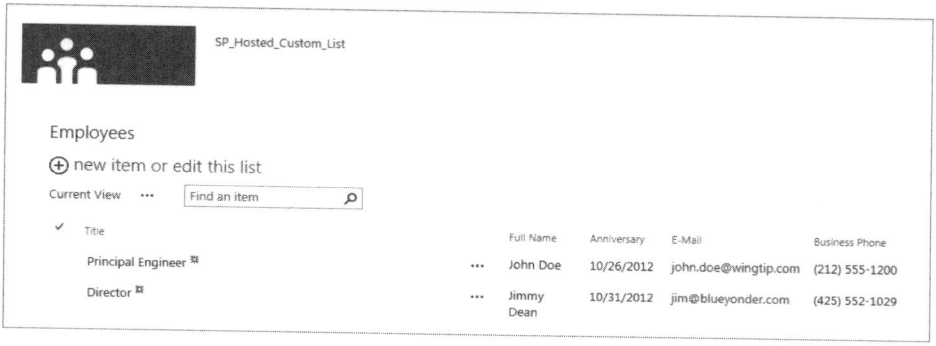

FIGURE 3-31

How It Works

The SharePoint-hosted app is meant to be for lightweight applications. The exercise you just completed leveraged the new list designer to add a custom list to your SharePoint site as well as a view to that list using an ASP.NET XSLT List View Web part — added to your ASP.NET `default.aspx` page through code. The XSLT View Web part is not new to SharePoint, but provides a way to surface a view of it in SharePoint Web pages. The list designer experience, however, will evolve the way in which you work with lists because it abstracts the XML representation of that list. For example, in previous versions of SharePoint, you would need to hand-code the XML for the list. The following is the top-level list template XML, to which a more complex XML schema is associated.

```
<?xml version="1.0" encoding="utf-8"?>
<Elements xmlns="http://schemas.microsoft.com/sharepoint/">
    <ListTemplate
        Name="Employees"
        Type="10000"
        BaseType="0"
        OnQuickLaunch="TRUE"
        SecurityBits="11"
        Sequence="410"
        DisplayName="Employees"
        Description="My List Definition"
        Image="/_layouts/15/images/itgen.png"/>
</Elements>
```

To see this XML, you can navigate to the new list you added and click the `Elements.xml` and `Schema.xml` files.

This exercise is useful not only to show you how to create a list, but also to show you the XML representation of that list. In a sense, this illustrates the way in which tooling is maturing around the SharePoint platform to make it easier for you to build SharePoint applications.

You're going to leverage more than just JavaScript and simple ASP.NET code when building Apps for SharePoint using Visual Studio 2012. For example, those familiar with SharePoint 2010 will remember the client-side object model (CSOM); you'll find that you use this API within the different hosted model apps (across JavaScript, Silverlight, and .NET). The following code snippet walks through setting the context for a SharePoint site, integrating the OAuth accessToken object within the context which is new to SharePoint 2013 and facilitates cross-domain app authentication. It then creates a Collaborative Application Markup Language (CAML) query, which is an XML language that enables you to build raw queries against SharePoint lists. The code also creates a query against a list and returns the items from the list. You can see a custom Customer object that is used to transpose the returned list items and bind them to a Listbox.

```
...
ClientContext clientContext =
            TokenHelper.GetClientContextWithAccessToken(sharepointUrl.ToString(),
 accessToken);
            Web web = clientContext.Web;
            clientContext.Load(web);
            List list = clientContext.Web.Lists.GetByTitle("Customers");
            CamlQuery camlQuery = new CamlQuery();
            camlQuery.ViewXml = "<View/>";
            ListItemCollection listItems = list.GetItems(camlQuery);
            clientContext.Load(list);
            clientContext.Load(listItems);
            clientContext.ExecuteQuery();

            foreach (ListItem listItem in listItems)
            {
                Customer tempCustomer = new Customer();
                tempCustomer.Name = listItem["Title"].ToString();
                tempCustomer.Company = listItem["Company"].ToString();
                listOfCustomers.Add(tempCustomer);
            }

            lstbxCustomerData.DataSource = listOfCustomers;
            lstbxCustomerData.DataBind();
```

OData is useful in a very similar way. You can use a REST URI to access data within lists and then cycle through the XML or JSON feed and integrate within your application. The following URI returns the list items in the Customers list.

```
https://me.sharepoint.com/sites/sp/_api/web/lists/getbytitle('Customers')/items
```

OTHER TOOLS FOR SHAREPOINT DEVELOPMENT

This chapter covers much about the core tools that are available for SharePoint development. Of course, you'll come across many other niche tools in addition to the main ones — some of which can be proprietary to your organization. Two of these lesser known tools are quite helpful in the right situation: Expression Blend, which is for design, especially when you're building out Silverlight-based applications, and Fiddler, for debugging.

Developing with Expression Blend

Visual Studio, SharePoint Designer, and Napa are your core developer tools for SharePoint, so you won't see as much coverage here for Expression Blend as you did for the aforementioned tools. However, getting at least an introduction to Expression is important, because it provides a great suite of applications offering Web, design, and encoding features.

One of the main reasons to introduce Expression Blend here is that it offers a great way to design Silverlight-based and Deep Zoom applications. Silverlight is a great way to create rich media and dynamic applications — and this dynamic user experience begins with the use of Expression Blend. Furthermore, Deep Zoom can also provide some interesting media experiences with images. For example, the Hard Rock Memorabilia site (`http://memorabilia.hardrock.com`) leverages the Deep Zoom capabilities within a Silverlight application embedded within an HTML page — see Figure 3-32.

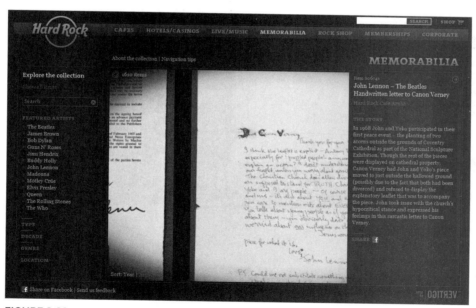

FIGURE 3-32

> **NOTE** *For more information on Silverlight and Deep Zoom, visit the following MSDN article:* `http://msdn.microsoft.com/en-us/library/cc645050(v=VS.95).aspx`.

The experience on the site enables you to zoom in on the different images on the page with remarkable clarity because the application refocuses each time it zooms into an image. Although you can create Deep Zoom applications like the one in Figure 3-32, you can also create more everyday business applications using Silverlight. For example, much like you would create a WinForm application using Visual Studio, you could just as easily create a Silverlight application using Expression Blend. The added value you get with Silverlight is additional rich-design functionality built into Expression that provides support for animation, behaviors, action triggers, gradient design, and so on — so it truly offers much more of a design experience than the designer that ships with the Silverlight templates within Visual Studio. Figure 3-33 shows how you can create dynamic controls in your Silverlight applications using Expression Blend.

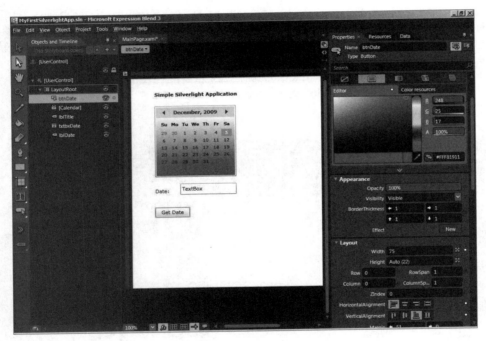

FIGURE 3-33

After you create these rich controls, you can then import them into Visual Studio and add event handlers to them as shown in Figure 3-34, enabling you to combine the design and development experience into one seamless, managed process.

Design is an important aspect of SharePoint development, and as you evolve in your SharePoint journey you will begin to look for more ways to enhance the design experience for your application development.

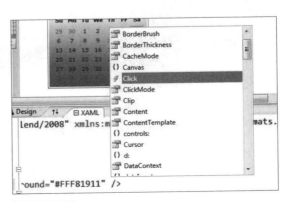

FIGURE 3-34

Debugging Using Fiddler

One other tool that you'll likely want to learn how to use is Fiddler, an HTTP debugging application written by Eric Lawrence. Fiddler is an excellent way to capture key statistics and metadata for network transactions, data packets (for example, XML or JSON data), performance and load times, and so on (see Figure 3-35). As you build and deploy your apps, especially now that you'll be focusing some of your time on cloud-based apps, tasks such as understanding how and where different traffic is being routed within your application, monitoring load times, and detecting bottlenecks, will be essential to building performing and usable apps. Fiddler provides these capabilities through its tracing functions (and more), as you can see in Figure 3-35.

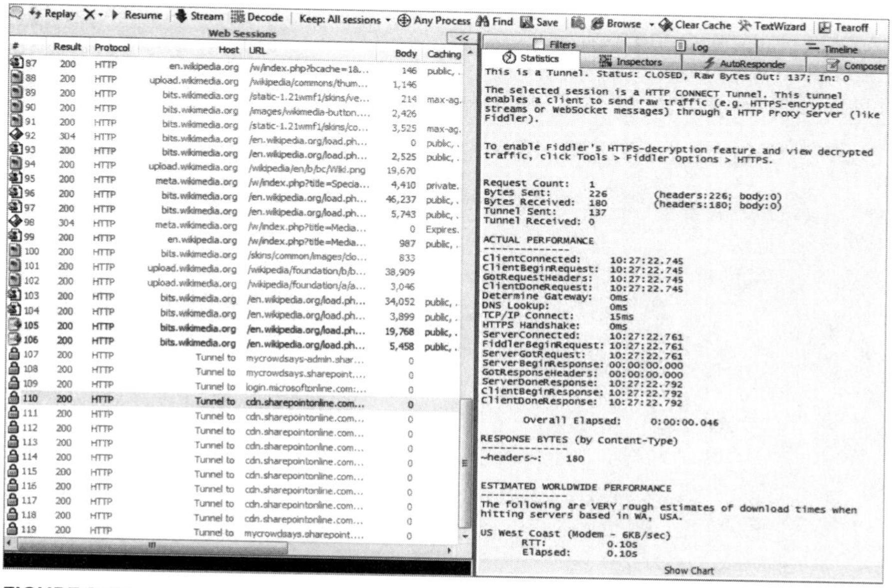

FIGURE 3-35

You can download Fiddler for free from: http://www.fiddler2.com/fiddler2/.

SUMMARY

Several major development tools are available to you in SharePoint 2013 with which you can perform different types of development — ranging from power use to a design to managing code. Some of these specific tools include Napa, SharePoint Designer, Visual Studio, Expression Blend, and Fiddler.

You will find more tools as you become an active part of the SharePoint developer community. The support for SharePoint development is growing, and with the release of Visual Studio 2012, good life-cycle and template support exists for those just getting into the world of SharePoint development.

In the next chapter, you take the next step in your SharePoint development journey and learn about the essential skills you'll need to pick up and how you should make choices against the range of solution and application types when building your SharePoint solutions.

EXERCISES

1. Describe the range of development tools that you can use for SharePoint development.

2. Summarize when you would use one tool over another.

3. Build out some simple applications leveraging the core project- and item-level templates in Visual Studio 2012.

▶ **WHAT YOU LEARNED IN THIS CHAPTER**

ITEM	DESCRIPTION
SharePoint Development	The spectrum of development ranges from power user to designer to managed code development.
Napa	This browser-based development tool enables you to build a variety of apps for SharePoint.
SharePoint Designer	You can use this designer tool to create and edit sites, pages, content types, and columns, build workflow, design master pages, and much more.
Visual Studio	This fully featured development IDE offers project- and item-level templates for you to build a variety of SharePoint apps and solutions.
Expression Blend	This rich design tool integrates with Visual Studio and enables you to build Silverlight and rich media applications.
Fiddler	You can use this Web-debugging tool to help you understand network traffic, metadata, and data transactions in your applications.

RECOMMENDED READING

Napa Overview — http://msdn.microsoft.com/en-us/library/jj220041%28v=office
.15%29.aspx
Visual Studio 2012 Overview — http://technet.microsoft.com/visualstudio/eng/whats-new
Getting Started with SharePoint 2013 Development — http://msdn.microsoft.com/en-us/
library/jj163980%28v=office.15%29.aspx
Fiddler Download — http://www.fiddler2.com/fiddler2/
Expression Blend Overview — http://expression.microsoft.com/en-us/cc507094.aspx

Understanding Your Development Options

WROX.COM CODE DOWNLOADS FOR THIS CHAPTER

The wrox.com code downloads for this chapter are found at: http://www.wrox.com/WileyCDA/WroxTitle/productCd-1118495845.html on the Download Code tab. The code for this chapter is divided into the following major examples:

➤   C4_Code_Options.zip

Thus far, you've been introduced to SharePoint 2013, learned about the different app models that are new to SharePoint, and walked through the tooling options for SharePoint. By now, you should have a pretty good understanding of the fundamentals from a development perspective. However, when you embark on your development journey with SharePoint you will be confounded with one question again and again: How should I develop *this* in SharePoint?

This might seem like a simple question, but the answer relies on factors not only within the technical scope of SharePoint features (that is, "What feature can I use to fulfill this business requirement?"), but it also relies on factors outside of your SharePoint project (for example, "Does this need to be in source code?" or "Can I accomplish this with an out-of-the-box feature?" and so on). To answer the question, you'll need to understand the features built into, for example, each SharePoint site template, what APIs to use when, and what solution type to use (*.WSP versus *.APP). Thus, knowing and understanding your options is key to successful development in the SharePoint world.

APPLICATION AND SOLUTION TYPES

When developing applications for SharePoint, remember that you have a few different ways to build and deploy a SharePoint application or solution. The following is a short list of the types of options — both historical and today:

➤ **Farm-level solution:** Typically associated with either SharePoint Server or SharePoint Foundation, this type of solution (.WSP or SharePoint feature) is an application that is installable and accessible across any site collection within a SharePoint farm.

➤ **Sandboxed solution:** Lightweight solution or feature that is deployed to a sandboxed environment (that is, a restricted execution environment that allows programs to access specific resources and data within the SharePoint site) and can be deployed to Office 365 or on-premises SharePoint installations.

➤ **SharePoint-hosted app:** Lightweight app (.APP) that is deployed to SharePoint but leverages client-side code such as HTML, JavaScript, and CSS.

➤ **Cloud-hosted app:** Apps (.APP) that are hosted in the cloud, but can be deployed to either SharePoint on-premises or Office 365. These are either Autohosted or Provider-hosted (as discussed in Chapter 2, "Overview of SharePoint 2013 App Model").

Each one of these options has pros and cons that you will need to understand — not only so you can choose between them, but also so you can really take advantage of all the services, APIs, or features that are available within each one of these options. You may also have combinations of a few of these options — you're not relegated to just using one or the other. For example, you may combine SharePoint-hosted with Cloud-hosted.

> **INSTALLATION TYPE MATTERS**
>
> The type of SharePoint installation (SharePoint Server or Office 365) also plays a role in choosing a development solution and choosing the APIs to use within that solution. For instance, if you're building an application for SharePoint Foundation or SharePoint Server, you can develop and deploy solutions that have farm-level scope (farm-level solution). You also can use a broader set of SharePoint-specific APIs; that is, you can use both the Server-Side Object Model and the Client-Side Object Model. If your target installation is Office 365, you will likely use Cloud-hosted apps, in which case you won't use the Server-Side Object Model, but design your apps using the Client-Side Object Model and more broadly the Windows Azure platform.

Table 4-1 further explores some of the differences you need to think about across the development options.

TABLE 4-1: Considerations Across SharePoint Deployment

CONSIDERATION	FARM-LEVEL SOLUTION	SANDBOXED SOLUTION	SHAREPOINT HOSTED	CLOUD HOSTED
App scope	Farm/site collection	Sandbox	Site	Site or tenancy
Architecture	Site	Site	Website	Multi-tenant app
Developer skills	Full stack	.NET	HTML/JS	Full stack
Server code	Yes	No	No	Yes
Key limitations	None	Limited OM, extensibility	No server code	Hosting expertise required

Note that if your target SharePoint installation is SharePoint Server, then you have the option of using the farm-level solution, which supports all the different types of app development. In regards to being able to leverage SharePoint APIs, services, and features, the farm-level solution is the most powerful out of the different solutions (as measured by the breadth of SharePoint API you can use).

Sandboxed solutions, inversely, are the most restricted. You can build some interesting applications with them, but they do not affect the whole server farm (unlike the farm-level solution), and they can be deployed by the site collection administrator and are isolated to resources within the site collection to which they are deployed. (You won't see too much coverage of sandboxed solutions in this book because Microsoft is emphasizing using the cloud-hosted app models moving forward and deprecating sandboxed solutions.)

You might think of SharePoint-hosted apps as sister apps to the sandboxed solutions. They are also lightweight apps that are meant to leverage site collection resources and artifacts; however, one of the key differences is that you typically leverage unmanaged code to build these apps. Also, as mentioned earlier, the cloud-hosted apps are pretty powerful; you can deploy them on full installations of SharePoint (for example, SharePoint Server) or you can deploy them in Office 365. They bring the broader elements of the cloud into SharePoint and can leverage some of the core REST APIs and client-side object model.

With these points in mind, you might be asking yourself in what situation do you use one over the other. Although Table 4-1 provides some measure of differentiation, Table 4-2 provides a little more guidance around when you might use one option over the other.

TABLE 4-2: Recommendations on When to Use Which Option

CONSIDERATION	WHEN TO USE
Farm-level solution	Use this solution for applications being deployed to SharePoint Server or SharePoint Foundation. Suitable for enterprise-grade solutions (such as Sales Management dashboard that is integrated with SAP) that require farm-level (or site-collection level) resource access, cross-site collection deployment, or need to execute server-side code.
Sandboxed solution	Given the strategic direction toward the cloud-hosted model, it is recommended that moving forward you should use the SharePoint-hosted model instead of the sandboxed solution. (While supported for backward compatibility, these are marked as deprecated in MSDN.)
SharePoint-hosted	Use when you have smaller, lightweight apps that are centric to a specific site collection or SharePoint page (for example, custom list view on a Web page or custom content type). If you have any server-side code requirements, you cannot use SharePoint-hosted apps.
Cloud-hosted	Use when you don't want any running code on the server, if you're targeting Office 365, or if you want to build a Web app on a different infrastructure (e.g., Google, Amazon, LAMP, etc.). Use Autohosted for smaller-scale apps (for example, ASP.NET data views or forms) and Provider-hosted for enterprise-grade cloud apps (for example, expense apps that use third-party state-level services to calculate tax). The client-side object model or REST APIs can substitute some of the server-side object model functionality (especially when interacting with list data). Also, you must manage your own hosting of the app for Provider-hosted apps and the permissions/app authentication for either Autohosted or Provider-hosted depending on what you're trying to accomplish in the app.

In general, you'll find that the more SharePoint applications you develop the better sense of what to use for a particular situation you'll have, and you'll begin to ask a specific set of questions as you start to gather requirements for your SharePoint applications. These questions will range from understanding the installation scenario to data security to business process and workflow to leveraging third-party services.

> **NOTE** *A word of advice to those of you starting out as SharePoint developers: always look to see whether what the business is asking for already exists within SharePoint before you re-create it. You will save time and money by leveraging the extensive amount of out-of-the-box features that are available to you.*

While understanding when to use a specific scenario is important, so are the common developer tasks and skills that you'll need to leverage in your day-to-day SharePoint development career.

With that in mind, let's talk about the more common tasks in which you can expect to engage as a SharePoint developer.

COMMON DEVELOPER TASKS

Although everything is technically an "app" in SharePoint 2013, you will find yourself building different types of apps, and when doing so, you will run into several of the same tasks many times over. It is helpful to identify these familiar tasks so that you can hone the skills associated with them, as you'll be using them often. Some of the more common tasks you'll likely find yourself doing are as follows:

- ➤ Creating Web Parts
- ➤ Creating SharePoint-hosted apps
- ➤ Accessing and managing data
- ➤ Creating cloud-hosted apps
- ➤ Creating event receivers
- ➤ Creating ASPX pages
- ➤ Creating master pages

Let's walk through each of these tasks and explore what they are and the skills required for your success in completing them.

Creating Web Parts

One of the most common developer tasks you'll likely engage in is the creation and deployment of a Web Part. This historically has been the key artifact that a developer develops and deploys to SharePoint.

In SharePoint 2013, you work primarily with three different types of Web Parts: Standard, Visual, and Silverlight. Many other SharePoint artifacts might *feel* like a Web Part, but in many cases these are ASP.NET objects, containers, or IFRAMEs that provide dynamic client-side code rendering and pass-through capabilities to other Web Parts or applications, or views to list data. Because of the rich designer capabilities, the Visual and Silverlight Web Parts will likely be your first choice; however, this section covers all three.

Standard Web Parts

A Standard Web Part provides the plumbing for you to create a Web Part and deploy it to SharePoint. When you create a Standard Web Part, you are creating most objects from scratch and assembling the Web Part without the aid of a designer. This can be good and bad. If you're a skilled developer and are familiar with the ASP.NET/SharePoint APIs and object model, then this won't be too much trouble. However, you do gain some advantage when using more designer-driven Web Parts, if nothing more than to improve your productivity around creating a user interface for your Web Part.

To follow is a short code snippet that includes a text box, label, and button control that are being instantiated, properties set, and a `Click` event that corresponds to the button control. In this code snippet, you can see that the four controls are declared at the class level, and then in the `CreateChildControls` method the properties for those objects are set, the `Add` method is called to add the controls to the `Controls` collection (to display them in the Web Part), and the `myButton_Click` event is called to render the user's entry as text in one of the labels. If you have not coded Web Parts before, this is pretty standard; that is, creating the controls, setting the properties for those controls, adding the controls to the `Controls` collection, and also adding any event handlers for those controls. This code illustrates the explicit code you need to write to generate the UI through ASP.NET objects:

```
namespace MyFirstDevTask.TaskOneWebPart
{
    [ToolboxItemAttribute(false)]
    public class TaskOneWebPart : WebPart
    {
        Label myLabel = new Label();
        TextBox myTextbox = new TextBox();
        Label myResponse = new Label();
        Button myButton = new Button();

        protected override void CreateChildControls()
        {
            myLabel.Text = "Enter Text:";
            myResponse.Text = "";
            myTextbox.Enabled = true;
            myTextbox.Text = "";
            myButton.Text = "Click Me";
            this.Controls.Add(myLabel);
            this.Controls.Add(myTextbox);
            this.Controls.Add(new LiteralControl("<br/>"));
            this.Controls.Add(myResponse);
            this.Controls.Add(new LiteralControl("<br/>"));
            this.Controls.Add(myButton);

            myButton.Click += new EventHandler(myButton_Click);
        }

        void myButton_Click(object sender, EventArgs e)
        {
            string userResponse = myTextbox.Text;
            myResponse.Text = userResponse;
        }
    }
}
```

Figure 4-1 shows the end result if you were to deploy this Web Part to SharePoint.

SimpleWebPart - MyFirstWebPart
Enter Text: Hello World!
Hello World!
Click Me

FIGURE 4-1

Visual Web Parts

The Visual Web Part is different from the Standard Web Part in that you have a designer experience for creating the user interface (UI) for the Web Part. This makes it very easy to add controls and code-behind for this type of Web Part. Because SharePoint is built on ASP.NET, you have many of the same underlying constructs and objects that you might have learned through ASP.NET for the creation of a Standard Web Part. You can create and apply many of the same objects and events when building out a Visual Web Part that you might have used when building out an older ASP.NET Web Part.

Using the designer experience in Visual Studio to create the Web Part UI, you can drag and drop a wide array of library controls from the toolbox onto the designer surface. Where you would manually write the code in the Standard Web Part to create controls or events, in the Visual Web Part you use a method with which you're likely familiar: drag and drop the control and then double-click the control in the designer to add the code-behind. For example, if you were to take the same functionality shown earlier in the Standard Web Part and implement it in the Visual Web Part, then you would have an ASP.NET user control (ASCX file) that represents the UI with a code-behind file. The ASCX user control code would look like the following:

```
<asp:Label ID="myLabel" runat="server" Text="Enter Text:"></asp:Label>
 <asp:TextBox ID="myTextbox" runat="server"></asp:TextBox>
<p>
    <asp:Label ID="myResponse" runat="server" Text="Label"></asp:Label>
</p>
<asp:Button ID="myButton" runat="server" onclick="myButton_Click"
    Text="Click Me" />
```

The code-behind for the ASCX user control would look like the following:

```
using System;
using System.Web.UI;
using System.Web.UI.WebControls;
using System.Web.UI.WebControls.WebParts;

namespace MyFirstDevTask.TaskTwoWebPart
{
    public partial class TaskTwoWebPartUserControl : UserControl
    {
        ...

        protected void myButton_Click(object sender, EventArgs e)
        {
            string userResponse = myTextbox.Text;
            myResponse.Text = userResponse;
        }

    }
}
```

Note that the control declarations do not appear in this specific ASCX code-behind (ASCX is the file extension for the ASP.NET user control file); however, a reference exists to the ASCX control in the core Web Part class that loads the user control you build with the designer experience at runtime. The following shows the code that represents this reference inside of the core Web Part class. Note that the _ascxPath object simply represents a filesystem path to the location of the ASCX file you created using the designer.

```
public class TaskTwoWebPart : WebPart
    {
        private const string _ascxPath =
@"~/_CONTROLTEMPLATES/MyFirstDevTask/TaskTwoWebPart/TaskTwoWebPartUserControl.ascx";

        protected override void CreateChildControls()
        {
            Control control = Page.LoadControl(_ascxPath);
            Controls.Add(control);
        }
    }
```

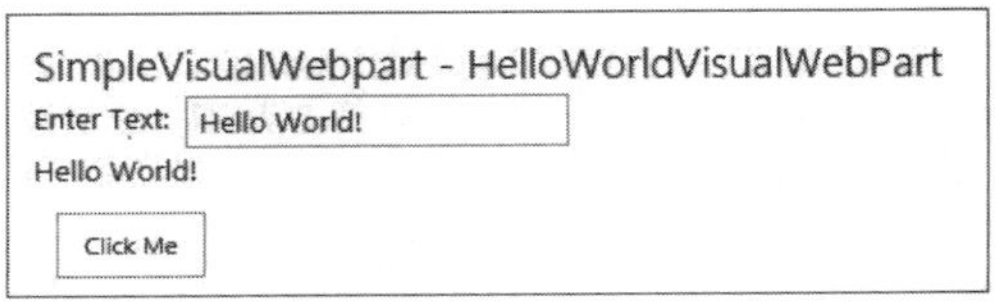

Figure 4-2 shows what this Visual Web Part looks like.

Now that you've seen a bit of code behind both a Standard and Visual Web Part, let's walk through an exercise to create a new Visual Web Part. This exercise assumes that you've created a SharePoint site (a developer site).

FIGURE 4-2

TRY IT OUT   Creating a Visual Web Part

Visual Web Parts provide a designer experience for your Web Part customization. To create a Visual Web Part, perform the following steps:

1. Open Visual Studio 2012.

2. Click File ⇨ New Project, navigate to Office/SharePoint ⇨ SharePoint Solutions, and then select SharePoint 2013 – Empty SharePoint Solution.

3. Provide a name for the project (**MyFirstSPProject**), as shown in Figure 4-3.

4. After the new project has been created, right-click the SharePoint project and select Add ⇨ New Item.

5. In the Add New Item dialog, select the Visual Web Part item template.

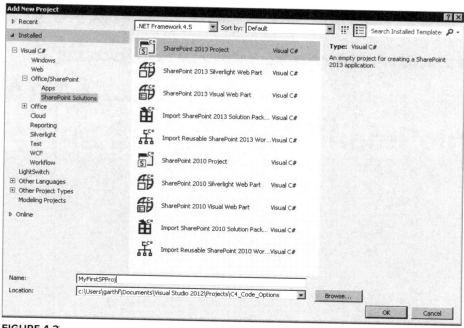

FIGURE 4-3

6. A prompt appears, asking you to designate the application as a sandboxed solution or a farm-level application. Select Deploy as a farm solution, and click Finish, as shown in Figure 4-4.

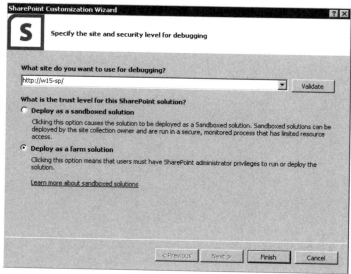

FIGURE 4-4

7. Provide a name for the Visual Web Part (**MyNewVisualWebPart**), and click Add. See Figure 4-5.

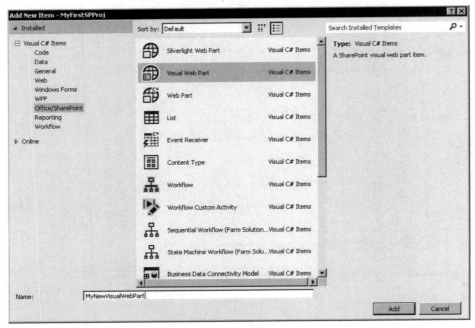

FIGURE 4-5

8. After the Visual Web Part is added to the project, right-click the SharePoint project and select Add ⇨ Class, and provide a name for the new class (**Sales**).

9. Click Add.

10. Add the bolded code as per the following code snippet:

```
using System;
using System.Collections.Generic;
using System.Linq;
using System.Text;
using System.Threading.Tasks;

namespace MyFirstSPProj
{
    class Sales
    {
        public int ID { get; set; }
        public string Quarter { get; set; }
        public string TotalSales { get; set; }
    }
}
```

11. Right-click the `Default.aspx` page and select View Designer. Click the Source tab and add the bolded code as per the following code snippet:

```
<%@ Assembly Name="$SharePoint.Project.AssemblyFullName$" %>
<%@ Assembly Name="Microsoft.Web.CommandUI, Version=15.0.0.0, Culture=neutral,
PublicKeyToken=71e9bce111e9429c" %>
…

<p style="font-family: calibri">
    My First Visual Web Part</p>
<asp:GridView ID="salesGridView" runat="server" CellPadding="4"
Font-Names="Calibri" Font-Size="Small" ForeColor="#333333" GridLines="None">
    <AlternatingRowStyle BackColor="White" ForeColor="#284775" />
    <EditRowStyle BackColor="#999999" />
    <FooterStyle BackColor="#5D7B9D" Font-Bold="True" ForeColor="White" />
    <HeaderStyle BackColor="#5D7B9D" Font-Bold="True" ForeColor="White" />
    <PagerStyle BackColor="#284775" ForeColor="White" HorizontalAlign="Center" />
    <RowStyle BackColor="#F7F6F3" ForeColor="#333333" />
    <SelectedRowStyle BackColor="#E2DED6" Font-Bold="True" ForeColor="#333333" />
    <sortedascendingcellstyle backcolor="#E9E7E2" />
    <sortedascendingheaderstyle backcolor="#506C8C" />
    <sorteddescendingcellstyle backcolor="#FFFDF8" />
    <sorteddescendingheaderstyle backcolor="#6F8DAE" />
</asp:GridView>
<br />
<asp:LinkButton ID="lnkGetSalesData" runat="server" Font-Names="Calibri"
Font-Size="Small">Get Sales</asp:LinkButton>
```

12. Double-click the `Default.aspx.cs` file and add the bolded code as per the following code snippet:

```
using System;
using System.ComponentModel;
using System.Web.UI.WebControls.WebParts;
using System.Collections.Generic;

namespace MyFirstSPProj.MyNewVisualWebPart
{
    [ToolboxItemAttribute(false)]
    public partial class MyNewVisualWebPart : WebPart
    {

        List<Sales> mySalesData = new List<Sales>();
        Sales FY11 = new Sales();
        Sales FY12 = new Sales();
        Sales FY13 = new Sales();

        public MyNewVisualWebPart()
        {
        }

        protected override void OnInit(EventArgs e)
        {
```

```
        base.OnInit(e);
        InitializeControl();
    }

    protected void Page_Load(object sender, EventArgs e)
    {
    }

    protected void lnkGetSalesData_Click(object sender, EventArgs e)
    {
        FY11.ID = 1;
        FY11.Quarter = "FY11";
        FY11.TotalSales = "$2,002,102.00";
        mySalesData.Add(FY11);

        FY12.ID = 2;
        FY12.Quarter = "FY12";
        FY12.TotalSales = "$2,500,201.00";
        mySalesData.Add(FY12);

        FY13.ID = 3;
        FY13.Quarter = "FY13";
        FY13.TotalSales = "$2,902,211.00";
        mySalesData.Add(FY13);

        salesGridView.DataSource = mySalesData;
        salesGridView.DataBind();
    }
  }
}
```

13. Right-click the SharePoint project and select Deploy. This builds and deploys the Visual Web Part to your SharePoint site.

14. After the Visual Web Part successfully deploys to the SharePoint site, navigate to the top-level SharePoint site.

15. Click Page and then Edit.

16. Click the Insert tab, and then select Web Part ⇨ Custom, and then add the newly deployed Visual Web Part. The result will look similar to Figure 4-6.

How It Works

In this exercise, you created a simple Visual Web Part. The Web Part uses a Sales object with three properties: a record ID, fiscal quarter, and sales figure, as shown in the following:

FIGURE 4-6

```
Class Sales
{
    public int ID {get; set;}
    public string Quarter {get; set;}
    public string TotalSales {get; set;}
}
```

The code then added three objects to a `List` collection that was then bound to the `GridView` object. This event was triggered by a `linkbutton`, which created the `List` collection and bound it to the `GridView`.

Silverlight Web Part

Beyond the Standard and Visual Web Parts, you can also use the Silverlight Web Part. The Silverlight Web Part provides a way to deploy rich media applications to SharePoint. The Silverlight Web Part combines a Web Part and Silverlight application into one project (so it uses the Web Part infrastructure to deploy the Silverlight application) that it then deploys to SharePoint. Behind the scenes, the Web Part represents a container that points to a Silverlight application that it deploys to SharePoint. Similar to the Visual Web Part, you can use a designer experience to build rich Web Parts (also ones that can leverage the CSOM API to interact with SharePoint data). Use the Silverlight Web Part for rich media applications, data-bound applications, and applications that you want to use across all versions of SharePoint.

FIGURE 4-7

Figure 4-7 shows a simple Silverlight Web Part that has been deployed to SharePoint.

Creating SharePoint-Hosted Apps

SharePoint-hosted apps are a newer breed of app in SharePoint 2013 and are generally a good fit across many developers' needs. This is because many SharePoint applications can be lightweight in nature, they leverage only client-side code, and they don't require heavy back-end processing elements. SharePoint-hosted apps are by far the easiest app to create and deploy; the contents of the app are deployed to a single SharePoint site.

A number of different elements can make up a SharePoint-hosted app. For example, in Figure 4-8 note the range of available options, such as Content Type, Workflow, or even App for Office.

Another reason that SharePoint-hosted apps are popular is that you can create some of the more common SharePoint artifacts you use on a regular basis; that is, lists, content types, and site columns, and then deploy them to a cloud-hosted or on-premises instance of SharePoint.

Lists are a core part of SharePoint and have a rich object model that you can use to code against them. As a potential part of lists, site columns are reusable column definitions that you can create and then repurpose across the SharePoint site. For example, if you need a very specific site column called Tax Rate that has a calculation embedded within it, you can use that site column to enforce some

FIGURE 4-8

level of consistency across your lists and sites. Content types are also a reusable object that you can repurpose across your SharePoint site. Content types can come in different shapes and sizes; for example, you might define a content type as a set of columns or as a custom document template. One common use of content types is for custom documents (for example, a legal contract with boilerplate text).You create the content type and bind that content type to a document library. You can create site columns, content types, and lists in a variety of ways. For example, you can create each one of these objects through the SharePoint Web interface. You can also leverage SharePoint Designer to create all of these objects or even Visual Studio to create content types and list definitions. Using Visual Studio makes it possible to begin integrating list definitions into other applications or redeploying a custom list definition across multiple SharePoint sites.

In the following Try It Out you take a look at how to use Visual Studio to build custom site columns for lists.

TRY IT OUT   Creating a Site Column Using Visual Studio 2012

The project templates in Visual Studio 2012 make it convenient for you to create site columns, content types, and lists. To create a custom site column using Visual Studio:

1. Open Visual Studio 2012, click File ⇨ New, and then click Project.

2. Select the Empty SharePoint Project in the SharePoint 2013 project node. Provide a name for the project (`SPH_Sales`) and click OK.

3. In the project creation wizard, make sure your SharePoint site is typed in correctly and then select the farm-level solution for the level of trust. Click Finish.

4. Visual Studio creates an empty SharePoint project for you. When it's done, right-click the top-level project node and select Add ⇨ New Item.

5. Select the Site Column template and provide a name for the file (`Sales`) and click Add — see Figure 4-9.

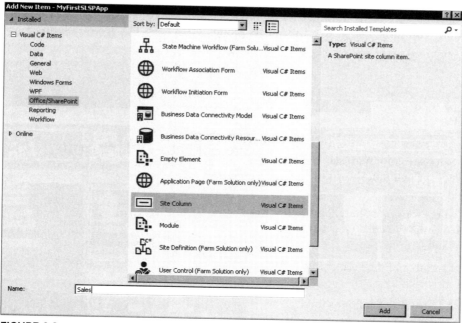

FIGURE 4-9

6. Add the following bolded code to the `Elements.xml` file that is created in the default project.

```xml
<?xml version="1.0" encoding="utf-8"?>
<Elements xmlns="http://schemas.microsoft.com/sharepoint/">
  <Field
      ID="{4c3a41d4-366d-44c7-910c-74716019ae75}"
      Name="Sales"
      DisplayName="Sales"
      Type="Choice"
      Required="FALSE"
      Group="Sales Levels">
    <CHOICES>
      <CHOICE>Premier</CHOICE>
      <CHOICE>Gold</CHOICE>
      <CHOICE>Silver</CHOICE>
      <CHOICE>Bronze</CHOICE>
      <CHOICE>Non-Affiliated</CHOICE>
    </CHOICES>
    <Default>Bronze</Default>
  </Field>
</Elements>
```

7. Press F6 to build the project. When the project successfully builds, click Build and then Deploy to deploy the site column to SharePoint.

8. Navigate to your SharePoint site and click Site Actions ⇨ Site Settings. Under Galleries, click Site Columns. You should now see a Customers group with a Sales Levels site column — see Figure 4-10.

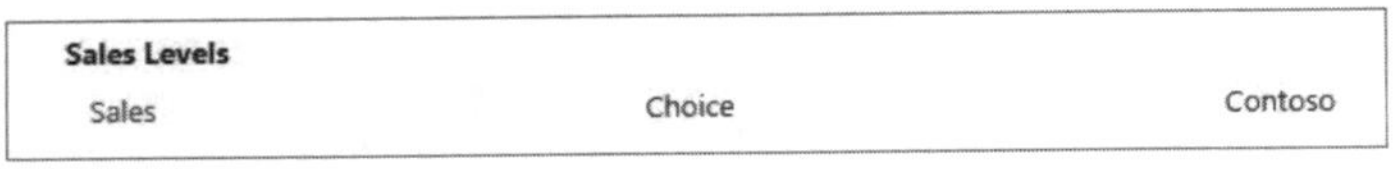

Sales Levels		
Sales	Choice	Contoso

FIGURE 4-10

9. Click the Sales site column to see the details of the column, shown in Figure 4-11.

10. Navigate to the top-level SharePoint site, click Add an App and create a new Custom List called **Sales**.

11. Click the List tab and then select List Settings.

12. Click the Add from site columns link.

13. In the Groups drop-down menu, select Sales Level and then select Sales Type. Click Add, as shown in Figure 4-12.

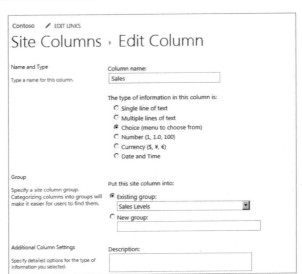

FIGURE 4-11

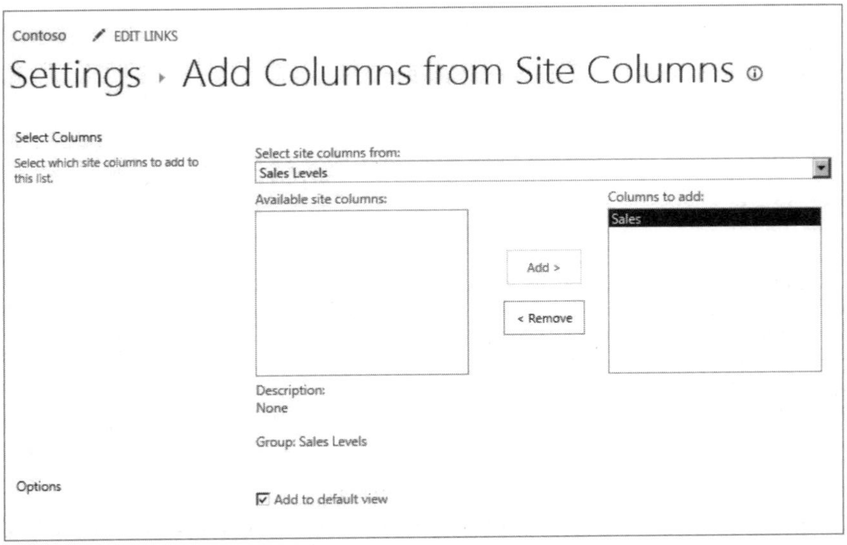

FIGURE 4-12

14. Click OK to add the new site column you created to the list.

15. Add a new item to the Sales list. You'll now see an option with the new site column, as shown in Figure 4-13.

16. Your newly amended list should now look similar to Figure 4-14.

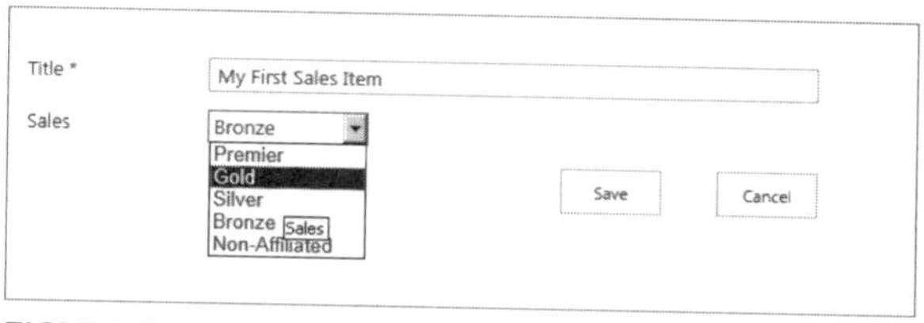

FIGURE 4-13

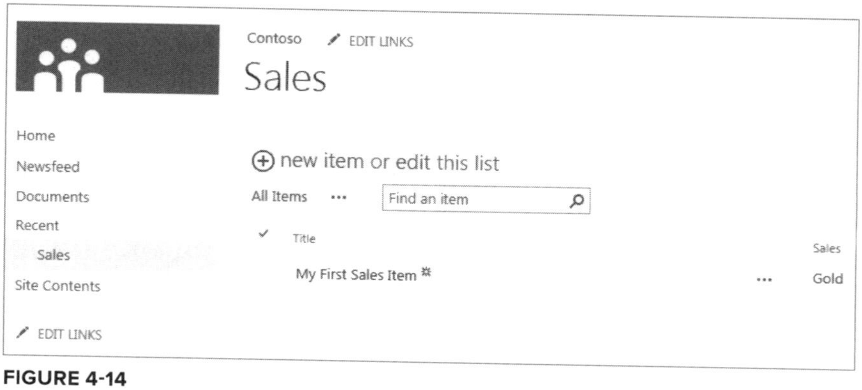

FIGURE 4-14

How It Works

A column is the constituent part of a list and is composed of one or more items. You create and store site columns at the site level, and thus you can reuse them across your SharePoint site. In this example, you created a site column and added it to the Sales list. You could also leverage this type of column in other lists across your site — thus making it a primary distinguishing factor across the normal and site columns.

Although you can create lists manually through the browser or in SharePoint Designer, you might have the need to create a site column, list definition, or content type using Visual Studio (for example, you want to package and distribute a content type with a larger solution). Using the out-of-the-box project templates, these objects are much easier to create than in past versions of SharePoint. When you do create objects such as site columns, list definitions, or content types using Visual Studio, you need to be familiar with the Collaborative Application Markup Language (CAML) syntax and structure for the objects you're trying to create (CAML is an XML syntax specific to SharePoint). For example, the following XML defines a site column that you can deploy to a SharePoint site and then reuse across the site. The site column defines a reusable list of Sales types for a program a company is running; it does this through the XML definition of the site column.

```
<?xml version="1.0" encoding="utf-8"?>
<Elements xmlns="http://schemas.microsoft.com/sharepoint/">
```

```
<Field ID="{4c3a41d4-366d-44c7-910c-74716019ae75}"
    Type= "Choice"
    FillInChoice="TRUE"
    Name="Sales"
    DisplayName="Sales"
    Group="Sales Levels">
  <CHOICES>
    <CHOICE>Premier</CHOICE>
    <CHOICE>Gold</CHOICE>
    <CHOICE>Silver</CHOICE>
    <CHOICE>Bronze</CHOICE>
    <CHOICE>Non-Affiliated</CHOICE>
  </CHOICES>
  <Default>Bronze</Default>
</Field>
</Elements>
```

You can create a site column manually in SharePoint Designer or in Visual Studio. In this exercise, you used Visual Studio, which treats the site column like any other SharePoint project; it creates a *feature* and then deploys the XML elements file (which represents the definition of the site column) to the appropriate place within SharePoint.

Working with SharePoint Data

One of the most common tasks when working with SharePoint is interacting with the various data sources such as lists or document libraries. The great thing about SharePoint is that you have a number of different options for interacting with this data. For example, you have the Server Object Model, the Client-Side Object Model (which has become more powerful since SharePoint 2010), REST (or OData) services, SharePoint Services (which ship out-of-the-box and cover a wide array of scenarios), and Business Connectivity Services or BCS (which provide a rich set of APIs for working with external data systems such as SAP, Microsoft Dynamics CRM, or PeopleSoft). You'll see each of these methods of working with data discussed throughout the book, but this section introduces you to a couple of select examples of tasks that you'll likely do on a daily basis across some of these services and APIs.

Before you can do anything with SharePoint programmatically, you need to establish a connection and context with your SharePoint site. For the most part, this means using (or adding) a reference in your project to `Microsoft.SharePoint.dll` or `Microsoft.SharePoint.Client.dll`. With the appropriate references added to your project, you can then begin to set the context and code within that context. For example, you can set the context for a SharePoint site using the Server Object Model by adding the `Microsoft.SharePoint.dll` to your project reference and then use the following `using` statements to wrap your code. In this code snippet, you set the site collection context and can either call the `OpenWeb` method on that site context, or use the `RootWeb` property to set the context of the `SPSite` object (that is, `mySiteCollection`). You would then add your code where the comment is marked.

```
using (SPSite mySiteCollection = new SPSite(mySiteUrl))
    {
        using (SPWeb mySPSite = mySiteCollection.RootWeb)
            {
//Code here.
            }
    }
```

NOTE *There is a separate set of DLLs for using the Client-Side Object Model with Silverlight. For more information, go here:* `http://msdn.microsoft.com/en-us/library/office/jj164060(v=office.15).aspx`.

The SharePoint Client-Side Object Model is a way to read and write data from SharePoint lists (and enables you to do it through remote client apps). After adding the `Microsoft.SharePoint.Client.Runtime.dll` and `Microsoft.SharePoint.Client.dll` references, you can use the following code to set the context with your SharePoint site. When you've created your application code, you then call the `ExecuteQuery` method to batch-process that code. The final statement (the `Close` method) disposes of the context from memory.

```
String mySiteUrl = "http://fabrikamhockey/acme";
ClientContext mySPSiteContext = new ClientContext(mySiteUrl);

//Code here.

mySPSiteContext.ExecuteQuery();
mySPSiteContext.Close();
```

You will find yourself using both the Server and Client-Side Object Model in different scenarios; for server-side only applications you can use the Server Object Model, and for remote client or cloud-hosted apps you can use the SharePoint Client-Side Object Model.

In SharePoint 2013, your options for interacting with lists expand to include REST. To use REST, which supports full create, read, update, and delete (CRUD) operations, you construct a RESTful HTTP request using the Open Data Protocol (OData) standard. This enables you to perform, for example, GET or POST operations against your SharePoint lists. The following REST URI retrieves all the items in the Customers list:

```
https://me.sharepoint.com/sites/sp/_api/web/lists/getbytitle('Customers')/items
```

The REST URI is quite versatile as well; you can use it in JavaScript or .NET apps to interact with your list data. The REST interface is efficient because it exposes all the SharePoint entities and operations — some of which are not available in the other APIs, and you can also manage the returned data through XML or through JSON, so programming your client apps is flexible (you can use client-side script or .NET apps against the REST URIs). The following code illustrates how you can make a GET request that returns a JSON representation of all of your site's lists by using jQuery:

```
$.ajax({
    url:http://myspsite/_api/web/lists,
    type: "GET",
    contentType: "application/json;odata=verbose",
    headers: {
            "ACCEPT","application/json;odata=verbose",
            "Authorization","Bearer" + accessToken
        },
    })
```

After you've obtained context with the SharePoint object model, you can interact with data that resides on SharePoint. For example, you can iterate over every list in SharePoint and get the title of the list, you can retrieve views of specific lists, or you can update properties or list items in lists programmatically. The following code snippet shows the use of the Server Object Model to obtain the SharePoint site context, but now you're iterating through the lists (see bolded code) on the SharePoint site and adding each list title to a list box.

```
string mySiteUrl = "http://intranet.contoso.com/acme/";
string myListItemInfo = "";

using (SPSite mySiteCollection = new SPSite(mySiteUrl))
    {
        using (SPWeb mySPSite = mySiteCollection.RootWeb)
            {
                foreach (SPList mySPList in mySPSite.Lists)
                    {
                        myListItemInfo = mySPList.Title.ToString();
                        lstbxListTitles.Items.Add(myListItemInfo);
                    }
            }
    }
```

Again, you can do similar types of list interaction by using the SharePoint Client-Side Object Model. The following code snippet shows the setting of the site context again but the bolded code retrieves a list called Inventory from SharePoint and then loads it with a query to filter on the Salmon field.

```
String spURL = "http://fabrikamhockey/acme";
ClientContext spSiteContext = new ClientContext(spURL);
List myProducts = spSiteContext.Web.Lists.GetByTitle("Inventory");
spSiteContext.Load(spSiteContext.Web);
spSiteContext.Load(myProducts,
list => list.Fields.Where(field => field.Title == "Salmon"));
spSiteContext.ExecuteQuery();
spSiteContext.Close();
```

When updating list data, you can choose between using the Server Object Model, CSOM, or REST services). One example is to use the Server Object Model and then call the Update method to update items on a SharePoint list. For example, the following code takes the same site context code shown earlier, but instead of iterating through the list, it now creates an instance of a specific list and then adds a record to the list comprising two fields (Product_Name and Product_SKU). You can see the final call in this case is the Update method to add the new item (newListItem) to the SharePoint site.

```
using (SPSite mySPSite = new SPSite("http://fabrikamhockey/acme"))
    {
        using (SPWeb mySPWeb = mySPSite.OpenWeb())
            {
        SPList productsList = mySPWeb.Lists["Products"];
        SPListItem newListItem = productsList.Items.Add();
        newListItem["Product_Name"] = "Salmon";
```

```
newListItem["Product_SKU"] = "SLM-30989";
newListItem.Update();
      }
  }
```

Depending on what API you use, you might come across the need to use Collaborative Application Markup Language (CAML) constructs, which can get a bit hairy. In essence, CAML enables you to build an XML-based query to return data from a SharePoint list. The following illustrates a CAML query that returns all the results (up to 100). You can construct CAML queries across any of the SharePoint APIs.

```
var camlQuery = new SP.CamlQuery();
camlQuery.set_viewXml('<View><RowLimit>100</RowLimit></View>');
this.collListItem = oList.getItems(camlQuery);
```

Beyond CAML queries, you can also use Language Integrated Query (LINQ) statements to query SharePoint list data. LINQ is a very effective way to query data, which is supported in SharePoint 2013. For example, the following LINQ statement retrieves the list item (from a list represented through the myCustomerList object) where the customer name (represented as c) is Acme.

```
var customers =
    from c in myCustomerList
    where c == "Acme"
    select c;
```

You'll find many different ways to interact with SharePoint lists. Becoming familiar with both a server-side and client-side way to do this is best.

Creating Cloud-hosted Apps

Chapter 2 covered cloud-hosted apps, so this section does not go into too much detail other than to say that you will be using this type of app quite a bit. A couple of things to call out here, though, are that you have the flexibility to use the CSOM and REST APIs within these apps. You must also manage OAuth (when your app calls back into SharePoint) and app permissions, which beyond moving to a more cloud-hosted model, is one of the key changes in SharePoint 2013.

Creating Event Receivers

SharePoint supports a wide array of *event receivers*, which are events that are triggered through a system or user action such as updating a list or adding a new document to a document library. You can create event receivers for a wide variety of objects such as lists, list items, sites, and so on. For instance, suppose you want to load external data as additional company metadata (such as company or national holidays) when a user creates a new calendar item. This requires a Web service call to load the data and an event receiver to load the data when the user creates a new list item. You might also want to log a transaction when certain lists are updated; this is another effective way to use event receivers. You can also build event receivers against feature activations or deactivations if you want. This can be particularly handy when you need to clean up dependent features or assemblies when a feature is activated or deactivated. The event receiver can help remove any ancillary files or dependent Web Parts from the Web Part gallery or the filesystem.

Event receivers are very easy to build and deploy to SharePoint: you create event receivers using the Visual Studio Event Receiver project or item template. Let's go ahead and create a simple event receiver in the following Try It Out to get you familiar with the process.

TRY IT OUT   Creating a Simple Event Receiver

Event receivers are effective ways to add triggers into your SharePoint solutions. To create a simple event receiver, perform the following steps:

1. Open your SharePoint site and create a new list called `TestList`.

2. Open Visual Studio 2012 and click File ➪ New Project, and select Event Receiver in the SharePoint 2013 project template folder.

3. Provide a name for your project (`MyFirstEventReceiver`) and click OK.

4. When prompted in the wizard, select the List Item Events option under the type of event receiver with which you want to associate your event, select the Document Library option under the event source, and select An item was added as the specific event (see Figure 4-15).

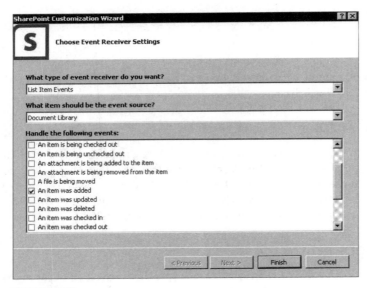

FIGURE 4-15

5. Click Finish.

6. In the `SPEventReceiver.cs` file, added the following bolded code. This applies some of the code discussed thus far and adds a new list item in another list.

```
using System;
using System.Security.Permissions;
using Microsoft.SharePoint;
```

```
using Microsoft.SharePoint.Utilities;
using Microsoft.SharePoint.Workflow;

namespace MyFirstEventReceiver.SPEventReceiver
{
    public class SPEventReceiver : SPItemEventReceiver
    {
        public override void ItemAdded(SPItemEventProperties properties)
        {
            base.ItemAdded(properties);
            logAnAnnouncementEvent(properties);
        }

        private void logAnAnnouncementEvent(SPItemEventProperties properties)
        {
            string eventTitle = properties.ListTitle;
            string mySiteUrl = "http://w15-sp/";

            using (SPSite mySiteCollection = new SPSite(mySiteUrl))
            {
                using (SPWeb mySPSite = mySiteCollection.RootWeb)
                {
                    SPList mySPList = mySPSite.Lists["TestList"];
                    SPListItem newListItem = mySPList.Items.Add();
                    newListItem["Title"] =
                    "Event triggered from the following list: " + eventTitle;
                    newListItem.Update();
                }
            }
        }
    }
}
```

7. Click Build and then Deploy to build and deploy the event receiver project to your Share Point site.

8. Navigate to the Documents list and click Add Item to add a new document. When done, click OK. Figure 4-16 illustrates what this looks like.

9. Navigate to the TestList list, and you can see a new list item — see Figure 4-17.

FIGURE 4-16

FIGURE 4-17

How It Works

An event receiver is in essence a custom DLL that gets deployed and called to the global assembly cache (GAC) within SharePoint. Visual Studio, using the project template, creates a feature that then references the custom assembly when the action that triggers the event occurs. In this example, you added an event that triggered whenever someone added an event to the Announcements list. Specifically, the `ItemAdded` event was a default event handler that was created; it is here where you can add your code. For example, the bolded method (`logAnAnnouncementEvent`) you added will have your event handler code in it (shown here). Note that you're passing the properties of the event, which you can use when building out your event handler code.

```
public override void ItemAdding(SPItemEventProperties properties)
{
    base.ItemAdding(properties);
    logAnAnnouncementEvent(properties);
}
```

Within the `logAnAnnouncementEvent` page, you can see in the following that the one property used is the Title of the list, which is then stored in the `eventTitle` object.

```
private void logAnAnnouncementEvent(SPItemEventProperties properties)
{
    string eventTitle = properties.Title;
    string mySiteUrl = "http://intranet.contoso.com/";

    using (SPSite mySiteCollection = new SPSite(mySiteUrl))
    {
        using (SPWeb mySPSite = mySiteCollection.RootWeb)
        {
            SPList mySPList = mySPSite.Lists["TestList"];
            SPListItem newListItem = mySPList.Items.Add();
            newListItem["Title"] = "Event triggered from the following list:
            " + eventTitle;
            newListItem.Update();
        }
    }
}
```

Most of the other code will now be familiar to you because you've already seen how you add an item to a list. As you explore event receivers, be sure to try out some other types of events that are more complex and involve other parts of the SharePoint site — or external data that you can leverage within your SharePoint site.

Creating ASPX Pages

Those of you familiar with ASP.NET might recognize the .ASPX extension; this is the core ASP .NET Web page. Because SharePoint is built on ASP.NET, the individual pages within SharePoint are of this specific type. What sets SharePoint ASPX pages apart from other ASP.NET sites is that you get a lot of native capabilities built into an ASPX page when you create it. For example, SharePoint ships with a number of capabilities such as edit functionality and Web Part capabilities, and when you create a new ASPX page it derives parent features and loads and registers dependent assemblies that are required to render the page and controls on that page correctly. If you examine the following code in the default Web Part ASPX page you can see that a number of directives exist that register specific assemblies to the page. SharePoint requires that these directives exist. Don't worry; you won't have to memorize what all of them are. SharePoint Designer creates many of them for you by default, so you can focus on page creation and customization.

```
<%@ Page language="C#" MasterPageFile="~masterurl/default.master"
Inherits="Microsoft.SharePoint.WebPartPages.WebPartPage,
Microsoft.SharePoint,Version=15.0.0.0,Culture=neutral,
PublicKeyToken=71e9bce111e9429c"
meta:webpartpageexpansion="full"
meta:progid="SharePoint.WebPartPage.Document" %>
<%@ Register Tagprefix="SharePoint" Namespace="Microsoft.SharePoint.WebControls"
Assembly="Microsoft.SharePoint, Version=15.0.0.0,
Culture=neutral, PublicKeyToken=71e9bce111e9429c" %>
<%@ Register Tagprefix="Utilities" Namespace="Microsoft.SharePoint.Utilities"
Assembly="Microsoft.SharePoint, Version=15.0.0.0,
Culture=neutral, PublicKeyToken=71e9bce111e9429c" %>
<%@ Import Namespace="Microsoft.SharePoint" %>
<%@ Assembly Name="Microsoft.Web.CommandUI, Version=15.0.0.0,
Culture=neutral, PublicKeyToken=71e9bce111e9429c" %>
<%@ Register Tagprefix="WebPartPages" Namespace="Microsoft.SharePoint.WebPartPages"
Assembly="Microsoft.SharePoint, Version=15.0.0.0,
Culture=neutral, PublicKeyToken=71e9bce111e9429c" %>
```

You can create a simple ASPX page for SharePoint without any of the frills that the Web Part pages deliver and the code for this type of page would look more readable (see the following). However, note that this page would not contain any of the standard SharePoint controls and would not inherit the structure and style that is laid out by the master page.

> **NOTE** *Web Part pages are a special type of ASPX page that provide structure using different Web Part zone layouts.*

```
<!DOCTYPE html PUBLIC "-//W3C//DTD XHTML 1.0 Strict//EN"
 "http://www.w3.org/TR/xhtml1/DTD/xhtml1-strict.dtd">
<%@ Page Language="C#" %>
<html dir="ltr" xmlns="http://www.w3.org/1999/xhtml">
<head runat="server">
<meta name="WebPartPageExpansion" content="full" />
<meta http-equiv="Content-Type" content="text/html; charset=utf-8" />
<title>Untitled 1</title>
</head>
<body><form id="form1" runat="server">
</form>
</body>
</html>
```

Although a couple of different paths exist for creating ASPX pages for SharePoint, using SharePoint Designer 2013 is the easiest. This is because not only is code like the preceding created for you, but you can also use templates to create Web Part pages — a special type of ASPX page that has Web Parts located in specific ways on the page. You could alternatively use Visual Studio 2012 to create ASPX pages, but you would have to manually add the preceding namespace registration directives and then manually add the page to the appropriate page on the site. By default, SharePoint Designer can save the ASPX pages you create in a number of places (for example, the Site Assets library).

Beyond the assemblies that are registered through the directives, you also have HTML markup interlaced with `ContentPlaceHolder` controls and ASP.NET controls. Again, if you're familiar with ASP.NET, then these concepts won't be new to you. If you're not, `ContentPlaceHolder` controls and ASP.NET controls are how you render functional controls or applications on the ASPX page. For example, one of the default `ContentPlaceHolder` controls is the search control, which is expressed in the following code:

```
<asp:Content ContentPlaceHolderId="PlaceHolderSearchArea" runat="server">
     <SharePoint:DelegateControl runat="server" ControlId="SmallSearchInputBox"/>
</asp:Content>
```

Depending on the level of complexity of your ASPX page, you might have more or fewer of the preceding controls — some that work independently of one another or others that work hand-in-glove with one another.

Creating Master Pages

Master pages are an ASP.NET creation that SharePoint inherits from being built on ASP.NET. SharePoint uses master pages to provide a consistent structure and layout for each of the pages in a SharePoint site. Similar to a single CSS file providing structure for many Web pages, a single master page can serve multiple sites and define the look, feel, and behavior that you want for all the pages of that site. Using the master page as the structural foundation of your site, you can then add other content or custom applications or Web Parts to your SharePoint site.

When you install SharePoint, it installs a single master page to your SharePoint site by default. You can then create a copy of the `default.master` master page and customize it to your liking or add a new, custom master page that provides the branding and behavior you want for your SharePoint site. SharePoint Designer provides some great capabilities for managing, creating, and editing master pages; for example, you can edit and view your changes from within SharePoint Designer and then check it in for approval to your SharePoint site.

When a user navigates to a SharePoint site, the site or content page references a master page, which is then merged with the page. This produces an output that combines the layout of the master page with the content from the site page. The following bolded code shows a token reference (the token being ~masterurl/default.master) to the master page that was used for that site:

```
<%@ Page language="C#" MasterPageFile="~masterurl/default.master"
Inherits="Microsoft.SharePoint.WebPartPages.WebPartPage,
Microsoft.SharePoint,Version=15.0.0.0,Culture=neutral,
PublicKeyToken=71e9bce111e9429c"
meta:webpartpageexpansion="full" meta:progid="SharePoint.WebPartPage.Document"  %>
```

A master page is characterized by the `.master` file extension. The master page itself can contain an array of objects. For example, the master page can contain HTML, JavaScript, CSS, and ASP. NET server controls. When you examine the syntax of the master page, you'll see text and controls that render a look and feel that is specific to SharePoint. This is especially true when you look at the `default.master` master page, which includes all the breadcrumbs and default menu and navigation options that are specific to SharePoint.

However, you'll also see a series of `ContentPlaceHolder` objects (discussed earlier) within a master page, which define regions where content or controls can appear. When you're customizing SharePoint master pages, you need to have a set of `ContentPlaceHolder` controls on the page, for example, global breadcrumb, top-level navigation, search, and title. You can add more `ContentPlaceHolder` controls than are required by default; however, you cannot remove the ones that are required or else your content or site pages might fail to render.

> **NOTE** For the complete list of required controls, go to the following MSDN article: `http://msdn.microsoft.com/en-us/library/ms467402.aspx`.

The following code snippet shows some of the different types of text and controls that you can find within a SharePoint master page. Note that these are taken from the `default.master`, which ships with all versions of SharePoint, so you can explore the full set of code and controls that ship with this master page by reviewing the file from within SharePoint Designer.

```
<title id="onetidTitle"><asp:ContentPlaceHolder id="PlaceHolderPageTitle"
runat="server"/>
</title>
<SharePoint:CssLink runat="server" Alternate="true"/>
<SharePoint:Theme runat="server"/>
<SharePoint:CssRegistration Name="minimalv4.css" runat="server"/>
<SharePoint:CssRegistration Name="layouts.css" runat="server"/>
<SharePoint:ULSClientConfig runat="server"/>
<span class="s4-notdlg">
<a href="javascript:;" onclick="javascript:this.href='#mainContent';"
class="ms-SkiptoMainContent" accesskey="<%$Resources:wss,maincontent_accesskey%>"
 runat="server">
<SharePoint:EncodedLiteral runat="server"
text="<%$Resources:wss,mainContentLink%>" EncodeMethod="HtmlEncode"/>
</a>
</span>
…
<asp:ContentPlaceHolder id="PlaceHolderWelcomeMenu" runat="server">
<div class="lb ms-mini-trcMenu">
<wssuc:Welcome id="IdWelcome" runat="server" EnableViewState="false">
</wssuc:Welcome>
<wssuc:MUISelector runat="server"/>
</div>
</asp:ContentPlaceHolder>
…
<div>
```

```
<asp:ContentPlaceHolder id="PlaceHolderTitleBreadcrumb" runat="server" />
</div>
...
<div id="DeveloperDashboard" class="ms-developerdashboard">
<SharePoint:DeveloperDashboard runat="server"/>
</div>
...
</body>
</html>
```

When managing your master pages, be mindful of any changes you make to the existing master pages. In fact, avoid at all costs editing any of the default master pages that ship with SharePoint and always copy and edit alternate, renamed copies so you never lose a snapshot to which you can safely return. If you're going to be doing a lot of master page customization in the future, start with a minimal master page (which contains the bare minimum set of controls necessary for a SharePoint site) and add onto that as practice to get familiar with how they work.

SUMMARY

There are many different types of options you have when developing SharePoint solutions, which range from farm-level to sandboxed to cloud-hosted to SharePoint-hosted. Each one of these options provides different levels of SharePoint API support and support for broader Web technologies (such as PhP or HTML5).

Regardless of the development option you choose, you will find yourself running into several common tasks you'll engage in as a SharePoint developer time and time again. These include creating Web Parts, creating SharePoint-hosted apps, accessing and managing data, creating cloud-hosted apps, creating event receivers, creating ASPX pages, and creating master pages. It is important to be familiar with these tasks to gain a fundamental base of development knowledge. Understanding how you can leverage different API choices within these tasks is also important for you to understand.

Many of the topics covered in this chapter resurface throughout the book as you write more code and explore more of the programmatic capabilities that SharePoint has to offer. Thus, as you move throughout this book, try and frame each application discussion with an understanding of the type of solution and how you might use the different SharePoint APIs within that solution.

EXERCISES

You can find answers to exercises in Appendix A.

1. Using Visual Studio 2012, create a simple Standard Web Part and Visual Web Part using the code snippets in this chapter.

2. Create a custom ASPX page that leverages two or more controls from the ASP.NET Toolbox and publish to SharePoint.

3. Create a simple master page that has a logo and some header text.

▶ WHAT YOU LEARNED IN THIS CHAPTER

ITEM	DESCRIPTION
Web Part	SharePoint leverages the ASP.NET framework and provides different types of Web Parts to use when building solutions. The most common Web Parts include the Standard Web Part (baseline Web Part available in SharePoint), Visual Web Part (adds a designer experience for the UI to Standard Web Parts), Silverlight Web Part, and Data View Web Parts (exposes list data in a custom-formatted way).
SharePoint-hosted app	This is a lightweight app you can deploy to a specific site collection (such as list view or content type).
Site column	You can reuse this custom column across a SharePoint site.
Content type	This is a custom object with metadata that can range from predefined columns to custom documents that you can reuse across a SharePoint site.
Cloud-hosted app	This is an Autohosted or Provider-hosted app that you build and deploy to the cloud (for example, Windows Azure).
List	This is a standard way of representing data in SharePoint. You interact with list data using the server-side object model, CSOM, or Rest APIs.
Event receiver	This is an event that is triggered when the system or user performs an action.
ASPX page	This is the standard page in SharePoint. Built on ASP.NET, SharePoint supports simple ASPX pages (no controls) or more complex pages that come predefined with controls and layouts (for example, Web Part page).
Master page	A master page provides a single point of branding and structure that you can leverage across a SharePoint site.

RECOMMENDED READING

Overview of cloud-hosted apps — `http://msdn.microsoft.com/en-us/library/fp179930 (v=office.15).aspx`

Event receivers — `http://msdn.microsoft.com/en-us/library/jj220051.aspx`

REST services for SharePoint 2013 — `http://msdn.microsoft.com/en-us/library/fp142386.aspx`

Overview of master pages for SharePoint 2013 — `http://msdn.microsoft.com/en-us/library/jj191506(v=office.15)`

5

Overview of Windows Azure for SharePoint

WHAT YOU WILL LEARN IN THIS CHAPTER:

➤ Defining cloud computing

➤ Using Windows Azure

➤ Understanding how to integrate SharePoint 2013 and Windows Azure

WROX.COM DOWNLOADS FOR THIS CHAPTER

The wrox.com code downloads for this chapter are found at `http://www.wrox.com/WileyCDA/WroxTitle/productCd-1118495845.html` on the Download Code tab. The code for this chapter is divided into the following major examples:

➤ MyFirstAzureApp.zip

➤ AzureClientAppWebPart.zip

➤ MyFirstAutohostedApp.zip

As you've seen thus far, the new SharePoint app model includes a rich cloud integration model (called *cloud-hosted applications*). Although you can leverage broader web strategies when building and deploying your SharePoint app, Windows Azure is one of Microsoft's primary cloud-based technologies that you'll need to be familiar with when building your apps; it is key to the development model in SharePoint 2013.

Windows Azure is Microsoft's cloud platform technology, and in and of itself, is a very powerful technology. It's not just a place to deploy your code; a whole set of services exists that you as a developer can use in your SharePoint solution development. This chapter provides a deeper look at Windows Azure so you can leverage more of its underlying platform services.

DEFINING THE CLOUD

To understand Windows Azure, you must first know a bit about the cloud. *Cloud computing* (a broader descriptor for the cloud) is all about leveraging the Web as a set of resources for the development and deployment of your solutions. Traditionally, cloud computing has been defined as categories of *services* — for example, Infrastructure as a Service (IAAS), Platform as a Service (PAAS), and Software as a Service (SAAS). Each one of these categories is fairly different in the context of development. For instance, you might think of IAAS as hosted virtual machines (VMs) you manage remotely; PAAS as where you deploy code, data, binary large objects (BLOBs), web apps, and other application artifacts to a cloud-based environment (such as Windows Server 2008 R2 and IIS); and SAAS as subscription-based services that you can sign up to use (for example, Office 365).

Although these three categories of services dominate the way in which the cloud is characterized, the cloud has four generally accepted *pillars*:

➤ Pool resources with other cloud users.

➤ Manage your own services and apps through the management portal.

➤ Apps and services can grow and contract with your business needs.

➤ Pay for only what you use in regards to the cloud.

Figure 5-1 illustrates these four core pillars of the cloud. You can apply each principle in some way to the categories of services.

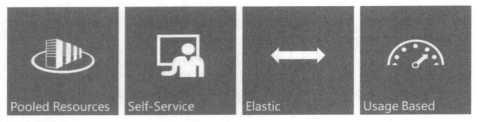

FIGURE 5-1

Both the categories of services and the core pillars of cloud computing apply to Windows Azure. For example, you can create and deploy a set of virtual machines to Windows Azure, build out a SharePoint farm on those virtual machines, and then manage it remotely. Within this virtualized farm, you're potentially pooling resources; you're managing the services through your portal or tools; you can grow or shrink the SharePoint farm (number of servers in the farm), therefore, it is elastic; and it is usage-based because you're only getting billed for what you use.

In addition to understanding the relationship across the cloud services (IAAS, PAAS, and SAAS) categories and the pillars that define cloud computing, getting beneath the surface area of the cloud and digging into Windows Azure is also important. This is not only because integrating the two technologies provides the developer with interesting and compelling solution opportunities, but it's also because now Windows Azure is a more native part of the SharePoint 2013 platform. Thus, it's critical that you understand how you can use Windows Azure in your SharePoint development.

DEFINING WINDOWS AZURE

Windows Azure is a flexible cloud-computing platform that provides services for virtualizing VMs; building, deploying, and managing resources, data, and services; and building cloud-based applications and websites. What all this means is that you can leverage physical data centers that Microsoft has built and supports globally (see Figure 5-2) and deploy your applications to run in geographically dispersed locations. Within each of these locations are racks of servers (for example, Windows Server 2008 R2) that enable you to deploy into these remote locations. This, in essence, represents the cloud (or at least Microsoft's cloud) and the benefits to the cloud: the fact that you have virtualized environments around the world that you don't need to physically manage, and with which you can start up and use in a matter of minutes.

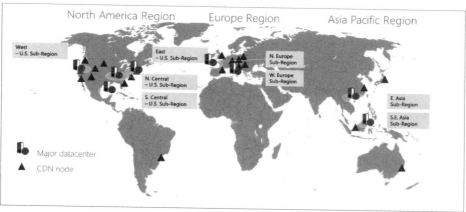

FIGURE 5-2

As Microsoft's key cloud platform, Windows Azure enables you to provision and scale resources to the cloud without having to worry about chasing and managing your on-premise hardware. When you use Windows Azure you not only get application scale (hardware needs expanding as your data and application needs grow), but you also get patching and operating-system management (your cloud-hosted environment is always up to date), and a 99.9 percent uptime guarantee.

You might think of Windows Azure as consisting of three major pieces:

➤ **A core set of platform services and capabilities:** A variety of core platform services (discussed later in this section) are available for use. Each of these services has a set of APIs and an SDK so you can take advantage of them.

➤ **Development and management tools:** You can download the Windows Azure SDK and Visual Studio companion tools, which make developing and deploying Windows Azure applications very easy.

➤ **The marketplace:** You can build and deploy applications and make them available in the Windows Azure marketplace.

As a developer, you also have a main web portal, which you use to manage your applications, services, database, websites, virtual machines, and so on. Additionally, you have a rich, underlying set of APIs (for example, REST and .NET) that support task automation (for example, creating a new virtual machine). Figure 5-3 illustrates what this web portal looks like. Note that clicking each of the available options on the left side of the portal invokes a view that displays meta data as well as performance and usage information, and enables you to configure properties of that service. It also provides you with the ability to create new service instances (for example, a website or SQL Database) and configure properties against those newly created services.

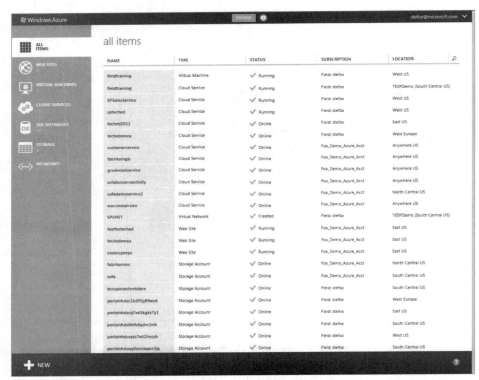

FIGURE 5-3

WINDOWS AZURE PLATFORM

The Windows Azure platform is composed of many different services. You can leverage them in your application design, deployment, and management. Figure 5-4 shows the different *layers* within Windows Azure: Data, Service, and Integration (the Client layer is any application that consumes the services within Windows Azure).

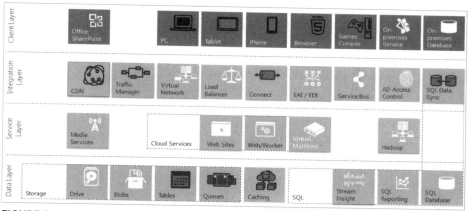

FIGURE 5-4

Data Layer

Within the Data layer are a number of different types of data storage mechanisms (or features that map directly to data storage) — both nonrelational and relational. The *nonrelational* storage features enable you to store assets such as virtual machine images (Drive) or images or videos (Blobs), create nonrelational tables, manage message queues along a service bus, and manage data caching in your distributed applications. The *relational* data features include the core Windows Azure SQL Database (think of this as the cloud version for the on-premises SQL Server), along with reporting services (SQL Reporting) and the ability to stream near real-time data streams from data transactions (Stream Insight). Throughout this chapter and indeed your broader development efforts you can use these core Windows Azure services in many different ways when building SharePoint applications — from learning solutions that leverage Media Services to synchronizing data in the cloud using the SQL Data Sync Service. A diverse set of services are available to build a wide array of applications.

Services Layer

The Services layer contains a number of default services that you can use when building your solutions, ranging from Media Services to core Cloud Services (including creating websites and Worker role classes, as well as leveraging Hadoop on Windows Azure to process Big Data requests). For many of these services, you can use baked-in functionality and a set of APIs within your application. For example, if you want to build a multimedia learning solution, you could leverage the Media Services to upload WMVs, transcode them to MP4s, save them to BLOB storage, create a public URL for access, and then stream them from Windows Azure to SharePoint.

Integration Layer

The Integration layer contains some fundamental services such as a geo-replicated content delivery network (CDN) or Traffic Manager — these are often core platform capabilities. Other important integration services are in this layer, too, such as Virtual Private Network (which enables you to connect a virtual machine to your on-premises system) or workflow and business process and integration services. All of these capabilities enable you to integrate systems or secure them.

DEVELOPING WINDOWS AZURE APPLICATIONS

Windows Azure is not just about services. It is an ever-evolving cloud platform that has a set of tools and SDKs that enable you to get started quickly developing cloud applications.

Getting started with Windows Azure requires the following:

➤ Visual Studio (2010 or 2012)

➤ Windows Azure SDK and Tools for Visual Studio

➤ Windows Azure subscription

You can also integrate different SDKs and tools with Visual Studio 2010 or Visual Studio 2012. The Windows Azure tools and SDK are free downloads. After you download the tools and SDK, you must set up a Windows Azure account. You can sign up for a free 90-day account to get started.

> **NOTE** *Remember that the cloud is about* pay-per-use: *as you use more compute, storage, data, and other service capabilities, the more you'll be charged per month.*

After you download the Windows Azure tools and SDK and create a Windows Azure account, you can use Visual Studio to build and deploy applications to your account. When you're ready you will be able to test, stage, and ultimately deploy your applications to a production environment. While you're developing (and especially while you're developing offline), you can use the emulator — an emulated Windows Azure environment that is installed with the tools — to test your applications locally.

Figure 5-5 illustrates at a high level the process of developing cloud applications. In the diagram, you can see the left side represents a local development environment. Installed in this environment are the tools, SDK, and emulator as well as the .NET and Visual Studio development toolset. (Windows Azure also supports PHP, Java, Node.js, and other types of non-Microsoft technologies through SDKs and community tooling.) You can build and test your applications locally, but at some point you'll need to deploy these apps to your production account, and which account you choose depends on what licensing structure your company has purchased (for example, basic subscription or pay-per-use account versus enterprise license account). In any case, you deploy into an account using a LiveID (or Microsoft account ID) username and password information. The Windows Azure account has a unique subscription ID and allows you to add co-admins so others can manage the services that are deployed to it. Note in the right side of Figure 5-5 how the cloud environment is hosted in a physical data center (as shown earlier in the chapter); thus your application, service, or data becomes available to others when you deploy into this production environment.

You can lock down the applications (using Windows Azure Active Directory technology) and have an authenticated, single sign-on experience, or you can have a fully anonymous-access site or service that is leveraged by your application.

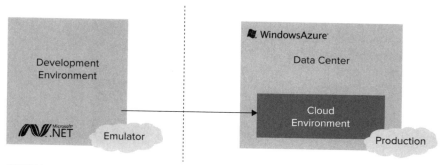

FIGURE 5-5

A number of elements must be in place to get started developing, so the following exercise walks you through where you can find the software to set up your development environment.

TRY IT OUT Setting Up Your Development Environment

To set up your Windows Azure development environment, you first install Visual Studio and then the Windows Azure tools install on top of it.

To install the trial version of Visual Studio:

1. Download and install Visual Studio 2012. At the time of this writing, you could get the trial edition at http://www.microsoft.com/visualstudio/en-us. You have your choice of different SKUs (or Visual Studio versions) available; choose Professional or above.

2. When you click the appropriate SKU, select Run when prompted. Visual Studio asks for a download location and begins installing the product.

To install the Windows Azure SDK and tools:

1. Download and install the Windows Azure tools for Visual Studio 2012. At the time of this writing, you could get the tools at http://www.windowsazure.com/en-us. You can also get the software and tools through the Web PI: http://www.microsoft.com/web/downloads/platform.aspx.

2. Click the Develop link, which takes you to all the available SDKs and tools. Under languages, click .NET, the first option shown in Figure 5-6.

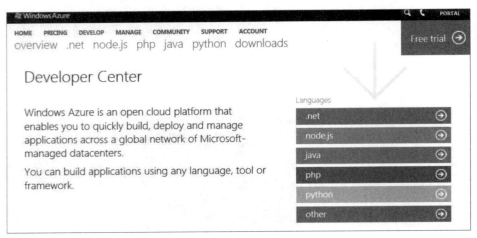

FIGURE 5-6

3. Click the Install button, and then select Install with Visual Studio 2012.

4. Select Run when prompted, which invokes the Web Platform installer.

5. Click Install, as shown in Figure 5-7, and then follow the wizard to accept the license and begin the installation process.

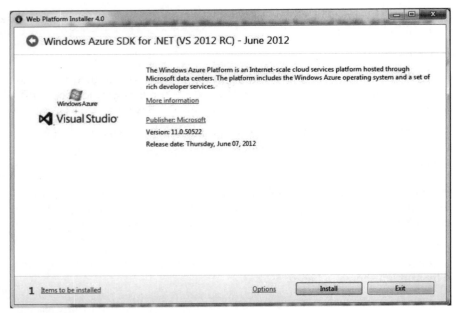

FIGURE 5-7

How it Works

The installation process is fairly self-explanatory; just follow the wizard. If you want to download a permanent version of Visual Studio, you can visit http://www.microsoft.com/visualstudio/en-us and you should be able to buy the most recent version. If you're an MSDN subscription holder, you should be able to download Visual Studio 2012 under your subscription license there.

After you've installed Visual Studio and the Windows Azure tools/SDK for Visual Studio, you need to sign up for a Windows Azure account. To do this, click the Home link on the main Windows Azure site, click the Free Trial button, and then click the Try it Free* button (see Figure 5-8). You'll be prompted for your LiveID and a wizard will walk you through a sign-up process. After you sign up, you'll then be able to navigate to your portal and begin creating cloud services, websites, and so on.

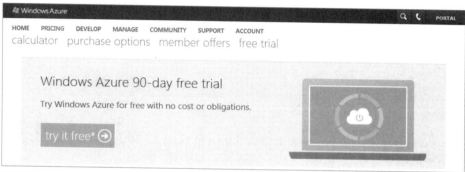

FIGURE 5-8

Now that you have your development environment up and running and a Windows Azure account ready to go, you'll want to get hands on with developing for Windows Azure. To do this, the following Try It Out walks you through creating your first Windows Azure application. The application is a simple REST-based Web API project that will return some hard-coded sales data.

TRY IT OUT Creating Your First Windows Azure Application

To create your first Windows Azure application, perform these steps:

1. Open Visual Studio 2012.
2. Click File ➪ New Project and select Visual Studio Solution.
3. Right-click the solution and select Add ➪ New Project.
4. Select Cloud, and provide a name for your project: **MyFirstAzureApp**.
5. Add a location and click OK (see Figure 5-9).

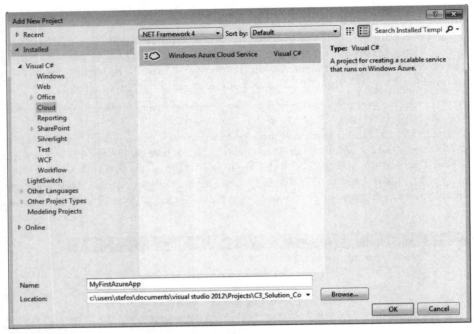

FIGURE 5-9

6. In the New Windows Azure Cloud Service dialog, shown in Figure 5-10, select the ASP.NET MVC 4 Web Role project.

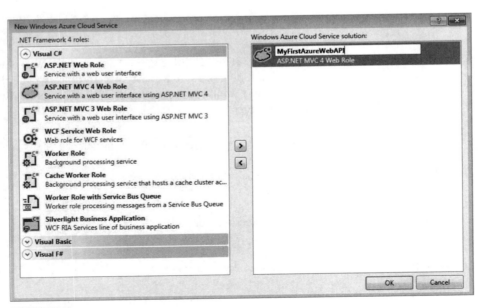

FIGURE 5-10

7. Click the right-arrow button to add the Web role to the Azure solution. Click the pencil icon to edit the name of the Web role (`MyFirstAzureWebAPI`).

8. Click OK.

9. In the New ASP.NET MVC Project dialog, select the Web API option.

10. Leave the default option, and click OK.

How it Works

Visual Studio creates the plumbing for a new Web API project, which includes a Windows Azure (Cloud) project and the Web API (MVC) project. Figure 5-11 highlights four parts of the solution for your benefit. The Cloud project represents a "wrapper" project around the Web API MVC project. The Cloud project contains configuration information and links

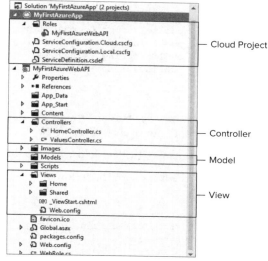

FIGURE 5-11

autodeployment and publishing features for developers to easily deploy their code to Windows Azure. The three other parts are standard MVC (that is, model, view, and controller) components. MVC components process incoming requests, manage user input and interactions, and execute application logic. The controller is typically separate and is created to generate an HTML view of the request. The model is, for example, a class that is used to model incoming or connected data. The view is what is displayed to the user.

The next series of steps in the process of creating an application with Windows Azure entails creating a simple model to represent data. The following exercise walks you through this process.

TRY IT OUT Creating a Model (MyFirstAzureApp.sln)

Now create a simple model to represent the data (which will be a small set of sales data), and then expose that data as a return value using the default controller. The example uses the default plumbing code as much as possible to keep things straightforward.

1. Right-click the Models folder and select Add ⇨ Class. Name the class `Sales` and then click Add.

2. Add the following bolded code to the `Sales` class, which provides you with a small set of properties for your custom `Sales` object.

```
using System;
using System.Collections.Generic;
using System.Linq;
using System.Web;

namespace MyFirstAzureWebAPI.Models
{
```

```
public class Sales
{
    public string Company { get; set; }
    public string FY09Sales { get; set; }
    public string FY10Sales { get; set; }
    public string FY11Sales { get; set; }
}
}
```

Now that you've created a model (or class), you'll use this class to create a return `List` collection object that your Web API service will return in JSON format.

3. Expand the Controllers folder and double-click the `ValuesController` class.

4. Amend the class with the following bolded code (note these are fictional companies and sales figures).

```
using System;
using System.Collections.Generic;
using System.Linq;
using System.Net;
using System.Net.Http;
using System.Web.Http;
using MyFirstAzureWebAPI.Models;

namespace MyFirstAzureWebAPI.Controllers
{
    public class ValuesController : ApiController
    {
        // GET api/values
        public List<Sales> Get()
        {
            List<Sales> mySales = new List<Sales>();

            mySales.Add(new Sales
            {
                Company="Contoso",
                FY09Sales="$9,020,398,122,332.00",
                FY10Sales="$10,111,309,312,998.00",
                FY11Sales="$11,033,990,102,443.00"
            });

            mySales.Add(new Sales
            {
                Company="Fabrikam",
                FY09Sales="$7,332,444,552,112.00",
                FY10Sales="$5,019,132,011,668.00",
                FY11Sales="$3,889,940,589,901.00"
            });

            mySales.Add(new Sales
            {
                Company = "Wingtip",
                FY09Sales = "$9,032,522,000,129.00",
                FY10Sales = "$9,115,339,990,899.00",
                FY11Sales = "$9,001,439,321,666.00"
```

```
        });

        return mySales;

    }
    ...

    }
}
```

The code that you added uses the `Sales` object to create a `List` collection object. When you append the Web API URI with `"api/values"` it will return the three `Sales` objects within the `List` collection as a JSON formatted object.

5. Press F6 to build.

6. When you've added and successfully compiled the code, press F5 to debug the cloud application. (The solution uses the local cloud emulator to debug the Web API.)

7. When debugging, you'll see the ASP.NET default page appear (within the 127.0.0.1 domain). When you append the `"api/values"` path to the URL (as in Figure 5-12), the Web API service passes back a JSON-formatted object.

FIGURE 5-12

How it Works

The MVC templates are a versatile set of ASP.NET Web templates, and the Web API is a specific template that enables you to easily build REST-based services for Windows Azure. You'll find that Cloud services (such as REST or WCF-based services) will be important to your cloud development efforts for a number of reasons, such as service reuse or application extensibility. In this exercise, you built a REST API with the scaffolding provided by the MVC templates, and the result was a REST service that returned a JSON object.

The JSON object, shown in the following code (with purely fictional data), reflects the `List` collection you created in the `Get` method. In essence, this is a small set of data that is returned to you via the REST service call.

```
[
{
"Company":"Contoso",
"FY09Sales":"$9,020,398,122,332.00",
"FY10Sales":"$10,111,309,312,998.00",
"FY11Sales":"$11,033,990,102,443.00"
},
{
"Company":"Fabrikam",
"FY09Sales":"$7,332,444,552,112.00",
"FY10Sales":"$5,019,132,011,668.00",
```

```
"FY11Sales":"$3,889,940,589,901.00"
},
{
"Company":"Wingtip",
"FY09Sales":"$9,032,522,000,129.00",
"FY10Sales":"$9,115,339,990,899.00",
"FY11Sales":"$9,001,439,321,666.00"
}
]
```

When deployed, the REST service would behave similarly, except the endpoint would be configured to a production URI (for example, `http://myapp.cloudapp.net`).

Congratulations! You've created your first Windows Azure application; that is, a REST-based Web API that returns JSON data. When you deploy it to a production environment, you can use the REST service from a multitude of clients and process the JSON data within your applications — whether it is SharePoint, Windows Phone, Windows 8, or other device/tablet applications.

Even before you deploy your first application to your Windows Azure account, you can use this REST service locally within the cloud emulator environment with other applications. Although you won't deploy this application to Windows Azure now (you'll have the opportunity to deploy many different applications to Windows Azure throughout the book), you can right-click the cloud project (MyFirstAzureApp) and select Publish. This invokes the Publish Windows Azure Application dialog, which enables you to walk through a wizard and deploy your application directly to your Windows Azure subscription — which you can then manage within the Windows Azure portal. See Figure 5-13 for the Start page of the Publish Windows Azure Application wizard.

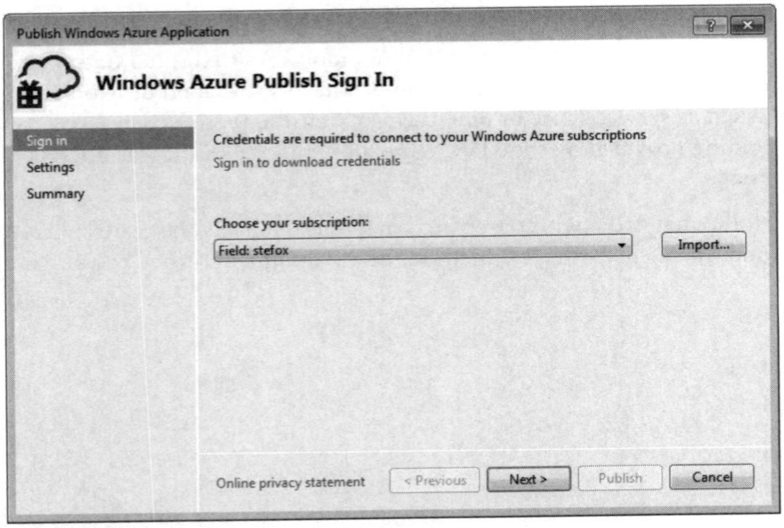

FIGURE 5-13

At this point, you should at least have a basic understanding of what Windows Azure is, how to set up the Windows Azure development environment, and the types of applications that you can build using Windows Azure. You might now be asking yourself, "Why all the Windows Azure hubbub?" When paired with SharePoint 2013, Windows Azure becomes important in two ways:

➤ It is natively integrated within the SharePoint application development and deployment experience — you use Windows Azure to build and deploy cloud-hosted applications.

➤ You can also use Windows Azure in the broader cloud application development experience — just like you could use an array of other Web technologies and standards.

The next section of this chapter covers how SharePoint and Windows Azure integrate both in general and through the two main app models: the *Autohosted* model and the *Provider-hosted* model, covered in Chapter 2, "Overview of the SharePoint 2013 App Model."

SHAREPOINT AND WINDOWS AZURE

SharePoint and Windows Azure are two sizeable platforms unto themselves. SharePoint is one of Microsoft's leading server productivity platforms — the collaborative platform for the enterprise and the Web. Windows Azure is Microsoft's operating system in the cloud. Separately, they have their own strengths, market viability, and developer following. Together, they provide many powerful benefits. For example:

➤ They help expand how and where you deploy your code and data.

➤ They increase opportunities to take advantage of the Windows Azure "metered usage" model while at the same time reducing the storage and failover costs of on-premises applications.

➤ They provide you with new business models and offerings that you can take to your customers to increase your own solution offerings.

SharePoint and Windows Azure have evolved quite a bit since mid-2010 (when Microsoft introduced the topic) into a mature set of integrated technologies. Figure 5-14 illustrates the fact that each of the three categories of Windows Azure can in some way, shape, or form be integrated with SharePoint. For example, within the IAAS category, you can stand up servers in Windows Azure with fully functional SharePoint farms (whether they are stand-alone servers or connected servers that include Web front ends, index servers, SQL Servers, and so on). You can see here it's possible to support SharePoint for Internet Sites (FIS) sites, or Business Intelligence (BI) servers that run SQL Reporting apps. You can also create development and test or training environments on Windows Azure Virtual Machine (or IAAS). Within PAAS, you use the core services within Windows Azure to build applications, so much of what you would do here to integrate with SharePoint apps or sites would be hosting WCF or REST services in the cloud, integrating with workflow, building media-rich applications, hosting data, and so on. Finally, the SAAS model extends on the subscription-based Office 365 core functionality to integrate with Windows Azure and build complete cloud-based solutions (for example, a training solution that uses Media Services to stream videos to your

SharePoint site) or line-of-business (LOB) applications such as Dynamics CRM integration or data-synchronized apps that reflect on-premises LOB applications.

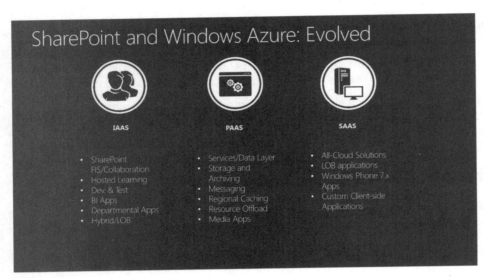

FIGURE 5-14

Windows Azure is not just about the integration of cloud apps with SharePoint though; it's also about extending your apps in other directions and to other endpoints. For example, you can also build services that not only integrate Windows Azure SQL Database data with SharePoint but also wrap cloud-based services that project to devices, phones, and Windows 8 tablets. With the integration of SharePoint and Windows Azure, cloud-based applications are entirely possible.

Understanding SharePoint Cloud-Hosted Apps and Windows Azure

In SharePoint 2010, Windows Azure and SharePoint were two distinct platforms and technologies; you could integrate them easily enough, but they were not part of the same "system." However, in SharePoint 2013 this has changed. As discussed in Chapter 1, "Introduction to SharePoint 2013," SharePoint 2013 introduces different types of "cloud" applications. In fact, you can build two types of Windows Azure integrated applications. Chapter 2 also covered these, but in this chapter you revisit them more in the context of Windows Azure. The first type of application is *Autohosted*, and the second is *Provider-hosted* (sometimes referred to as self-hosted). The major difference between the two is that *Autohosted applications* natively support a set of Windows Azure features (for example Web Sites and SQL Database) with the SharePoint development and deployment experience, and *Provider-hosted applications* are meant to integrate with a broader set of web technologies and standards than Autohosted applications, one of which is Windows Azure. Thus, you can take advantage of the entire Windows Azure stack when building Provider-hosted apps that use Windows Azure.

To show just how closely integrated Windows Azure and SharePoint have become, for the Autohosted app model, Office 365 has its own flavor of a Windows Azure site that it uses behind the scenes. You can use it to effectively leverage the core Windows Azure features. Not only is this important from the feature-sharing aspect between the two platforms, but it's also important from a security perspective — HTTPS is supported across these two connected domains.

This HTTPS support extends to Provider-hosted applications that are deployed to Windows Azure as well. For example, if you build and deploy a Windows Azure Web Site, you'll note that it natively supports HTTP *and* HTTPS. This has significant implications for when you want to secure your web assets and have them conversant with SharePoint. That is, you don't have to purchase a certificate from a trusted body such as GoDaddy, upload it, build it into your Windows Azure application, and so on. All you need to do is deploy your website to Windows Azure and then register the HTTPS-based URL with SharePoint and connect the applications.

You use the Autohosted cloud app model to build and deploy smaller, cloud-hosted apps to SharePoint. The Autohosted app leverages a smaller subset of the Windows Azure platform — namely Web Sites and SQL Database. Using these areas, you can build some lightweight, data-driven apps where the code lives in Windows Azure and the configuration for that code lives in SharePoint. Figure 5-15 illustrates how an app deployed to SharePoint comprises two main parts: the .APP that is deployed to SharePoint, which contains configuration and registration information, and the functional code, which is deployed to Windows Azure.

One of the principal items to keep in mind with Autohosted apps is that they're an evolution towards a more cloud-hosted model. When you compare Autohosted apps to Sandboxed solutions, for example, you have much more power and developer capability at your fingertips with the former. But similar to Sandboxed Solutions, Autohosted apps get your code off of the server, while still allowing you to build interesting applications.

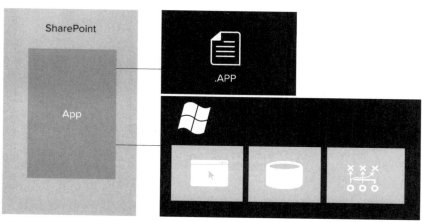

FIGURE 5-15

Autohosted apps are different from Provider-hosted apps in that the SharePoint environment executes code that is deployed to Windows Azure; this is abstracted from the view of the developer but is still a native part of Windows Azure. This is really good for singular deployment and billing, and enables you to build once, but automatically deploy to the right places.

Provider-hosted apps are a slightly different breed with which you can build more broad-reaching web apps that integrate with SharePoint. Within Provider-hosted apps, you're managing your own hosted web environment and then integrating the applications, services, or data from those separate domains with SharePoint (for example, one domain being SharePoint and the other being Windows Azure). Thus, using a Provider-hosted app is not as simple as using the Autohosted app in regards to integrating Windows Azure. The Autohosted app model automatically registers the code that is deployed to Windows Azure, but in the Provider-hosted model you need to configure the registration of the Windows Azure application to authenticate the app and the events in that app such that they can fire within the SharePoint environment. As discussed previously though, there are mechanisms between Windows Azure and SharePoint that make the authentication process a smooth one (such as HTTPS support across SharePoint and Windows Azure Web Sites). Also, the SharePoint client-side APIs facilitate cross-domain events such as reading or writing list items.

Provider-hosted apps are also different because you can deploy and integrate apps that go beyond Windows Azure. Thus, it's not just about Windows Azure; the Provider-hosted apps support PHP, Java, and so on.

Throughout this book you will learn how to create a variety of different Autohosted and Provider-hosted apps as well as how to use OAuth and other security and token providers to register the app and the events within that app for SharePoint. To get started, this chapter introduces you to two simple examples. The first example uses the native Windows Azure integration built into SharePoint 2013 (the Autohosted app), and the second example shows you how to create a lightweight connection with SharePoint 2013 using the Client App Web Part. Given the first part of this book focuses on the fundamentals, the exercises here are more basic, and therefore the more advanced examples for Provider-hosted apps aren't covered until later in the book.

Creating a Simple Autohosted SharePoint App

In the Autohosted cloud app model, as discussed earlier, part of the application you create is auto-deployed to Windows Azure and the other part is deployed to SharePoint. To help illustrate this process, create an Autohosted application in the following example.

TRY IT OUT   Building Your First Autohosted App (MyFirstAutohostedApp.sln)

To create your first Autohosted app:

1. Open Visual Studio 2012.
2. Select File, and then New Project.
3. Expand the Office/SharePoint node and select Apps, as shown in Figure 5-16.

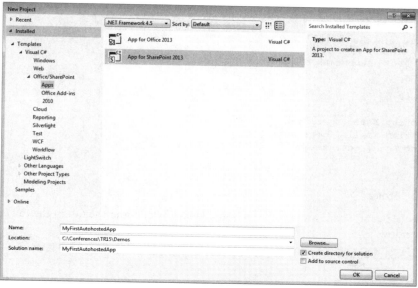

FIGURE 5-16

4. Type `MyFirstAutohostedApp` as the project name.

5. Select the App for SharePoint 2013 project, and click OK.

6. In the New App for SharePoint dialog, enter the name of the app, the SharePoint site you'll be using for debugging and deployment, and select Autohosted in the drop-down box, as shown in Figure 5-17. When done, click Finish.

FIGURE 5-17

7. Right-click `MyFirstAutohostAppWeb` and select Add New, and then select Class.

8. Call the class **People**, and then click Add.

9. In the newly added `People` class, insert the following bolded code.

```
...
public class People
{
        public string Name { get; set; }
        public string Email { get; set; }
        public int Age { get; set; }
}
...
```

10. Press F6 to build the project.

11. Right-click the `Default.aspx` page and switch to Source view by clicking the tab in the lower part of the main window.

12. Insert the following bolded line of code into the `Default.aspx` page.

```
...
<html xmlns="http://www.w3.org/1999/xhtml">
<head runat="server">
<title></title>
</head>
<body>
    <form id="form1" runat="server">
    <div>
        <asp:GridView ID="grdViewPeople" runat="server"></asp:GridView>
    </div>
    </form>
</body>
</html>
```

13. Press F6 to build the project.

14. Double-click the `Default.aspx.cs` file. This is the code-behind for the `Default.aspx` page.

15. Insert the following bolded code into the `Default.aspx.cs` file. Leave all the other code that was created by default there.

```
using System;
using System.Collections.Generic;
using System.Linq;
using System.Web;
using System.Web.UI;
using System.Web.UI.WebControls;

namespace MyFirstAutohostedAppWeb.Pages
{
    public partial class Default : System.Web.UI.Page
    {
        List<People> myPeeps = new List<People>();

        protected void Page_Load(object sender, EventArgs e)
```

```
        {
            var contextToken = TokenHelper.GetContextTokenFromRequest(Page.Request);
            var hostWeb = Page.Request["SPHostUrl"];

            using (var clientContext = TokenHelper.GetClientContextWithContextToken
            (hostWeb, contextToken, Request.Url.Authority))
            {
                clientContext.Load(clientContext.Web, web => web.Title);
                clientContext.ExecuteQuery();
                Response.Write(clientContext.Web.Title);
                clientContext.ToString();
            }

            GeneratePeepsData();
            DataBindPeepsData();

        }
        private void GeneratePeepsData()
        {
            People clsPeep1 = new People();
            clsPeep1.Name = "John Doe";
            clsPeep1.Age = 24;
            clsPeep1.Email = "john.doe@contoso.com";
            myPeeps.Add(clsPeep1);

            People clsPeep2 = new People();
            clsPeep2.Name = "Jane Doe";
            clsPeep2.Age = 22;
            clsPeep2.Email = "jane.doe@contoso.com";
            myPeeps.Add(clsPeep2);
        }

        private void DataBindPeepsData()
        {
            grdViewPeople.DataSource = myPeeps;
            grdViewPeople.DataBind();
        }
    }
}
```

16. Press F6 to build the project.

17. Right-click `MyFirstAutohostedApp`, and select Publish. In the Publish Office Apps dialog, select Finish. This builds and packages the SharePoint app, but does not deploy it. Windows Explorer automatically opens when the build and package process is complete. Copy the folder path in Windows Explorer; you'll need this later on in this exercise.

18. Navigate to your SharePoint Online Developer Site home page, and click New apps to deploy.

19. In the Deploy App dialog, select the upload link, click Browse when prompted, and then click Deploy.

20. When prompted, click Trust It, as shown in Figure 5-18.

When the app is installed, click the link to the app. Something similar to Figure 5-19 appears.

Congratulations! You've built your first Autohosted app.

FIGURE 5-18

How It Works

In the earlier exercise where you created a Windows Azure MVC4 application, you used the Windows Azure Cloud template to create the Windows Azure project. However, when you create a SharePoint Autohosted app, the deployment and packaging process automatically manages the deployment of part of the project to SharePoint and the other part to Windows Azure. Therefore, in this exercise `MyFirstAutohostedApp` was packaged and deployed to SharePoint, and `MyFirstAutohostedAppWeb` was packaged and deployed to Windows Azure automatically.

FIGURE 5-19

Within the `Default.aspx` page (which is deployed to Windows Azure), you added a simple class object to represent a person. The person had three properties: a name, email address, and age.

```
public class People
{
    public string Name { get; set; }
    public string Email { get; set; }
    public int Age { get; set; }
}
```

To keep things simple, you then created two helper methods that were called when the default pages were loaded. The first one, `GeneratePeepsData`, created two instances of the `People` object, populated the properties, and then added the newly created objects to the `List<People>` collection object. The second method, `DataBindPeepsData`, data-bound the `List<People>` collection object to the data grid you added to the `Default.aspx` page.

You might be curious to understand how SharePoint knows to point off to the page you deployed to Windows Azure, and how it allows the cross-domain access. This is defined automatically for you in the AppManifest configuration file. You can see the following XML snippet that shows the default `remoteAppUrl` token (which is auto-created by Visual Studio) and a pointer to the `Default.aspx` page. The `StandardTokens` token then adds some additional information to the URL such as SharePoint host URL and language.

```
...
<Properties>
 <Title>MyFirstAutohostedApp</Title>
 <StartPage>~remoteAppUrl/Pages/Default.aspx?{StandardTokens}</StartPage>
</Properties>
...
```

Let's now walk through a second example that more explicitly splits the Windows Azure piece from the SharePoint piece. In this example, you'll again use the Autohosted template, but this time you'll first publish the Windows Azure application you created earlier and then use the Client App Web Part to integrate the Windows Azure application with SharePoint. This is the most lightweight way to integrate Windows Azure with SharePoint (and is tantamount to an `iframe` object that registers the Windows Azure application with SharePoint).

This example is composed of two parts:

- ➤ An application that has been built and deployed to Windows Azure
- ➤ A lightweight configuration application that will be deployed to SharePoint

For the Windows Azure application, you can use the web page you created and published to Windows Azure in the first exercise or create a new one using the method described earlier for creating and publishing an application to Windows Azure. Either way, you should have a web page that is deployed to Windows Azure. When deployed, you can see from Figure 5-20 that the URL in SharePoint includes both the SharePoint site URL and the URL for the Windows Azure application.

FIGURE 5-20

TRY IT OUT   Building A Client App Web Part (SPClientAppWebPartForAzure.sln)

To create a Client App Web Part that loads a Windows Azure site, perform the following steps:

1. Open Visual Studio 2012 and create a new solution project called `SPClientAppWebPartForAzure`.

2. After the solution is created, right-click the solution and click Add ➪ New Project and select Cloud, .NET Framework 4.0, and Windows Azure Cloud Service.

3. Provide a name for the project (`SPAzureClientAppWebPart`) and click OK.

4. In the New Windows Azure Cloud Service dialog, select the ASP.NET Web Role and click the right-arrow button.

5. Edit the name of the new project (`GetPeople`) and click OK.

6. After the project has been created, right-click the `App_Data` folder and select Add ➪ New Item.

7. Select Data, and then click XML File. Provide a name for the XML file (`People.xml`), and click Add.

8. Add the following XML to the `People.xml` file.

```
<?xml version="1.0" encoding="utf-8" ?>
<People>
  <Peep Name="John Doe" Email="john@contoso.com" />
  <Peep Name="Jane Doe" Email="jane@fabrikam.com"/>
  <Peep Name="Cooper McGovern" Email="cooper.mcgovern@acme.net" />
  <Peep Name="Satya Saiid" Email="satya@fabrikam.com" />
  <Peep Name="Fred Nietzche" Email="fred.neitzche@postmodern.net" />
  <Peep Name="Aaron Schtick" Email="aarons@postcolonial.com" />
</People>
```

9. Double-click the `Default.aspx` page, click the Source tab, and replace the default markup with the following code.

```
<%@ Page Title="Home Page" Language="C#" MasterPageFile="~/Site.Master"
AutoEventWireup="true"
CodeBehind="Default.aspx.cs"
Inherits="GetPeople._Default" %>
<asp:Content runat="server" ID="FeaturedContent" ContentPlaceHolderID="FeaturedContent"
>
    <section class="featured">
        <div class="content-wrapper">
            <h2>My Peeps</h2>
            <asp:GridView ID="grdPeopleData"
                runat="server">
            </asp:GridView>
        </div>
    </section>
</asp:Content>
```

10. Right-click `Default.aspx` and select View Code.

11. Replace the default code with the following bolded code.

```
using System;
using System.Collections.Generic;
using System.Linq;
using System.Web;
using System.Web.UI;
using System.Web.UI.WebControls;
using System.Xml.Linq;

namespace GetPeople
{
    public partial class _Default : Page
    {
        protected void Page_Load(object sender, EventArgs e)
        {
            GetPeopleData();
        }

        private void GetPeopleData()
        {
            var xDoc = XDocument.Load(Server.MapPath("App_Data/People.xml"));
            var query = from p in xDoc.Descendants("Peep")
                        orderby p.Attribute("Name").Value
                        select new
                        {
                            Name = p.Attribute("Name").Value,
                            Description = p.Attribute("Email").Value
                        };
            grdPeopleData.DataSource = query;
            grdPeopleData.DataBind();

        }
    }
}
```

12. Press F6 to build the Windows Azure application, and then press F5 to run the application in debug mode.

13. To publish your Windows Azure application, right-click the Windows Azure project and select Publish. Click Finish when you're ready to publish the app to the cloud.

After you've published your Windows Azure application, you're ready to create the SharePoint application.

14. Create a new Visual Studio 2012 project.

15. Select Office/SharePoint ⇨ Apps ⇨ Apps for SharePoint 2013.

16. Provide a name for the project (**AzureClientAppWebPart**) and click OK.

17. Leave the defaults, except in the hosting options select Autohosted as shown in Figure 5-21.

18. Click Finish.

FIGURE 5-21

19. Right-click the Web Part of the project, and select Remove.

20. Right-click the SharePoint project, and select Add ⇨ New Item.

21. In the Add New Item dialog, select Office/SharePoint and then click Client Web Part (Host Web).

22. Provide a name for the Client Web Part (**MyAzureApp**) and click Add.

23. Right-click the `AppManifest.xml` file and select View Designer.

24. Under Permission Requests, select Web as the scope and then Read as the level of permissions.

25. Right-click the `AppManifest.xml` file and select View Code.

26. Amend the `StartPage` property so that it points to your Windows Azure website as shown by the following bolded code.

```
<?xml version="1.0" encoding="utf-8" ?>
<App xmlns="http://schemas.microsoft.com/sharepoint/2012/app/manifest"
     Name="AzureClientAppWebPart"
     ProductID="{50be3f58-ee99-420e-af96-85cf73904fa1}"
     Version="1.0.0.0"
     SharePointMinVersion="15.0.0.0">
  <Properties>
    <Title>AzureClientAppWebPart</Title>
    <StartPage>http://myazuresite.cloudapp.net/?{StandardTokens}</StartPage>
  </Properties>

  <AppPrincipal>
    <AutoDeployedWebApplication/>
  </AppPrincipal>

  <AppPrerequisites>
    <AppPrerequisite Type="AutoProvisioning" ID="RemoteWebHost" />
  </AppPrerequisites>
<AppPermissionRequests><AppPermissionRequest
Scope="http://sharepoint/content/sitecollection/web"
Right="Read" />
</AppPermissionRequests></App>
```

27. Right-click the `Elements.xml` file in the newly added Client Web Part and amend the Content property to include the Windows Azure Web page as show in the following bolded code.

```
<?xml version="1.0" encoding="utf-8"?>
<Elements xmlns="http://schemas.microsoft.com/sharepoint/">
  <ClientWebPart Name="MyAzureApp" Title="MyAzureApp Title"
    Description="MyAzureApp Description" DefaultWidth="300" DefaultHeight="200">
    <Content Type="html" Src="http://myazuresite.cloudapp.net" />
  </ClientWebPart>
</Elements>
```

28. Press F6 to build after you've amended these files.

29. When you've successfully built the app, right-click the SharePoint project, select Publish, and then click Finish. The result should look something like Figure 5-22.

30. After your project publishes, follow the same steps to upload and deploy the project into your SharePoint developer site as you did in steps 16 onwards in the previous Try It Out.

FIGURE 5-22

You should now see the newly published app in SharePoint, as shown in Figure 5-23

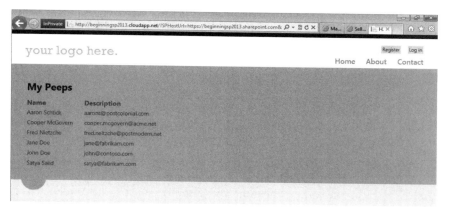

FIGURE 5-23

How it Works

The Client App Web Part is an alternate way to expose Windows Azure applications in SharePoint. This exercise illustrated how you walk through creating a Windows Azure app and then integrate it with SharePoint using the Client App Web Part. You might think of it as an `iframe` of sorts.

If you click the deployed app from within Apps in Testing, you won't see the default SharePoint UI built around the app; it is redirected from SharePoint to load the remotely hosted domain. However, if you copy and paste the URL after the Windows Azure page loads, you should see something similar to `http://myazuresite.cloudapp.net/?SPHostUrl=https://myazuresite.sharepoint` `.com&SPLanguage=en-US`. This shows that the Windows Azure website, although remotely hosted in a separate Windows Azure domain, is registered and loaded as a SharePoint application.

However, clicking the Page tab, selecting Edit ➪ Insert ➪ App Part, and selecting the Client Web Part you just created and deployed to SharePoint adds the Web part that integrates the Windows Azure application with SharePoint. Figure 5-24 shows what this integration looks like.

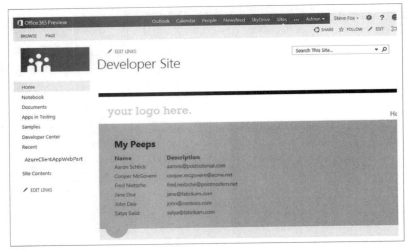

FIGURE 5-24

With the SharePoint Client App Web Part, you can see that the Windows Azure website or application appears with the SharePoint UI and navigation around it.

SUMMARY

This chapter provides a first look at Windows Azure, Microsoft's key cloud platform technology. Within the broader area of cloud computing, you can develop many different types of cloud-based solutions using Windows Azure.

You can integrate Windows Azure with SharePoint 2013, both generally and specifically. Generally, you use the Autohosted and Provider-hosted app models to leverage the power of Windows Azure in the cloud-hosted app models. Two specific ways to integrate with SharePoint using the Autohosted cloud app and the Client App Web Part. Key to understanding this integration is knowing that SharePoint natively uses Windows Azure in the Autohosted project template, but that you can use the Client App Web Part to integrate remotely hosted Windows Azure applications or use the provider-hosted project template to create this integration. As you progress throughout the book, you'll return to the Provider-hosted app as it is a more advanced topic requiring some additional configuration and setup.

EXERCISES

Answers to Exercises can be found in Appendix A.

1. Identify the core categories of cloud computing and Windows Azure.

2. What are some of the key features available in Windows Azure?

3. What are the two key cloud apps in SharePoint 2013 where you can integrate Windows Azure?

4. Build an Autohosted application that uses Windows Azure Web Sites and the REST service you built in the first exercise.

▶ **WHAT YOU LEARNED IN THIS CHAPTER**

ITEM	DESCRIPTION
Cloud Computing	Using web-based resources to deliver applications, services, and data.
Windows Azure	Microsoft's key cloud computing platform technology.
Autohosted Cloud App	A new type of SharePoint cloud app that uses Windows Azure natively to deploy code.
Provider-Hosted Cloud App	A new type of SharePoint cloud app that enables you to integrate broader web technologies such as Windows Azure, HTML5 PHP, Java, and so on into SharePoint.
SharePoint Client App Web Part	A new type of SharePoint artifact that you can use to surface Windows Azure apps inside of SharePoint.

RECOMMENDED READING

Overview of SharePoint and Office App development: `http://msdn.microsoft.com/en-us/library/office/apps/jj220030`

SharePoint 2013 Developer MSDN site at `http://msdn.microsoft.com/en-us/library/jj163794(v=office.15)`

Steve Fox's blog (which shows how to integrate SharePoint and Windows Azure in more general ways) at `http://blogs.msdn.com/steve_fox`

Windows Azure Developer Portal at `http://www.microsoft.com/windowsazure`

PART II
Fundamental SharePoint 2013 Development Building Blocks

Developing, Integrating, and Building Applications in SharePoint 2013

WHAT YOU WILL LEARN IN THIS CHAPTER:

➤ Understanding the basics of the new SharePoint application model in SharePoint 2013

➤ Understanding the fundamental building blocks of application development in SharePoint 2013

➤ Building your first SharePoint 2013 application

WROX.COM CODE DOWNLOADS FOR THIS CHAPTER

The wrox.com code downloads for this chapter are found at `http://www.wrox.com/Wiley CDA/WroxTitle/productCd-1118495845.html` on the Download Code tab. The code for this chapter is divided into the following major examples:

➤ Dataintegration.zip

➤ EventsandLogicintegration.zip

➤ UserInterfaceintegration.zip

As you read in Chapter 2, "Overview of SharePoint 2013 App Model," SharePoint applications forge a new path for developers in the SharePoint 2013 release. They are designed to take custom code out of the running SharePoint processes to increase stability and security, and at the same time offer more flexibility to developers. In SharePoint 2010 and earlier, developers were forced to write code that was limited to the confines of what SharePoint allowed. For example, in SharePoint 2010 the version of the .NET Framework was 3.5

and developers couldn't write code that used the 4.0 Framework because the SharePoint process wouldn't allow for it. Many of these limitations have plagued SharePoint developers for years. The new SharePoint application model allows developers' code to run outside of the SharePoint processes, thus freeing them from these limitations. Developers are free to use whatever version of the .NET Framework they desire. In fact, they could write all their applications' code in PHP or Java if they so desired. This freedom is a huge plus for developer happiness and productivity. However, along with this fundamental shift in the way custom applications are built come some limits in the way that code can integrate with SharePoint that experienced SharePoint developers will notice from previously writing full-trust applications.

This chapter covers the various options the new SharePoint application model offers for integrating and extending SharePoint, including many of the fundamental techniques, tools, and building blocks that the new model offers and how they map to the common application layers of UI, events, and data.

DEVELOPMENT MODELS AVAILABLE IN SHAREPOINT 2013

In Chapter 2 you learned about the new application model for SharePoint solutions. This new model differs both in architecture and capability from traditional full-trust solutions offered in SharePoint 2007 and SharePoint 2010. As you start developing solutions for SharePoint 2013 you need to decide which of the following two models best suits your needs:

➤ A full-trust solution

➤ A new SharePoint application

Each has its respective pros and cons and you must carefully weigh which will suit your purposes best. One of the driving design decisions behind SharePoint applications was to provide a development model that was agnostic to whether the application was being used in SharePoint on premises or to Office 365 in the cloud. This point is extremely important to keep in mind as you decide how to build your application, and you are advised to seriously consider future plans for using SharePoint Online. Your organization might very well want to move to SharePoint Online in the coming years and will need many of its apps to go with it.

Although both the older full trust–style apps and the newer SharePoint applications offer some of the same capabilities, they differ in several areas. Table 6-1 summarizes some of the high-level components, or building blocks, that each offers.

TABLE 6-1: Full Trust Solutions versus SharePoint Applications

COMPONENT	SHAREPOINT APPS	FULL TRUST SOLUTION
Web Parts		X
App parts	X	
ASP.NET server controls		X
ASP.NET user controls		X
List and library templates	X	X

Content types	X	X
Event handlers		X
Remote event receivers	X	
Pages and page layouts		X
Files	X	X
Master pages		X
Ribbon and list actions	X	X
Workflows		X
Apps for Office	X	
Custom JavaScript list view renderings	X	
Custom JavaScript column renderings	X	

All SharePoint 2013 solutions are made up from a combination of one or more of the preceding building blocks. Typically, a solution built on SharePoint consists of three high-level application layers, not unlike solutions built with other technologies:

➤ User interface

➤ Logic

➤ Data storage

The developer's task is to decide what SharePoint components best fulfill the requirements for each of the preceding application layers. A solution might, for example, mean using a Web Part for display purposes, an event receiver for processing and logic, and a list for storing and managing the solutions data. These basic architectural decisions don't change based on your decision to build a full-trust solution or SharePoint application. You must still map your requirements to each of the capabilities these models provide to ensure it is suitable for your needs.

APPLICATION INTEGRATION OPTIONS IN SHAREPOINT 2013

The new application model in SharePoint 2013 offers a number of options for your application to deeply integrate with SharePoint, other systems, and data. These options fall into the following categories:

➤ User interface integration

➤ Events and logic integration

➤ Data integration

When you think about building a solution, you must evaluate your options for how you want to surface your application inside SharePoint (UI), how you want to call code and process actions when a user uses your application (events and logic), and how and where you store and work with your application's data and data that resides in other systems (data). Understanding what options are available and how they work is critical when designing your application.

The following sections cover some of the most common options you have for each of the layers (UI, events, and data) in the new SharePoint application model.

User Interface Integration

Three main integration points are available to you in the SharePoint user interface as part of the SharePoint application model:

- ➤ App Parts and Pages
- ➤ Ribbon and Action menus
- ➤ Navigation

App Parts and Pages offer you the ability to surface your applications' user interface to your users. For people familiar with SharePoint 2010, App Parts are similar to Web Parts. Navigation lets users find your application, and integrating with the Ribbon and Action menus lets your users take actions in the same familiar location that they do elsewhere in SharePoint. Using one or more of these building blocks enables you to integrate your application's user interface with that of SharePoint's and expose your app to its users.

App Parts and Pages

App Parts are reusable and configurable windows into your application. They are analogous to Web Parts in SharePoint 2010; however, the UI is generated and served remotely within your application as opposed to being generated from code running in the SharePoint process. Typically, the interface is rendered from another environment such as Windows Azure in the cloud or IIS on premises. Additionally, App Parts show in the Web Part gallery alongside all the other Web Parts in SharePoint, so they are easy to find and add to your SharePoint pages. Your solutions can consist of one or more App Parts, which should typically surface parts of your application that make sense to show alongside other Web Parts, such as a summary of data or a small set of controls. Figure 6-1 shows a weather App Part that has been added to the homepage of a site. It acts much like a Web Part would except that the UI of your application is embedded within the part via an iFrame. This means your application UI can be served from anywhere you choose, as long as it is accessible from the user's browser. As you will see later in this section, part of an App Part's configuration is the URL that the iFrame should be pointed at. Along with this URL you can feed additional parameters that your App's logic can pick up from the query string. These can be properties set via the App Parts property panel, for example.

FIGURE 6-1

> **NOTE** *When designing your application try to think about how parts of your application and its data might be useful in other places, and use an App Part if appropriate.*

Pages are much like an App Part except that they are viewed in a larger, fuller window style. Unlike with an App Part though, when someone launches your app's page via a navigation link or similar method, the whole browser is directed to your app's page thus giving your app full control over what is displayed. This ability enables you to include and show much more of your application to the user. Using Pages is good for when you need a lot of room to do things such as have the user fill in a large form or show a lot of data. Additionally, parameters can be passed along on the URL much like with an App Part. SharePoint provides a number of controls to assist you in branding your application so that it fits well with the look and feel of SharePoint. This includes a top navigation bar, as shown in Figure 6-2.

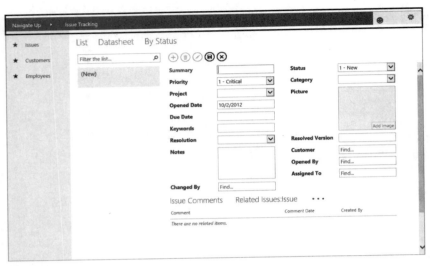

FIGURE 6-2

> **NOTE** *To maintain a consistent user experience in your solutions, App Parts and Pages in SharePoint 2013 allow you to include a "Chrome Control" that adds a top navigation bar and defines standard styles for your application. This helps you make your application UI look consistent with that of SharePoint's.*

To get a better feel for how App Parts and Pages work, try your hand at creating an app and adding these new elements to it. The following activity walks you through the process.

TRY IT OUT   **Building Your First SharePoint Application (UserInterfaceIntegration.zip)**

In this exercise you create a new SharePoint application, add an App Part to it, and deploy it to SharePoint Online. Prior to beginning this exercise you should have already signed up for and created your developer Office 365 SharePoint site. You can do that via the `http://msdn.microsoft.com/sharepoint` website.

1. Run Visual Studio 2012 as Administrator.

2. Select File ⇨ New ⇨ Project.

3. In the New Project dialog, expand Templates ⇨ Visual C# ⇨ Office/SharePoint ⇨ Apps.

4. Select App for SharePoint 2013 and enter the Name, `MyFirstSharePointApp`. Click OK.

5. In the Specify the App for SharePoint settings dialog, provide the URL to your Office 365 developer site and click the Validate button to confirm connectivity to the site.

6. For the question, "How do you want to host your app for SharePoint?" select Autohosted, and then click Finish.

7. Right-click the `MyFirstSharePointApp` project and select Add ⇨ New Item. In the Add New Item dialog select Client Web Part and name it `MyAppPart`. Click Add.

8. Open the `Elements.xml` under `MyAppPart` if it is not already open.

9. Replace the `<Content Type="html" Src="" />` block with the following and save the file:

```
<Content Type="html" Src="~remoteAppUrl/Pages/Default.aspx?{StandardTokens}" />
```

10. Open the `Default.aspx` page.

11. Replace everything after the line starting with `<%@ Page` with the following code:

```
<!DOCTYPE html PUBLIC "-//W3C//DTD XHTML 1.0
Transitional//EN" "http://www.w3.org/TR/xhtml1/DTD/xhtml1-transitional.dtd">
<html xmlns="http://www.w3.org/1999/xhtml">
<head runat="server">
    <title></title>
    <script src="https://ajax.aspnetcdn.com/ajax/4.0/1/MicrosoftAjax.js"
type="text/javascript"></script>
    <script type="text/javascript"
src="https://ajax.aspnetcdn.com/ajax/jQuery/jquery-1.7.2.min.js"></script>

    <script type="text/javascript">
        var hostweburl;

        $(document).ready(function () {
            hostweburl = decodeURIComponent(getQueryStringParameter("SPHostUrl"));
            var scriptbase = hostweburl + "/_layouts/15/";

            var dclink = document.createElement("link");
            dclink.setAttribute("rel", "stylesheet");
            dclink.setAttribute("href", scriptbase + "defaultcss.ashx");

            var head = document.getElementsByTagName("head");
            head[0].appendChild(dclink);
        });

        function getQueryStringParameter(paramToRetrieve) {
            var params = document.URL.split("?")[1].split("&");
            var strParams = "";
            for (var i = 0; i < params.length; i = i + 1) {
                var singleParam = params[i].split("=");
                if (singleParam[0] == paramToRetrieve)
                    return singleParam[1];
            }
        }
    </script>

</head>
<body>
    <form id="form1" runat="server">
    <h1 class="ms-core-pageTitle">Your First SharePoint Application!</h1>
    <h1 class="ms-accentText">Put your app UI here.</h1>
    <div>
        <h2 class="ms-webpart-titleText">Use the SharePoint CSS</h2>
        <a class="ms-commandLink" href="#">links</a>
        <br />
        You can use the SharePoint CSS in your app by referencing it in your pages.
    </div>
    </form>
</body>
</html>
```

12. Press F5 to compile, package, deploy, and debug your application. When the process is complete, a browser launches to a page asking, "Do you trust `MyFirstSharePointApp`?" Click Trust It to continue. You should see your application listed, as shown in Figure 6-3:

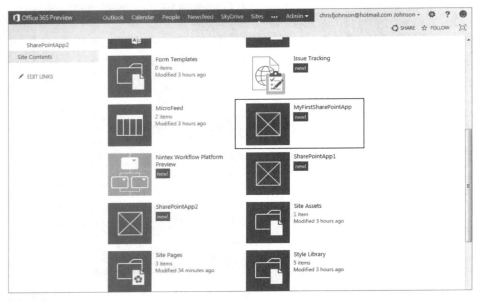

FIGURE 6-3

13. Click on your app's tile image to navigate to it. You might see a security certificate warning as shown in Figure 6-4. This is because your app isn't correctly secured with SSL while running in your development environment. Click the Show content button to continue.

FIGURE 6-4

You should see your page render as shown in Figure 6-5. It is using the SharePoint style sheet.

14. Navigate back to your SharePoint site.

15. Navigate to your site's homepage by clicking the Home link in the Quick Navigation on the left side of the page.

16. Click the Page ribbon and select Edit. You will now add your new App Part to your site's homepage.

FIGURE 6-5

17. Click the Insert Ribbon tab and click the App Part button.

18. Select MyAppPart from the list of parts and click Add to add the part to your page.

19. Click Save in the ribbon when the operation completes.

You should now see your new App Part displayed on the page with both the name of your site displayed and "My application goes here!" as shown in Figure 6-6. Congratulations — you have just created a SharePoint application!

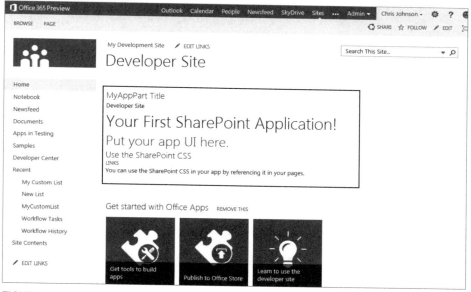

FIGURE 6-6

How It Works

In this exercise you first created a new project using one of the new project templates in Visual Studio 2012 for SharePoint application development. These templates provide the starting point for any new app, a project for packaging the declarative parts of your application that don't include compiled code for installation into SharePoint, and a Web project for your app's code for Provider-hosted and auto-hosted applications. When you run the solution, Visual Studio packages up these projects and deploys the app project package (.app file in the bin directory) to your SharePoint site's application gallery. Alongside that process it runs your app's code in a Web project on your local development IIS instance. Ultimately, after your Autohosted application is packaged for release that project will be packaged up for deployment into a location in Azure where it will run instead.

The App Part you created is simply an HTML <iframe> window into your application as specified by the src property on the Content node of your App Parts elements.xml file. However, it also adds some special tokens to the URL query string of that page to pass it additional information about who the caller is. This information is then used by the TokenHelper.GetClientContextWithContextToken helper function to assist in the construction of a CSOM client context that makes calls to SharePoint authenticated as that application and caller. This ensures your app's code can make only operations it has been allowed to do. Chapter 10, "Overview of OAuth in SharePoint 2013," covers this topic in depth. The JavaScript and markup that you added to the `Default.aspx` page dynamically added a style sheet link to the page, the source of which was the CSS from your SharePoint site. It defines the styles it uses to show the UI with the same fonts and styles as SharePoint.

As with traditional Web Parts, you may also configure App Parts with custom properties. You can do this in the `Elements.xml` file for the App Part. App Parts support the following types of custom properties:

➤ **String:** Gives a simple text box input field

➤ **Int:** Renders as an input field that only accepts integers

➤ **Boolean:** Renders as a check box field

➤ **Enum:** Renders as a drop-down field

For example, if you wanted your App Part to accept a configuration property where the user could choose from one of three options, you could use the following XML:

```
<Property Name="colorProp" Type="enum" RequiresDesignerPermission="true"
DefaultValue="R" WebCategory="My App Part Settings"
WebDisplayName="Fav Color">
  <EnumItems>
    <EnumItem WebDisplayName="Red" Value="R"/>
    <EnumItem WebDisplayName="Green" Value="G"/>
    <EnumItem WebDisplayName="Blue" Value="B"/>
  </EnumItems>
</Property>
```

This code would render as shown in Figure 6-7.

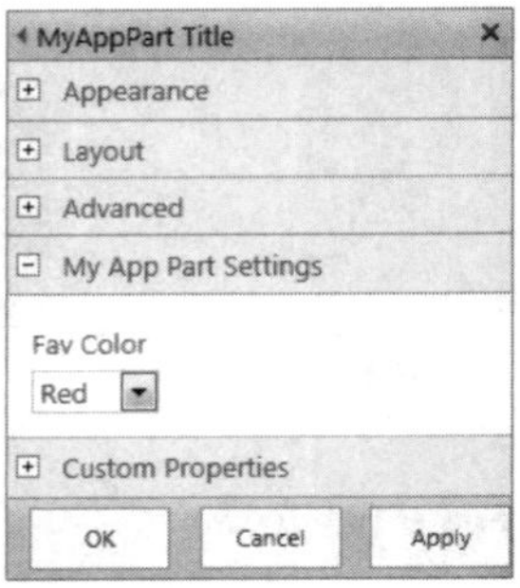

Additionally, you can choose to pass the value set for these properties to your App Part via the URL by setting them as tokens in the `Src` attribute on the `Content` node in the `Elements.xml` file:

FIGURE 6-7

```
<Content Type="html"
Src="~remoteAppUrl/Pages/Default.aspx?{StandardTokens}& Property1=_ colorProp _" />
```

Ribbon and Action Menus

The ribbon was first introduced in SharePoint 2010 and provides the central location for all actions that a user may want to take on documents and other data. In SharePoint 2010, developers could include custom actions for their applications in the ribbon; SharePoint applications also allow this customization. This enables you to include actions where users expect them, alongside all the other standard actions SharePoint provides (see Figure 6-8).

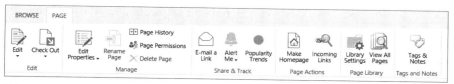

FIGURE 6-8

> **NOTE** *When designing your SharePoint application consider including your application's common actions on the ribbon. Doing so makes them easy for users to find and provides a consistent user experience.*

The Action menu is a context-aware menu on items in a SharePoint list or library. For example, in a SharePoint document library the Action menu exposes common functions such as Check In and Check Out (see Figure 6-9). Another term commonly used for this menu is ECB (Edit Control Block). SharePoint applications allow you to include additional actions on this menu. For example, it is a great location to expose your application's functions that apply to a single list item. You should also consider including the action in the ribbon for consistency; however, the ECB offers quicker access for the user, so including it in both locations is advised.

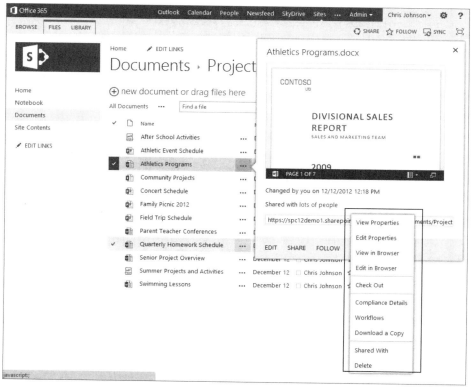

FIGURE 6-9

To get a feel for how to develop with the Ribbon in a SharePoint application try the following exercise that walks you through the process.

TRY IT OUT Adding a Custom Action to Your Application

In this exercise you add a new Ribbon action to your application that, when clicked, will call your application. You must have completed the App Part exercise, "Building Your First SharePoint Application," in the previous section before starting this example.

1. Ensure you have the `MyFirstSharePointApp` solution open in Visual Studio 2012.

2. Right-click the `MyFirstSharePointApp` project and select Add ⇨ New Item. In the Add New Item dialog select UI Custom Action (Host Web) and name it **MyAppAction**. Click Add.

3. Open the `Elements.xml` under `MyAppAction` if it is not already open.

4. Replace the entire contents of the file with the following code. This defines your Ribbon button. The `CustomAction` node contains information specifying that the action resides in the ribbon and should be present on all custom lists as defined by the `RegistrationId` attribute. The `CommandUIDefinition` node defines the button and that it should reside inside the Manage tab in the list item Ribbon. Finally, the `CommandUIHandler` node specifies the URL that should be called when the action is initiated. In this example, you also pass the IDs of the list and list item to the page so that they can be used in the action code.

```xml
<?xml version="1.0" encoding="utf-8"?>
<Elements xmlns="http://schemas.microsoft.com/sharepoint/">
  <CustomAction Id="00ec7345-f310-4fb1-a836-5cef4d0ad2fa.MyAppAction"
                RegistrationType="List"
                RegistrationId="100"
                Location="CommandUI.Ribbon"
                Sequence="100"
                Title="MyAppAction action">
    <CommandUIExtension>
      <CommandUIDefinitions>
        <CommandUIDefinition Location="Ribbon.ListItem.Manage.Controls._
children">
          <Button
              Id="Ribbon.Library.Connect.PropertyViewer"
              Alt="MyAppAction action"
              Sequence="115"
              Command="Invoke_CustomAction"
              LabelText="MyAppAction action"
              TemplateAlias="o1"/>
        </CommandUIDefinition>
      </CommandUIDefinitions>
      <CommandUIHandlers>
        <CommandUIHandler
            Command="Invoke_CustomAction"
            CommandAction="~remoteAppUrl/Pages/Default.aspx?{StandardTokens}
&amp;ListURLDir={ListUrlDir}&amp;SelectedListID={SelectedListId}
&amp;SelectedItemID={SelectedItemId}"/>
      </CommandUIHandlers>
    </CommandUIExtension>
  </CustomAction>
</Elements>
```

5. Open the `Default.aspx.cs` page.

6. Replace the entire `Page_Load` method with the following code:

```
protected void Page_Load(object sender, EventArgs e)
{
    var contextToken = TokenHelper.GetContextTokenFromRequest(Page.Request);
    var hostWeb = Page.Request["SPHostUrl"];

    using (var clientContext = TokenHelper.GetClientContextWithContextToken (
hostWeb,contextToken, Request.Url.Authority))
    {
        clientContext.Load(clientContext.Web,
            web => web.Title);

        clientContext.ExecuteQuery();
        Response.Write(clientContext.Web.Title);
        clientContext.ToString();

        if (Page.Request["SelectedListID"] != null)
        {
            Guid listId = Guid.Parse(Page.Request["SelectedListID"]);

            Microsoft.SharePoint.Client.List list =
clientContext.Web.Lists.GetById(listId);

            clientContext.Load(list,
                l => l.Title);

            clientContext.ExecuteQuery();

            Response.Write("<p>Action taken on:" + list.Title + "</p>");
        }
    }
}
```

7. Press F5 to compile, package, deploy, and debug your application. When the process completes, a browser launches to a page asking, "Do you trust `MyFirstSharePointApp`?" Click Trust It to continue. You should see your application listed when the compile and deploy operation is complete.

8. Click the Add an app link and select a Custom List. Call it **My Custom List** and then click Create.

9. Click My Custom List from the list.

10. Click the Items ribbon tab. You should see your custom action within the Manage group as shown in Figure 6-10.

FIGURE 6-10

11. Click the MyAppAction ribbon action. If a security warning appears, click the option to continue to the site. (This warning appears if your application site is not correctly secured with SSL in your development environment.)

12. You should see your application with the text "Action taken on: My Custom List" on the page. The application has used the Client-Side Object Model to call back into SharePoint and retrieve the name of the list from which your application custom action was triggered.

How It Works

In this exercise you added a custom action button to the SharePoint Ribbon. As part of the button configuration you specified a page in your application as the destination when the button is clicked. Passed along on the query string was an additional piece of information about the ID of the list that was in the user's context when it was clicked. The app's page code used that ID to call back into SharePoint via a CSOM call to retrieve the list's DisplayName. Similar to the previous exercise, the Ribbon button definition was packed up as part of your app's package and deployed to SharePoint. There are many different locations where you can choose to place custom Ribbon buttons. You can find a list of these on MSDN (http://msdn.microsoft.com/en-us/library/ee537543.aspx).

Navigation

To ensure a consistent way for users to find and interact with apps, SharePoint 2013 provides two standardized navigational elements:

➤ Quick Launch navigation (see Figure 6-11)

➤ All Site Content tiles (see Figure 6-12)

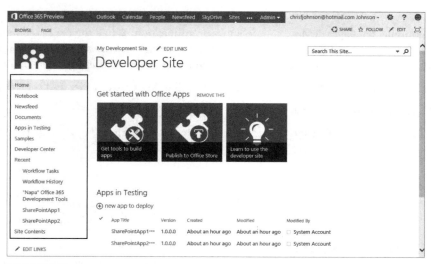

FIGURE 6-11

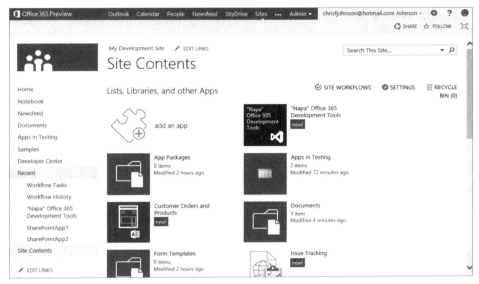

FIGURE 6-12

App developers have little control over the style and location of the Quick Launch navigation because it is provided by SharePoint and the inclusion of your app in this navigation is dictated by the user. However, app developers have more control over the appearance of their application's tiles available in the Site Contents section of a SharePoint 2013 site. You are able to specify the name and tile icons shown.

As a developer you can specify the following properties via the `AppManifest.xml` file in your application:

➤   Name

➤   Title (shown in the SharePoint site UI)

➤   Tile icon (96 × 96 PNG)

Try out the following exercise to learn how to change the look of your application with a custom tile and name.

TRY IT OUT   Customizing Your Application's Name and Tile

In this exercise you set a new tile image for your application. You must have completed the "Building Your First SharePoint Application" in the "App Parts and Pages" section before starting this example.

1.   Ensure you have the `MyFirstSharePointApp` solution open in Visual Studio 2012.

2.   Locate and double-click the `AppManifest.xml` file in the MyFirstSharePointApp project to open it in Design view.

3.   Change the title of the application to `My First SharePoint Application`.

4. Click Browse next to the Icon path text box. From the downloaded code package for this chapter locate the `MyAppIcon.png` file, select it, and click Open.

5. Press F5 to package and deploy your application.

FIGURE 6-13

6. After the app deploys, you should see its new title and icon displayed (see Figure 6-13).

How It Works

In this exercise you customized the title and icon for your application. A SharePoint application's configuration properties are stored in the `AppMenifest.xml` file. Visual Studio 2012 provides a designer-based interface over this file so you can configure these properties easily; however, you can also go into the XML itself to set them.

Events and Logic Integration

Providing a UI for users is usually the most prominent aspect of any application. However, responding to the actions users take either within an application, or to interact with an application, is also extremely important. SharePoint applications provide the ability to both respond to activities within your application (such as a button click) and respond to activities within SharePoint (such as a document being checked out).

Responding to activities within your application is very straightforward. Your application's UI and code run remotely from SharePoint and are simply surfaced via App Parts and Pages. For that reason, responding to an event such as a button being clicked in your application is entirely tied to your application's programming framework. For example, if your app is built with ASP.NET then you simply catch the `OnClick` event for an ASP.NET button. SharePoint does not get in your way for these types of events.

The following exercise shows you how to add code behind a button in your SharePoint application that responds when it is pressed.

TRY IT OUT **Responding to Events Within Your Application (EventsandLogicintegreation.zip)**

In this exercise you add a button to your application and include code that is run when it is pressed. You must have completed the "Building Your First SharePoint Application" in the "App Parts and Pages" section before starting this example.

1. Ensure you have the `MyFirstSharePointApp` solution open in Visual Studio 2012.

2. Open the `Default.aspx` file under the `MyFirstSharePointAppWeb` project.

3. Insert the following code directly after `</div>`.

```
<asp:Button ID="Button1" runat="server" Text="Do Something"
OnClick="Button1_Click" /><br />
<asp:Label ID="txtUser" runat="server" Text=""></asp:Label>
```

4. Open the `Default.aspx.cs` file.

5. Replace the `Page_Load` method with the following code:

```
protected void Page_Load(object sender, EventArgs e)
{
    var contextToken = TokenHelper.GetContextTokenFromRequest(Page.Request);
    var hostWeb = Page.Request["SPHostUrl"];

    if (!IsPostBack)
    {
        Button1.CommandArgument = contextToken;


        using (var clientContext =
TokenHelper.GetClientContextWithContextToken(hostWeb, contextToken,
 Request.Url.Authority))
        {
            clientContext.Load(clientContext.Web, web => web.Title);
            clientContext.ExecuteQuery();
            Response.Write(clientContext.Web.Title);
            clientContext.ToString();
        }
    }
}
```

The `Button1.CommandArgument = contextToken;` line ensures that the `contextToken` is stored for later use on postback events when the button is clicked. You need it to make subsequent CSOM calls.

6. Add the following new method after the `Page_Load` method:

```
protected void Button1_Click(object sender, EventArgs e)
{
    var contextToken = ((Button)sender).CommandArgument;
    var hostWeb = Page.Request["SPHostUrl"];

    using (var clientContext =
TokenHelper.GetClientContextWithContextToken(hostWeb, contextToken,
 Request.Url.Authority))
    {
        clientContext.Load(clientContext.Web.CurrentUser);
        clientContext.ExecuteQuery();

        txtUser.Text = clientContext.Web.CurrentUser.LoginName;
    }
}
```

7. Press F5 to package and deploy your application.

8. After your app deploys, add your app's App Part to the homepage of your site by clicking Page ⇨ Edit ⇨ Insert ⇨ App Part. Select MyAppPart from the list and then click Add.

9. Inside your App Part you should now see a button called Do Something. Click it.

10. You should now see your full login name displayed directly below the button, as shown in Figure 6-14.

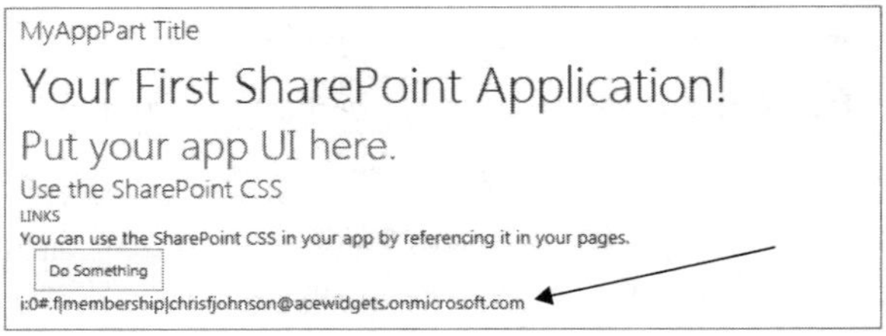

How It Works

In this exercise you added a button to your application and responded to it being clicked. Nothing is particularly special about this button over and above a standard ASP.NET

FIGURE 6-14

button; however, it is worth understanding the role of the `contextToken` and the need to keep it between postbacks to your code so that further calls to the CSOM can be made. In the exercise you stored it in the `CommandArgument` for the button; however, the same could have been achieved in a variety of other ways, such as a hidden control on the page. The important thing is that it is in a location that you are able to retrieve at a later time during a postback event — you need this context in order to call SharePoint via the CSOM on subsequent requests.

For responding to events that occur inside SharePoint, such as a document's being saved or updated, SharePoint provides *event receivers*. In SharePoint 2010 developers could use event receivers to receive events from SharePoint when a user took certain actions such as checking in a document or saving a list item. SharePoint 2013 also provides event receivers that allow applications to respond to events occurring within a SharePoint site. The primary difference from SharePoint 2010 is that event receivers now trigger code that runs remotely outside the SharePoint process in your application's code. They do this via a commonly defined Web service interface. This means the code that you want to respond to events could reside in almost any system you like, as long as it is callable over HTTP/HTTPS from the SharePoint Server or Office 365. An example might be your application code that runs in Windows Azure.

> **NOTE** *For a deeper look into remote event receivers please read Chapter 12, "Remote Event Receivers in SharePoint 2013."*

Data Integration

At the heart of every application is data, which is typically what users want to work with within your application. SharePoint provides a number of out-of-the-box options for storing and working with data. These options fall into two categories:

➤   Storing and manipulating data within SharePoint

➤   Working with data that lives external to SharePoint

From the very first version of SharePoint, the goal has been to make working with data simple and straightforward for users. The simplest example of this is the concept of list data. Users are able to store and work with tabular style data via a common Web interface. Many see using lists analogous to using a table of data in a database. SharePoint applications can also take advantage of these same data storage capabilities natively. By using lists SharePoint offers developers the ability to take advantage of many of the data storage capabilities that SharePoint provides without having to reinvent the wheel. If used properly, SharePoint can save time and effort and potentially reduce the management and support costs of your operation.

At the core of the data storage capabilities within SharePoint are the following:

➤ **Lists:** For storing structured data, much like in a table

➤ **Libraries:** For storing unstructured data, such as in a document or file

SharePoint provides a comprehensive set of APIs for developers to use within applications to interact with and manipulate data that resides in SharePoint. For SharePoint applications those APIs are exposed in the Client-Side Object Model (CSOM).

> **NOTE** Chapter 9 goes more in depth on Client-Side Object Model (CSOM) and the various APIs available in it.

To get a better feel for the data storage capabilities SharePoint provides, try out storing data in lists within SharePoint in the following exercise.

TRY IT OUT **Storing Data in SharePoint Using the Client-Side Object Model (DataIntegration.zip)**

In this exercise you create new items in a SharePoint list using the CSOM API set. You must have completed the "Building Your First SharePoint Application" in the "App Parts and Pages" section before starting this example.

1. Ensure you have the `MyFirstSharePointApp` solution open in Visual Studio 2012.

2. If you haven't already done so in a previous exercise create a new custom list in your site called My Custom List (choose Site Contents ➪ Add an App ➪ Custom List. Call it **My Custom List** and then click Create.)

3. Open the `Default.aspx` file under the MyFirstSharePointAppWeb project in Visual Studio.

4. Open the `Default.aspx.cs` file and replace the `Button1_Click` method with the following:

```
protected void Button1_Click(object sender, EventArgs e)
{
    var contextToken = ((Button)sender).CommandArgument;
    var hostWeb = Page.Request["SPHostUrl"];

    using (var clientContext =
TokenHelper.GetClientContextWithContextToken(hostWeb, contextToken,
 Request.Url.Authority))
    {
        Microsoft.SharePoint.Client.List list =
clientContext.Web.Lists.GetByTitle("My Custom List");

        for (int i = 0; i < 10; i++)
```

```
        {
            ListItemCreationInformation itemCreateInfo =
new ListItemCreationInformation();
            Microsoft.SharePoint.Client.ListItem newListItem =
list.AddItem(itemCreateInfo);
            newListItem["Title"] = "New Item " + i.ToString();
            newListItem.Update();
        }

        clientContext.ExecuteQuery();
    }
}
```

5. Press F5 to package and deploy your application.

6. After the app deploys, add your app's App Part to the homepage of your site by selecting Page ⇨ Edit ⇨ Insert ⇨ App Part. Select MyAppPart from the list, and then click Add.

7. Inside your App Part you should now see a button called Do Something. Click it. A ServerUnauthorizedAccessException error appears, as shown in Figure 6-15. This is because your application currently only has Read access to your SharePoint site. You need to modify your app's permissions.

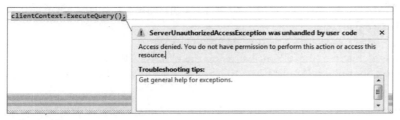

FIGURE 6-15

8. Click Stop Debugging in Visual Studio.

9. Double-click the AppManifest.xml file under MyFirstSharePointApp.

10. Under Permission Settings, add the following options:

➤ Scope: List

➤ Permission: Write

11. Press F5 to package and deploy your application.

12. Notice that SharePoint now asks you which list you want to allow it access to edit or delete items in. Select My Custom List from the drop-down menu. Click Trust It to continue.

13. You might need to re-add your App Part due to the change in app security settings.

14. Click Do Something in your App Part.

15. After the operation completes, open My Custom List in the SharePoint site. You should see that ten items have been added to the list, as shown in Figure 6-16.

How It Works

In this exercise you added list items to a SharePoint list. You configured your application to ask for permission to have edit rights on the list. SharePoint apps can ask for access to various security scopes of varying levels. Your application should only demand the permissions it needs to operate correctly. An app asking for too many permissions might make a user unwilling to grant them and therefore unable to use the app. Additionally, users cannot grant applications permission to resources that they themselves do not have appropriate access to.

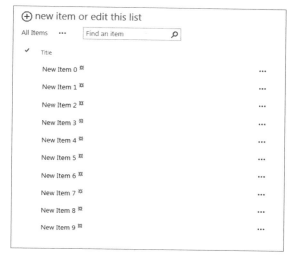

FIGURE 6-16

> **NOTE** *You can read more about all the available permission scopes and rights on MSDN* (`http://msdn.microsoft.com/en-us/library/fp142383(v=office.15).aspx`).

Additionally, SharePoint offers developers a range of mechanisms and APIs for integrating with data that lives outside of SharePoint. Although the data exists external to SharePoint, these APIs and features offer the ability to integrate with data much the same way you would with data stored inside SharePoint itself. The capability is called Business Connectivity Services and you can read more about these advanced data integration options in Chapter 13, "Building Line-of-Business Solutions Using Business Connectivity Services."

SUMMARY

SharePoint development has fundamentally shifted its focus to provide a model that is better suited to running SharePoint in the cloud. SharePoint applications solve many of the issues of running code in the cloud by extracting the run time of that code out of the core SharePoint process and into either Windows Azure or another hosting environment of your choice.

Like many application frameworks, SharePoint provides the key mechanisms for building out your UI, event, and data layers and integrations through the use of tiles and App Parts, remote event receivers, and a comprehensive Client-Side Object Model that your application can use to call into and manipulate data in SharePoint lists and libraries, respectively.

Whether you are building a complex CRM system or a much simpler application, you should certainly consider building a SharePoint application. Your code will be transportable to SharePoint Online and available to users in that environment.

EXERCISES

You can find answers to exercises for this chapter in Appendix A.

1. What are the high-level differences of the SharePoint application model versus the older full-trust model?

2. Describe the three types of high-level integration available for SharePoint applications.

3. How does an App Part differ from a traditional Web Part?

4. How are permissions granted to an application and who can grant them?

5. How can you visually style your apps like SharePoint with little effort?

► WHAT YOU LEARNED IN THIS CHAPTER

ITEM	DESCRIPTION
SharePoint application	Applications are a reusable unit of application functionality that is installable in a SharePoint site.
User interface integration points	SharePoint applications are able to surface UI in SharePoint sites using App Parts and Pages.
Event integration	SharePoint applications can respond to events in their user interface and be called by remote event receivers in SharePoint.
Data integration	SharePoint offers a wide range of APIs that SharePoint applications can use via the Client-Side Object Model.
Full-trust code	Full-Trust code is custom code that runs within the SharePoint runtime process.

RECOMMENDED READING

Develop apps for SharePoint — `http://msdn.microsoft.com/en-us/library/jj163794 (v=office.15).aspx`

App permissions in SharePoint 2013 — `http://msdn.microsoft.com/en-us/library/ fp142383(v=office.15).aspx`

App for SharePoint UX design guidelines — `http://msdn.microsoft.com/en-us/library/ jj220046(v=office.15).aspx`

Packaging and Deploying SharePoint 2013 Apps

WHAT YOU WILL LEARN IN THIS CHAPTER:

➤ Packaging an application you have built

➤ Deploying each SharePoint application type

➤ Creating a private app catalog

WROX.COM DOWNLOADS FOR THIS CHAPTER

The wrox.com code downloads for this chapter are found at http://www.wrox.com/ WileyCDA/WroxTitle/productCd-1118495845.html on the Download Code tab. The code for this chapter is divided into the following major examples:

➤ MyAutoHostedApp.zip

➤ MySharePointHostedApp.zip

➤ SharePointProviderHostedApp.zip

➤ SharePointAppPackage.app

In SharePoint 2010 and earlier, code and artifacts were packaged and deployed to the SharePoint farm as either full-trust solutions or sandbox solutions. In both cases the assets in the solutions were extracted and installed upon installation, or at runtime in the case of sandbox solutions. Additionally, code assets were deployed and at runtime were loaded and run from within the SharePoint code processes. This meant that great care had to be taken so the code didn't break any of the rules of best practice; otherwise, you would face a poorly performing solution. In the new app model, things are similar in that some assets are deployed when an application is installed; however, how apps are built, packaged, and where and how they are deployed are significantly different. The new app model has been fundamentally designed to address the concerns and issues of running code in the SharePoint execution processes, thus allowing more flexible deployment options, cloud-enabled applications, and better APIs and programming models for developers.

Much of the content in this book focuses on SharePoint apps and the options they offer developers. This chapter is all about what makes up an application from the inside out and how to deploy applications in a variety of scenarios.

ANATOMY OF AN APP

For any SharePoint 2013 apps to deploy and be of use to anyone, they must be first packaged into .app packages, which in turn are Open Packaging Convention (OPC) packages, and therefore Zip files in disguise. If you rename them with a .zip extension you can open and extract them much like you would any other Zip package. The OPC packaging format is fully documented and standardized. You can read more about it and working with packages at: http://msdn.microsoft.com/en-us/magazine/cc163372.aspx.

A SharePoint app package has four main parts:

➤ Manifest

➤ SharePoint solution package

➤ Web deploy package

➤ Database package

For those developers familiar with full-trust solution .wsp files in SharePoint 2010, this concept of a single file containing multiple subparts might seem familiar (excluding the database package portion). In SharePoint 2010, WSP solutions also included a manifest, files and assets, and code packages (DLLs). However, in SharePoint 2013 the format and deployment of these assets varies greatly.

The *manifest* in an app package contains important information such as the app's name and version.

The *SharePoint solution package* contains XML-based declarations for SharePoint components such as lists and content types that should be deployed as part of the app.

The *Web deploy package* is the code portion of your app. It is the package that will be deployed to Azure as part of an Autohosted app.

Finally, the *database package* contains the SQL Azure deployment package that deploys and creates a database as part of an Autohosted app deployment, and might include post deployment scripts to populate tables with data.

To better understand the format and contents of an app package, take a look inside one in the following Try It Out.

TRY IT OUT Exploring an App Package (SharePointAppPackage.app)

In this exercise you open an `.app` package file and explore its parts. You will use the prebuilt and provided `.app` file found in the code downloads for this chapter called `SharePointAppPackage.app`.

1. Copy the `SharePointAppPackage.app` file to a location on your hard drive; for example, `c:\tmp\SharePointAppPackage.app`.

2. Right-click the file and choose Rename.

3. Remove the `.app` extension and replace it with `.zip`. You might need to turn on Show file extensions in Windows Explorer options if you don't see the `.app` extension when you go to rename it.

4. If you are asked whether you are sure you want to rename the file choose OK.

5. After renaming it, open the Zip file. You should see a set of files similar to the one shown in Figure 7-1.

6. Select all the files and copy them to a new location outside of the Zip file. This step assists with opening and exploring them.

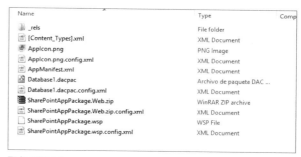

FIGURE 7-1

7. Open the `AppManifest.xml` file. You will see the manifest markup as shown in the following code snippet. This contains the name of the app, ID, version, and other information about the app code and where it's located.

```xml
<?xml version="1.0" encoding="utf-8"?>
<App xmlns="http://schemas.microsoft.com/sharepoint/2012/app/manifest"
Name="SharePointAppPackage" ProductID="{6b80672f-3edc-409c-94fe-608ee4264280}"
Version="1.0.0.0" SharePointMinVersion="15.0.0.0">
  <Properties>
    <Title>SharePointAppPackage</Title>
    <StartPage>~remoteAppUrl/Pages/Default.aspx?{StandardTokens}</StartPage>
  </Properties>
  <AppPrincipal>
    <AutoDeployedWebApplication />
  </AppPrincipal>
  <AppPermissionRequests>
    <AppPermissionRequest Scope="http://sharepoint/content/sitecollection/web"
Right="FullControl" />
  </AppPermissionRequests>
  <AppPrerequisites>
    <AppPrerequisite Type="Capability" ID="A83C8D70-71DE-4260-9FB8-677418EB47F2" />
    <AppPrerequisite Type="Feature" ID="5B79B49A-2DA6-4161-95BD-7375C1995EF9" />
    <AppPrerequisite Type="AutoProvisioning" ID="Database" />
    <AppPrerequisite Type="AutoProvisioning" ID="RemoteWebHost" />
  </AppPrerequisites>
</App>
```

How It Works

The fundamental part of an app package is the `app.manifest` file. As you have seen in this example it is straightforward to open and look around inside an app package. It is also recommended you take a look inside the `SharePointAppPackage.Web.zip` file. This is the app code and pages packaged in a Web deploy package.

The `Database1.dacpac` file is the SQL Database project for the app that will be deployed to SQL Azure when the application is installed.

The last important element is the `SharePointAppPackage.wsp` file. This is the SharePoint Solution package that contains definitions for things such as content types, columns, lists/libraries, and features.

In the following sections you will explore each of these main components that go into an app package in more detail and also try out building your own.

Manifest and Assets

At the heart of an `.app` file is the app manifest file. This file is the central location that SharePoint reads from when interrogating an app. The manifest contains things such as the app name, product ID, version, security information, and information about the starting page of the app. An example of a simple app manifest follows:

```xml
<?xml version="1.0" encoding="utf-8"?>
<App xmlns="http://schemas.microsoft.com/sharepoint/2012/app/manifest"
Name="SharePointAppPackage" ProductID="{6b80672f-3edc-409c-94fe-608ee4264280}"
Version="1.0.0.0" SharePointMinVersion="15.0.0.0">
  <Properties>
    <Title>SharePointAppPackage</Title>
    <StartPage>~remoteAppUrl/Pages/Default.aspx?{StandardTokens}</StartPage>
  </Properties>
  <AppPrincipal>
    <AutoDeployedWebApplication />
  </AppPrincipal>
  <AppPermissionRequests>
    <AppPermissionRequest Scope="http://sharepoint/content/sitecollection/web"
Right="FullControl" />
  </AppPermissionRequests>
  <AppPrerequisites>
    <AppPrerequisite Type="Capability" ID="A83C8D70-71DE-4260-9FB8-677418EB47F2" />
    <AppPrerequisite Type="Feature" ID="5B79B49A-2DA6-4161-95BD-7375C1995EF9" />
    <AppPrerequisite Type="AutoProvisioning" ID="Database" />
    <AppPrerequisite Type="AutoProvisioning" ID="RemoteWebHost" />
  </AppPrerequisites>
</App>
```

In this example you can see in the app node the name of the application specified; the product ID, which uniquely signifies this app; the version of the app; and the minimum version of SharePoint that is required. Although at the time of writing there is only one version of SharePoint 2013, in the future developers will be able to target their apps at a minimum version to ensure compatibility.

Additionally, in the `AppPermissionRequests` node an application can specify the minimum permissions it needs granted for it to work correctly. In this case it is asking for full control permissions on the host Web. Finally, the manifest specifies a number of `AppPrerequisites`. These are IDs of features and capabilities that must be enabled or turned on in the SharePoint site and farm so that the app can run. For example, the sample code is requesting that the Media Player Web Part feature be activated and as well as the Managed Metadata Service Capability. As a developer you don't need to know the IDs by GUID. The Visual Studio tools assist with this via a GUI-style property panel.

When you deploy an app to SharePoint the first thing SharePoint does is unpack and take a look at the manifest file. This tells SharePoint what sort of app it is, such as Autohosted. Additionally, SharePoint looks for the other deployment assets such as a SharePoint solutions package, a Web deploy package, and a database package. Each of these are deployed differently and are discussed in the following sections.

SharePoint Solution Package

An `.app` file may also contain a SharePoint solution package, which would in turn contain a variety of SharePoint components such as the following:

➤ Lists/libraries

➤ Site columns

➤ Content types

➤ Event receivers

➤ Modules

➤ UI actions

Much like in SharePoint 2010 full-trust applications and sandbox solutions, the aforementioned components are defined declaratively using XML and packaged in a `.wsp` file, which makes up the SharePoint Solution file. In fact, in many regards the new app model's `.wsp` packages are the next generation of solution package formats that started with custom template `.stp` files in SharePoint 2003. Much of the declarative XML contained within these new packages shares historical roots in the earlier template formats. However, don't be fooled — many of the techniques and options you might have used in the past are no longer supported or available in the new packaging format, so caution is advised.

In the past, understanding the structure of a `.wsp` file was important, and in many ways it still is for those looking to do more advanced debugging and diagnosis. However, the SharePoint tools in Visual Studio have developed so much in the 2012 edition that the packaging format is largely taken care of for you along with inclusion of the `.wsp` inside an app package.

Similar to an `.app` file, a `.wsp` file is another type of file in disguise — in this case a `.cab` file. These can be simply renamed and opened with Windows Explorer. Also like an `.app` file, a `.wsp` file contains a manifest and other supporting assets.

Along with the manifest file, a `.wsp` file contains XML definitions for the components it contains, which are grouped into Features. A Feature can be activated or deactivated through the SharePoint UI and is a fundamental building block of SharePoint solutions. When you're building apps many of the same Feature constructs apply. Components are grouped into Features, which are packaged into a `.wsp`. Visual Studio takes care of much of the Feature creation for you; however, it is worth being familiar with the contents of a `.wsp` so that if you need or want to learn about how something works under the hood you know where to look.

During installation of an app the `.wsp` package is used to deploy the Features and artifacts to the app Web, which is the SharePoint site that is created for the instance of the application. Note the `.wsp` isn't deployed to the host Web, which is the site that the application is installed in. Therefore, lists, content types, and so on that are defined in this package will be deployed to the app Web only.

Only two types of components can be deployed into the host Web versus the app Web. Those are:

➤ Client Web Part (Host Web) also known as App Parts

➤ Custom UI Action (Host Web)

These are not included in the `.wsp` but rather included in the app package as Features without a parent `.wsp`.

Web Deploy Package

If you are building an Autohosted application then the app package produced by Visual Studio will contain a Web deploy package containing your app code and pages. Web Deploy is a tool produced by Microsoft that can take Web deploy packages and deploy the contents to an Internet Information Server (IIS) enabled server. It is also a packaging format that can be used for deploying to Azure. Because Autohosted apps use Azure, your code and pages are packaged as a Web deploy package for automated deployment to Azure when an Autohosted app is installed. When the app is installed, SharePoint Online takes the Web deploy package included in the app's `.app` file and automatically deploys it to Azure. This creates a running website with your app's code and pages in it. Additionally, SharePoint Online creates a new client ID and client secret and sets up the app with it so that the OAuth and API calls all work (read more about OAuth, client IDs, and client secrets in Chapter 10, "Overview of OAuth in SharePoint 2013"). Likewise, when the app is uninstalled, the website in Azure is removed. This entire process is managed by SharePoint Online without any user or developer involvement, hence the name Autohosted model.

If you take a look inside an `.app` file for an Autohosted app, you will find the Web deploy package contained within it packaged into a `.zip` file and named the same name as the app in Visual Studio with a ".web" appended. For example, `SharePointAppPackage.Web.zip` file shown the in the file list in Figure 7-2 is the Web deploy package.

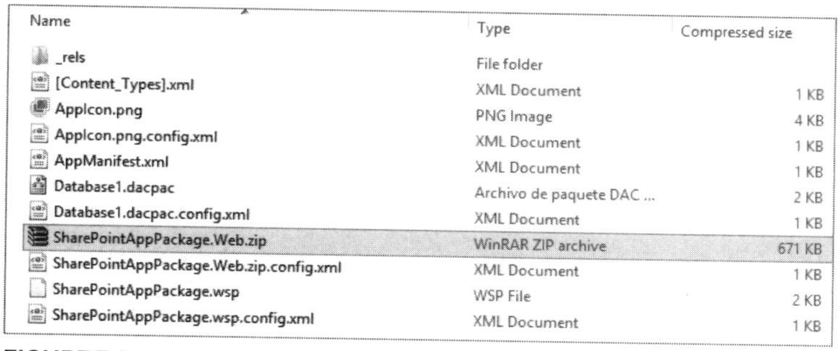

Name	Type	Compressed size
_rels	File folder	
[Content_Types].xml	XML Document	1 KB
AppIcon.png	PNG Image	4 KB
AppIcon.png.config.xml	XML Document	1 KB
AppManifest.xml	XML Document	1 KB
Database1.dacpac	Archivo de paquete DAC ...	2 KB
Database1.dacpac.config.xml	XML Document	1 KB
SharePointAppPackage.Web.zip	WinRAR ZIP archive	671 KB
SharePointAppPackage.Web.zip.config.xml	XML Document	1 KB
SharePointAppPackage.wsp	WSP File	2 KB
SharePointAppPackage.wsp.config.xml	XML Document	1 KB

FIGURE 7-2

Database Package

Like Web deploy packages a database package may be included in an Autohosted app's .app package. This is commonly called a DACPAC because it's a file with a .dacpac extension, but it is the packaging name for the Data-tier Applications technology (DAC for short, chosen because DTA was already taken), introduced in SQL Server 2008 R2. Essentially a DACPAC is a packaging format for databases.

> *A DAC is a self-contained unit of SQL Server database deployment that enables data-tier developers and database administrators to package SQL Server objects into a portable artifact called a DAC package, also known as a DACPAC.*
>
> "DATA-TIER APPLICATIONS." MICROSOFT TECHNET LIBRARY

For developers, Visual Studio supports building .dacpac files with the SQL Server Database Project type. SQL Azure also supports deploying DACPACs, hence the use of DACPACs in Autohosted app packages.

In the same way code packages work, if SharePoint Online detects a DACPAC in the app package it will extract it, create a database in SQL Azure, and deploy the DACPAC. This, in turn, creates the tables, relationships, and associated SQL objects needed in the database to support the application.

A question you might be asking yourself at this point is, "How does my SharePoint app know where the database is?" SharePoint will replace a specially named connection string in your app's web.config file after the database has been set up and configured. To ensure this works correctly you *must* have a connection string property named SqlAzureConnectionString and configured in the app's web.config file as follows:

```
<add key="SqlAzureConnectionString" value="Data
Source=(localdb)\MyDatabaseProjName;Initial
Catalog=AutohostedAppDatabase;Integrated Security=True;Connect
Timeout=30;Encrypt=False;TrustServerCertificate=False" />
```

> **NOTE** As of this writing, Microsoft has indicated that the use of the `SqlAzure` `ConnectionString` configuration property is subject to change moving forward.

After you have the database connection string, you can treat the database and access it like any other SQL Azure database, and all the same data access and query techniques apply.

> **WARNING** When thinking about developing Autohosted applications, it is impor-tant to consider the life cycle of an Autohosted app and the impact it has on data stored in the SQL database. Like the Web deploy package for an Autohosted app, the SQL database is also deleted after the app is uninstalled. This causes data loss, and there is no way to get it back.

PACKAGING AND PUBLISHING AN APP

Now that you understand the four main parts of an app you can begin the process of packaging and publishing your own app. When you package an app you essentially take the Web deploy package, database package, SharePoint solution package and `app.manifest` and combine them into an `.app` file. After you have an `.app` file you are ready to publish it to a location where users can install it. You can publish an app either using a private app catalog or the public SharePoint store. The following sections walk you through publishing to a private app catalog and Chapter 8, "Distributing SharePoint 2013 Apps," discusses publishing to the public SharePoint store.

Packaging an App

After you have completed developing an app and are ready to deploy it to either an on-premises SharePoint farm or to SharePoint Online, you need to get it ready for deployment by packaging it.

As Chapter 3, "Developer Tooling for SharePoint 2013" discusses, Visual Studio 2012 provides some excellent tools to increase your productivity when writing SharePoint apps, but the help doesn't stop there. Visual Studio provides a number of tools to help you package your apps into `.app` files for either automated or manual deployment. In fact, when you press F5 to debug an application, Visual Studio packages the app and deploys it automatically to SharePoint for you!

Visual Studio provides integrated publishing wizards that guide you through the process of packaging your application. This wizard varies depending on the type of application you have built, but in each type the process starts by using the Publish function available when you right-click your application project. See Figure 7-3.

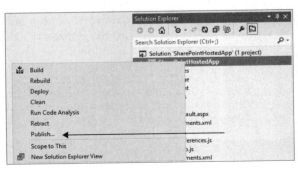

FIGURE 7-3

Depending on the type of app you have built, the deployment wizard varies and requires different information. For example, in some cases it asks for a client ID and client secret whereas in SharePoint-hosted apps no additional information is needed at all. The following section, "Deploying an App," explores the deployment process in more detail for each type of application package and walks through examples of each.

Private Publishing in an App Catalog

Before an application can be installed you must publish it to either a private app catalog, on premises or in SharePoint Online, or in the public Marketplace provided by Microsoft. Many organizations may want to build applications that only they intend to use, or they may turn off the ability to purchase apps from the Marketplace and only offer apps they provide in the private app catalog. The app catalog enables organizations to offer a private and curated app catalog that they control to users in the organization.

An app catalog is simply a SharePoint site based on a provided template. An organization can create and configure an app catalog in a few simple steps and offer users a curated list of apps with which the organization is comfortable with. After you create the apps, installing them from the catalog into a site is seamless and integrated into the existing app installation process.

In following exercise you will learn how to create a new app catalog for privately deploying apps to.

TRY IT OUT   **Creating a Private App Catalog in Office 365**

In this example you create an app catalog for SharePoint Online. You need a SharePoint Online site prior to starting this exercise.

1. Navigate to `portal.microsoftonline.com` and log in with your Office 365 credentials. You must be a tenant administrator in order to do this exercise.

FIGURE 7-4

2. Under the Admin menu in the top navigation, click SharePoint to go to the SharePoint Online tenant admin pages as shown in Figure 7-4.

3. Click apps in the left-side navigation in the screen that appears.

4. Click the App Catalog link.

5. Select the Create a new app catalog site option and then click OK.

6. On the Create page, enter **Contoso App Catalog** in the Title field.

7. Ensure `/sites/` is selected in the drop-down list and then type in `AppCatalog` in the box to the right. This is the site collection URL for the site.

8. Enter your name in the Administrator field and make sure it resolves to the correct account using the provided tick button to the right. The form should look like the one shown in Figure 7-5.

9. Click OK to create the catalog; the site will start to be created.

Create App Catalog Site Collection

Title	Contoso App Catalog
Public Website Address	https:// sharepoint.com
	/sites/ AppCatalog
Language Selection	Select a language: English
Time Zone	(UTC-08:00) Pacific Time (US and Canada)
Administrator	Chris Johnson
Storage Quota	500 MB of 22450 MB available
Server Resource Quota	300 resources of 5300 resources available

OK   Cancel

FIGURE 7-5

10. After the process completes, go back into the app configuration settings in your tenant admin by clicking the apps link in the left-side navigation.

11. Click the App Catalog link. The catalog site that you just created appears. You have now created a private app catalog for your organization and can start to populate it with apps.

How It Works

An app catalog is simply a SharePoint collection based on a particular template. In this exercise you created the catalog site collection via the SharePoint Online tenant admin site. This instructed SharePoint to create the site and configure it to be the catalog for your tenancy. It is now ready for apps to be deployed to it.

DEPLOYING AN APP

The options available for deploying apps depend on your deployment scenario and application type. There are three main application types and each one requires a different deployment scenario. Table 7-1 summarizes these various scenarios.

TABLE 7-1: Application Deployment Summary

APP TYPE	APP CODE DEPLOYED TO	APP PACKAGE DEPLOYED TO
SharePoint-hosted	N/A	App catalog or Marketplace
Provider-hosted	Azure or other	App catalog or Marketplace
Autohosted	Azure	App catalog or Marketplace

SharePoint-hosted apps are a bit simpler than the others given that there isn't any Web deploy package to have deployed, and because they generally consist of HTML pages and JavaScript only. SharePoint-hosted apps don't have any other dependencies on a runtime environment for this reason.

Provider-hosted apps are a bit more complex and consist of just an app package without any Web deploy package in it. This is because the provider of the app is already required to be hosting it either in Azure or some other Internet-accessible location. The provider of the app manages running the code for the app and any associated databases or dependent resources.

Autohosted app packages are the only ones that contain Web deploy packages and/or database packages. This is because Autohosted apps are the only app types where SharePoint needs to take both the Web deploy package and database package and deploy them to Azure when the app is installed. Azure is currently the only option for autodeployment in the Autohosted scenario.

SharePoint-Hosted App Deployment

SharePoint-hosted apps are the simplest of the three app types to package and deploy because of the lack of a code package and associated deployment steps. All that is required is to package the application using the Publish wizard in Visual Studio and then deploy the app to either the Marketplace or an app catalog. After the app is deployed, users can install the app on their site. When this occurs, SharePoint takes the app package, creates a new app Web for that instance of the application, and provisions the pages and content from the app package into it. Any custom UI actions and App Parts are also deployed to the host Web.

Try your hand at deploying a SharePoint-hosted app in the next exercise to learn how straightforward the process is.

TRY IT OUT　　Deploying a SharePoint-Hosted App

In this example you create a very basic SharePoint-hosted app using Visual Studio 2012 development tools and deploy that new app to the app catalog. You will need to use the app catalog created from the previous Try It Out, "Creating a Private App Catalog in Office 365."

1. Ensure you have created an app catalog. See the earlier exercise, "Creating a Private App Catalog in Office 365."

2. Open Visual Studio and create a new app for a SharePoint 2013 project called SharePoint Hosted App by selecting File ➪ New Project ➪ App for SharePoint 2013. In the Name field enter `MySharePointHostedApp`.

3. In the New Project wizard specify SharePoint-hosted as shown in Figure 7-6.

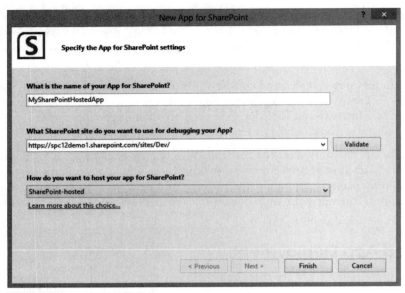

FIGURE 7-6

4. After the project has been created, right-click the project and select Publish. The publishing wizard for the application launches; see Figure 7-7.

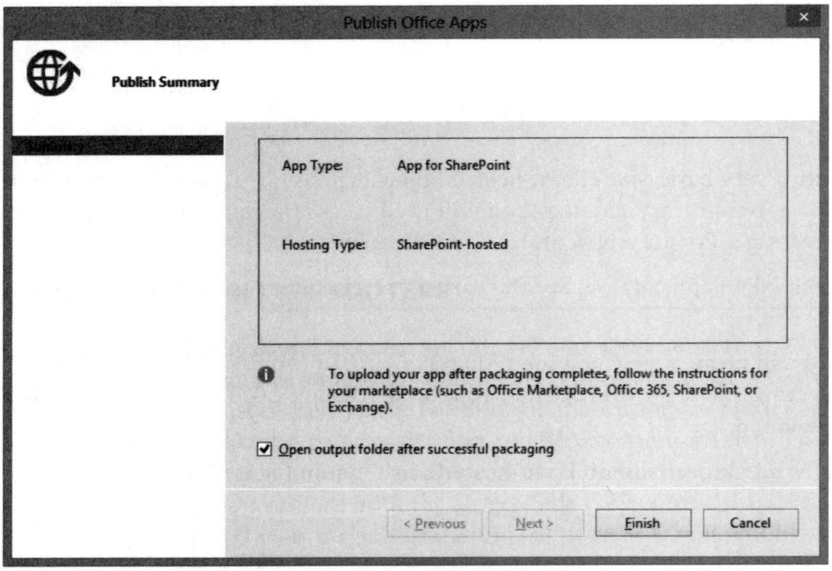

FIGURE 7-7

5. Click Finish. A new Windows Explorer window opens with your application package called `MySharePointHostedApp.app` showing.

6. Open a browser window and navigate to the tenant admin portal for your Office 365 environment at: `http://portal.microsoftonline.com`.

7. Under the Admin menu in the top navigation, click SharePoint to go to the SharePoint Online tenant admin pages.

8. Click apps in the left-side navigation.

9. Click the App Catalog link. The app catalog you created in the previous exercise appears.

10. Click the Distribute apps for SharePoint tile.

11. Click the New App button. A prompt appears asking you to pick the `.app` file for your application.

12. Click Browse and select the `.app` file that Visual Studio packaged for you in step 5. Click OK. A dialog appears asking for information about your application, as shown in Figure 7-8.

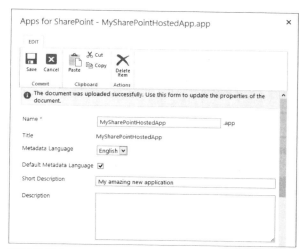

FIGURE 7-8

13. You are not required to enter any information unless you want to. Click Save to proceed. You should now see your application in the app catalog, as shown in Figure 7-9.

FIGURE 7-9

14. Navigate to your development site in SharePoint Online.

15. Click Site Contents in the left-side navigation.

16. Click Add an App.

17. Click From Your Organization in the left-side navigation and you should see your newly added application listed, as shown in Figure 7-10.

18. Click the tile for the application and click Trust It when prompted. SharePoint Online begins to provision your app in the site.

19. When the process completes, click the newly installed app tile. The Start page for your application appears; your username will be listed as shown in Figure 7-11.

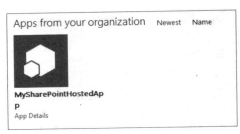

FIGURE 7-10

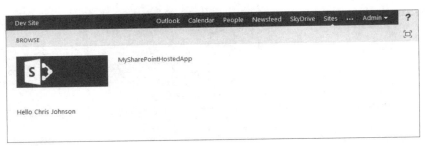

FIGURE 7-11

How It Works

In this exercise you created a rudimentary SharePoint-hosted app that simply lists the name of the currently logged-in user. You packaged the app ready for deployment using the Publish wizard in Visual Studio and then uploaded and configured the app in the app catalog in SharePoint Online. You then installed the app on a SharePoint Online site. Behind the scenes, SharePoint created a new SharePoint site specifically for this installation of the application and deployed the application's assets, such as pages and JavaScript, to the appropriate places. You can see in the URL for the app the domain name created and set up specifically for the app instance. These steps are done on demand each time a SharePoint-hosted app is installed. When the application is run it uses the JavaScript Client-Side Object Model to make a call to `web.get_currentUser();` to retrieve the currently logged-in user. This code is in the `/Scripts/App.js` file in the Visual Studio project.

Provider-Hosted App Deployment

Provider-hosted applications are the most complex of the three app types because hosting and running the application code is up to the developer, rather than allowing SharePoint and Azure do these things for you. However, with the increased complexity comes increased flexibility, because you manage your application's back end. This means that making fixes or updates to it is straightforward, and the ultimate user for the application might never know or care to know about the changes being made to the application. Only if you make changes to the components of your app that reside within the SharePoint site itself would you need to issue an update to the application package in the app catalog or Marketplace. However, you should consider that you might need to deal with multi-tenancy issues, such as tenant specific–data partitioning, given that an app may be installed on multiple sites.

Deploying a Provider-hosted application happens in two main stages:

1. Deploying the application back end
2. Deploying the SharePoint application package

The application backend can theoretically be any technology and is not limited to Internet Information Server. The only stipulation is that the SharePoint farm or SharePoint Online must be able to communicate with it over HTTP (port 80) and HTTPS (port 443).

For on-premises applications, Provider-hosted applications are the only choice when back-end code is involved. This requires setting up server-to-server authentication (see Chapter 10).

Now try out deploying a Provider-hosted application in the following exercise using SharePoint Online and Windows Azure.

TRY IT OUT   Deploying a Provider-Hosted App

In this example you create a very basic SharePoint Provider-hosted application using Visual Studio and Azure Web Sites. You need a SharePoint Online tenant set up as well as an Azure account with Azure Web Sites enabled. You also need to have the app catalog created from the previous exercise, "Creating a Private App Catalog in Office 365," prior to starting this exercise.

1. Log into the Azure management portal and create a new Azure Web Site as shown in Figure 7-12. You must give it a unique URL, so remember to write it down because you will need it later on.

FIGURE 7-12

2. After the site is created, go into the Azure dashboard for the site and download the publishing profile for Visual Studio using the Download publish profile link. Save the file locally somewhere.

3. Navigate to SharePoint Online's tenant admin screens by logging into: `http://portal.microsoftonline .com`, clicking the Admin menu in the top right of the homepage and then selecting SharePoint. Create a new SharePoint Developer site by clicking into the Site Collections management page, and then click the New button and select Private Site Collection, as shown in Figure 7-13.

FIGURE 7-13

4. Give your site a title; for example, **My New Site**, as well as a URL, such as **mydevsite**. Select the Developer Site template from the list of available templates, as shown in Figure 7-14, and then click OK.

FIGURE 7-14

5. After the site has been created, navigate to it and then navigate to the following page in the browser:
`https://<my SPO site url>.sharepoint.com/sites/mydevsite/_layouts/15/appregnew.aspx`.

6. After the form appears, complete it by clicking the Generate button to create the client ID and secret for you.

7. Give your application a name such as **My Awesome App**.

8. In the App Domain box specify the exact URL for the Azure Web Site you created in step 1. The form should look like Figure 7-15.

FIGURE 7-15

9. Click Create to create the application registration. For more details on app IDs, see Chapter 10.

```
The app identifier has been successfully created.
App Id:        b148d816-ab5f-44f8-97a0-40dacedc3c13
App Secret:    loGoNVdXMmGmZBWjEGk0A2p2ynRTaNxGE0E3h6lM84g=
Title:         Foo
App Domain:    myawesomeapp.azurewebsites.net
Redirect URI:  https://myawesomeapp.azurewebsites.net/Pages/Default.aspx
```

FIGURE 7-16

10. Copy all the details provided about the application registration. Figure 7-16 shows an example.

11. Create a new SharePoint app in Visual Studio using the App for SharePoint 2013 template.

12. Enter the name of your app in the first box; for example, `My Awesome App`.

13. Enter the URL to your SharePoint Online development site.

14. Select Provider-hosted from the app type drop-down list. When it's complete, the form should look similar to Figure 7-17.

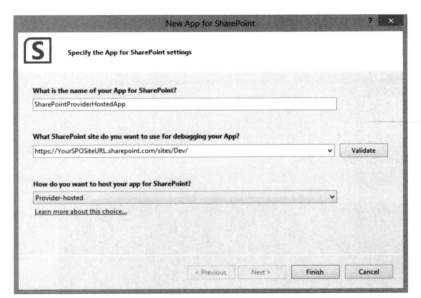

FIGURE 7-17

15. Click Finish.

16. Right-click the Web project in the solution and select Publish as shown in Figure 7-18.

17. Click the Import button and select the profile file you downloaded from Azure previously. Download it from Azure if you skipped this step earlier. Validate the connection to make sure it's working by clicking the Validate Connection button as shown in Figure 7-19.

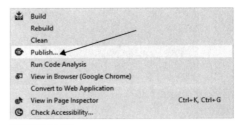

FIGURE 7-18

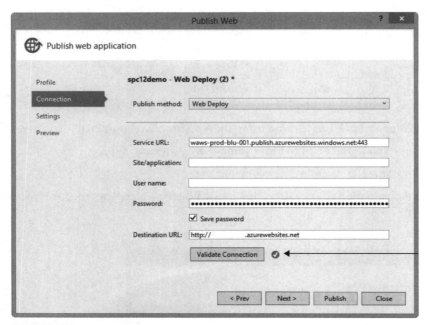

FIGURE 7-19

18. Click Publish and let your site deploy. When the deployment finishes, a browser should pop up a screen like the one shown in Figure 7-20.

FIGURE 7-20

19. Go back into the Azure management dashboard for your site and click the Configure tab. Create the ClientId and ClientSecret app settings and copy in the App ID and App Secret you generated in step 10 (see Figure 7-21). Azure Web Sites reads them from here even if you have them in your `web.config`. Not configuring the settings in Azure will mean your app crashes.

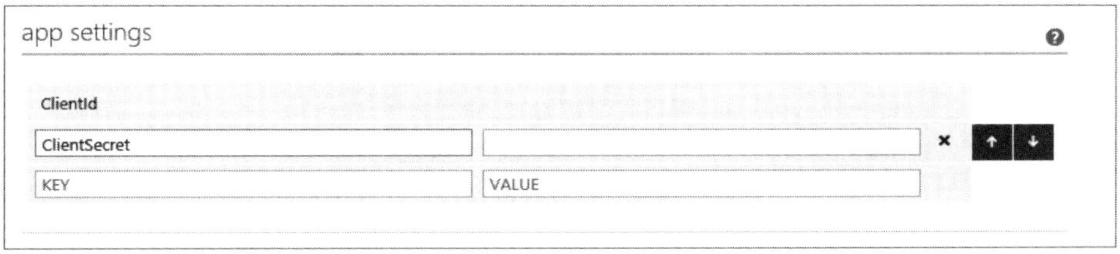

FIGURE 7-21

20. Click the Save button to commit the settings to Azure.

21. Right-click the SharePoint app project in Visual Studio and choose Publish. If the Publish wizard is not already on the profile page, click profile in the left-side navigation to get to the Start screen.

22. Type a new profile name; for example, **Office 365 Profile**, and click Next.

23. On the Hosting page enter the full URL to your Azure Web Site, including the **/pages/default .aspx**; for example, **https://cjsproviderhostedapp.azurewebsites.net/pages/default. aspx**. See Figure 7-22.

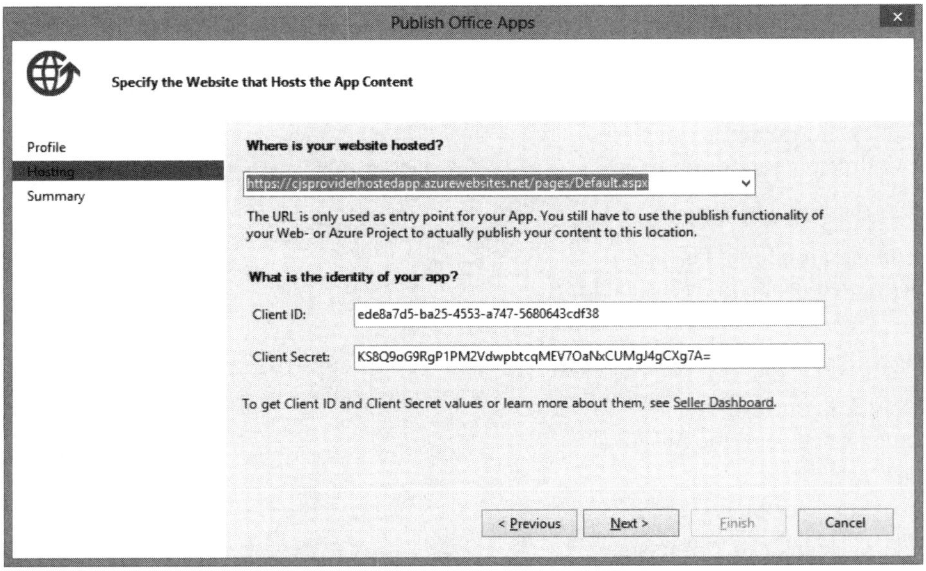

FIGURE 7-22

24. Enter the App ID you generated into the Client ID field and the App Secret into the Client Secret field.

25. Click Next. A summary page appears like the one shown in Figure 7-23.

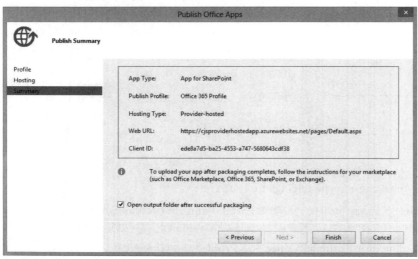

FIGURE 7-23

26. Click Finish. A new Windows Explorer window opens with your application package called `MySharePointProviderHostedApp.app`.

27. Open a browser window and navigate to the tenant admin portal for your Office 365 environment at: `http://portal.microsoftonline.com`.

28. Under the Admin menu in the top navigation, click SharePoint to go to the SharePoint Online tenant admin pages.

29. Click Apps in the left-side navigation.

30. Click the App Catalog link. The app catalog you created in the previous exercise appears.

31. Click the Distribute apps for SharePoint tile.

32. Click the New App button. You are prompted to pick the `.app` file for your application.

33. Click Browse and select the `.app` file that Visual Studio packaged for you in step 26. Click OK. A dialog appears asking for information about your application, as shown in Figure 7-24.

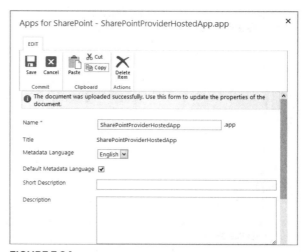

FIGURE 7-24

34. You are not required to enter any information, but you can enter the information if you want to, and then click Save. Your `SharePointProviderHostedApp` application appears in the app catalog.

35. Navigate to your development site in SharePoint Online.

36. Click Site Contents in the left-side navigation.

37. Click Add an App.

38. Click From Your Organization in the left-side navigation; you should see your newly added application listed.

39. Click the tile for the application. A prompt appears asking whether to trust your app.

40. Click Trust It, as shown in Figure 7-25. Your new app appears listed in the site contents.

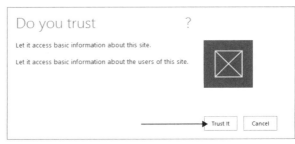

FIGURE 7-25

41. Click it. You are redirected to your app and should see the title (whatever you called your site when you created it) of your site written to the page, as shown in Figure 7-26.

FIGURE 7-26

How It Works

In this exercise you created a rudimentary SharePoint Provider-hosted app that simply lists the name of the host site that app is installed in. You created, packaged, and deployed the code portion of your application to an Azure Web Sites site and configured the client ID and secret in the settings for that application. You then packaged and deployed the SharePoint app using Visual Studio's Publish wizard. Once the packaging process was complete you uploaded the newly created app package to the app catalog in SharePoint Online.

Behind the scenes Visual Studio uses Web Deploy to deploy the app code to the Azure Web Site. When the application ran, it used the Client-Side Object Model (CSOM) combined with OAuth to call back to SharePoint and retrieve the name of the host Web SharePoint site. It did this using the client ID and secret you set up in the Azure settings along with the `TokenHelper` class provided in the app template project in Visual Studio (read more about client IDs and secrets in Chapter 10).

Autohosted App Deployment

Autohosted application deployment is almost as straightforward as SharePoint-hosted application deployment. This is because SharePoint Online takes care of all the heavy lifting deploying the code and database packages to Azure for you as well as creating and managing client IDs and secrets.

In the following exercise you will give creating a simple Autohosted app a go and deploy it into SharePoint Online using a private app catalog.

TRY IT OUT Deploying an Autohosted App

In this example you create a very basic SharePoint Autohosted application using Visual Studio. You need a SharePoint Online tenant set up as well as the app catalog created from the previous exercise, "Creating a Private App Catalog in Office 365," prior to starting this exercise.

1. Create a new SharePoint app in Visual Studio using the App for SharePoint 2013 template by selecting File ➪ New Project ➪ App for SharePoint 2013.

2. Enter the name of your app in the first box; for example, **MyAutoHostedApp**.

3. Enter the URL to your SharePoint Online developer site.

4. Select Autohosted from the app type drop-down list. When you have completed the form it should look similar to Figure 7-27.

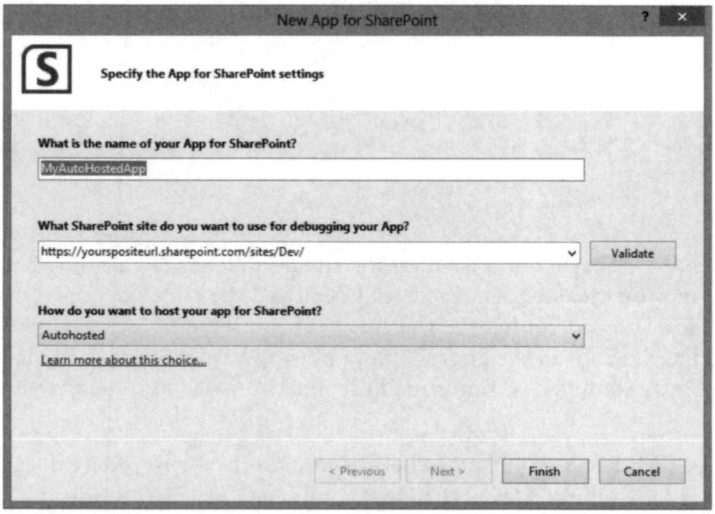

FIGURE 7-27

5. Click Finish.

6. Right-click the Web project in the solution and select Publish.

7. Click Next. A summary page appears like the one shown in Figure 7-28.

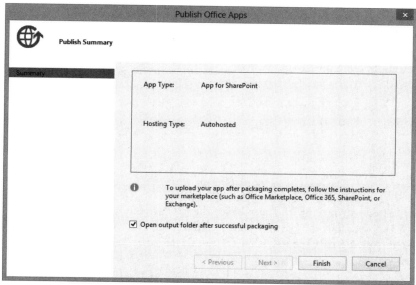

FIGURE 7-28

8. Click Finish. Once the wizard completes a new Windows Explorer window opens with your application package called MyAutoHostedApp.app showing.

9. Open a browser window and navigate to the tenant admin portal for your Office 365 environment at: http://portal.microsoftonline.com.

10. Under the Admin menu in the top navigation, click SharePoint to go to the SharePoint Online tenant admin pages.

11. Click Apps in the left-side navigation.

12. Click the App Catalog link.

13. Click the Distribute apps for SharePoint tile.

14. Click the New App button. A prompt appears asking you to pick the .app file for your application.

15. Click Browse and select the .app file that Visual Studio packaged for you in step 8. Click OK. A dialog appears asking you to enter information about your application, as shown in Figure 7-29.

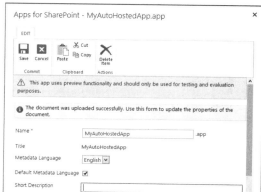

FIGURE 7-29

16. You are not required to enter any information, but if you want, enter the information and then click Save to proceed. You should now see your `SharePointAutoHostedApp` application in the app catalog.

17. Navigate to your development site in SharePoint Online.

18. Click Site Contents in the left-side navigation.

19. Click Add an App.

20. Click From Your Organization in the left-side navigation; you should see your newly added application listed.

21. Click the tile for the application. A pop-up dialog opens, asking whether you trust your app.

22. Click Trust It, as shown in Figure 7-30. Your new app becomes listed in the site contents.

FIGURE 7-30

23. Click it. You are redirected to your app and should see the title of your site written to the page, as shown in Figure 7-31. Note that the URL of your app pages sits in `o365apps.net`. This is the SharePoint Online–controlled Azure tenancy that your code package was automatically deployed to during installation.

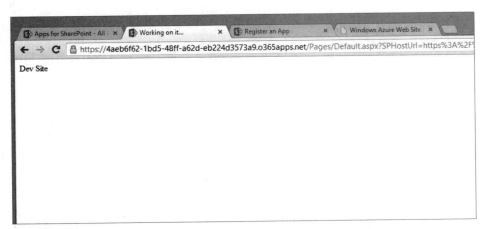

FIGURE 7-31

How It Works

In this exercise you created a rudimentary SharePoint Autohosted app that simply lists the name of the host site that app is installed in. You packaged the app using the Visual Studio Publish wizard and then deployed to your app catalog in SharePoint Online. When you installed the application, SharePoint

Online took the code package from the app package and deployed it to Azure for you. It then installed the application in your SharePoint site. Note that in this example you didn't need to deal with client IDs and secrets. That is because SharePoint Online creates and configures those for you in the Autohosted scenario. When the application ran it used the Client-Side Object Model (CSOM) combined with OAuth to call back to SharePoint and retrieve the name of the host Web SharePoint site.

SUMMARY

Visual Studio 2012 combined with SharePoint 2013 provides a robust and comprehensive set of development tools for SharePoint applications. Whether you decide to create a SharePoint-hosted, Provider-hosted or Autohosted application, the options and publishing tools available in Visual Studio make packaging and publishing your application package a straightforward process.

For organizations and individuals looking to build an application just for themselves or provide a curated set of applications to their users, then the private app catalog provides a seamless way to publish those applications. Chapter 8, "Distributing SharePoint 2013 Apps," discusses the options available to publish applications to a wider audience with the app store or Marketplace in SharePoint Online.

EXERCISES

You can find the answers to exercises for this chapter in Appendix A.

1. What are four main components of an `.app` package file?

2. Describe the architecture of a Provider-hosted application.

3. What types of SharePoint components are able to be deployed to the host Web during app installation?

▶ **WHAT YOU LEARNED IN THIS CHAPTER**

ITEM	DESCRIPTION
App Catalog	This is a private catalog of selected applications deployed by an administrator and installable in a site.
App Package	This is the packaging and file format for SharePoint apps.
Database Package	This contains the SQL Azure deployment package that deploys and creates a database as part of an Autohosted app deployment, and might include post deployment scripts to populate tables with data.
Manifest	This is an app package that contains important information such as the app's name and version.
SharePoint Solution Package	This contains XML-based declarations for SharePoint components such as lists and content types that should be deployed as part of the app.
Web Deploy Package	This is the code portion of your app. It is the package that will be deployed to Azure as part of an Autohosted app.

RECOMMENDED READING

How to package apps for SharePoint for publishing by using Visual Studio — `http://msdn.microsoft .com/en-us/library/office/apps/jj220044.aspx`

8

Distributing SharePoint 2013 Apps

WHAT YOU WILL LEARN IN THIS CHAPTER:

➤   Distributing apps via the SharePoint Store

➤   Licensing and managing apps in the Store

WROX.COM CODE DOWNLOADS FOR THIS CHAPTER

The wrox.com code downloads for this chapter are found at: `http://www.wrox.com/WileyCDA/WroxTitle/productCd-1118495845.html` on the Download Code tab. The code for this chapter is divided into the following major examples:

➤   SharePointAppPackage.app

So you have built the next million-dollar idea into a SharePoint app and you want to make sure the world buys it. The SharePoint Store is a good starting point for making sure the largest number of people sees your app. But how do you take your app and distribute it through the SharePoint Store? What are your licensing options? How can you manage your apps after they are out in the wild being used by millions of happy users? This chapter provides guidance and answers for these questions.

Over the past five years, the app phenomenon has taken the world by storm. The concept of an app isn't new — it has been around for decades, ever since the first personal computer. What makes the app concept so popular today is the ease of finding and buying low-cost and (mostly) high-value apps easily and quickly. Today that concept centers mostly on smartphones; however, ecosystems are quickly developing around other types of computing, such as social computing and gaming. Although they are not the first to the game enterprise, software vendors are starting to take notice and make sure they offer their users additional capabilities and options not available out of the box with their products through reusable, additive, and easily discovered components — also known as apps. Many people are already used to paying for apps because of their familiarity with the concept from the smartphone world, and vendors are benefiting from this familiarity by taking a percentage of the sale for themselves. The marketplace is selling access to their user base and benefitting financially from it. To warrant the marketplace provider taking a percentage, a compelling and sizable audience must exist for the developers.

Enter SharePoint — one of the most widely used and popular enterprise software platforms on the planet today. Hundreds of millions of licenses to it have been sold. Thousands of huge organizations use it to do everything from team collaboration to building their Internet site. One of the challenges independent software vendors (ISVs) have had is getting their products out in front of all those users. Many have done very well at this challenge and profited immensely from it, but many haven't. Microsoft is finally letting developers and ISVs get a front-and-center stage for their products right within the product itself — the SharePoint Store (see Figure 8-1).

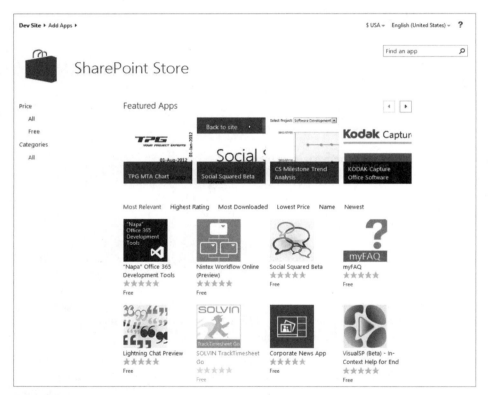

FIGURE 8-1

The SharePoint Store offers users and IT departments the ability to find, buy, install, and manage apps. IT can configure the store so it is in charge of what is purchased, or it can let users do the same. As you have read in this book, the app model offers a tightly controlled method for integrating with SharePoint that preserves the sanctity of organizations' data while also allowing them to offer additional capabilities and services that users might want.

This chapter delves into how you can apply, submit, publish, and manage apps in the SharePoint Store. This marketplace is open to everyone, and Microsoft actively encourages not only large ISVs, but also smaller independent developers to build and submit apps to the Store. All you need is a great idea, a bit of time, and a store account.

PUBLISHING APPS IN THE SHAREPOINT STORE

When you have completed developing your app and are ready to publish the next thing you need to do is to sign up and get access to the Seller Dashboard. The Seller Dashboard is the back-end entry point for developers and ISVs to access the SharePoint Store. It's where you can submit, publish, and manage your apps.

To apply for access you simply create an account with Microsoft on the website at: `http://sellerdashboard.microsoft.com`. You must sign in with a Microsoft account and answer some questions about yourself or the company you are registering. After you're registered you receive access to the Seller Dashboard. However, this access doesn't let you start publishing applications immediately. Microsoft conducts a verification process to ensure you are who you say you are and that you have completed the information sufficiently. You will be notified when this process is complete via e-mail.

After you successfully log in to the Store, you will see the Seller Dashboard, as shown in Figure 8-2.

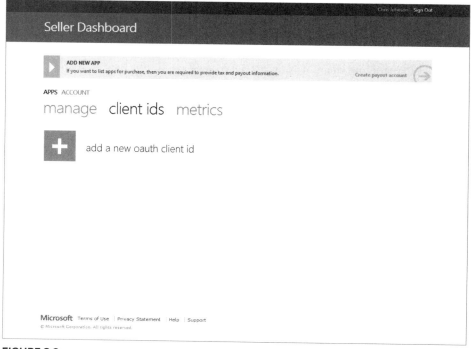

FIGURE 8-2

> **WARNING** *At the time of this writing only SharePoint-hosted and Provider-hosted app types are supported in the SharePoint Store. Microsoft has indicated this restriction will be lifted at a later date after the new SharePoint Online is out of preview. This means Autohosted apps are not currently allowed to be submitted to the store for publication.*

You are now ready to start submitting apps. The two high-level steps in this process are:

1. Creating a client ID
2. Submitting an app package

Chapter 10, "Overview of OAuth in SharePoint 2013," discusses client IDs in detail, but for now all you need to know is that they provide an identity used in the authentication and authorization process between an app and SharePoint. On the other hand, Chapter 7, "Packaging and Deploying SharePoint 2013 Apps," discusses what the various packaging and deployment options are for applications. Understanding these concepts prior to building and submitting an app is important, so if you haven't read Chapter 7 yet please do so. The remainder of this chapter assumes you have read Chapter 7 and therefore understand these concepts.

Creating a Client ID and Secret

A client ID and client secret form a critical component of how the OAuth authentication and authorization flows work between apps and SharePoint. They are used to secure and verify calls as well as identify apps when calls are made.

For Provider-hosted apps you are required to apply for a client ID and secret prior to submitting the app. This is because you need to both supply them as part of the app package and, more importantly, you need to configure them in your app's back-end code. The back-end code of your application must be up and running prior to submission so that Microsoft can successfully test the application and verify it.

When you're creating private apps, you create a client ID and secret through the `appregnew.aspx` page (see Chapter 10 for more detail on this process). For apps you want to distribute through the SharePoint Store, you need to obtain the client ID and secret from the Seller Dashboard. This is a straightforward process (as shown in the following Try It Out) and requires you to supply a friendly name, the domain name on which the app code back end will be hosted, and the period for which the ID/secret should be valid for.

TRY IT OUT   **Creating a New Client ID through the Seller Dashboard**

In this example you create a new client ID and secret combination using the Seller Dashboard. You first need a Seller Dashboard account to get these items.

1. Log in to the Seller Dashboard on the `http://sellerdashboard.microsoft.com` website.
2. Click the Client IDs link.

3. Click the Add a new oauth client id link as shown in Figure 8-3.

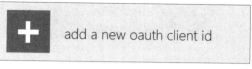

4. Enter a friendly name for the client ID; for example, `MyAppKeys`.

FIGURE 8-3

5. In the App Domain field enter the domain name of where your Provider-hosted application code resides; for example, `myapp.contoso.com`.

6. In the App Redirect URL field enter the fully qualified domain name and path to the redirect URL page in your app code. This field accepts authorization codes from SharePoint (see Chapter 10). Note that it must be HTTPS; for example, `https://myapp.contoso.com/redirecturi.aspx`.

7. Pick the duration you want the client ID and secret to be valid for. The default is one year.

8. After it's complete, the form should look like the one shown in Figure 8-4.

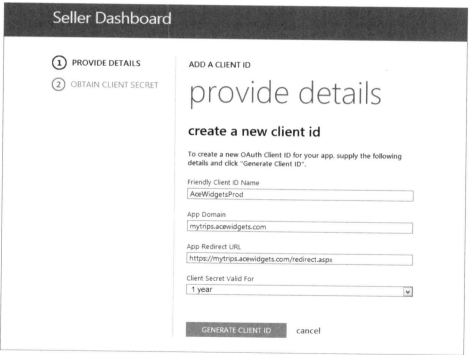

FIGURE 8-4

9. Click the Generate Client ID button. A confirmation screen with your client ID and secret appears, as shown in Figure 8-5.

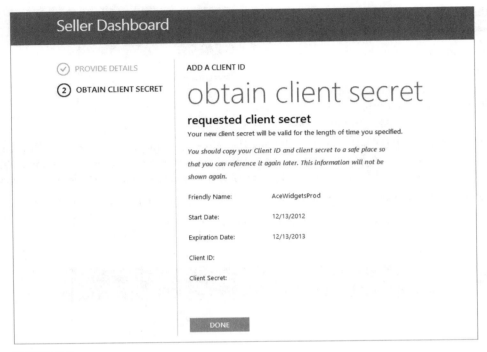

FIGURE 8-5

10. Make a copy of this page and store these details somewhere safe. This is very important! No way exists to retrieve them again after you have dismissed this screen.

11. After you have made a safe and secure copy of the details shown, click Done.

12. You can now configure your Provider-hosted app with the client ID and secret combination you generated.

How It Works

In this exercise you created a new client ID and secret through the Seller Dashboard. In the background the Seller Dashboard keeps a record of the combination for use when your app code talks to SharePoint. You need to manually create a combination for Provider-hosted apps because you need to manually set them in your app code project. For SharePoint-hosted and Autohosted apps, the client ID and secret are created automatically upon installation and you never need to worry about them.

Pricing and Licensing Apps

After you have created a client ID and client secret, but before you submit an app to the Store, you need to make some important decisions about how you will price and license the app. The first question to ask yourself is whether your app will be free or not. There is a lot to consider when making this decision. You might want to make the app free and make money by having ads in the app. Alternatively, you could offer a free version that supports in-app purchases that cost money and unlock additional functionality in your application.

For paid apps you can offer a price per user and set an upper bound for the most an organization will pay for your app. This method allows you to say, for example, that for above 500 users, the app costs the same no matter how many users it is for.

> **NOTE** *At the time of this writing the SharePoint Store does not support commerce or licensing support for in-app purchases. This capability is possible through the use of a third-party payment system and licensing checks, but it is outside the boundary of the SharePoint Store and Seller Dashboard and is up to the developer to provide and manage.*

You might also want to support offering a trial of your application. The SharePoint Store supports the ability to limit the use of the trial to a particular time period and a number of users.

Another important point to consider is that app developers must include code-based checks in their code to check for a valid license. This ensures the individual or organization has purchased the appropriate license for your app. This isn't enforced by SharePoint itself and is the developer's responsibility. This is done in two steps:

1. Request the licenses from SharePoint.

2. Verify the licenses with the Store.

To request the licenses from SharePoint you make a call using the Client-Side Object Model (CSOM) as follows:

```
ClientResult<AppLicenseCollection> licenses =
Microsoft.SharePoint.Client.Utilities.Utility.GetAppLicenseInformation(ctx, productId);
ctx.ExecuteQuery();
```

This returns the list of licenses that the user has for the application. The next step is to verify those licenses. To do that you need to submit the license to the validation Web service hosted and run by Microsoft. The REST-based call to verify a license is at: `https://verificationservice` `.officeapps.live.com/ova/verificationagent.svc/rest/verify?token={token}`.

The `{token}` parameter is a URI-encoded representation of the license token (.NET uses `Uri.EscapeDataString` or something similar). The response from the service includes information about whether the license is valid or has expired, the license type, number of seats, and when it expires. You can then make determinations based on this information in your application code to decide what you want to do. Some considerations include:

➤ Revoking access

➤ Allowing access

➤ Turning on or off features based on whether the users are paid or free

➤ Turning on features if users have bought more than a certain number of seats

➤ Warning users their license is going to expire soon and they should consider buying a new one

The options are limitless, which is why leaving it up to the developer to decide what to do and enforce those options through code is part of the app model design. You are not limited to the decision-making process. You could, for example, confer with another system as part of the process such as another licensing system or in-app payment system. These are just examples, but the final pricing and licensing decisions will vary based on the individual app.

Submitting Apps

Once you make a decision on pricing and licensing your app, you are ready to submit it. The two main steps for submitting and publishing an app through the Seller Dashboard are the following:

1. Submit the app.

2. Receive app validation.

You are responsible for submitting the app, and Microsoft is responsible for validating and approving the app.

To submit an app, you must provide details about your application. Some of these include:

➤ App type

➤ Title

➤ Description

➤ Logo and graphics

➤ App package

➤ OAuth client ID and secret details (Provider-hosted apps)

➤ Pricing and licensing information

Some of these details are easier to answer than others, and thinking them through prior to submitting your app is advisable. Don't worry if you get stuck, however; you can save your submission as a draft and come back to it at a later date.

In this next exercise you will try out the process of submitting an app to the SharePoint Store. The example will only submit a test application and won't submit the app for final validation with Microsoft, however, the application won't end up being published to the SharePoint Store.

TRY IT OUT **Submitting an App to the Store**

In this example you submit a Provider-hosted app package to the store for publishing. You need a valid `.app` package, artwork, and associated app details. You also must have created a client ID in the Seller Dashboard (see the "Creating a Client ID and Secret" section earlier in this chapter).

1. Log in to the Seller Dashboard on the `http://sellerdashboard.microsoft.com` website.

2. Click the Add a new app link. A page appears prompting you to choose an application type, as shown in Figure 8-6.

3. Select App for SharePoint from the list and click Next.

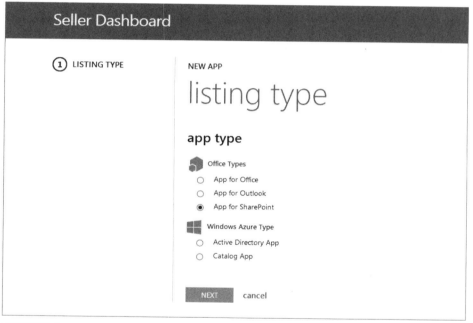

FIGURE 8-6

4. Now it's time to start entering all the data about the application. Enter **My App** into the Title field and **1** in the Version field. Select Travel + Navigation from the Category drop-down list.

5. Click the + in the logo area. This prompts you to pick a logo. The logo must be 96 × 96 in size. A logo in the correct dimensions is available in the source code download package for this chapter (`applogo.png`).

6. Click the app package icon and select the `SharePointAppPackage.app` file from the download package for this chapter.

7. Click the "My app is a service and requires server to server authorization" check box. This specifies that your app is Provider-hosted and an OAuth client ID and secret is required. Select the client ID you created earlier, as shown in Figure 8-7.

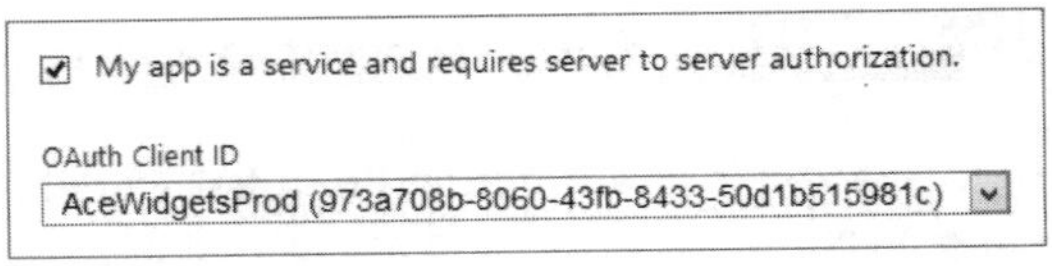

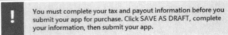

☑ My app is a service and requires server to server authorization.

OAuth Client ID

AceWidgetsProd (973a708b-8060-43fb-8433-50d1b515981c) ▼

FIGURE 8-7

8. Click Next.

9. On the details screen enter a short and a long description for the app. These can be anything you like.

10. You need to specify at least one screenshot of 512×384 dimensions for the application in order to submit an app. Click the + on the first screenshot and select screenshot1.png from the download package for this chapter.

11. In the support URL field enter the URL of your website where users can get assistance on your application; for example, http://www.acewidgets.com.

12. Click Next.

13. Select the pricing and licensing for the application. In this example, make it a paid-for application, so select the "My app is for purchase" option.

14. Select 1.99 in the Price per User drop-down list.

15. Select 50 in the Price Threshold drop-down list. This number signifies that the most an organization will need to purchase is 50 licenses.

16. At this point you might see a warning about your payout information not being complete (see Figure 8-8). If you see this warning, click "My app is free" so that you can move on.

! You must complete your tax and payout information before you submit your app for purchase. Click SAVE AS DRAFT, complete your information, then submit your app.

FIGURE 8-8

17. Click Save as Draft, unless this is for a real app submission, in which case, click Submit for Approval. You can now see your newly created app submission in draft status in the manage section, as shown in Figure 8-9.

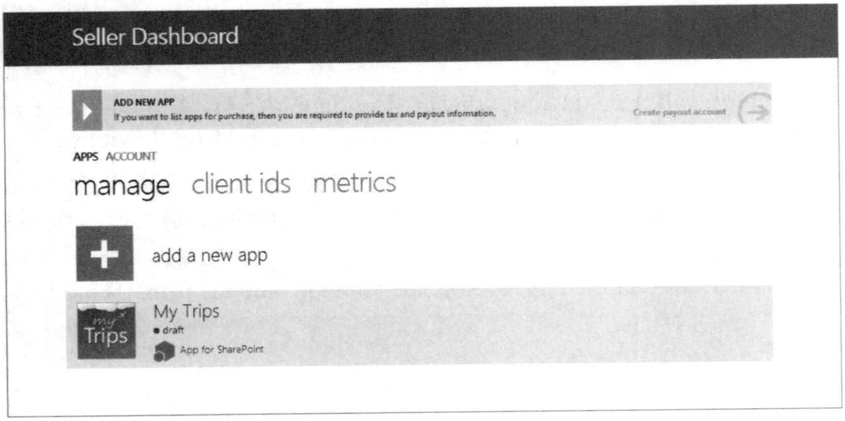

Seller Dashboard

▶ ADD NEW APP
If you want to list apps for purchase, then you are required to provide tax and payout information.   Create payout account ⟶

APPS ACCOUNT

manage client ids metrics

➕ add a new app

Trips   My Trips
● draft
App for SharePoint

FIGURE 8-9

How It Works

In this exercise you prepared an application submission to the SharePoint Store by providing the details for the application and associated artwork such as the logo and screenshots. Behind the scenes Microsoft keeps a catalog of these details. When, and if, you submit the application for final validation, Microsoft's test and verification teams receive your application and then install it on a set of test systems for verification and testing. In this example you didn't submit the sample application for verification, however, for a production application you would.

After your application has been submitted, validated (more on that in the next section), and published, the Apps page in the Seller Dashboard gives you the ability to edit the application's details or unpublish the app. See Figure 8-10 for an example of a published app page in the Seller Dashboard.

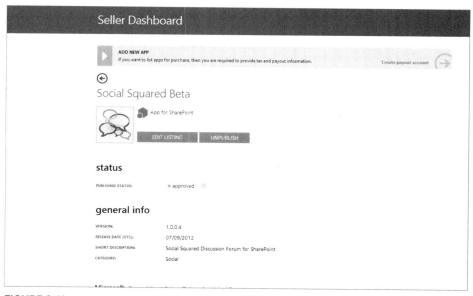

FIGURE 8-10

Getting Apps Validated

When you submit an application for publishing in the store by Microsoft, the app goes through a series of checks and tests. Microsoft conducts these tests to ensure apps are high-quality and that they meet the rules and policies Microsoft has put in place.

App developers must ensure their creations meet Microsoft's rules and regulations. If your app fails one or more of these rules, it will be rejected and you will be notified with details of the failure and the policy that the app didn't pass. You can correct the issue and resubmit the app when it's ready.

The rules that your app must adhere to fall into the following high-level categories:

- **App value:** Does it provide value to the customer?
- **Advertising rules:** Does your app show ads in an appropriate manner?
- **In-app purchases:** Does the description of your app state what is for sale in your app?
- **Reliability and performance:** Does your app error out?
- **Predictability:** Does the app do only what it says it does — for example, with customer data?
- **Customer in control:** Does your app ask for permission to do things with customer data?
- **Content:** Does your app contain adult or obscene content?
- **Accuracy:** Does the name and marketing information of your application accurately represent the app?
- **Updates:** Does an update to your app remove functionality?
- **Supported capabilities:** Does your app use only supported APIs?

You can view a comprehensive list of rules and policies online on the MSDN website at: `http://msdn.microsoft.com/en-us/library/office/apps/jj220035.aspx`. As of this writing these rules are at version 1.2, but are subject to change at any time by Microsoft.

APPLICATION LIFE CYCLE

After you have an application in the store, keeping track of any issues and problems people are having with it and submitting updates to add new functionality or correct any issues is very important. It is generally well understood that a popular application in any ecosystem often has a responsive developer who is assisting customers with issues they are having and releasing updates to fix common issues. Additionally, customers love buying an app and then seeing ongoing value delivered through regular updates and feature additions.

The Seller Dashboard gives app publishers some tools to assist with the life-cycle process:

- Metrics about your apps
- App update process

These tools are discussed at length in the following sections.

Using Seller Dashboard Metrics

The Store captures a number of helpful metrics that can help with giving you insights into how your app is being used and whether any issues are occurring. The following are a few of the metrics that are gathered:

- ➤ Downloads
- ➤ Purchases
- ➤ Trials
- ➤ Purchased seats
- ➤ Installs
- ➤ Uninstalls
- ➤ Runtime errors

Figure 8-11 shows an example of the metrics overview page showing all your apps in the Seller Dashboard.

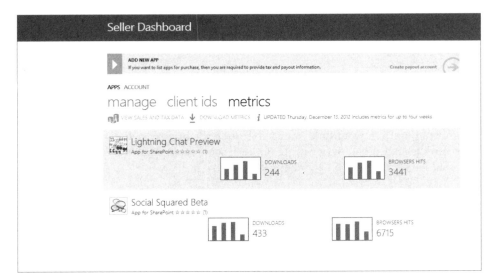

FIGURE 8-11

Figure 8-12 shows an example of the detailed metrics for a given application in the Seller Dashboard.

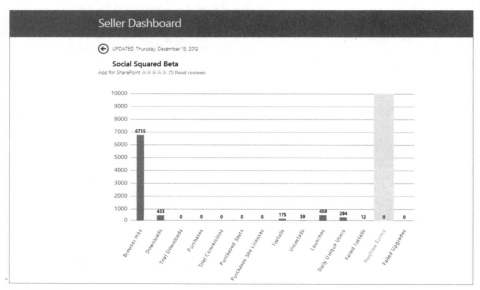

FIGURE 8-12

Capturing additional information and metrics to help you run your apps is also highly advisable. You can use tools such as Google Analytics to monitor usage of an app because app pages and App Parts are Web pages.

Gathering information about crashes or errors that occur in an app is also extremely important so that you can make further diagnoses. Having a customer complaining about an app crashing and not having any visibility into why it might be happening can be infuriating to a developer. Capturing more information than you think you need is often the best plan. Following on from that, monitoring your error logs and proactively getting in touch with customers who are experiencing an issue often goes a long way toward keeping a happy customer.

Upgrading Apps

From time to time you will either want to release a new feature in an app or release a new version to fix a found bug or issue. To update an app, simply submit a new version of your app package using the same Product ID (in the app manifest file). Doing this signifies that it is an update and not a new application.

In many cases, however, you might not need to submit an update. For Provider-hosted apps, the only time you need to submit an update is if the components in the app package change, not if the back end of the app changes. The reason is that with a Provider-hosted app, you can change the back end of the app, any pages, code, databases, and assets without needing to touch any of the parts that are deployed to SharePoint. This capability can be extremely helpful when resolving issues, can be done quickly, requires no input or effort from the customer, and can be controlled by you. However, in some instances this capability can cause issues. Think about the scenario when you do update the SharePoint components of an app and change its behavior for some reason. Now your back-end code must support those who have installed version 1 of the application and also version 2! Be careful not to make breaking changes to the back end code without thinking through the ramifications of doing so.

When you do submit an app update to the store or app catalog, the user will see a visual indicator beside the app that an update is available and will be prompted to update it.

After the update starts, SharePoint locks the application while the update is in progress. This stops people from inadvertently trying to launch the app while the update is happening.

What happens during the update depends on the application type. The following summarizes at a high level what occurs for each:

For Provider-hosted and SharePoint-hosted apps (apps with a WSP in them):

➤ A backup of the application's SharePoint site is taken.

➤ The update is applied to the backup.

➤ If the update succeeds, the update is applied to the primary application's SharePoint site.

➤ SharePoint executes the PostUpdate Web service, if one is provided.

For Autohosted apps:

➤ SharePoint updates the SQL Azure database if the app contains a DACPAC (see Chapter 7 for more on this topic).

➤ SharePoint then runs the same steps as for Provider-hosted and SharePoint-hosted apps (see the preceding bulleted list).

The PostUpdate Web service referenced in the earlier steps is one of several events that are raised in the life cycle of an application. These are calls that are made by SharePoint to remote Web services that you as an app developer host and run, which means you are notified when these events occur. These events include the following:

➤ App Installed (InstalledEventEndpoint node in the app manifest)

➤ App Uninstalling (UninstallingEventEndpoint node in the app manifest)

➤ App Upgraded (UpgradedEventEndpoint node in the app manifest)

You can use these events to do things such as:

➤ Set up data when a customer installs an app.

➤ Remove data when a customer uninstalls an app.

➤ Change data when a customer upgrades.

➤ Record the version a customer is using when he upgrades.

How to use these events is up to the developer. Even if you only use them to record what installs have taken place and what version customers are running, this information might come in handy for debugging and diagnosis purposes.

SUMMARY

The SharePoint Store offers developers and ISVs access to the potentially hundreds of millions of SharePoint customers and users around the world, creating a global marketplace for components, add-ons, and a full line of business apps. The store is an unprecedented channel to get these reusable and resalable components into customers' hands.

For users of SharePoint it provides a single trusted location for procurement of apps. Today, users generally need to research and find components themselves and then go through the common and often arduous process of asking their IT department to install the component on their SharePoint farm. The IT department often balks at the task, given the risk involved in installing others' code on the SharePoint servers and so typically only the most popular apps ever see the light of day in SharePoint. The store helps fix that situation by offering a sandboxed and secure location for installing components where the IT department can have a level of trust that the apps won't bring down the SharePoint farm due to poor programming or the like. However, apps may still be able to read, edit, copy, and delete data depending on the permissions they ask for and are granted, so caution is still advised. To assist with this problem SharePoint provides the ability for the IT department to shut off access to the store and only provide apps through a curated private app catalog experience that IT controls.

Developers should seriously consider offering applications to others through the store, thus helping others with their innovative apps and also potentially making money in the process.

EXERCISES

You can find answers to the exercises for this chapter in Appendix A.

1. What app type requires a pre-created client ID and secret prior to submission to the SharePoint Store?

2. What are some of the options you have as an app publisher for monetizing your application through the store?

3. What are the Web services available to catch the life-cycle events of an application?

▶ WHAT YOU LEARNED IN THIS CHAPTER

ITEM	DESCRIPTION
Pricing and licensing	The store offers the ability to publish free and paid-for application types.
Validation	Apps must not violate a set list of policies set by Microsoft for inclusion in the marketplace.
Submission	The submission process includes creating client IDs and secrets (Provider-hosted apps only) and then submission of the app and its assets.

RECOMMENDED READING

How to create or edit your seller account in the Microsoft Seller Dashboard — `http://msdn`
`.microsoft.com/en-us/library/office/apps/jj220034.aspx`
Licensing apps for Office and SharePoint — `http://msdn.microsoft.com/en-us/library/`
`office/apps/jj163257.aspx`

Overview of the Client-Side Object Model and REST APIs

WHAT YOU WILL LEARN IN THIS CHAPTER:

➤ Understanding the API options available in SharePoint 2013

➤ Learning how to use the new CSOM APIs

➤ Learning about REST and OData support in SharePoint 2013

WROX.COM CODE DOWNLOADS FOR THIS CHAPTER

The wrox.com code downloads for this chapter are found at: `http://www.wrox`
`.com/WileyCDA/WroxTitle/productCd-1118495845.html` on the Download Code tab. The
code for this chapter is divided into the following major examples:

➤ MyODataJavaScriptApp.js

➤ MyFirstCSOMConsole.zip

➤ JavaScriptCSOMApp.js

SharePoint applications begin a fundamental shift away from building code that runs within
the SharePoint process. Along with this shift comes the start of a movement away from
using the historical API sets that don't provide support for this newly decoupled code. In
this chapter you learn about and explore the updated and new options available for working
with SharePoint at a programmatic level. You also learn when is best to use the various
options, how they work, and most importantly, how to use them to your advantage. As this
chapter explains, many of the design philosophies, technologies, and principles that went into
SharePoint are shared with services on the Internet with which developers are already familiar,
such as Twitter and Facebook. This means learning them should be more straightforward and
far simpler than learning a proprietary system.

INTRODUCING REMOTE APIS IN SHAREPOINT 2013

When SharePoint first started gaining traction with users all across the world around the year 2002, the product was very different than the developer friendly platform it is today. Initially, SharePoint wasn't built with developers in mind. It didn't offer good extensibility points or customization techniques, which lead to people's customizing SharePoint in unsupported and often fragile ways. Microsoft heard loud and clear from people all over the world that they wanted to be able to do things such as change the branding and make templates for parts of SharePoint. As a result, releases such as SharePoint 2007 and the move from ASP to ASP.NET represented great steps forward, and new options for extensibility emerged. People were able to build Web parts and had access to SharePoint's Server-Side Object Model (Server OM) that allowed them to call into SharePoint data and perform operations programmatically. These features enabled developers to build solutions of all kinds. However, this code that leveraged the Server OM ran as part of SharePoint's processes. The code would load within SharePoint, which made it vital to ensure that it was of high quality; otherwise, the code could adversely affect SharePoint. Issues such as high memory consumption and high CPU load became prevalent. In fact, Microsoft has often acknowledged that many of the critical support issues customers raised with them had their root cause identified as issues with custom code in the SharePoint process. This was, of course, not a good thing for SharePoint's image and reputation. Matters were further complicated by the fact that, at times, the Server OM was hard to use. For example, developers needed to know how and when to dispose of objects correctly. Not doing so could lead to high memory consumption. Conversely, disposing of the wrong thing could cause crashes.

Additionally, SharePoint has for some time provided a set of SOAP-based Web services that enable users to do some, but by no means all, of the same things the Server OM provided. These Web services revolved around sending and receiving a SOAP-formatted XML payload to and from SharePoint. These services have not stood the test of time well though. They are bulky and cumbersome and have been in dire need of an upgrade.

In the SharePoint 2013 release, those same Web services exist for backward compatibility. In fact, in SharePoint 2013 Microsoft has signaled it is deprecating these older SOAP-based services, which means you are unlikely to see them in future releases. Deprecating is a warning to stop using these services and to start thinking about shifting your code to the newer, more modern APIs.

Because the Server Object Model and the SOAP Web services are the two main APIs available for programmatically integrating with SharePoint, and because both of these options have significant drawbacks in their approach given modern recent developments in API and protocol design, SharePoint 2013 addresses these issues head-on. The new release of SharePoint provides a new, consolidated set of APIs for developers based on newer Web standards and modern coding practices, and targets integration scenarios that are the most prevalent and common. For developers who build solutions that integrate with SharePoint this is good news.

The rest of this chapter is dedicated to walking you through SharePoint 2013's API improvements, assisting you with learning about them, and providing guidance on where and when to use them.

CLIENT-SIDE OBJECT MODEL (CSOM) BASICS

In SharePoint 2010 Microsoft took the first steps toward providing better remote API options to developers with the introduction of the Client-Side Object Model, or CSOM. The CSOM came in three varieties:

➤   Managed Code (.NET)

➤   ECMA Script (also known as JavaScript)

➤   Silverlight

This model provided developers with the ability to access some functionality of SharePoint from remote code applications. For example, a Silverlight application running on a Web page could call back into SharePoint and retrieve data, or another system written in a .NET language could do the same. In fact, the underlying protocols that the CSOM used to talk to SharePoint were XML and JSON (JavaScript Object Notation) and were fully documented so that other systems capable of HTTP requests could make the same calls if they wanted. This was a huge step ahead of the SharePoint Server OM because your code could run remotely. It also hid much of the pain and overhead of having to deal with the SOAP Web services. However, the first version had one major drawback: it only provided API coverage to features in SharePoint Foundation such as sites, lists, and documents, and not to features available in the SharePoint Server standard or enterprise versions of the software.

SharePoint 2013 has added focus on remote APIs with the CSOM and its underlying protocols as *the* primary API for interacting with SharePoint moving forward. SharePoint 2013 provides access to its APIs in several forms to assist developers:

➤   Managed code assemblies (.NET)

➤   JavaScript

➤   REST/OData

➤   Windows Phone assemblies

➤   Silverlight assemblies

Depending on your solution or project you must decide on the suitability and applicability of using one or more of the preceding to accomplish your tasks. For example, if you are building a Windows Forms application for Windows with C# you would use the Managed CSOM. If you are building a Web Part/app part for SharePoint you can use the JavaScript CSOM in your app's front-end code and the Managed CSOM for the server-side code.

If you find that an applicable precompiled library doesn't exist for the platform you are using then you must consider the REST/OData endpoints. They provide Web standards–based HTTP/HTTPS endpoints that are platform agnostic.

Underlying all of these choices is a standards-based protocol based on REST, OData, and XML. Each of the libraries simply abstracts the complexity of calling the underpinning services for you and adds a layer of helper libraries to nicely package those up.

At the heart of the new API set is _API. This is a consolidated single endpoint for all remote APIs in SharePoint 2013. _API refers to the location from which it is accessible in the SharePoint URL structure: http://*yourservername*/*sitename*/_api.

Although _API provides the central location for API services, SharePoint 2010 also supported (in a more limited manner) some REST services with the ListData.svc service. Those of you who are familiar with the ListData.svc service will be glad to hear backward compatibility has been preserved in SharePoint 2013 by leaving the ListData.svc path in place.

_API is fully REST and OData enabled. REST stands for Representational State Transfer, and people commonly refer to an API as RESTful when it meets the definition laid out as part of the founding REST principles. You can read more on the background of REST in the creator's dissertation on the topic at: http://www.ics.uci.edu/~fielding/pubs/dissertation/rest_arch_style.htm.

The Open Data Protocol (OData) specifies a protocol for requesting and working with data over commonly accepted Web protocols such as HTTP, JSON, and XML. OData builds on the principles of REST to provide a common resourcing URL structure and parameter system to make querying and working with data simpler. This chapter goes into more detail on this topic later.

_API builds on the foundation laid in the SharePoint 2010 CSOM by providing access to many more areas of SharePoint, including the following, which are all discussed in detail later in the chapter:

- ➤ Lists and libraries
- ➤ User profiles
- ➤ Search
- ➤ Workflow
- ➤ Publishing
- ➤ Social feeds and sharing
- ➤ Taxonomy
- ➤ Web
- ➤ Business data

_API provides a consistent and unified place where SharePoint provides access to its remote APIs. Each of the CSOM libraries and object models discussed in the rest of this chapter build on a common foundation of API design based on standards-based protocols such as HTTP, REST, OData, and XML to provide an open and accessible API infrastructure.

MANAGED CODE (.NET)

In SharePoint 2010 Microsoft provided a version of the managed code CSOM for developers of .NET applications. This library has been rebuilt for SharePoint 2013 and is provided as part of the SharePoint installation. As in the 2010 release, it is provided as part of a redistributable package for developers to include in their applications.

It is made up of the following .NET assemblies:

➤ `Microsoft.SharePoint.Client.Runtime.dll`

➤ `Microsoft.SharePoint.Client.dll`

➤ `Microsoft.SharePoint.Client.DocumentManagement.dll`

➤ `Microsoft.SharePoint.Client.Publishing.dll`

➤ `Microsoft.SharePoint.Client.Taxonomy.dll`

➤ `Microsoft.SharePoint.Client.UserProfiles.dll`

➤ `Microsoft.SharePoint.WorkflowServices.Client.dll`

Later in this chapter you learn about which parts of the CSOM are in what DLL and namespace, but the naming of the DLLs should also give you a few hints.

Setup

You can install the DLLs on any computer by downloading the SharePoint Client Components SDK available at: `http://www.microsoft.com/en-us/download/details.aspx?id=30355`.

Additionally you can find them in the following location on a machine with SharePoint installed, as shown in Figure 9-1:

`%ProgramFiles%\Common Files\Microsoft Shared\web server extensions\15\ISAPI`

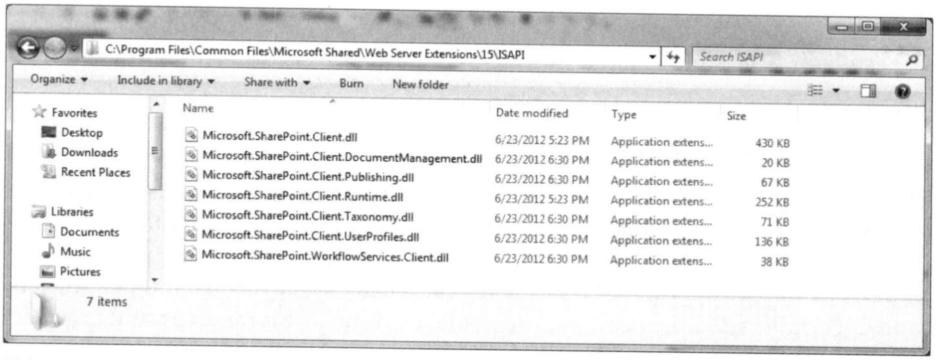

FIGURE 9-1

After you have added references to these DLLs from your .NET application such as a Windows Forms application or console application, you can add a `using` statement as follows:

`using Microsoft.SharePoint.Client;`

In managed code one of the first things you must do to make calls to SharePoint is to establish a `ClientContext`. It sets up things such as the URL to your SharePoint site and the authentication details needed to communicate with the services. You can instantiate a `ClientContext` object along with the URL of your site as shown here:

```
ClientContext context = new ClientContext("http://MySharePointSite");
```

After you have established a `ClientContext` the next thing most people want to know is how to interact with SharePoint data. The core set of SharePoint data objects in the CSOM are as follows:

➤ Site

➤ Web

➤ List

➤ ListItem

If you are familiar with the SharePoint Server-Side Object Model these items will all sound familiar. However, the naming convention is slightly different, and in the CSOM the "SP" on the front is omitted. However, they map one to one with their server-side equivalent.

In an installation where your SharePoint Server uses Windows Authentication (NTLM) to secure it, the CSOM passes the authentication context of the application process along with it. For example, if you ran your console application under your account the CSOM would be running as you are making the calls to SharePoint. This means you would need to have the correct privileges in SharePoint for the operations or data you were trying to access or you would receive an access denied exception. So, for example, if you were trying to manipulate ListItem object data with the CSOM you would need the corresponding security privileges on those list items in SharePoint.

Querying

The CSOM has been built from the ground up with two important features in mind:

➤ Batching

➤ Returning only the data that you need

When you work with remote systems and call them over potentially latent and unknown bandwidth connections, these two things are very important. You must be able to keep the number of calls and responses to a minimum and you should only bring back the minimum amount of data you need to do your job. For this reason the CSOM only executes calls when you ask it to and includes all statements and operations since the last time you made it execute. This might at times seem cumbersome to someone new to using the CSOM; however, it enforces the developer's involvement in these choices and ultimately helps make better performing code.

The core object required to work with almost every aspect of the CSOM is a Site or Web object. Because all SharePoint data is stored in sites these objects are usually the first ones you need to instantiate.

You can do it by querying the context for the Site and Web objects corresponding to the URL with which you constructed the `ClientContext`. You do this with the `.Site` and `.Web` properties like so:

```
ClientContext clientContext = new ClientContext("http://MySharePointSiteUrl");
Site site = clientContext.Site;
Web web = clientContext.Web;
```

Once you have your Site and Web context objects you are ready to start working with data in them. As mentioned previously the CSOM only brings back the data you ask it to. You use the Load method on the ClientContext to do this as follows:

```
List list = web.Lists.GetByTitle("Movies");
ListItemCollection listItems = list.GetItems(CamlQuery.CreateAllItemsQuery(50));
clientContext.Load(listItems, items => items.Include(item => item["Title"]));
clientContext.ExecuteQuery();
```

In the Load statement the Include command instructs the CSOM to include that property in the results. In the example this instructs the CSOM to load the Title property. Now you are ready to execute the operation against the SharePoint Server. Remember, the CSOM only sends commands to SharePoint when you are ready. Calling Load does not do that. The transaction only executes when you call the ExecuteQuery method, like this:

```
ClientContext clientContext = new ClientContext("http://MySharePointSiteUrl");
Web web = clientContext.Web;
clientContext.Load(web);
clientContext.ExecuteQuery(); // this line executes the instructions
```

By making the developer explicitly request that the instructions be carried out, the CSOM enables you to batch your commands into appropriate sets and thus minimize the number of requests and responses to and from the server. On a highly latent connection this can save many seconds of transmission time and thus help keep your application speedy.

> **NOTE** *If you attempt to use a property on a CSOM object and get a* PropertyOrFieldNotInitializedException *you likely have not asked for it to be returned and loaded by specifying it in a* Load *command.*

This same technique is applicable in other scenarios and operations, such as bringing back only the properties you desire; for example:

```
ClientContext clientContext = new ClientContext("http://MySharePointSiteUrl");
Web web = clientContext.Web;
clientContext.Load(web, w => w.Title, w => w.Description);
clientContext.ExecuteQuery();
```

Here the Load method is called, passing along a description of the properties to return. If you don't specify these properties only the default ones will be returned.

The CSOM also allows for operations such as creating data. Because you don't have a reference to an existing object, the CSOM instead uses a creation information object such as ListItemCreationInformation to capture all the information, such as the column data, about the ListItem.

The following example shows a basic use of the `ListItemCreationInformation` class to insert a new row into a list:

```
ClientContext clientContext = new ClientContext("http://MySharePointSiteUrl");
Web web = clientContext.Web;
List list = web.Lists. GetByTitle("Tasks")
clientContext.Load(web);
clientContext.Load(list);
ListItemCreationInformation itemCreateInfo = new ListItemCreationInformation();
ListItem listItem = list.AddItem(itemCreateInfo);
listItem["Title"] = "New Announcement!";
listItem.Update();
clientContext.ExecuteQuery();
```

Some other examples of creation information classes include:

➤ `ListCreationInformation`

➤ `WebCreationInformation`

➤ `ViewCreationInformation`

➤ `FileCreationInformation`

To try a practical example of using the CSOM in a console application, work through the following exercise.

TRY IT OUT   **My First CSOM Console App (MyFirstCSOMConsole.zip)**

In this exercise you create a console application that uses the Managed .NET CSOM to talk remotely to a SharePoint on-premises server. You need a SharePoint 2013 site, Visual Studio 2010 or 2012, and the SharePoint Client Components SDK installed. You can find the completed code for this exercise in the `MyFirstCSOMConsole.zip` file included with the code download for this chapter.

1. In your SharePoint site create a new Custom list called Movies by clicking in Site Contents ➪ Add App, then pick Custom List from the list and call it **Movies**. Click Create.

2. Click on the List tab of the ribbon and choose Create Column.

3. Select Number and call the column **Length**. Click OK to create the new column.

4. Add three or four new list items to the list for your favorite movies along with their lengths.

5. Open Visual Studio and create a new project by choosing Visual C# ➪ Windows ➪ Console Application project. Call it **MyFirstCSOMConsole**. Click OK to create the project.

6. Right-click References, then choose Add Reference.

7. Click Browse and browse to the `%ProgramFiles%\Common Files\Microsoft Shared\web server extensions\15\ISAPI` folder.

8. Select `Microsoft.SharePoint.Client.Runtime.dll` and `Microsoft.SharePoint.Client.dll`. Click Add.

9. At the top of your `Program.cs` file add using `Microsoft.SharePoint.Client;`.

10. In the `Main()` function of your app add the following code. This code queries your SharePoint site for its Title and queries the Movies list for its items, only bringing back the ID, Title, and Length fields. You need to replace *servername* and *sitename* with your own SharePoint Server details.

```
ClientContext clientContext = new ClientContext("http://servername/sitename");
Site site = clientContext.Site;
Web web = clientContext.Web;
clientContext.Load(web, w => w.Title);

List list = web.Lists.GetByTitle("Movies");
ListItemCollection listItems = list.GetItems(CamlQuery.CreateAllItemsQuery(50));
clientContext.Load(listItems, items => items.Include(item => item["Title"],
item => item["Length"], item => item.Id));

clientContext.ExecuteQuery();

Console.WriteLine(web.Title);

foreach (ListItem item in listItems)
{
    Console.WriteLine(string.Format("Item: {0}, {1}, {2}", item.Id,
item["Title"], item["Length"]));
}

ListItemCreationInformation itemCreateInfo = new ListItemCreationInformation();
ListItem listItem = list.AddItem(itemCreateInfo);
listItem["Title"] = "Diamonds Are Forever";
listItem["Length"] = 120;
listItem.Update();

clientContext.Load(listItems, items => items.Include(item => item["Title"],
item => item["Length"], item => item.Id));
clientContext.ExecuteQuery();

Console.WriteLine("Added Movie: " + listItem["Title"]);
```

11. Press F5 to run your console application. The Title of your site appears followed by a row for each movie in the Movies list. Finally, you can also see that your new ListItem was added to the list. Figure 9-2 outlines what you should see in the console window.

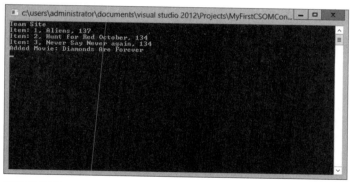

FIGURE 9-2

How It Works

In this exercise you created a console application that used the Managed .NET CSOM to query your SharePoint Server. You limited the data you received back by indicating in the Load statements just the properties you wanted and only executed the calls when ready with the ExecuteQuery statement.

Behind the scenes the CSOM is constructing queries to the SharePoint Server with XML and sending them to the _vti_bin/Client.svc CSOM endpoint. SharePoint is then interpreting the calls and returning the results in a JSON payload that the CSOM then unpacks into the resultant CSOM objects.

JAVASCRIPT

Alongside the Managed .NET Client-Side Object Model (Managed CSOM) is the JavaScript Client Object Model (JS CSOM).

> **NOTE** See the previous section, "Managed Code (.NET)," for background foundational information about the CSOM that isn't repeated in this section.

The primary purpose of the JS CSOM is to allow JavaScript code running on pages within the context of SharePoint to talk back to SharePoint without requiring a full-page postback. It is not designed or intended for developers to use outside of the context of pages served from SharePoint.

Similar to the Managed CSOM, the JS CSOM also is built to batch requests to ensure performance. However, one of the fundamental differences is that the JS CSOM is designed with asynchronous calls and callbacks in mind. This ensures that transactions that take some time to complete don't potentially block the calling thread, possibly impacting the UI of your application.

To access the JS CSOM the calling page must reference the following two files:

➤ SP.Runtime.js

➤ SP.js

Each of these is located in the /_layouts/15/ directory under each SharePoint site; for example, http://myserver/sitename/_layouts/15/SP.js.

You can also find these files on any SharePoint 2013 server in the following location:

```
%ProgramFiles%\Common Files\Microsoft Shared\
web server extensions\15\TEMPLATE\LAYOUTS
```

> **NOTE** Although the JS CSOM libraries are available, sometimes simple REST/OData HTTP-based calls might be just as easy for you to use. If you are familiar with making REST/JSON-based calls then they might also be worth considering. However, you would lose some of the benefits of the CSOM, such as automatic batching.

Setup

By default, pages that run within the context of SharePoint typically have the appropriate JavaScript references already defined in the master page. This means you shouldn't need to reference them in each page of your application. However, understanding what it means to be within the context of SharePoint is important. It means that the page is served from the same domain as SharePoint, rather than from another location such as in Azure. In cloud-hosted SharePoint apps, this is the default. Pages are loaded and served from SharePoint, which is possible because they can contain only out-of-the-box SharePoint controls, HTML, and JavaScript, so no custom code runs within the SharePoint process itself.

One way to tell whether your page uses the SharePoint master page is to look for the following `Page` declaration at the top of the page:

```
<%@ Page Inherits="Microsoft.SharePoint.WebPartPages.WebPartPage,
Microsoft.SharePoint, Version=15.0.0.0, Culture=neutral,
PublicKeyToken=71e9bce111e9429c"
MasterPageFile="~masterurl/default.master" language="C#" %>
```

If you have a page that doesn't inherit the SharePoint master page then you must include references to the appropriate JavaScript CSOM files. An example of this would be in an App Part when you don't want the full SharePoint master page wrapping your App Part's user interface.

To add the references manually you must include the following script references:

```
<script type="text/javascript"
src="https://ajax.aspnetcdn.com/ajax/4.0/1/MicrosoftAjax.js"></script>
<script type="text/javascript" src="/_layouts/15/sp.runtime.debug.js"></script>
<script type="text/javascript" src="/_layouts/15/sp.debug.js"></script>
```

If your page is served from outside of the SharePoint site, such is the case with Autohosted apps (served from Azure) or Provider-hosted apps, then you must dynamically generate the script includes in JS to ensure they include the fully qualified domain name (FQDN) in the URL. This is because you need to have the JS files served from the SharePoint Server itself to ensure the browser doesn't block the JS CSOM calls because of cross-site scripting protections.

To do this you can use the `SPHostUrl` query string parameter passed to your SharePoint app as follows:

```
<script type="text/javascript">
    var hosturl;
    $(document).ready(function () {
        hosturl = decodeURIComponent(getQueryStringParameter("SPHostUrl"));
        var scriptbase = hostweburl + "/_layouts/15/";

        $.getScript(scriptbase + "SP.Runtime.js",
            function () {
                $.getScript(scriptbase + "SP.js", scriptLoaded);
            }
        );
    });

    function scriptLoaded () {
```

```
    // your code goes here
    }

    function getQueryStringParameter(paramToRetrieve) {
        var params = document.URL.split("?")[1].split("&");
        var strParams = "";
        for (var i = 0; i < params.length; i = i + 1) {
            var singleParam = params[i].split("=");
            if (singleParam[0] == paramToRetrieve)
                return singleParam[1];
        }
    }
</script>
```

In the preceding code the JQuery `$(document).ready` method is called when the page has loaded and it's safe for the script to continue. The code then uses the `getScript` method to dynamically load the JavaScript files. It also uses the `SPHostUrl` query string parameter passed to dynamically ensure it is retrieving the files from the originating SharePoint site. After that call completes, the `scriptLoaded` method is called. The `ScriptLoaded` method is the location you can safely place your JS CSOM code.

> **NOTE** For demonstration purposes all the examples in the rest of this chapter use a cloud-hosted SharePoint app in Office 365 and use the Napa Office 365 development tools. These items enable you to develop lightweight cloud-hosted apps within a browser in a SharePoint Online developer site.
>
> These items are available in the Office 365 app marketplace. Install them into your developer site prior to continuing.

Querying

Similarly to the Managed CSOM, the JS CSOM also includes built-in batching and filtering. These features are especially important in client applications where the browser executing the code is always remote and often on an unknown quality of connection. To ensure your application stays responsive and fast you must take measures to make as few requests as possible and only return the data you really need.

Prior to making any requests you must set up a `ClientContext`. To get the context associated with the site and page the script is running on, use the `get_Current()` method:

```
var clientContext = context = new SP.ClientContext.get_current();
```

You can then start requesting data. One of the simplest requests you can make is for the information about the site, like so:

```
var web;
web = clientContext.get_web();
clientContext.load(web);
```

Now you are ready to make the request to the server. Because you don't want to block the application thread processing while this potentially long-running task is in progress, you provide callback functions that will be called either after the operation completes or if an error occurs.

To do this, make a call to executeQueryAsync like this:

```
clientContext.executeQueryAsync(
        myQuerySucceeded,
        myQueryFailed);
```

In the myQuerySucceeded function you can start using the objects you asked for:

```
function onQuerySucceeded() {alert(this.web.Title);}
```

Additionally, your application should be able to handle when errors occur. This might be due to connectivity issues, for example, like the following:

```
function myQueryFailed(sender, args) {alert('Call to SharePoint failed :(');}
```

When querying lists and libraries you have the choice of querying for a specific item whose ID you already know using the getItemById(id) method, or with a query using the getItems(query) method. The latter is slightly more complex in that you need to set up the query against that list using CAML syntax. The following sample code shows querying a simple list for all items whose Title column equals "Foo":

```
var list = listContext.get_web().get_lists().getByTitle('My Custom List');

var camlQuery = new SP.CamlQuery();

camlQuery.set_viewXml(
'<View><Query><Where><Eq><FieldRef Name=\'Title\'/>' +
'<Value Type=\'Text\'>New Item 1</Value></Eq></Where></Query>' +
'<RowLimit>10</RowLimit></View>' );

items = list.getItems(camlQuery);

context.load(items);
context.executeQueryAsync(myQuerySucceeded, myQueryFailed);
```

You can use the CAML query to carefully construct the exact query against the list you want to make and also the data you want to bring back.

To create and manipulate list items, use the ListItemCreationInformation object as shown in the following code example. This gives you a context object that allows you set up the item prior to sending it to the server along with the data you want to create:

```
var newListItem;

function createItems()
{
    var listContext = new SP.AppContextSite(context, hostUrl);
    var list = listContext.get_web().get_lists().getByTitle('My Custom List');

    var itemCreateInfo = new SP.ListItemCreationInformation();
    newListItem = list.addItem(itemCreateInfo);
```

```
            newListItem.set_item('Title', 'Created via JS CSOM!');
            newListItem.update();
            context.load(newListItem);
            context.executeQueryAsync(onCreateListItemsSuccess,onCreateListItemsFail);
            }

function onCreateListItemsSuccess() {
    alert('New ListItem created: ' + newListItem.get_id());
}

// This function is executed if the above call fails
function onCreateListItemsFail(sender, args) {
    alert('Failed to create list item. Error:' + args.get_message());
}
```

For updates you simply get the list item in question, make the update to the data, and then call `update()` on it like so:

```
var listItem = list.getItemById(1);
listItem.set_item('Title', 'Updated via JS CSOM');
listItem.update();
```

You can try out these APIs and techniques in the following exercise to get a better feel for how they work with SharePoint Online using the new Napa developer tools.

TRY IT OUT **Using the JavaScript Client-Side Object Model in a SharePoint-Hosted App Using Napa for Office 365**

In this exercise you create a SharePoint application using only JavaScript and the Napa Office 365 development tools. You must have the Napa application installed from the Office 365 marketplace prior to starting this exercise. The full JavaScript source for this exercise is available in the code download in the `JavaScriptCSOMApp.js` file.

1. Ensure you have Napa Office 365 Development Tools installed in your development site in Office 365.

2. Click Site Contents in your site navigation to see a list of all apps installed in your site.

3. Locate Napa Office 365 Development Tools in the list and click it as shown in Figure 9-3.

FIGURE 9-3

4. Click Add New Project.

5. Select App for SharePoint and enter **MyFirstJavaScriptApp** in the Project name box. Click Create to continue. Napa creates a set of template files and folders for you. Explore the structure and get familiar with the layout of the application.

6. Open the `Scripts` folder and then open the `App.js` file. This is the default file that contains the JavaScript for your application.

7. At the bottom of the file add the following code:

```
function getParameterByName(name)
{
  name = name.replace(/[\[]/, "\\\[").replace(/[\]]/, "\\\]");
  var regexS = "[\\?&]" + name + "=([^&#]*)";
  var regex = new RegExp(regexS);
  var results = regex.exec(window.location.search);
  if(results == null)
    return "";
  else
    return decodeURIComponent(results[1].replace(/\+/g, " "));
}
```

8. Replace the `sharePointReady()` function with the following code. This gets the host URL for use later.

```
var hostUrl;

function sharePointReady() {
    context = new SP.ClientContext.get_current();
    web = context.get_web();
        hostUrl = getParameterByName('SPHostUrl');
    createList();
}
```

9. Directly after the `sharePointReady()` function insert the following code. This creates a new list.

```
var newList;

function createList() {
    var hostContext = new SP.AppContextSite(context, hostUrl);
    web = hostContext.get_web();

    var newListInfo = new SP.ListCreationInformation();
    newListInfo.set_title('My Sample List');
    newListInfo.set_templateType(SP.ListTemplateType.genericList);

    newList = web.get_lists().add(newListInfo);

    context.load(newList);
    context.executeQueryAsync(onCreateListSucceeded, onFailed);
}

function onCreateListSucceeded() {
    alert('New list created: ' + newList.get_title());
}

// This function is executed if the above call fails
function onFailed(sender, args) {
    alert('Failed. Error:' + args.get_message());
}
```

10. Click the Run Project button in the bottom left of the window to test out the application. When it completes, a message appears like the one shown in Figure 9-4.

11. Right-click the launch link and open your app in a new window to start your application.

12. A JavaScript alert message appears, stating, "`Failed. Error: Access denied. You do not have permission to perform this action or access this resource.`" This is

FIGURE 9-4

supposed to happen. The reason is that you have not yet given your application permissions to create lists in the app's host Web. Click OK to continue then close the window. Click Close in the Launch App dialog in Napa to get back to your code.

13. In the lower left of the window click the wrench icon to open the Property panel for your application, as shown in Figure 9-5.

14. Click into the Permissions tab and set the permissions for Web under Content to Full Control.

FIGURE 9-5

15. Run the project again using the Run Project button in the bottom left of the window. A permissions request window appears, asking you to grant the application full control of the site. Click Trust It.

16. An alert window appears, stating, "`New list created: My Sample List.`" Click OK.

17. Check that your list was created by clicking the link in the top left of the page to get to your developer site. Click `Site Content` and find the new list called `My Sample List`. Click it to open the list. Currently, no data is in it.

18. Within the `sharePointReady` function, change the `createList();` call to `createItems();`.

19. After the `sharePointReady` function, add the following code:

```
function createItems()
{
    var listContext = new SP.AppContextSite(context, hostUrl);
    var list = listContext.get_web().get_lists().getByTitle('My Sample List');

    for(var i=0; i < 10; i++)
    {
        var itemCreateInfo = new SP.ListItemCreationInformation();
        var newListItem = list.addItem(itemCreateInfo);
            newListItem.set_item('Title', 'Created via JS CSOM! - ' + i);
        newListItem.update();
            context.load(newListItem);
    }
        context.executeQueryAsync(onCreateListItemsSuccess,onFailed);
}

function onCreateListItemsSuccess() {
    alert('New ListItems created');
}
```

20. Run and launch the app again using the Run Project button in the bottom left of the window. This time an alert appears stating, "`New ListItems created.`"

21. Check the list in the SharePoint site to ensure the data has been created. You should see ten new items created in the list.

22. Within the `sharePointReady` function, change the `createItems();` call to `updateListItem();`.

23. Directly after the `sharePointReady` function, insert the following code:

```
var updatedItem;

function updateListItem() {
    var listContext = new SP.AppContextSite(context, hostUrl);
    var list = listContext.get_web().get_lists().getByTitle('My Sample List');

    var listItem = list.getItemById(1);
    listItem.set_item('Title', 'Updated via JS CSOM');
    listItem.update();

    context.load(listItem);
    context.executeQueryAsync(onUpdateItemSucceeded, onFailed);
}

function onUpdateItemSucceeded() {
    alert('Updated item!');
}
```

24. Run and launch the app again. This time an alert appears stating, "`Updated item!`". Again, check the SharePoint list to see that the first item in the list has been updated.

25. Within the `sharePointReady` function, change the `updateListItem();` call to `getItems();`.

26. Directly after the `sharePointReady` function, insert the following code:

```
var items;

function getItems()
{
    var listContext = new SP.AppContextSite(context, hostUrl);
    var list = listContext.get_web().get_lists().getByTitle('My Sample List');

    var camlQuery = new SP.CamlQuery();
    camlQuery.set_viewXml(
        '<View><Query><Where><Eq><FieldRef Name=\'Title\'/>' +
        '<Value Type=\'Text\'>Updated via JS CSOM</Value></Eq></Where></Query>' +
        '<RowLimit>10</RowLimit></View>'
    );
    items = list.getItems(camlQuery);
    context.load(items);
    context.executeQueryAsync(onGetListItemsSuccess,onFailed);
}

function onGetListItemsSuccess() {
```

```
    var listItemEnumerator = items.getEnumerator();

    while (listItemEnumerator.moveNext()) {
        var item = listItemEnumerator.get_current();
        alert(item.get_item('Title'));
    }
  }
}
```

27. Run and launch the app again. An alert appears stating, "`Updated via JS CSOM`" indicating that the app was able to query the list for the item it previously updated.

How It Works

In this exercise you created a SharePoint-hosted app using the new Napa tools available in Office 365. These tools allow for lightweight application development within a browser environment without requiring any client-side installation. The app used the JavaScript CSOM and then created a new list using the `SP.AppContextSite` method to call into the host Web and create and manipulate data. This call is necessary to ensure SharePoint brokers the calls to the host Web. If you attempted to make the calls directly to the host Web the browser would stop you due to cross-site scripting security requirements because the two sites are on a different domain.

The app first created a brand-new list based on the generic list type (the same as creating a custom list via the Web UI) and then inserted 10 new list items into it. Finally, the app updated one of those list items and then queried the list for that newly updated item. The JS CSOM wraps the underlying API calls to SharePoint for you and provides convenient wrapper objects and methods.

When you ran the application Napa packaged the application into an application package (`.app` file) and then deployed and installed it in SharePoint for you.

WATCH THE JAVASCRIPT CSOM AT WORK WITH FIDDLER

If you are interested in seeing the underlying API calls to SharePoint from the JavaScript CSOM you can do so with a tool called Fiddler. You can download Fiddler from: `http://www.fiddler2.com`. Using Fiddler you can see all the HTTP traffic between your computer and another such as Sharepoint.com, where Office 365 is hosted. When watching Fiddler look for requests to URLs with paths that end in: `/_vti_bin/client.svc/ProcessQuery`. You will see XML payloads being sent to SharePoint along with JSON responses.

Security and Cross-Domain Calls

JavaScript engines in modern browsers include security mechanisms that do not allow JavaScript to make calls across domains. This means that scripts can only get data from the domain where they were served. For example, if your page is served from `http://www.myserver.com` then JavaScript will not be allowed to make calls to `http://www.someotherserver.com`. This is to stop *cross-site scripting attacks* (XSS). Because of this limitation SharePoint also provides some mechanisms that let your SharePoint JS calls get at information in other domains including:

➤ `SP.AppContextSite`

➤ Web proxy

The `SP.AppContextSite` helper allows you to set up the CSOM `ClientContext` to make calls to other SharePoint sites. This site could be the host website or another site collection or server entirely. This helper proxies the calls you make via the SharePoint site on the domain where your JavaScript was served, thus getting around the cross-site scripting issues. You must use this technique if you are using Office 365 and your app is hosted on another domain, or if you are using app isolation for application deployment on premises. The latter option creates a subdomain just for your application. Your script will, therefore, need to call out beyond its own domain, and `AppContextSite` helps with that.

Additionally, you can use the Web proxy SharePoint to call other non-SharePoint endpoints. To use it you must create an `SP.WebRequestInfo` object and set up the URL and method for the call you want to make as follows:

```
var context = SP.ClientContext.get_current();

var crossDomainRequest = new SP.WebRequestInfo();

crossDomainRequest.set_url("http://looselytyped.net/feed/");
crossDomainRequest.set_method("GET");

var response = SP.WebProxy.invoke(context, crossDomainRequest);
```

This code proxies the call to the remote endpoint via SharePoint and returns the results. You can use this technique to call out to any HTTP/HTTPS-enabled endpoint; however, always remember the call goes through SharePoint and is therefore open to being viewed by someone with access to that server/service. HTTPS will not help because the call to SharePoint will be terminated and decrypted on the SharePoint Server prior to the request being made to the destination endpoint. However, this feature allows developers to get around many of the intricacies of cross-site scripting that are otherwise too complex to solve.

WINDOWS PHONE

Like with the .NET managed code and JavaScript CSOMs, CSOM libraries are available for both Windows Phone and Silverlight. This availability allows developers to use the same common library and patterns to integrate Windows Phone mobile apps in almost the same way they would in a JavaScript-based SharePoint-hosted application. The reason mobile apps are not exactly the same is because a developer must take into consideration a few additional things in mobile scenarios that are not as prevalent in other types of applications. For example, you must think about scenarios where the phone is not connected to a data network. Will it support offline data sync? What about on different types and speeds of data network? How do you connect to the SharePoint Server while you are not on the same network and possibly behind a firewall? Finally, what about your authentication options? These are all things you must consider and design for in your mobile applications.

The Windows Phone CSOM assists you with some of these issues; however, many others are up to you as a developer to work out how you want to support them. The Windows Phone CSOM offers support for new authentication options by supporting forms authentication, basic authentication, and Office 365 authentication. Previously, there wasn't a CSOM library that would run on Microsoft's Windows Phone, and communication was limited to Web service calls. Additionally, authentication was very hard, nearing impossible for many. Additional products that facilitated transforming forms authentication to Windows authentication put it out of reach for most. The new Windows Phone CSOM solves this problem by wrapping each of the authentication options for you so that you don't have to do the plumbing work. However, they still might offer some challenges such as not supporting Windows authentication (NTML), which many on-premises SharePoint implementations rely on. However, the authentication options that are supported certainly cover many of the scenarios that are more broadly applicable in mobile scenarios where the user is out of the office and connecting over the Internet.

Additionally, the Microsoft SharePoint SDK for Windows Phone 7.1 adds support in Visual Studio 2012 for SharePoint mobile project templates that allow you to get building applications faster with some convenient templates you can extend and build on.

The improvements offered for Windows Phone mobile applications with the 2013 release include:

➤ Visual Studio templates to get you started

➤ SharePoint Client-Side Object Model support

➤ Extended authentication support (forms, basic, Office 365)

Setup

To start building Windows Phone applications that communicate with SharePoint you need the following components:

➤ Visual Studio 2010

➤ Windows 7 or Vista

➤ A SharePoint Server on premises or an Office 365 site

➤ SharePoint SDK for Windows Phone 7.1

➤ Windows Phone SDK 7.1

> **NOTE** *SharePoint does not support being run on a Windows 7, Windows 8, or Vista operating system. If you don't have access to another machine running SharePoint 2013 then a good option is to sign up for Office 365.*

After you have the requisite applications and SDKs installed you can find the CSOM libraries for referencing in the following:

```
%ProgramFiles (x86)%\Microsoft SDKs\SharePoint\v15.0\Phone\v7.1\Libraries
```

This directory includes the three main DLLs you need:

➤ `Microsoft.SharePoint.Client.Phone.dll`

➤ `Microsoft.SharePoint.Client.Phone.Runtime.dll`

➤ `Microsoft.SharePoint.Phone.Application.dll`

Much like the Managed CSOM, you must reference these DLLs in your application to get access to the CSOM types required.

You may also start your project from one of the provided Visual Studio templates:

➤ The Windows Phone empty SharePoint application

➤ The Windows Phone SharePoint List application

These templates, by default, reference the required CSOM assemblies for you. The empty application, as its name suggests, gives you a blank canvas to create your application, whereas the list application template lays down some starter files to get you started building an app that reads and saves data in a SharePoint list. It walks you through a series of steps in a wizard that allows you to pick your SharePoint site, list, and fields with which you want to interact and then builds the appropriate views and view models using a Model-View-ViewModel (MVVM) design pattern (see Figure 9-6).

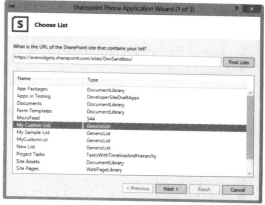

FIGURE 9-6

Querying

The only major difference between the Windows Phone CSOM and the Managed CSOM that you will not be familiar with from previous releases is in how you set up authentication. This step is required prior to making any CSOM calls. To do it you first pick the authentication option that your SharePoint site uses. You create a `ClientContext` object and then set up the `Credentials` property on it. In the following example the `Credentials` property is set to authenticate using Office 365:

```
ClientContext context = new ClientContext("https://contoso.sharepoint.com/");
Authenticator auth = new Authenticator();

auth.AuthenticationMode = ClientAuthenticationMode.MicrosoftOnline;
context.Credentials = auth;
```

> **NOTE** *The Windows Phone CSOM library assists your authenticating with SharePoint Online by opening a Sign In window that allows the user to sign in to the SharePoint site, as shown in Figure 9-7. Providing a username and password and circumventing this user interaction are not possible at this time.*

FIGURE 9-7

Alternatively, if your SharePoint Server uses forms authentication, then you can supply a username and password as follows:

```
auth.AuthenticationMode = ClientAuthenticationMode.FormsAuthentication;

auth.UserName = "Your_UserName";
auth.Password = "Password";
```

After you indicate your authentication options you are ready to start making CSOM calls to SharePoint. The code is almost the same as what you would use with the JavaScript or Managed CSOM; however, because Windows Phone Silverlight requires all network calls to be made asynchronously, you must cater callbacks in that manner for when your CSOM call succeeds or fails. To illustrate this process the following code makes a CSOM call to retrieve a list from the SharePoint Server:

```
List list = context.Web.Lists.GetByTitle("My Custom List");

// Load the query and execute the request to fetch data.
context.Load(list);

context.ExecuteQueryAsync((object obj, ClientRequestSucceededEventArgs args) =>
    {
        // success
        var SiteId = list.Id;
    },
    (object obj, ClientRequestFailedEventArgs args) =>
    {
        // query failed.
    });
```

As you can see the code defines a success and a failure function inline using a lambda expression. In your success function you can query and use the now "full" objects you asked for in your CSOM query.

The Windows Phone Silverlight Client-Side Object Model provides a great set of functionality to quickly get you up and running querying and interacting with SharePoint. You must take into account some differences with authentication and some runtime subtleties such as asynchronous callbacks. However, for the most part you can use the CSOM the same way you use the Managed CSOM.

REST AND ODATA

REpresentational State Transfer (REST) is a prevalent pattern for designing easily consumed data APIs over the Internet. You might hear an API described as RESTful if it is designed to be used over HTTP protocols and is in line with the principles of REST. These principles are as follows:

➤ **Client-Server:** The client is unaware of how the server stores or manages the data and doesn't need to know in order to use the API.

➤ **Stateless:** The server does not store any context or state about the calling client.

➤ **Cacheable:** The results of the calls to the API define themselves as being cacheable, or not.

➤ **Layered:** The client does not mind whether the call to the API is transmitted via common Internet technology such as load balancers.

➤ **Uniform Interface:** This provides a simple and known way to access data through standard URI addressing and self-describing so that a client can discover how to access data.

Many services offer REST-based APIs to ease access to their systems in a commonly understood manner. SharePoint 2013 builds on this foundation to offer access in a "RESTful" way to allow remote systems to interact with it in a platform agnostic and open way. For developers this means that using other helper libraries and frameworks for working with REST is a viable method, and the time to become proficient in a proprietary API is decreased.

OData or Open Data Protocol is a protocol definition for querying, finding, and updating data over HTTP. It offers defined methods for specifying common query operations and defines the format in which data is returned. SharePoint 2013 uses WCF Data Services v5.0 which implements the OData v3 specification. For more information on OData you can visit: `http://www.odata.org`.

Combining a RESTful Web API with OData gives a powerful combination of simple and easy-to-use APIs that have a well-defined interface and interaction model. In practical terms, having access to a RESTful OData-based API means the following for SharePoint developers:

➤ Standard URIs for addressing data

➤ Simple use of `GET`, `POST`, `PUT/MERGE`, and `DELETE HTTP` methods

➤ JSON or XML (ATOM) responses

➤ Simple query/filter semantics

The following sections describe each of the preceding points with simple-to-follow examples of how they are addressed in SharePoint 2013's implementation of its REST/OData Web API endpoints.

Getting Started with REST and OData

You can find SharePoint's REST/OData APIs in the `_API` URL space under each SharePoint site. For example:

```
https://servername/sitename/_api/
```

`_api` is the root URI for all REST/OData calls. SharePoint also supports calls to the `_vti_bin/client.svc/` URI to maintain backward compatibility with the previously available but more limited REST API in SharePoint 2010.

To query for data, issue a `GET` request. To update data you use either a `PUT` or `MERGE` request passing the data you want to update. But first you must specify which namespace it belongs in, such as Web, Site, or Search. Other groups include:

➤ `_api/web`

➤ `_api/site`

➤ `_api/search`

➤ `_api/publishing`

After you specify a namespace you must address an object, method, indexer, or property on it. Figure 9-8 depicts the URI address system.

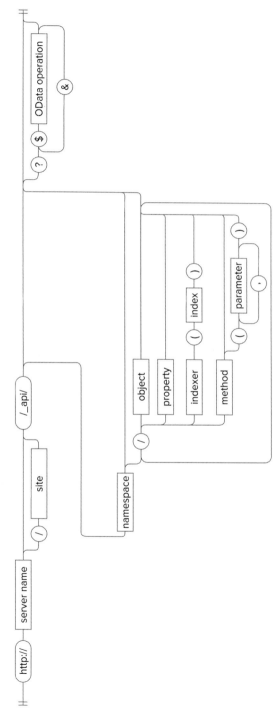

FIGURE 9-8

To retrieve the list of lists on a SharePoint site simply issue a GET request to the following:

```
https://servername/sitename/_api/web/lists
```

To retrieve the details about a list simply make a GET request to that list's URI indicated in the previous response's id property. For example:

```
https://servername/sitename/_api/Web/Lists(guid'f57d3ddc-4522-4145-a0fe-72abbd6ea8fc')
```

This example uses the Lists method with a parameter to specify the ID of the list. You could also use the list's entity name; for example:

```
https://servername/sitename/_api/Web/Lists/MoviesList
```

Additionally, you can address a list by name using the getbytitle function as follows. This addresses the list with its name versus its entity name:

```
https://servername/sitename/_api/Web/Lists/getbytitle('movies')/items
```

To access the items within a list add /items to the URI:

```
https://servername/sitename/_api/Web/Lists/MoviesList/Items
```

By default you will receive an ATOM feed XML response containing the lists in your site. If you want to receive a JSON payload instead, set the HTTP Accept header to application/json;odata=verbose. This signals that you want JSON instead of the default ATOM payload. JSON is typically lighter weight and better suited to mobile scenarios where speed is important.

Filtering and Selecting

When you query for data it's important to ask for only the data you really need. This keeps payload sizes down and speeds up delivery of the data. _Api uses OData semantics to let you do this by filtering records and selecting properties you want. The common operators you can use for manipulating the result set include the following:

- ➤ $filter, for filtering results
- ➤ $select, for selecting properties to return
- ➤ $expand, for expanding properties to return
- ➤ $orderby, for ordering results
- ➤ $top, for taking the top X results

The simplest way to learn about these operations is to try them out for yourself, as shown in the following exercise.

TRY IT OUT **OData Operations on Data**

In this exercise you try out querying and filtering for data using the REST/OData _Api in SharePoint 2013.

1. Create a new list in your SharePoint 2013 site by clicking Site Contents from the Quick Launch navigation.

2. Click Add an App.

3. Choose Custom List and call it **Movies**.

4. After the list is created, add some list items to it of your favorite movie titles.

5. Modify the URL to navigate to the following URI. Review the payload XML that is returned:

```
https://servername/sitename/_api/Web/Lists/MoviesList/Items
```

6. Modify the URL by adding (1) on the end (shown in the following code). This returns the first item in the list:

```
https://servername/sitename/_api/Web/Lists/MoviesList/Items(1)
```

7. Modify the URL and add a $filter parameter like the following, specifying the title of one of the movies you added earlier:

```
?$filter=Title eq 'Aliens'
```

8. Add a $select parameter to just select the Title property of the list item:

```
https://servername/sitename/_api/Web/Lists/_api/Lists/ /Items?
$filter=Title eq 'Aliens'&$select=Title
```

You should see a payload similar to the following:

```
<?xml version="1.0" encoding="utf-8" ?>
<feed xml:base="https://servername/sitename/_api/"
xmlns="http://www.w3.org/2005/Atom"
xmlns:d="http://schemas.microsoft.com/ado/2007/08/dataservices"
xmlns:m="http://schemas.microsoft.com/ado/2007/08/dataservices/metadata"
xmlns:georss="http://www.georss.org/georss" xmlns:gml="http://www.opengis.net/gml">
<id>0d01b697-f8f4-496a-bc66-81e4ab7d8208</id>
<title />
<updated>2012-11-03T07:07:21Z</updated>
<entry m:etag="""2""">
<id>f6126125-fddb-4651-bedd-d797c6ef06f4</id>
<category term="SP.Data.MoviesListItem"
scheme="http://schemas.microsoft.com/ado/2007/08/dataservices/scheme" />
<link rel="edit"
href="Web/Lists(guid'f57d3ddc-4522-4145-a0fe-72abbd6ea8fc')/Items(1)" />
<title />
<updated>2012-11-03T07:07:21Z</updated>
<author>
<name />
```

```
</author>
<content type="application/xml">
<m:properties>
<d:Title>Aliens</d:Title>
</m:properties>
</content>
</entry>
</feed>
```

Notice that only the `Title` property is returned.

9. Modify the `querystring` as follows to order your movie titles alphabetically:

```
?$select=Title&$orderby=Title
```

10. Modify the `querystring` as follows to just retrieve the first movie:

```
?$select=Title&$orderby=Title&$top=1
```

How It Works

In this exercise you queried SharePoint list data using the REST/OData API. When a request is made to SharePoint via this API, SharePoint uses WCF Data Services support for OData to parse and interpret the query on the URL. It then uses that information to translate the query into an internal SharePoint list query (called a `CAML` query) and executes the query. By adding OData support parameters to the URL you are able to refine the query you make to SharePoint and just return the data you specifically need.

Creating, Updating, and Deleting

The REST endpoints also accept requests to create, update, and delete data using `POST`, `PUT`, and `PATCH` commands.

➤ `POST` is used for creating data

➤ `PUT` is used for updating (all property values specified)

➤ `PATCH` is used for updating (specified properties only)

When using any of the preceding commands from JS running on a SharePoint page, you also must include the form digest from the page in the appropriate HTTP header:

```
X-RequestDigest: formDigest
```

You can get the `formDigest` from the object returned from a `POST` call to `/_api/contextinfo`, or if you are building a SharePoint-hosted app then you can simply get the value of the `formDigest` with this JQuery function:

```
$('#__REQUESTDIGEST').val()
```

You are then ready to send your create, update, or delete command to SharePoint. To practice doing so, take a look at the following activity.

TRY IT OUT   Creating a New List in the Host Web

In this example you use a SharePoint-hosted app using the Napa Office 365 Development Tools and use the REST/OData API to create a new list in the host Web. You must have the Napa application installed from the Office 365 marketplace prior to starting this exercise. The full JavaScript source for this exercise is available in the code download in the `MyODataJavaScriptApp.js` file.

1. Ensure you have Napa Office 365 Development Tools installed in your development site in Office 365.

2. Click Site Contents in your site navigation to see a list of all apps installed in your site.

3. Locate "Napa" Office 365 Development Tools in the list and click it, as shown in Figure 9-9.

4. Click Add New Project in the screen that appears.

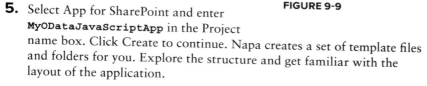

FIGURE 9-9

5. Select App for SharePoint and enter **MyODataJavaScriptApp** in the Project name box. Click Create to continue. Napa creates a set of template files and folders for you. Explore the structure and get familiar with the layout of the application.

6. In the lower left of the window click the wrench icon to open the Property panel for your application as shown in Figure 9-10.

FIGURE 9-10

7. Click the Permissions tab and set the permissions for Web under Content to Full Control.

8. Open the `Scripts` folder and then open the `App.js` file. This default file contains the JavaScript for your application.

9. Add the following code to the bottom of the file. This helps you get the various parameters that were passed to the page from the `querystring`:

```javascript
function getParams() {
    var params = {};
    location.search.split('?')[1].split('&').forEach(function (param) {
        var key = param.split('=')[0],
            val = decodeURIComponent(param.split('=')[1]);
        params[key] = val;
    });
    return params;
}
```

10. Replace the `sharePointReady()` function with the following. This code loads the `SP.Request Executor.js` JavaScript file that helps with cross-domain calls. The app needs this to call into the host Web because it's on a different domain name:

```
var params;
var scriptbase;

function sharePointReady() {
    context = new SP.ClientContext.get_current();
        params = getParams();
    scriptbase = params.SPHostUrl + "/_layouts/15/";
        $.getScript(scriptbase + "SP.RequestExecutor.js", execCrossDomainRequest);
}
```

11. Add the following new function. This uses a POST command to post a JSON payload with the new list information to the host web's REST API:

```
function execCrossDomainRequest()
{
    var executor;
    executor = new SP.RequestExecutor(params.SPAppWebUrl);

    var data = JSON.stringify({ '__metadata': { 'type': 'SP.List' },
        'AllowContentTypes': true, 'BaseTemplate': 100,
        'ContentTypesEnabled': true, 'Description': 'My list description',
        'Title': 'My New List' });

    var requestUri = params.SPAppWebUrl +
        "/_api/SP.AppContextSite(@target)/web/lists?@target='"
        + params.SPHostUrl + "'";

    executor.executeAsync(
        {
            url: requestUri,
            method: "POST",
            body: data,
            headers: {
                "accept": "application/json;odata=verbose",
                "content-type":"application/json;odata=verbose",
                "content-length": data.length,
                "X-RequestDigest": $('#__REQUESTDIGEST').val()
            },
            success: successHandler,
            error: errorHandler
        }
    );
}

function successHandler(data) {
    alert('success');
}

function errorHandler(data, errorCode, errorMessage) {
    alert("Failed :( Error:" + errorMessage);
}
```

12. Click the Run Project button in the bottom left of the window to test out the application. When it completes a message appears like the one shown in Figure 9-11.

13. Right-click the launch link and open your app in a new window to start your application. When you are prompted to trust your app, click Trust It to continue.

14. A JavaScript alert message appears, stating "Success." The app has created the list in the host Web.

15. Navigate to the host website by clicking the title of your site in the navigation.

16. Click Site Content to see a list of the apps/lists in your site. You can see the new list called My New List that your app created, as shown in Figure 9-12.

FIGURE 9-11

FIGURE 9-12

How It Works

In this exercise you created a SharePoint-hosted app that created a new list in the host or parent Web. To do this it used the REST/OData API and a POST command to post the creation information as a JSON payload in the request. Because the request was from one domain to another, you used the SP.RequestExecutor framework to proxy the call via the app Web to the host Web. This step was necessary due to the cross-domain security boundary browsers put on JavaScript.

The JSON payload consisted of a JSON representation of an SP.List object, along with the properties needed for creation such as the BaseTemplate ID and the Title.

By making a POST request along with this JSON to the /_api/SP.AppContextSite(@target)/web/lists URI, SharePoint proxies the request to the host Web for you along with the JSON. Because the request is a POST SharePoint knows you want to create something. SharePoint knows you want to create a list because the URI specifies the /web/list REST endpoint. SharePoint looks in the body of the request for the details on the list you want to create and creates it.

WATCH THE REST/ODATA CALLS WITH FIDDLER

If you are interested in seeing the HTTP(S) calls to SharePoint from the JavaScript you can do so with a tool called Fiddler. You can download Fiddler from http://www.fiddler2.com. Using Fiddler you can see all the HTTP traffic between your computer and another such as Sharepoint.com, where Office 365 is hosted. When watching Fiddler look for POST requests to /_api/SP.AppContextSite(@target)/web/lists. You can see JSON payloads being sent and received from SharePoint.

CLIENT-SIDE OBJECT MODEL API COVERAGE

As previously mentioned in this chapter, one of the original drawbacks with the prior implementation of the Client-Side Object Model was its lack of coverage for SharePoint APIs and access to functionality. In the past the CSOM was limited to mostly site, Web, and list operations as part of SharePoint Foundation.

SharePoint 2013's implementation of the CSOM significantly builds on the coverage of functionality available. It has now expanded to cover most of the surface area of SharePoint Server, not just SharePoint Foundation.

The CSOM is split into a number of different DLLs and namespaces based on functional areas they cater to, which are outlined for you in the following lists. Because the API coverage is so vast in 2013, these lists are only a summary of the most important and widely used areas. They are not exhaustive so you should check MSDN for full reference documentation. Discussing every area of the CSOM would be a whole book on its own so this section is designed to point you in the right area of the CSOM to look for the functionality you desire, as opposed to showing you examples of every area included.

Core functionality contains all the base-level CSOM functionality that you need for working with sites and data. These classes are included in `Microsoft.SharePoint.Client.dll`:

➤ Administration

➤ Event receivers

➤ Sharing

➤ Web Parts

➤ Analytics

➤ Business Data Catalog (BDC)

➤ Apps

➤ Lists

➤ Site

➤ Web

➤ User

➤ Site health

Content contains APIs for working with SharePoint's vast document management features such as Document Sets. These build on the foundation provided by the list and file classes with the features found in SharePoint Server Standard and Enterprise. Significant new features in 2013 surface in these classes with new APIs for managing metadata-driven navigation, video, and legal discovery features. These are included in `Microsoft.SharePoint.Client.Publishing.dll`, `Microsoft.SharePoint.Client.DocumentManagement.dll`, `Microsoft.SharePoint.Client.Taxonomy.dll`, and `Microsoft.Office.Client.Policy.dll`:

- ➤ Document management
- ➤ Discovery
- ➤ Document Sets
- ➤ Information policy
- ➤ Publishing
- ➤ Publishing navigation
- ➤ Taxonomy
- ➤ Video

User Profiles provide access to do things such as read and write to the microfeed on people's My Sites, access and update user profile information, and work with social data such as whom people follow and what they like. These classes are included in `Microsoft.SharePoint.Client .UserProfiles.dll`:

- ➤ Social
- ➤ User profiles
- ➤ Microfeed
- ➤ Reputation model

Search enables you to search and find information and documents in the search index. This is a great way to make fast queries for information in lieu of creating queries over lists and libraries in sites. The Query class can be found in `Microsoft.SharePoint.Client.Search.dll`.

Workflow classes let you find, start, create, and query for the status of workflows running in SharePoint. The Workflow Services classes are included in `Microsoft.SharePoint.Client .WorkflowServices.dll`.

Work Management in SharePoint 2013 offers enhanced capabilities for managing work in teams with features such as task lists and tracking. These classes are included in `Microsoft.SharePoint .WorkManagement.Client.dll`:

- ➤ Work management
- ➤ Tasks

Application Services is where services with APIs surface in the CSOM. A new service API in 2013 is the ability to submit jobs for automated translation. The Translation classes can be found in `Microsoft.Office.Client.TranslationServices.dll`.

Education in SharePoint 2013 adds site templates and features for managing classes in an education environment. These APIs let you manage things such as classes, lessons, assignments, communities, events, and grades. Education-related classes can be found in `Microsoft.Office.Client .Education.dll`.

SUMMARY

Building solutions that communicate with a remote system always hinges on that system providing great remote API support. SharePoint 2013 builds on the foundation laid in SharePoint 2010 and brings full support for the highly popular Internet API standards REST and OData. This offers developers new opportunities to interact with SharePoint like never before.

For those who are developing systems in .NET or Windows Phone, that same support is extended with the Managed Client-Side Object Model and Windows Phone CSOM to wrap the underlying protocol calls for you. It also adds out-of-the-box support for batching requests so that you don't need to think as much about ensuring your app performs the best it can.

For those building SharePoint apps, the CSOM is fully embraced because the JavaScript CSOM brings the benefits of batching and filtered results with the ease of the CSOM wrappers. Whether you are building a SharePoint-hosted App or a Provider-hosted app you can take advantage of these benefits to interact with SharePoint.

Finally, SharePoint 2013 has a robust and wide array of API coverage across the product, not just the list and data APIs in the previous release.

All of these improvements together provide a comprehensive and sophisticated API set that should meet the needs of almost all who want to interact with SharePoint remotely. All are conveniently located at _Api and based on open and documented standards over Internet standard protocols.

EXERCISES

Answers to Exercises can be found in Appendix A.

1. What are three types of Client-Side Object Model libraries provided in SharePoint 2013?

2. What additional capabilities does OData offer on top of the REST support provided in SharePoint?

3. What types of operations are supported with REST and OData in SharePoint 2013?

4. What are the key benefits of using the provided CSOM libraries versus rolling your own calls to the REST/OData APIs?

▶ WHAT YOU LEARNED IN THIS CHAPTER

ITEM	DESCRIPTION
CSOM	Client-Side Object Model libraries providing API access to SharePoint.
REST	REpresentational, State Transfer protocol. An API that adheres to REST principles laid out by the protocol's creator.
OData	Open Data Protocol for enhanced querying and resulting data over a REST API. A standard proposed by Microsoft and others to the OASIS standards consortium.
JSON	JavaScript Object Notation. A text standard-based representation of data and objects in a JavaScript-friendly format.
Cross-Site Scripting	When JavaScript code attempts to call code or endpoints in another domain from which it was served.
_API	The location at which all REST and OData API endpoints are surfaced by SharePoint 2013.

RECOMMENDED READING

Work with data in SharePoint 2013 — `http://msdn.microsoft.com/en-us/library/fp179893(v=office.15).aspx`

How to access SharePoint 2013 data from remote apps using the cross-domain library — `http://msdn.microsoft.com/en-us/library/fp179927(v=office.15).aspx`

10

Overview of OAuth in SharePoint 2013

WHAT YOU WILL LEARN IN THIS CHAPTER:

➤ Getting to Know OAuth

➤ Discovering how SharePoint 2013 uses OAuth

➤ Seeing how to use OAuth in Apps for SharePoint

WROX.COM CODE DOWNLOADS FOR THIS CHAPTER

The wrox.com code downloads for this chapter are found at: `http://www.wrox.com/ WileyCDA/WroxTitle/productCd-1118495845.html` on the Download Code tab. The code for this chapter is divided into the following major examples:

➤ SharePointTokenCacheApp.zip

➤ Tokens.zip

➤ S2SScript.txt

As you read in Chapter 9, "Overview of the Client-Side Object Model and REST APIs," SharePoint 2013 provides a new, rich set of APIs that you can use to work with SharePoint data and functionality. Key to using these APIs is the ability to securely call them and receive access when doing so. Additionally, SharePoint provides the ability to secure content to groups and individuals, and it is critical that anyone calling code be subject to the same set of authorization criteria as anyone using the SharePoint Web browser user interface. This ensures information is kept secure and that only people with the correct privileges can access it. To do this effectively SharePoint 2013 has built-in support for the common and open authorization standard OAuth 2.0.

This chapter explains the new application authentication and authorization features available to developers. You will learn how applications can make calls to SharePoint to perform operations such as retrieving data as part of building SharePoint applications. This chapter also provides a brief overview of OAuth and explains how to set up OAuth to grant applications access to resources in SharePoint.

INTRODUCTION TO OAUTH

OAuth is an open standard managed by the Internet Engineering Task Force and is designed to allow applications to access services in a Web-friendly manner on behalf of an application or user.

Some might ask, "Why not just give the caller my username and password?" This unfortunately poses some issues that OAuth avoids:

➤ The app can do everything and anything your account can do. This means that if the calling code had your username and password it could, for example, change your password or do things that you would rather it didn't have access to. Because the app has your username and password it is as if you are making the calls and the service has no idea who the real caller is.

➤ To the service, all calls look the same whether it is you or the calling app making the calls. This means keeping an audit trail is almost pointless because there is no way to tell who the caller really was if the same username is being used each time. Additionally, if you give your username and password to multiple services and one of them deletes information, you have no way to know which one it was. Obviously, this could cause some problems if you are not careful.

➤ You can't revoke access to a particular service without changing your password. This means that you would need to update your password on all those services that you want to continue working. If a few services are involved this task can be error-prone and cumbersome.

Here is a simple analogy to help explain this concept. Imagine an office building that is secured using swipe cards. A lot of sensitive information is stored in this office building and many people work in it each day. Now imagine each of those workers were issued the exact same swipe card. From the door lock–system logs you couldn't tell who was accessing the building and when. Additionally, if you fired a worker and she didn't give her swipe card back you would need to reissue everyone one else a new key. This is the same as sharing your username and password.

To solve these issues, OAuth introduces the concept of an *application identity* or *application principle*. This is simply an identity given to an app much the same way a user has a username and password. It offers the ability to control and manage access to resources at an application level versus a user level, and therefore you don't need to give an app your username and password to access any desired resources. Furthermore, this means an app's access can be monitored, audited, and revoked if needed. For an app to gain access to a service the user must deliberately grant that specific application access to that specific service. Access is only granted once that app identity is checked and verified as valid with permissions to the resource. This access may be scoped to specific resources within the service. This means, for example, that the user could grant the app access to some data, but not to change the user's password. This also means that a user may revoke an app's access to the service at any time without needing to affect other applications' access.

So, revisiting the analogy, if the building security system used an OAuth style access system, each worker in the building would be granted an ID, and then his swipe card with that ID on it would be granted access to the particular areas of the building that he was allowed to be in. When a worker is revoked access, the building owner simply revokes access for that worker's ID in the system. That way when the worker tries to swipe in he is denied access. Or, in the case when a worker changes departments, the building owner simply signifies that for that particular ID the person is now denied access to Level 1, for example, and is allowed access to Level 2. It's the same in OAuth. Each app (the equivalent of a person in the analogy) is granted an ID and a set of privileges. When the caller tries to access a resource, the ID is verified and a check is made to ensure he is allowed access to that particular resource. If access is allowed, the call proceeds and if not, the caller is denied.

OAuth is supported and used by many large services on the Internet today such as Facebook and Twitter. Numerous open source libraries exist for various languages to assist with the standard OAuth messages involved in authorizing and calling a service. The SharePoint 2013 app framework and tools also include many helper libraries and functions to wrap a lot of the underlying OAuth protocol exchanges. In many cases a developer might never be aware of the communication and messages OAuth uses behind the scenes.

OAUTH IN SHAREPOINT 2013

SharePoint apps use OAuth to authorize calls to SharePoint APIs. When an app calls an API in SharePoint to, for example, get some list data, SharePoint checks that the app identity is valid and has permissions to the resource; for example, a list. Additionally, the app may pass information about what the calling user identity is so that SharePoint can also check that the user has access to the resource. When discussing OAuth in the context of SharePoint, the following standard naming conventions are commonly used and therefore worth understanding:

➤ *Content owner*: The user who installs the app and grants the application access to particular resources.

➤ *Client app*: The SharePoint app that uses an API to access and make calls to the content server (SharePoint).

➤ *Content server*: The SharePoint environment that has the resources the client app wants to access.

➤ *Authentication server*: A service that both the client app and content server trust that creates the various tokens used in the OAuth process. In SharePoint the Authentication server is either Azure Access Control Services (ACS) in the case of Office 365 or a Security Token Service (STS) hosted with SharePoint in the case of SharePoint on premises.

When you're building SharePoint apps, the three different app types fall into two distinct categories in regard to authentication and authorization:

➤ **Internally authenticated apps:** Includes SharePoint-hosted apps

➤ **Externally authenticated apps:** Includes Autohosted and Provider-hosted apps

The key difference between these two categories is that externally authenticated apps must explicitly authenticate with SharePoint, whereas internally authenticated apps do not. Take, for example, the case of a SharePoint-hosted app with some client-side code that uses the JavaScript Client-Side Object Model (CSOM) to create a SharePoint list item. In this case the JS code doesn't need to authenticate explicitly with SharePoint. This is considered internal authentication because the code is served from the SharePoint domain.

An externally authenticated app is one where the code runs outside of the security boundary of SharePoint. For example, when your app code is running in Azure, that code must authenticate with SharePoint using OAuth prior to making API calls. As part of this process several important IDs, secrets, and "tokens" are used to authenticate and authorize a user and calls to the APIs:

➤ Client ID

➤ Client secret

➤ Context token

➤ Access token

The *client ID* and *client secret* are pre-issued identifiers and secret strings that only SharePoint and the app know about. These are shared and are used to sign the various tokens involved in the process.

The *context token* includes information about who the caller is and the Security Token Service (STS) that signed and issues tokens for this server. It also includes a "refresh token" that is used to request access tokens.

The *access token* is a token passed when accessing an API and is requested from the STS by the app when it needs to make calls.

The following sections show you how to create and manage client IDs and secrets, how the various parts of the authentication flows work, and how apps are granted access to various SharePoint resources.

CREATING AND MANAGING APPLICATION IDENTITIES

In the previous section you saw how applications have an identity as well as users. When an app takes an action in the context of a user, SharePoint records this information. For example, when a SharePoint list item is created or modified and you later view that list item, you will see the Last Modified and Created information listed as "by *My Simple App* on behalf of *Joe Bloggs*," where *My Simple App* is the name of the application (application principle) and *Joe Bloggs* is the name of the user for whom the app made the request. The following activity shows how this works in practice and helps you get started working with application identities by creating a simple application and an associated application identity.

TRY IT OUT Application Identities (ApplicationIdentity.js)

In this exercise you create a simple SharePoint-hosted application that uses the JavaScript CSOM to talk to SharePoint using the Napa tools in Office 365. You need the Napa application installed from the Office 365 marketplace prior to starting this exercise. You can find the completed code for this exercise in the ApplicationIdentity.js file included with the code download for this chapter.

1. In your SharePoint site create a new Custom list called Gadgets. Do this by clicking in Site Contents, and click Add App. Select Custom List from the list and call it **Gadgets**. Click Create.

2. Ensure you have Napa Office 365 Development Tools installed in your development site in Office 365.

3. Click Site Contents in your site navigation to see a list of all apps installed in your site.

4. Locate Napa Office 365 Development Tools in the list and click it.

5. Click Add New Project.

6. Select App for SharePoint and enter **MyNewApp** in the Project name box. Click Create to continue. Napa creates a set of template files and folders for you. Explore the structure and get familiar with the layout of the application.

7. Open the Scripts folder and then open the `App.js` file. This default file contains the JavaScript for your application.

8. Replace the contents of the file with the following code:

```
var context;
var web;
var user;

// This code runs when the DOM is ready. It ensures the SharePoint
// script file sp.js is loaded and then executes sharePointReady()
$(document).ready(function () {
    SP.SOD.executeFunc('sp.js', 'SP.ClientContext', sharePointReady);
});

var hostUrl;

function sharePointReady() {
    context = new SP.ClientContext.get_current();
    web = context.get_web();
    hostUrl = getParameterByName('SPHostUrl');
    createItems();
}

function createItems()
{
    var listContext = new SP.AppContextSite(context, hostUrl);
    var list = listContext.get_web().get_lists().getByTitle('Gadgets');
    var itemCreateInfo = new SP.ListItemCreationInformation();
    var newListItem = list.addItem(itemCreateInfo);
    newListItem.set_item('Title', 'Microsoft Surface 32GB with Touch Cover');
    newListItem.update();
    context.load(newListItem);
    context.executeQueryAsync(onCreateListItemsSuccess,onFailed);
}

function onCreateListItemsSuccess() {
    alert('List Item created');
}

// This function is executed if the preceding call fails
function onFailed(sender, args) {
```

```
      alert('Failed. Error:' + args.get_message());
}


function getParameterByName(name)
{
  name = name.replace(/[\[]/, "\\\[").replace(/[\]]/, "\\\]");
  var regexS = "[\\?&]" + name + "=([^&#]*)";
  var regex = new RegExp(regexS);
  var results = regex.exec(window.location.search);
  if(results == null)
    return "";
  else
    return decodeURIComponent(results[1].replace(/\+/g, " "));
}
```

9. In the lower left area of the window click the wrench icon to open the Property panel for your application.

10. Click the Permissions tab and set the permissions for Web under Content to Full Control.

11. Run the project using the Run Project button in the bottom left of the window; a permissions request window appears, asking you to grant the application full control of the site. Click Trust It.

12. An alert window appears showing, "List Item created." Click OK.

13. Check that your list was created by clicking the link in the top left of the page to get to your developer site. Click Site Content and find the Gadgets list. You should see the new list item that was created.

14. View the list item by clicking the "..." beside the list item and selecting View Item.

15. Review the Created At information at the bottom of the page. It will say "by `MyNewApp` on behalf of."

How It Works

In this exercise you created a SharePoint-hosted application using the Napa tools that created a new list item in a SharePoint list. The app created the list item on behalf of the user, and you can see this information in the Created By and Modified By fields on the newly created list item. This is because when the app makes the CSOM call, the application identity is passed and SharePoint understands that the call is being made on behalf of a user via an application.

An application identity consists of an ID, name, and a domain where the app is hosted. The type of application and environment will dictate a particular method for creating new application identities/registrations.

The manual options for creating new registrations include the following:

➤ Manually register a new identity in SharePoint.

➤ Obtain a new identity for the app market from the Seller Dashboard.

➤ Register a new identity using PowerShell.

In some scenarios, creation of an app identity is automated for you. Those are as follows:

➤ Deploying and debugging via Visual Studio during development

➤ Using the Autohosted app type

During development Visual Studio takes care of temporarily creating an app identity for you during the deployment and configuration of your application so that you don't have to. A new one is created each time you deploy, but you can't rely on these identities for long periods of time. SharePoint Online will also take care of the creation of an app identity for you upon deployment and installation of an Autohosted app, however you must create an app identity when you are *not* building an Autohosted app *and* when one or more of the following apply:

➤ You have completed development and are ready to deploy your app.

➤ You are building a Provider-hosted app for either SharePoint Online or SharePoint on premises.

➤ You are building an app for the marketplace in SharePoint Online.

> **NOTE** *If you are packaging your application and will be distributing it via the marketplace in SharePoint Online you must obtain an application identity via the Seller Dashboard. To read more about this process refer to Chapter 8, "Distributing SharePoint 2013 Apps."*

If you want to deploy the app locally on a SharePoint on-premises deployment or privately (not via the marketplace) in SharePoint Online then you must manually register a new application identity. You can do it via the `AppRegNew.aspx` page, which is located at: `http://yourservername/_layouts/15/appregnew.aspx`. `AppRegNew.aspx` and allows you to either specify or generate a client ID (another name for app ID) and a client secret. Additionally, it requires you to specify a friendly name for the app and the domain that hosts the app. After you complete a new registration, a page appears listing the details. You should make a note of these somewhere safe. You need them to update the manifest files in Visual Studio.

After you have a static client ID and client secret you then must update the values in the following locations:

➤ In the app project `AppManifest.xml` file, change the `AppPrincipal`, `RemoteWebApplication` client ID node as follows:

```
<AppPrincipal>
    <RemoteWebApplication ClientId="<Client ID Here>"/>
</AppPrincipal>
```

➤ In the `Web.config` file in the app code project, change the `AppSettings`, client ID, and client secret nodes as follows:

```
<appSettings>
    <add key="ClientId" value="<Client ID Here>" />
    <add key="ClientSecret" value="<Client Secret Here>" />
</appSettings>
```

➤ The app domain is the host name of where your application remote Website and code is hosted. This could be a Website in Azure; for example, www.contoso.com.

➤ The redirect URI is used for when apps request permissions on the fly versus explicitly in the app manifest file. This should be the URL of the page that accepts the authorization code postback from SharePoint after the authorization has been processed. This field can be left blank if you are not requesting permissions on the fly from SharePoint.

The following exercise walks you through creating an application identity in SharePoint Online.

TRY IT OUT   **Creating an App Identity**

In this exercise you create a new application identity registration in SharePoint Online. You need a SharePoint Online site and need to be a site collection administrator.

1. In your SharePoint site navigate to /_layouts/15/appregnew.aspx.

2. Click Generate beside App ID and App Secret.

3. In the Title field type **My First App**.

4. In the App Domain, type the domain name of the location you will deploy your Provider-hosted app to; for example, **www.contoso.com**.

5. Leave the Redirect URI blank.

6. Click Create.

7. A set of information appears about your application identity. Copy this information to a safe location. It will look similar to the following:

```
The app identifier has been successfully created.
App Id:  b5759c4d-9572-4154-a569-8ad254c2c7ca
App Secret:  U6xxmVq1txVitMiqTffVt/G9c+JjXbMwNFijziv2YxU=
Title:  My First App
App Domain:  www.contoso.com
Redirect URI:
```

How It Works

In this exercise you created a new application identity. Behind the scenes SharePoint creates the registration and then saves it by way of the application management shared service. It is persisted to the services database and can be read from any of the SharePoint Servers in the farm.

You can also look up some of the details about a registered app using the AppInv.aspx page, which is located at: http://yourservername/_layouts/15/appinv.aspx. You must supply the client ID for the app. Note that the page doesn't provide the client secret of your app, just the display name and host domain information.

APPLICATION AUTHENTICATION

Now that you understand what application identities are and how to create and set them up in SharePoint, you can take a look at how those identities are used as part of the authentication between applications and SharePoint.

Whenever an app that is subject to external authentication needs to make an API call into SharePoint it must first confirm it has a valid and usable set of authentication tokens to do so. The two key tokens are:

➤ Context token

➤ Access token

The *context token* is passed when an application is launched. It contains information about who the calling user is and details about the SharePoint site where the application was launched. The *access token* is used when an application makes a call to a SharePoint API.

Several steps make up the authentication flow when these two tokens are issued and used, but there are five main occurrences that make up high-level flow when a user launches an app in SharePoint:

1. User logs into SharePoint.

2. SharePoint gets a context token for the user.

3. Context token is passed to the app when launched.

4. App uses the context token to request an access token.

5. Access token is passed with API calls.

The full process for app authentication is slightly more complex, as shown in Figure 10-1. This detailed, step-by-step version of process is explained in the following steps:

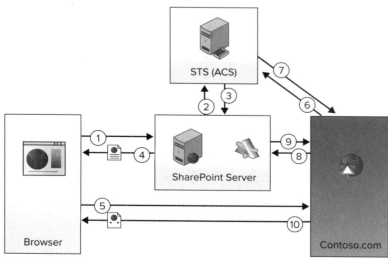

FIGURE 10-1

1. User requests a SharePoint page with an App Part included.

2. SharePoint requests a context token from ACS for the user, including context information about the user and a refresh token that can be used for requesting access tokens.

3. ACS returns the signed context token to SharePoint.

4. SharePoint returns the page with an iFrame for the App Part, including the content token as a query string parameter on the URL for the iFrame source.

5. The browser renders the page and iFrame, and a request to the remote app is made to render the App Part iFrame contents. The context token is passed on the URL.

6. The app code validates the content token to ensure its authenticity using a shared secret that only the app and SharePoint/ACS know. The app then uses the refresh token to request an access token from ACS.

7. ACS returns an access token. These can be cached and used multiple times. The expiry time is provided in the token so the app knows when to request a new one.

8. The app makes an API call to SharePoint such as a CSOM call or REST API request. The access token is included in the authorization HTTP header.

9. The SharePoint API call returns the data requested.

10. The app renders the page content and the result is returned.

> **NOTE** *Both the context token and access tokens are Base64-encoded JavaScript Object Notation (JSON) objects that follow the JSON Web Token (JWT) format. If you are interested in viewing the full structure of the tokens you can Base64-decode the tokens, which gives you the JSON-formatted token.*

In the case of SharePoint Online Azure Control Services (ACS), the STS is involved in creating both the context token and access tokens. In purely on-premises situations, SharePoint acts as the STS. You can find more on this topic later in this chapter in the "On-Premises App Authentication" section.

To assist with the various token-centric processes, such as validating tokens and requesting new ones from code, the default Visual Studio 2012 SharePoint application templates provide a helper class called TokenHelper. It wraps up the calls to ACS and so on to simplify the process for you.

The best way to illustrate some of the helper functions and classes that TokenHelper.cs provides is to walk through an example exercise, as follows.

TRY IT OUT   Using TokenHelper (Tokens.zip)

In this exercise you create a simple SharePoint Autohosted application and use the TokenHelper class to access the ContextToken passed. You can find the code for this exercise in the download package for this chapter in the file called Tokens.zip.

1. Create a new SharePoint app project in Visual Studio by choosing File ➪ New ➪ Project. Pick the App for SharePoint 2013 project template.

2. Name your app **SharePointApp** and click OK.

3. If required, specify the URL of your SharePoint online site for the site to use for debugging.

4. Ensure Autohosted is selected in the hosting type drop-down menu.

5. Click Finish.

6. Locate and open the `TokenHelper.cs` file.

7. Find the `CreateJsonWebSecurityTokenHandler` function and make the function public instead of private as follows:

   ```
   public static JsonWebSecurityTokenHandler CreateJsonWebSecurityTokenHandler()
   ```

8. Locate and open the `Default.aspx.cs` file.

9. Replace the `Page_Load` function with the following code:

   ```
   protected void Page_Load(object sender, EventArgs e)
   {
       var contextToken = TokenHelper.GetContextTokenFromRequest(Page.Request);
       var hostWeb = Page.Request["SPHostUrl"];

       JsonWebSecurityTokenHandler tokenHandler =
       TokenHelper.CreateJsonWebSecurityTokenHandler();
       SecurityToken securityToken = tokenHandler.ReadToken(contextToken);
       JsonWebSecurityToken jsonToken = securityToken as JsonWebSecurityToken;
       SharePointContextToken token = SharePointContextToken.Create(jsonToken);

       Response.Write("<b>Context Token:</b> " + contextToken);
       Response.Write("<b>STS:</b> " + token.SecurityTokenServiceUri);
   }
   ```

10. Press F5 to run and debug the project.

11. If prompted to trust the application, click Trust It.

12. When presented with the list of apps in your site, locate and click your new application.

13. A Web page appears that contains the Base64-encoded context token and the URL of the STS that issued the token. In the case of ACS it is as follows:

    ```
    https://accounts.accesscontrol.windows.net/tokens/OAuth/2
    ```

14. Copy the `ContextToken` value to the clipboard.

15. In a new window, navigate to `www.base64decode.org` and paste the `ContextToken` into the Value to decode box.

16. Click Decode to decode the Base64-encoded string. A JSON representation of your `ContextToken` appears, and you can see where all the values passed are included.

How It Works

In this exercise you created a new application that accepted the `ContextToken` from SharePoint. You used the `TokenHelper` class to assist with decoding and parsing out the `SharePointContextToken` object. Contained within the decoded context token is information about the token, including the issuing party — in this case, Azure Access Control Services acting as the STS.

App and User Context in API Calls

SharePoint provides the ability for apps to make calls to SharePoint with access tokens that are either on behalf of a user or without user context, also known as app-only context. When an access token is used that is on behalf of a user, SharePoint treats the call as if the user is making the call. This means it is subject to the same permissions that user has. Additionally, an app can make an app-only call to SharePoint, which means no user context is passed and only the permissions that the app has been granted apply.

The `TokenHelper` class provides helper methods for getting each of these types of tokens. To get an access token that includes the calling user's context, use the following method:

```
TokenHelper.GetAccessToken
```

To get an app-only access token, use the following method:

```
TokenHelper.GetAppOnlyAccessToken
```

See the "Application Authorization" section later in this chapter for more on app and user authorization and how permissions are determined by SharePoint.

Managing Tokens in Your Application

As previously mentioned, when an application is launched by a user a context token is passed to it. After this has happened it is up to the application to handle the tokens and potentially store them for future use or pass between app pages. These tasks are left to the application to manage because SharePoint has no knowledge of the inner workings of the application. The developer must decide how she wants to manage these tokens when the application passes them after it is launched. Some basic options are available, including the following:

- ➤ Cache the token for a period of time.
- ➤ Pass the token around as needed but don't store it.

To assist with caching, the tokens provide a `CacheKey` and an expiry that can make caching more straightforward for the developer. The `CacheKey` is a property on the token that is unique to that particular token. It can be used, as the name suggests, as a primary key for that token in a cache of the developer's choosing, such as ASP.NET application state. Additionally, the expiry time can be used in the application to flush the old tokens from the cache after they have expired.

CACHE THE REFRESH TOKEN

As part of the context token, SharePoint provides another token called a refresh token. This token is typically valid for six months and can be used to request access tokens for a particular user. This capability is very handy if your app needs to make calls into SharePoint as a particular user when the user isn't using the app; for example, on a timed basis such as a timer job.

The following exercise walks through a simple example of how to use ASP.NET application state to cache the appropriate tokens so that they can be used between page requests.

TRY IT OUT   Caching Tokens (TokenCache.zip)

In this exercise you create an Autohosted application that, when run, receives and then caches the ContextToken using application state. You can find the code for this exercise in the download package for this chapter in the file called TokenCache.zip.

1. Create a new SharePoint App project in Visual Studio by choosing File ➪ New ➪ Project. Select the App for SharePoint 2013 project template.

2. Name your app **SharePointTokenCacheApp** and click OK.

3. If required, specify the URL of your SharePoint online site for the site to use for debugging.

4. Ensure Autohosted is selected in the hosting type drop-down menu.

5. Click Finish.

6. Locate and open the TokenHelper.cs file.

7. Find the CreateJsonWebSecurityTokenHandler function and make the function public instead of private as follows:

```
public static JsonWebSecurityTokenHandler CreateJsonWebSecurityTokenHandler()
```

8. Locate and open the Default.aspx file and add the following code inside the <div> tags:

```
<asp:Button ID="Button1" runat="server" Text="Process" OnClick="Button1_Click"/>
```

9. Locate and open the Default.aspx.cs file and replace the contents with the following code:

```
using System;
using System.Collections.Generic;
using System.IdentityModel.Tokens;
using System.Linq;
using System.Web;
using System.Web.UI;
using System.Web.UI.WebControls;
using Microsoft.IdentityModel.S2S.Tokens;

namespace SharePointTokenCacheAppWeb.Pages
{
```

```
public partial class Default : System.Web.UI.Page
{
    protected void Page_Load(object sender, EventArgs e)
    {
        if (!this.IsPostBack)
        {
            var contextToken =
            TokenHelper.GetContextTokenFromRequest(Page.Request);
            var hostWeb = Page.Request["SPHostUrl"];

            JsonWebSecurityTokenHandler tokenHandler =
            TokenHelper.CreateJsonWebSecurityTokenHandler();
            SecurityToken securityToken = tokenHandler.ReadToken(contextToken);
            JsonWebSecurityToken jsonToken =
            securityToken as JsonWebSecurityToken;
            SharePointContextToken token =
            SharePointContextToken.Create(jsonToken);

            Application[token.CacheKey] = contextToken;

            Button1.CommandArgument = token.CacheKey;

        }
    }

    protected void Button1_Click(object sender, EventArgs e)
    {
        var contextToken =
        (string)Application[((Button) sender).CommandArgument];
        var hostWeb = Page.Request["SPHostUrl"];

        using (var clientContext =
        TokenHelper.GetClientContextWithContextToken(hostWeb, contextToken,
        Request.Url.Authority))
        {
            clientContext.Load(clientContext.Web, web => web.Title);
            clientContext.ExecuteQuery();
            Response.Write(clientContext.Web.Title);
            clientContext.ToString();
        }
    }
}
```

10. Press F5 to run and debug the project.

11. If prompted to trust the application, click Trust It.

12. When presented with the list of apps in your site, locate and click your new application.

13. A Web page appears with the Process button on it. Click the button. The page will display the Title of your Website.

How It Works

In this exercise you created a new application that cached the `ContextToken` passed to it in the ASP .NET application cache. It used the `CacheKey` property to uniquely key the token in the cache. This allowed subsequent page requests to locate the `ContextToken` in the cache and use it to make API calls to SharePoint. Without caching the `ContextToken` in this manner, subsequent page requests or postbacks wouldn't include the `ContextToken` in the `POST` parameters and API calls wouldn't be possible.

APPLICATION AUTHORIZATION

After an application call to a SharePoint API has been authenticated, the next step in the chain of security processing is to check whether the app and user have the appropriate rights to the resources they are attempting to access. These permissions can be assigned two ways:

➤ Statically

➤ Dynamically

Statically assigned permissions are defined as one or more permission requests in the `AppManifest.xml` file. They are defined by the application developer and are the permissions that the app requests when it is installed. When a user adds the app to the site, she is presented with a consent dialog screen, as shown in Figure 10-2, asking for the user to grant the permissions being asked for.

FIGURE 10-2

Note that granting permissions is an "all or nothing" operation. A user cannot, for example, only grant one of the two permissions being asked for. This is another example of why asking only for the permissions that app needs at a minimum to run is important.

After a user grants the application the appropriate permissions, they are recorded in SharePoint in the application management shared service. They are then referred to when an app makes an API call for access to resources.

Additionally, an application may dynamically request permissions on the fly during execution. This allows for scenarios where the application might not know what resources it needs to begin with, or when it might start with only basic rights and then request more as appropriate. This is discussed more in the next section, "Requesting Permissions Dynamically."

> **NOTE** *When designing your application, only statically define the minimum permissions the app needs to run. Defining permissions that give the application full control over an entire site will cause the user and admin concern if these permissions are not needed.*

Permission requests for apps are analogous to granting permissions for a user to access a resource. For example, granting a user contributor access on a document library is the same as granting an application read/write-access on that library.

You statically define permission requests in the `AppManifest.xml` file. Here is an example:

```
<AppPermissionRequests>
  <AppPermissionRequest Scope="http://sharepoint/content/sitecollection/web"
  Right="FullControl" />
</AppPermissionRequests>
```

Two pieces of information are needed in a permissions request:

➤ Scope

➤ Right

The *scope* defines what component the permission request is for. It is *not* a URL although it looks like one. These components (also referred to as a permissions provider) are from a defined list. They cover various aspects of SharePoint such as sites, lists, and libraries. Some example scopes include the following:

➤ `http://sharepoint/search`

➤ `http://sharepoint/content/sitecollection/web`

➤ `http://sharepoint/content/sitecollection/web/list`

➤ `http://sharepoint/projectserver`

➤ `http://sharepoint/social/microfeed`

➤ `http://sharepoint/taxonomy`

> **NOTE** *The preceding list is not exhaustive and only shows a short list of the possible scopes.*

The *right* defines what level of access is being requested. For example, the application might be asking only for read-access to a particular resource versus read/write access. The various rights available vary for each particular scope. The most common rights are:

➤ Read

➤ Write

➤ Manage

➤ FullControl

By combining a scope with a right, developers can define a vast number of permissions.

Requesting Permissions Dynamically

Many situations exist where an application might not know ahead of time what permissions it needs. Take, for example, the situation where an app reads documents in document libraries and does something with them. In this situation the app will not know ahead of time what document libraries those documents reside in, or how many document libraries they are stored in. This means the application might need to request permissions dynamically from the user. SharePoint 2013 has a method for doing this by prompting the user to allow additional permission requests by redirecting the user to another consent dialog. The `TokenHelper` class has a helper method to assist with constructing the URL for the consent page:

```
TokenHelper.GetAuthorizationUrl(sharePointSiteUrl.ToString(),
"Web.Read List.Write",
"https://myapp.com/RedirectAccept.aspx"));
```

This helper method returns a URL pointing at the `OAuthAuthorize.aspx` page along with the permissions you are requesting, the app client ID, scope, and the redirect-accept URI. You can then direct the user to that URL using `Response.Redirect()`. Another possibility is to pop up a modal dialog with JavaScript containing an iFrame to this page. After the permissions request is complete, SharePoint redirects back to the URI you specify (in the preceding example, `RedirectAccept.aspx`) along with an authorization code.

```
https://myapp.com/RedirectAccept.aspx?code=authcode
```

That authorization code found in the query string parameter `code` can then be used to request an access token that includes those additionally granted permissions. The `TokenHelper` class has a method for assisting with this:

```
TokenHelper.GetAccessToken(authorizationCode, targetPrincipalName,
targetUri.Authority, targetRealm, redirectUri).AccessToken;
```

This access token is also cacheable. It will expire, however, so you should also cache the refresh token given back, which will allow the app to request additional access tokens when they expire.

`TokenHelper` also has a method for getting a CSOM `ClientContext` object directly using the authorization code:

```
TokenHelper.GetClientContextWithAuthorizationCode(targetUrl,targetPrincipalName,
authorizationCode, targetRealm, redirectUri)
```

App-Only Policy

The three "contexts" in which authorization is validated in SharePoint are as follows:

➤ User-only policy

➤ App+user policy

➤ App-only policy

User-only policy is what is evaluated when users are using the SharePoint Web UI. SharePoint checks their permissions to do certain actions/activities and either allows or denies the activity.

The *app+user policy* is typically used when an app makes an API call to SharePoint. In this policy both the app and the user must have appropriate permissions/rights in SharePoint to complete the action successfully. If the call is being made to a document library the user does not have access to, the call will fail — access is denied. Likewise, if the app does not have permissions, the call will also fail.

In some situations an application might not want or need to act on behalf of a user. Additionally, there may be instances when you want to temporarily allow users to take actions on resources that they don't have explicit permissions on. This later scenario is analogous to temporarily elevating permissions using the full-trust code model of the past.

In these scenarios the application model allows apps to make calls to SharePoint only in the context of the application and not the user. This is called "app-only" context. Therefore, *app-only policy* means that only the app's permissions are checked when the call is made, so if the user does not have access to a resource but the app does, the call will still succeed. As mentioned earlier, this is a good way to temporarily elevate permissions for a user. The app can be granted permissions on things that the user doesn't normally have access to. An example of when this could be useful is for situations such as submitting a document to a secure location or perhaps approving a document that the user doesn't have access to via SharePoint and only has access to via the application.

To use the app-only policy you must do two things:

➤ Allow app-only permission in the app manifest.

➤ Create an app-only access token.

An app defines that it needs app-only access in the `AppManifest.xml` file by the developer setting the `AllowAppOnlyPolicy` attribute as follows:

```
<AppPermissionRequests AllowAppOnlyPolicy="true">
```

> **NOTE** *Because of the additional capabilities this access allows, only certain site collection administrators can grant applications requesting this permission.*

At run time an app-only access token must be created in order to make calls just like the application does. Again, the `TokenHelper` class makes this easy with the following helper function:

```
TokenHelper.GetAppOnlyAccessToken(contextToken.TargetPrincipalName,
sharepointUrl.Authority, contextToken.Realm).AccessToken;
```

ON-PREMISES APP AUTHENTICATION WITH S2S

In some situations an organization might need its SharePoint environment and solutions to be purely on-premises. This could be for security reasons, technical reasons such as in disconnected network situations, or simply because on-premises solutions are the company policy. In these situations, using Office 365, Azure Access Control Services (ACS), and apps hosted in Azure will not work. An alternative is to host the apps on premises along with the SharePoint sites and to use Server to Server (S2S) authentication. S2S effectively removes reliance on Azure Access Control Services (ACS). In its place SharePoint acts as the Security Token Service (STS) and predefined certificates are used to sign and verify the tokens that are generated. S2S uses extensions to the OAuth 2.0 protocol that are not (at the time of this writing) currently part of the OAuth 2.0 standard, but have been submitted by Microsoft for future inclusion.

Applications that run using S2S are also said to be "high-trust" apps. High-trust apps must authenticate users independently themselves versus being passed a trusted identity as part of the context token from SharePoint. Typically, applications would authenticate a user using Windows Authentication (NTLM) or a similar scheme. High-trust apps are considered "high trust" because SharePoint trusts the application and trusts that it has authenticated and identified the user context being passed as part of an API call.

Part of the reason why high-trust apps establish the identity of users themselves is because of other authentication/authorization needs in on-premises scenarios. Take, for example, the scenario where a financial organization needs to keep all its data on premises for regulatory reasons. It builds an app that works with data in a variety of other on-premises systems and its organization uses Active Directory (AD) to manage users and security in those systems. A high-trust app would use a user's Windows identity to authenticate him and check his permissions; that same identity could also be used for downstream systems such as SQL Server.

This means that high-trust apps can play in the same playground as other on-premises applications and, most importantly, use the same internally mandated authorization and authentication system.

Setting up S2S authentication requires a number of manual setup steps for it to work properly. Following them correctly is important to ensure proper authentication operation.

You must setup and configure two items prior to starting the S2S configuration:

- ➤ User Profile Service Application
- ➤ App isolation

For more setup steps for app isolation, see the following MSDN document: `http://msdn` `.microsoft.com/en-us/library/office/apps/fp179923.aspx`.

After you have the prerequisites set up then you can complete the following:

1. Create and export a certificate.
2. Register the app (see the previous section, "Creating and Managing Application Identities").
3. Create a Provider-hosted app.

After completing the preceding items, you can start building Provider-hosted apps that are deployed on premises with IIS and SharePoint. The app and SharePoint are able to generate and verify the tokens required based on the trust set up with the certificate. You'll need to create a certificate so that your app can generate and verify the tokens. You can either create a self-signed certificate or use a certificate obtained from a certificate issuing authority. A self-signed certificate is simply a certificate that you sign yourself rather than obtaining it from a trusted issuing authority, and, for the purposes of these steps, is adequate to use. To create a self-signed certificate, follow these steps (Windows Server 2012):

1. Open IIS Manager.
2. Click Server Certificates.
3. Select Create Self-Signed Certificate from the action menu.
4. Give your certificate a name, such as **MyAppCert**. Click OK and when complete you will see your new certificate listed.

5. Open your new certificate by double-clicking it.

6. Click Copy to File.

7. Click Next, leaving the fields with their defaults.

8. Click Next again, leaving the fields with their defaults.

9. Give your certificate a filename, such as `c:\MyAppCert.cer`.

10. Right-click your certificate in IIS Manager and choose Export.

11. Give it a filename such as `c:\MyAppCert.pfx`.

12. Provide a password and remember it.

You are now ready to register a new app identity in SharePoint. To do this, you can use the following PowerShell script. You need to generate a new GUID for the `$clientid` value, set the path to your certificate, and set the name of the app appropriately. (You can find the following script in the download materials for this chapter in the `s2sscript.txt` file.)

```
$clientid = "7c17e591-f4da-46fc-b85c-a22a6b09c059"
$publicCertificatePath = "C:\MyAppCert.cer"

$certificate = Get-PfxCertificate $publicCertificatePath
$web = Get-SPWeb "http://servername"
$realm = Get-SPAuthenticationRealm -ServiceContext $web.Site
$fullAppIdentifier = $issuerId + '@' + $realm

New-SPTrustedSecurityTokenIssuer -Name "My App"
-Certificate $certificate -RegisteredIssuerName $fullAppIdentifier

Register-SPAppPrincipal -NameIdentifier $fullAppIdentifier -Site $web
-DisplayName "My App"

$serviceConfig = Get-SPSecurityTokenServiceConfig
$serviceConfig.AllowOAuthOverHttp = $true
$serviceConfig.Update()
```

The preceding script does the following:

➤ Sets up a new trusted security token issuer.

➤ Creates a new app identity/registration.

➤ Turns off SSL for OAuth for development purposes.

> **NOTE** *Turning off SSL for OAuth makes it easier when developing to get your application up and running. No SSL certificates are needed which simplifies setup and configuration on developer machines with different machine names.*

Now you are ready to create a Provider-hosted app in Visual Studio using the Microsoft Office Developer Tools for Visual Studio 2012 - Preview 2. Follow these steps:

1. Create a new SharePoint App project with Visual Studio.

2. Specify Provider-hosted as the app type during creation.

3. When you are asked whether you want to Use a Certificate to authenticate, say that you do and specify the path to the PFX certificate file you exported. Provide the password you also specified during the export.

4. Enter the `$clientid` GUID you created for the earlier PowerShell script into the Issuer ID field in the wizard.

5. Complete the wizard and complete your application development.

6. Click F5 to deploy and test your application.

For more detailed step-by-step instructions on the preceding task, go to the MSDN site at: `http://msdn.microsoft.com/en-us/library/office/apps/fp179901.aspx#Cert`.

SUMMARY

OAuth in SharePoint 2013 offers many new opportunities for integrating with both SharePoint Online and SharePoint on premises. The introduction of an application identity gives developers and administrators alike new opportunities for authenticating and authorizing access to content and information in SharePoint. By building on the already-large ground swell of developer support for OAuth in the community, SharePoint can offer access to its APIs in a standards-based and well-understood manner, thus reducing the complexity and proprietary nature of the process. The authorization system built into SharePoint 2013 offers developers flexibility and control over asking for access to resources while at the same time balancing that with the security needs and controls needed by users and IT professionals running SharePoint environments.

The OAuth system is part of the new framework for building applications; however, the effects of offering standardized, remotely callable APIs is also further reaching, enabling developers a wider range of integration options dependent on their environment and scenarios.

EXERCISES

Answers to Exercises for this chapter can be found in Appendix A.

1. How can you create new application identity registrations in SharePoint 2013 and what are the uses of the client ID and client secret?

2. Describe the three main token types that comprise the OAuth flow.

3. How can the application principal be used to elevate permissions for a calling user?

4. What OAuth tokens can be cached and for how long?

▶ WHAT YOU LEARNED IN THIS CHAPTER

ITEM	DESCRIPTION
OAuth	An open protocol to allow secure authorization in a simple and standard method from Web, mobile, and desktop applications.
Application principal	An application identity giving the ability to grant access to resources on a per-application basis.
Server to Server authentication	The on-premises model for setting up application authentication between a SharePoint Server and application code.

RECOMMENDED READING

Authorization and authentication for apps in SharePoint 2013 — http://msdn.microsoft.com/en-us/library/office/apps/fp142384.aspx

OAuth authentication and authorization flow for cloud-hosted apps in SharePoint 2013 — http://msdn.microsoft.com/en-us/library/office/apps/fp142382.aspx

How to create high-trust apps for SharePoint 2013 using the server-to-server protocol — http://msdn.microsoft.com/en-us/library/office/apps/fp179901.aspx

PART III
Advanced Developer Topics in SharePoint 2013

11

Developing Integrated Apps for Office and SharePoint Solutions

WHAT YOU WILL LEARN IN THIS CHAPTER:

➤ Creating integrated Office 2013 solutions using the new app model

➤ Understanding the new app model concepts and JavaScript object model (JSOM) for Office

➤ Learning when and how to use the common patterns for developing and deploying Apps for Office 2013

WROX.COM CODE DOWNLOADS FOR THIS CHAPTER

The wrox.com code downloads for this chapter are found at `http://www.wrox.com/WileyCDA/WroxTitle/productCd-1118495845.html` on the Download Code tab. The code for this chapter is divided into the following major examples:

➤ CompositeOSPAutoHosted.zip

➤ ExploreMailApp.zip

➤ ExploreOfficeAPI.zip

➤ FirstApp.zip

The Microsoft Office desktop applications are used by millions of individuals worldwide. Whether it's a teenager putting his first PowerPoint presentation together for a class project, a doctoral candidate writing her thesis in Word, or a Wall Street financial analyst performing Monte Carlo simulations within Excel, the Office desktop applications are a valued tool in the hands of their user. Through their use, people express their ideas, document their theories and discoveries, and make decisions based on analyzed results. Because of this widespread popularity, it is a good idea to land SharePoint 2013 and Office 2013 integrated solutions within the context of the user's productivity tools. This is where you want to integrate the reach of the Web with the rich collaboration features of SharePoint in a way never before possible.

This chapter shows you how solutions built using the new app model for Office 2013 can be combined with SharePoint 2013 to bring a host of new business solution opportunities to end users. Although you can still build integrated solutions that use Visual Studio Tools for Office (VSTO) or Visual Basic for Applications (VBA) for that matter, the new Office app model provides a way to bring the power of the Web into Office. Think of this as a modern browser being hosted inside of Office 2013 (Microsoft Word, Excel, Outlook, and Project) that fully supports HTML5 and JavaScript. The new app model also includes a unified JavaScript object model (JSOM) that is shared across the aforementioned Office 2013 applications that enables the hosted web page and document, or e-mail in the case of Outlook, to interact! With this new app model you can build an app for Office or couple it with an app for SharePoint for an integrated solution. The app can either be standalone (as in the case of an app for Office) or deployed as part of an app for SharePoint 2013, but in either case it can be distributed to potentially millions of users via the Office Store on Office .com or directly to enterprises via an established sales relationship. Building integrated apps for Office and SharePoint is truly worth your consideration since the market for these app business solutions encompasses on-premises installations of SharePoint 2013 and Office 365 tenancies as well.

THE NEW APP MODEL FOR OFFICE

The new app model for Office 2013 works in a similar manner as the new app model for SharePoint 2013 to mitigate many of the challenges developers have faced in the past. The result has become a better platform for developers to include a broader set of technologies in their solutions while not having the risk of impacting the core runtime environments of SharePoint and the Office clients. In Chapter 2, "Overview of the SharePoint 2013 App Model," you learned how the new app model for SharePoint 2013 helps to improve some problem areas that SharePoint 2010 had around full-trust deployments that could impact server and end-user performance if code misbehaved. It also allows developers to move beyond the restrictions imposed by sandboxed solutions. In the same way, the new app model for Office 2013 addresses a number of challenges developers and IT have faced historically in Office with add-in installations, but it also is forward-looking in its adoption of web-based standards such as HTML5, CSS, JavaScript, and so on, which can now better facilitate web developers in surfacing valued cloud-based assets inside of Office.

The new app model for Office can be considered an evolutionary and logical step in the programmability/extensibility model for the Office clients. As the desktop, laptop, and other device form factors have evolved, so have the underlying hardware architectures. For instance, Office now runs on Windows RT which utilizes the ARM architecture that thin, lightweight tablet and PC devices are built on. However, the ARM architecture does not support the traditional extensibility models for Office: VBA and VSTO. Therefore, solutions that developers have built using VBA and VSTO are lost to users of these devices. The new app model for Office is the extensibility model that bridges this hardware/software divide. It now brings a new class of developer solutions to both the platforms that Office traditionally ran on as well as ARM devices and even the services layer to include the Office Web Apps where a version of Excel, Word, PowerPoint and Outlook run in the browser.

The new app model addresses a few other typical challenges for the developer and for IT. Take VBA solutions and VSTO add-ins for example: these are written to provide powerful business solutions, and VBA and VSTO developers write code specific to each Office client. The deep object model is not the same for Word as for Excel or PowerPoint, so a developer codes and maintains a different solution for each client. Additionally, with the advent of the Office Web Apps available in SharePoint 2010, the VBA code and COM-based add-ins became incompatible with the Web server environment. Essentially, a VBA solution or add-in developed for the rich client had no future with respect to being deployed to run within the Office server-side services on SharePoint.

Identifying the add-ins installed throughout the enterprise has been a challenge for IT, but due to the add-ins' tight coupling with the Office client, a need exists to fully test add-ins with each new version release of Office. Historically, these challenges have made rolling out a new version of Office across the enterprise difficult.

The new app model for Office nicely mitigates the challenges for both the developer and IT. For the developer, the object model and unified JSOM for Office is consistent across the clients. The intent is that with the unified JSOM, the app can run across the desktop applications that support Apps for Office without any changes — something that could not be done with VSTO add-ins. Also, because the app is essentially running in a browser inside Office, the added benefit is that the app can run equally well in the Office Web App under SharePoint. Although all the Office Web Apps don't yet have this functionality in the Office 2013 release, this is the direction for the new app model. Therefore a developer's solution written with the new app model is intended to run anywhere the Office client runs as well as in the server environment where the Office Web Apps run. The solution will not need to be altered to run in any of the locations. It's just going to take some time to attain parity across all the platforms.

IT benefits from the new application model because by its nature, there is no footprint on the Office client itself: Apps for Office do not require an install. IT chooses how Apps for Office are made available within the enterprise, providing central management and governance. As apps are made available in the enterprise, users can discover and access them from within the Office client. The client understands how to instantiate an app for Office, monitor the app's behavior, and provide telemetry information to IT for reporting and decision making. For more information on telemetry, monitoring, and reporting of Apps for Office, please see the recommended reading list at the end of this chapter.

Now that you have access to all these benefits that the new Office app model brings forth, it is worth taking a look at how simple it is to build your first app for Office. The following activity walks you through this process.

TRY IT OUT   Building Your First App for Office (FirstApp.zip)

Imagine extending Office by merely composing and using standard web technologies with no programming environment except a text editor! This exercise shows the simplicity of the new Office app model where an app can be broken down into a simple equation: Office = 1 manifest file + 1 HTML page + 1 Office client. To create one just follow these steps:

1. Create a new folder on your local disk and name it **AppManifests**.

2. Right-click on the folder and select Share with ⇨ Specific people. Type **Everyone** in the text box, click the Add button, and then click Share.

3. Create another new folder on your local disk and name it **FirstApp**.

4. Create the following markup document in your text editor, and save the document as `FirstApp`
`.html` in the `FirstApp` folder:

```html
<!DOCTYPE html>
<html xmlns="http://www.w3.org/1999/xhtml">
    <head>
        <meta charset="UTF-8" />
        <meta http-equiv="X-UA-Compatible" content="IE=9"/>
        <link rel="stylesheet" type="text/css" href="Program.css" />
    </head>
    <body>
        <p>My First app for Office!</p>
    </body>
</html>
```

5. Create the following CSS document in your text editor, and save the CSS document in the same
folder where you saved the previous HTML document, as **Program.css:**

```css
body
{
    position:relative;
}
li :hover
{
    text-decoration: underline;
    cursor:pointer;
}
h1,h3,h4,p,a,li
{
    font-family: "Segoe UI Light","Segoe UI",Tahoma,sans-serif;
    text-decoration-color:#4ec724;
}
```

6. Using Microsoft Paint or any application that can create a `.PNG` file, create a 32×32 pixel
image, and save the file in the same folder where you saved the previous CSS document, as
FirstApp.png.

7. Enter the following XML in your text editor to create a manifest document, and save this file in
the `AppManifests` folder with the name `FirstApp.xml`: be sure to replace *[YourDriveLetter]*
in the following XML with the actual letter of your local drive where you saved the `FirstApp`
folder.

```xml
<?xml version="1.0" encoding="UTF-8"?>
<OfficeApp xmlns="http://schemas.microsoft.com/office/appforoffice/1.0"
xmlns:xsi="http://www.w3.org/2001/XMLSchema-instance"
xsi:type="TaskPaneApp">
  <Id>c6ec2456-9fca-4f27-85c3-4623b25ef0ae</Id>
  <Version>1.0</Version>
  <ProviderName>Microsoft</ProviderName>
  <DefaultLocale>en-US</DefaultLocale>
  <DisplayName DefaultValue="My First App" />
  <Description DefaultValue="My first app for Office."/>
  <IconUrl DefaultValue="[YourDriveLetter]:\FirstApp\FirstApp.png" />
  <Capabilities>
    <Capability Name="Workbook" />
    <Capability Name="Document" />
```

```
</Capabilities>
<DefaultSettings>
  <SourceLocation DefaultValue="[YourDriveLetter]:\FirstApp\FirstApp.html" />
</DefaultSettings>
<Permissions>ReadWriteDocument</Permissions>
</OfficeApp>
```

Now that you have the files created for your first app for Office, you need to wire up the Office client so it knows where to look for app manifests.

To set the Trusted Catalog Location, follow these steps in either Word or Excel:

8. From the File menu, select Options ⇨ Trust Center.

9. On the Trust Center page, click the Trust Center Settings button.

10. In Trust Center, click Trusted App Catalogs and in the Catalog URL type: `\\[YourMachineName]\AppManifests\` and click the Add Catalog button. Click the check box beside the newly added item so it will show up in the menu, and then click OK on the screen, again when prompted, and a third time on the Options dialog. Then close Word or Excel.

Now you can use your first app for Office by following these steps:

11. Open Word or Excel. From the Insert menu, select Apps for Office ⇨ See All.

12. Click Shared Folder and then click Refresh.

13. Click `My First App` and then click the Insert button.

Your first app for Office should resemble Figure 11-1 in Word 2013.

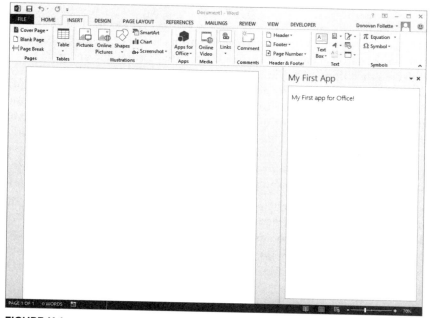

FIGURE 11-1

How It Works

In this exercise you first created a network share as a trusted catalog location for storing Apps for Office manifest files. This is essentially an easy way for an enterprise to make Apps for Office available to employees, although it is not the only way. Alternatively, if an organization has a SharePoint 2013 site or Office 365 SharePoint Online site, it can make Apps for Office available by setting up SharePoint to be the trusted catalog location for manifest files. For apps purchased directly from the Office Store by individuals, Office.com serves as the trusted catalog location for these manifests. Also, because the apps are purchased using a Microsoft LiveID, they roam with the user. If users log in to Office with that same LiveID on any machine, all their Apps for Office will be available to them!

Following the creation of the network share, you created four very simple files. For an app for Office, only three of them are actually required: the manifest .xml, .icon, and .html file. The .css file is optional. In this Try It Out you simply used a text editor so you could see the core components without having any tooling overhead. But as you will see, using a tool like Visual Studio helps make this much easier and provides structure and validation while building you Apps for Office.

Because an app for Office is simply a web page being rendered inside of Office, you can build your web pages using any web technology that will render in Internet Explorer version 9.0 (or later) or an equivalent browser. Therefore, Apps for Office can use any features supported by HTML5 and JavaScript. What is not supported in the Office clients are ActiveX controls embedded in web pages. ActiveX controls are blocked from rendering in the Office clients for security purposes.

You'll notice the manifest file is an extremely lightweight .xml file that serves to identify the app for Office to the host Office client applications. Although some of the XML elements in the manifest file are quite self-explanatory, there are a few worth highlighting:

➤ The element OfficeApp has an attribute xsi:type set to TaskPaneApp. The xsi:type is used to identify how the app for Office is to render within the Office client. In the preceding activity you chose the TaskPaneApp. Other valid types are ContentApp and MailApp. A task pane app renders in the Office clients in the same way that you traditionally see with various add-ins. Task pane apps are docked by default on the right-hand side of the client, but can be undocked so they float, too. Alternatively, content apps are inserted onto the document itself. Essentially, think of these like you would a chart or picture that the user has complete control over. Content apps for Office are printed and saved with the document just like any other inline object associated with a document. MailApp renders in the Office mail clients only when specific patterns for app activation are met within the mail item. You will see how this works in the mailbox app example later.

➤ The id element must contain a globally unique value. In the preceding example you simply used a GUID provided and this sufficed for an example on your local machine. However, for your real-world app for Office, you use a tool to generate a GUID. This unique id value identifies your app for Office in the Office Store or in your corporation trusted catalog location.

➤ Each `xsi:type` called out earlier has a specific set of `Capabilities` that designate the contexts within which it can be rendered. The `Capabilities` element is the location where you identify `Capability` elements. For instance, the `TaskPaneApp` has the capability to only render in a client that supports a workbook, document, or project. Here in the manifest you designate these. Sometimes your app for Office might only target a workbook whereas other times your app can be used in one or more of the other options. By listing each `Capability` here, when a user clicks the Insert ⇨ Apps for Office button on the ribbon in a client, if that Office client supports the `xsi:type`/`Capability` combination, then your app for Office will show as one of the available apps for that client. Table 11-1 shows the mapping between `xsi:type` and `Capabilities`. You can anticipate these to broaden and deepen over time across more Office clients.

TABLE 11-1: XSI:TYPE to Capability Mapping

XSI:TYPE	WORKBOOK	DOCUMENT	PROJECT	PRESENTATION	MAILBOX
TaskPaneApp	X	X	X	X	
ContentApp	X				
MailApp					X

➤ As mentioned previously, the beauty of Apps for Office is that there is no install on the Office client. Also, the `SourceLocation` element is where the magic of your app for Office meets with the power of the new Office clients. You simply designate the URL or location where you want Office to retrieve your web application, and the user can then begin to interact with Office and your productivity solution.

➤ Lastly, security and protection for the user is of utmost importance. The manifest file is where the `Permissions` element defines what type of permissions your app for Office will need to interact with the Office client. You'll see these permissions described in detail later, but knowing that the manifest file is where you'll identify the permissions for your app for Office is important.

Before the Office clients start "looking" for Apps for Office available to users within an organization on SharePoint, either on premises, in Office 365, or on a network fileshare, you must first set up the Trusted App Catalog location in at least one of the Office clients installed on the user's machine. After you designate this location, all the other client applications that support Apps for Office will use this setting and render the appropriate selections for apps that target that specific Office client. In the preceding activity you set this location manually through the Trust Center; however, in an enterprise it can be pushed out via Active Directory Group Policy. In this way IT can maintain control and governance over the Apps for Office allowed within the enterprise and can completely turn off the ability for employees to browse the Office Store if that's the restriction IT wants to enforce. After the Trusted App Catalog designation is set, the Office client applications are ready to render any Apps for Office that a user has available to select!

Now that you have the fundamental components identified for building an app for Office, check out the following introduction to the JavaScript object model and how Visual Studio helps enable developing integrated solutions using the new app model for Office.

THE OFFICE JAVASCRIPT OBJECT MODEL

The Office JavaScript Object Model provides the ability for your web application and the Office host application to interact, and that's where the creativity and innovation of your web-based solution can intersect with the creativity and innovation of the Office user.

You can think of Apps for Office in two ways: those that will interact with documents (document based) and those that will interact with mail items (mailbox based). At the time of this writing, document-based apps include Word, Excel, PowerPoint, and Project. The `xsi:type TaskPaneApp` and `ContentApp` are document-based apps for Office. The mailbox-based app, `xsi:type MailApp`, is, of course, associated with the Outlook rich client and companion Outlook Web App (OWA). Therefore, although the Office JSOM is a unified object model, due to the differences between the sheer nature of a document and a mailbox item, you will use different parts of the Office API depending on which Office applications your app for Office will target.

Fortunately, you do not need to build the manifest file and all the constituent parts in a raw text editor for an app for Office as you did in the previous Try It Out, but you instead have the power of Visual Studio to make this job much less tedious. With the Apps for Office tools installed in Visual Studio, the File ⇨ New Project process is a guided experience that automatically generates an appropriate manifest file for a `TaskPaneApp`, `ContentApp`, or `MailApp`. You then have an immediate F5, debug runtime experience. Of course, you can go on to fine-tune and customize the manifest and build out your app, but Visual Studio provides for you a solid starting point.

Document-based Apps

The Office JSOM provides many capabilities for document-based apps for Office. With Office JSOM, your web application can programmatically interact with a selection the user has made, read or write to your document, react to events as the user enters a specific location or changes data in the document, save one or more settings in the document so that they are persisted for the next time the document is opened, and much more. However, the thing to keep in mind, especially for those who have written VBA or built add-ins in the past, is that the Office JSOM is not for automation of the Office client itself, but for enabling programmatic interaction between the document and your task pane or content app. Everything you do using the Office JSOM is focused around the user and the document, and should enable that experience to be a productivity gain for the user.

The `Microsoft.Office.WebExtension` namespace contains the JavaScript objects needed to programmatically interact with the Office client applications that support Apps for Office. In code, this namespace is referred to by the alias `Office`. The Visual Studio app for Office project template includes the `Office.js` library in the `Scripts/Lib` folder for the Web project. Figure 11-2 shows the core objects in the API.

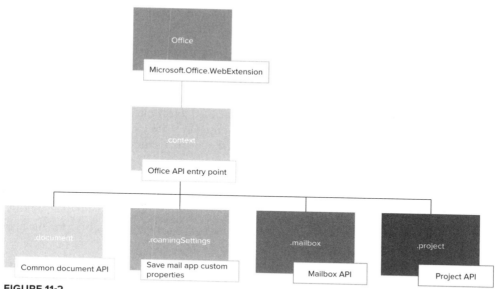

FIGURE 11-2

The main objects you will use for document-based apps are Office, .context, and .document. When your App for Office is specific to Microsoft Outlook, then you will use the .mailbox object to access the APIs specific to programming against the mail client — but this object is covered in further detail later. If you are creating Apps for Office specifically for Microsoft Project, you will use the .project part of the Office API.

To keep this discussion straightforward, for Microsoft Word and Excel, the document object provides the functional capabilities needed for document interaction. With this you can read and write an active selection, bind to named locations in the document, and react to events at the document or bound-location level. Almost all methods in the Office JSOM are asynchronous to not tie up the UI as your method call executes. A typical line of code used to retrieve the data the user has selected in the document looks like this:

```
Office.context.document.getSelectedDataAsync(…)
```

Although not a lot of methods are in the API, they provide the fundamental building blocks for you to build your solution — it's up to your imagination on how you stitch them together to meet a business need. Let's now explore what Visual Studio provides for Apps for Office and explore the API.

TRY IT OUT Using the Office JSOM for Document-based Apps (Explore Office API.zip)

Here you will get a feel for the baseline App for Office's project template that Visual Studio sets up for you. Then you will add some additional code to explore the API for Office.

1. Run Visual Studio 2012 as Administrator. Select New Project.

2. In the New Project dialog, expand the Templates ⇨ Visual C# ⇨ Office/SharePoint ⇨ Apps nodes. Select App for Office 2013 and provide the Name: **ExploreOfficeAPI**. Click OK.

3. In the Create App for Office dialog, leave the default Task pane app selected, but uncheck Project and PowerPoint because you will not be targeting these Office clients. Click Finish.

Before you press F5, take a quick look at the boilerplate app and the artifacts in the solution. The solution contains two projects. The first project, ExploreOfficeAPI, has only the manifest file in it. If you double-click the ExploreOfficeAPI.xml file you see a nice UI to set the values in the manifest file. You can, of course, view the raw XML by expanding the node and clicking on the XML file itself. You will also notice the second project called ExploreOfficeAPIWeb. This project is a boilerplate "remote web" application in that it must ultimately be hosted on a remote web server. For the F5 experience, it runs in IIS Express on the local machine. You can use this web project to build your web application or you could ultimately replace it with another one of your own. As you browse through the project you'll see that Visual Studio has provided a number of folders with the files needed to serve as the basis for an app for Office. A discussion about these various files appears later.

4. Press F5 to start debugging. (Internet Explorer must have script-debugging enabled for the app to run.)

5. By running the app from Visual Studio, the app is automatically registered with the Office client it is targeted for and inserted into the client. Click on any cell in the spreadsheet and click the Set Data button.

6. Click on any other cell in the spreadsheet and type any text value. Press Enter so the value saves into the cell. Re-select the cell by clicking on it and then press the Get Data button. The value of the cell is loaded into the TaskPaneApp text box.

7. Close the Excel application to stop the debugging session.

8. To explore the API, in the Solution Explorer expand the ExploreOfficeAPIWeb node, expand the Pages node, and click the ExploreOfficeAPI.html file to open it.

9. In the HTML page, locate the entire `<div id="Content">` element and replace it completely with the following code:

```
<button onclick="writeToDoc()"> Write to Document </button><br/>
<button onclick="readFromSelection()"> Read from Document Selection
</button><br/>
<button onclick="bindToData()"> Bind to User-selected Data </button><br/>
<button onclick="readFromBoundData()"> Read from Bound Data </button><br/>
<button onclick="addAnEvent()"> Add an Event </button><br/>
<span>Show: </span><div id="show"></div>
```

10. In the Solution Explorer under the Scripts/Office node, open the ExploreOfficeAPI.js file and replace all the code with the following:

```
Office.initialize = function (reason) {
    $(document).ready(function () {
        showResult('Document Ready');
    });
};


function writeToDoc() {
```

```
      Office.context.document.setSelectedDataAsync([["apples"],
  ["pears"], ["oranges"], ["cherries"]], function (asyncResult) {
          if (asyncResult.status === "failed") {
              showResult('Error: ' + asyncResult.error.message);
          }
      });
  }

  function readFromSelection() {
      Office.context.document.getSelectedDataAsync("matrix",
  function (asyncResult) {
          if (asyncResult.status === "failed") {
              showResult('Error: ' + asyncResult.error.message);
          }
          else {
              showResult('Read from Selection: ' + asyncResult.value);
          }
      });
  }

  function bindToData() {
      Office.context.document.bindings.addFromSelectionAsync("matrix",
  { id: 'fruitBinding' },
          function (asyncResult) {
              if (asyncResult.status === "failed") {
                  showResult('Error: ' + asyncResult.error.message);
              } else {
                  showResult('A binding type of ' + asyncResult.value.type
                      + ' was added with an id of ' +
                      asyncResult.value.id);
              }
          });
  }

  function readFromBoundData() {
      Office.select("bindings#fruitBinding").getDataAsync({
  coercionType: "matrix" },
          function (asyncResult) {
              if (asyncResult.status === "failed") {
                  showResult('Error: ' + asyncResult.error.message);
              } else {
                  showResult('Value of bound selection: ' + asyncResult.value);
              }
          });
  }

  function addAnEvent() {
      Office.select("bindings#fruitBinding").addHandlerAsync(
  "bindingDataChanged", fruitHandler, function (asyncResult) {
          if (asyncResult.status === "failed") {
              showResult('Error: ' + asyncResult.error.message);
          } else {
              showResult('New event handler added for binding.');
          }
      });
```

```
        }
        function fruitHandler(eventArgs) {
            eventArgs.binding.getDataAsync({ coerciontype: "matrix" },
        function (asyncResult) {

                if (asyncResult.status === "failed") {
                    showResult('Error: ' + asyncResult.error.message);
                } else {
                    showResult('Show bound data change: ' + asyncResult.value);
                }
            });
        }

        function showResult(text) {
            document.getElementById('show').innerText = text;
        }
```

11. Press F5. When the Excel document loads, click each button from top to bottom to see how the API allows programmatic interaction with the document. Once you add the event, type inside the bound area and change one of the fruit entries and press enter. You'll see the results show in the task pane with your change. Close Excel.

12. Now to show the benefit of the unified object model across the Office client applications, click on the ExploreOfficeAPI project. In the Properties pane find the Start Action property and set it to Microsoft Word. Press F5.

13. Click down through the buttons again from top to bottom. After you add the event, change a value within a cell, but you need to click outside the table for the event to fire in Word. Close Word.

14. In Visual Studio click open the ExploreOfficeAPI.js if it is not already open.

How It Works

The [YourAppnameHere].js is the JavaScript file that Visual Studio generates specifically for your app. For this Try It Out the name is ExploreOfficeAPI.js. All the other files in the Scripts folder by default are for reference purposes so you can readily take advantage of the jQuery and ASP.NET AJAX libraries. But this specific JavaScript file is where you write the code for your app.

Looking at the ExploreOfficeAPI.js file, a document-ready function executes as the initialize process completes after the app is started. In this function you simply wrote to the web page indicating that the document is loaded and ready.

Let's take a look into each of the functions. Notice that the writeToDoc function just passes in a hard-coded array of string values. This automatically creates a matrix structure for the data: in this case a single column with four rows. A matrix is a static two-dimensional structure of columns and rows. You could have multiple columns in the matrix by following the pattern such as [["apple", "red"], ["banana", "yellow"]] for two columns and two rows and so on. The Office.context.document.setSelectedDataAsynch method does the work for you to create the matrix within the document at any location where the cursor is located.

The readFromSelection function requires the CoercionType to be passed in to the Office.context.document.getSelectedDataAsynch method. Here you see the first parameter of this method uses `matrix` because the selected data, in this case it is in a columns and rows form. Other coercion types are `Text`, which can be a single word or any number of paragraphs, and a `Table` data type that is also a two-dimensional array but differs from a matrix structure in that it supports named columns and rows. It also is dynamic in that it will grow and shrink as additional rows are added or deleted. So when a table is bound, the binding automatically adjusts as the table shrinks or grows. A matrix binding remains static with the originally set number of columns and rows. Word also supports `HTML` and `Ooxml` data types so you can get selected data in HTML or Open XML form.

Any data that the user selects on the screen can be bound so that you can essentially get a programmatic handle for it to refer to in your code. In the `bindToData` function, you called the `Office.context.document.bindings.addFromSelectionAsync` method and passed in the coercion type of `matrix` with an `id` that is your specific name for the binding. To retrieve the contents of the bound data at any time as shown in the `readFromBoundData` function, you use `Office.select` where you identify the specific binding by the `id` you want and the coercion type.

Lastly, you added an event to your specific binding so that any time data changes within the binding you can take action upon it. Here again you used `Office.select` identifying the specific binding you want the `bindingDataChanged` event to fire on.

Functional Capabilities by Office Client

A number of other functional capabilities are available in the API but these are so numerous that they will need to be left to your own discovery. `http://dev.office.com` has the full documentation for the Apps for Office JSOM. Table 11-2 identifies some of the more popular additional functional capabilities and shows how they map to the Office client applications.

TABLE 11-2: Functional Areas vs. App Support Summary

FUNCTIONAL AREA	WORD	EXCEL/EXCEL WEB APP	PROJECT	POWERPOINT	OUTLOOK/OWA
Set/Get data as HTML, OOXML	X				
Get File	X			X	
Custom XML parts	X				
Bindings	X	X			
Settings	X	X		X	X
Set/Get data as text, table, matrix	X	X	X	X	
App-specific API			X		X

Mailbox-based Apps

Certainly as widely used by business professionals as Excel is for number crunching and Word is for authoring documents, a vast number of people exist whose days are built around communicating, scheduling, managing contacts, and ordering their day's tasks with Outlook. Therefore, historically, Outlook has been one of the most targeted Office clients for third-party add-ins. Outlook tends to be a hub application in the business person's day and a primary point of reference. Plus, if for some reason during the day a person doesn't have access to his or her desktop, a web companion called Outlook Web Access is available as long as he or she has access to a browser and an Internet connection. This tight bond between business people and their Outlook is what makes it such a key new opportunity for landing your app for Office.

The MailApp for Office differs from the TaskPaneApp and the ContentApp in a couple of ways. First, it is not associated with a document, and second, it does not render in a task pane in Outlook nor on the surface of a mail item like the ContentApp does in a workbook. Rather, MailApps are activated in the Outlook, OWA, or Outlook mobile UI based upon activation rules defined in your app for Office manifest file. This declarative set of rules evaluates contextual content within an e-mail message or appointment item when it is opened. If the contextual content within the item matches one or more of the activation rules then the MailApp will be automatically activated and show in the UI. This differs from the document-based apps for Office that must be manually selected and inserted via the ribbon by the user. Lastly, another significant difference is that the manifest file is deployed to an Exchange server, App Catalog, rather than to SharePoint or a network share. Microsoft has pre-installed at least four mailbox-based apps to the Office 365 Exchange App Catalog for each tenancy. These Apps for Office — Action Items, Bing Maps, Suggested Meetings, and Unsubscribe — are found in the Exchange admin center under Organization ⇨ Apps. Although the Office 365 Exchange administrator can globally disable these apps for their tenancy, they cannot be uninstalled. However, given that they are available to users, they will automatically activate for a user when the activation rules are met within a mail item.

For a mailbox-based app, the activation rules act on contextual information within the mail item and provide the unique opportunity to build genuine productivity solutions for those who live in their Outlook. You can use several built-in, well-known entity types to activate a MailApp. These include URL, contact, task suggestion, meeting suggestion, phone number, address, and e-mail address. In your app manifest, using the `Rule` element, you would include the evaluation of one or more of these in the form of `<Rule xsi:type="ItemHasKnownEntity" EntityType="Contact" />`, for instance. You can further scope the activation rule by adding an additional attribute of `RegExFilter` where the rule will only activate if, say, the `RegExFilter="ID"`. With this rule the intent is that you are only interested in identifying contacts from the state of Idaho. Hence, your MailApp would activate only when contact information contains an uppercase ID value. Although the well-known entity types will save you a ton of code writing, you will sometimes, of course, want a fully customized rule. Suppose you want to provide a convenient way for an Outlook user to interact with a back-end Line of Business (LoB) application or your Software as a Service (SaaS) application when the system sends an autogenerated e-mail to a stakeholder. In these situations you build your own rule using the `ItemHasRegularExpressionMatch` type. With this type you provide your own `RegExValue` to pattern match against the contextual information in the item body (whether HTML or plain text), subject, or sender's SMTP address. This fully customized rule, as with any other rule, can then stand alone or be combined with other rules in a rule collection. You can combine the `RuleCollection` type using a `Mode` of `And` or `Or` with other rule collections to create complex rules. This flexibility in rule and rule collection construction provides you the ability to control precisely what needs to be in the mail or appointment item for your MailApp to activate. When a rule is not met, the MailApp will not show in the UI.

From an app model perspective, you still have a manifest file and you write your mailbox-based app using your favorite web technologies and host the app on any server you like. From a JSOM perspective you still use the Office JSOM but you use the `Office.context.mailbox` object. From the mailbox object you can get information relating to the specific message or appointment item and access a limited set of profile information about the user. For more advanced scenarios you can call back into Exchange using Exchange Web Services (EWS) where you can create new e-mail messages and appointments to provide a more deeply integrated mailbox-based app for Office. For now, in the following Try It Out, you can explore well-known entities, rules and rule collections, and regular expressions for customized pattern matching.

TRY IT OUT   Using the Office JSOM for Mailbox-based Apps (Explore MailApp.zip)

In this exercise you work with the fundamentals of MailApps using a complex rule in the manifest file, retrieving information from the mail item, and displaying the information in a web page for the user to see. Because MailApps deploy to the Exchange App Catalog, you will deploy it to your Office 365 developer tenancy Exchange Server. Just follow these steps:

1. Run Visual Studio 2012 as Administrator. Select New Project.

2. In the New Project dialog, expand the Templates ⇨ Visual C# ⇨ Office/SharePoint ⇨ Apps nodes. Select App for Office 2013 and provide the Name: **ExploreMailApp**. Click OK.

3. In the Create App for Office dialog, select Mail app in. Click Finish.

4. The `ExploreMailApp.html` file should be displayed by default. If it's not, open it from the Pages folder and replace the entire `<body>...</body>` contents with the following:

```
<body>
    <div id="Content">
        <h4>Display some of what's available to developers:</h4>
        User Profile name: <span id="displayName"></span>
        <br />
        User Profile time zone: <span id="timeZone"></span>
        <br />
        Email item Subject: <span id="subject"></span>
        <br />
        Email item From: <span id="from"></span>
        <br />
        Email item To: <span id="to"></span>
        <table>
            <tr><td>Urls</td><td id="urls" /></tr>
            <tr><td>Contact Names and Addresses</td><td id="contactNames" /></tr>
            <tr><td>Invoices</td><td id="regexInvoices" /></tr>
        </table>
    </div>
</body>
```

5. Open the `ExploreMailApp.xml` manifest file and replace the entire `<Rule>...</Rule>` rule collection node with the following:

```xml
<Rule xsi:type="RuleCollection" Mode="And">
  <Rule xsi:type="RuleCollection" Mode="Or">
    <Rule xsi:type="ItemIs" ItemType="Message" />
    <Rule xsi:type="ItemIs" ItemType="Appointment" />
  </Rule>
  <Rule xsi:type="RuleCollection" Mode="Or">
    <Rule xsi:type="ItemHasKnownEntity" EntityType="Contact"
RegExFilter="ID" FilterName="state" IgnoreCase="false" />
    <Rule xsi:type="ItemHasKnownEntity" EntityType="Url" />
    <Rule xsi:type="ItemHasRegularExpressionMatch"
    PropertyName="BodyAsHTML" IgnoreCase="true"
    RegExName="Invoices"
    RegExValue="\bINVOICE#\s*([0-9][0-9][0-9][0-9][0-9][0-9])+\b"/>
  </Rule>
</Rule>
```

6. Open the JavaScript file and replace the entire contents with the following:

```javascript
Office.initialize = function () {
    $(document).ready(function () {
        var userProfile = Office.context.mailbox.userProfile;
        $('#displayName').text(userProfile.displayName);
        $('#timeZone').text(userProfile.timeZone);

        var item = Office.context.mailbox.item;
        $('#subject').text(item.normalizedSubject);
        $('#from').text(item.from.displayName);
        $('#to').text(item.to[0].displayName);

        //Get all the well-known entities to show this pattern and use for URLs.
        var myEntities = item.getEntities();

        // Build an array of Urls using the Urls entity.
        var myUrls = myEntities.urls;
        // Loop over the myUrls array.
        var myString = "";
        for (i = 0; i < myUrls.length; i++) {
            myString += "<a href='" + myUrls[i] + "'>" + myUrls[i]
+ "</a>" + " <br />";
        }
        // Write the Contacts found to the web page
        $('#urls').html(myString);

        // Build an array of Contacts by directly accessing the filtered entity
        // by name.
        var myContacts = item.getFilteredEntitiesByName("state")
        // Loop over the myContacts array.
        myString = "";
        for (i = 0; i < myContacts.length; i++) {
            myString +=
                    myContacts[i].personName + ", " + myContacts[i].addresses
+ " <br />";
        }
```

```
            // Write the Contacts found to the web page
            $('#contactNames').html(myString);

            // Handle invoices from RegEx matches
            var myInvoices = item.getRegExMatches();
            //Loop over the myInvoices collection.
            myString = "";
            for (var i in myInvoices.Invoices) {
                myString += myInvoices.Invoices[i] + ", ";
            }
            // Write the invoices found to the web page
            $('#regexInvoices').text(myString);

        });
    };
```

7. Before you run this, click on the `ExploreMailApp` node in the Solution Explorer and view the Properties. Notice that the Start Action is set to start using Microsoft Outlook Web Access. You could set the Start Action to Microsoft Outlook, but using OWA is best for testing to avoid any impact on your current Outlook configuration.

8. Press F5 to start debugging. (Internet Explorer must have script debugging enabled for the app to run.) Visual Studio immediately prompts you for your mailbox credentials. Enter your Office 365 developer subscription in the form of `YourO365UserName@YourO365DeveloperDomain` `.onmicrosoft.com` and the password for the account. If you choose the Remember my e-mail option, you won't be bothered by Visual Studio any longer with this prompt, but if you ever want the prompt back to possibly deploy to another mailbox, then delete this e-mail address from the E-mail Address property for the `ExploreMailApp` node.

9. After your browser opens, log in to Office 365 using the same account and password from step 8.

10. Because you might not have any e-mail items already in your mailbox that will fire the activation rules you're using, create and send a new e-mail to your Office 365 account with each of the following on a separate line in the e-mail body exactly as they are shown here:

    a. `http://bing.com`

    b. Joe Doe, 1234 SW East ST, Boise, ID, 88763

    c. Jon Doe, 624 West South ST, Sturgis, SD, 55557

    d. INVOICE# 000768, Invoice# 023457, invoice# 009888, invoice# 987

11. When you receive the e-mail, click on it. In the location above the body where MailApps render, you'll see a tab labeled `ExploreMailApp`. Click on this tab to see your MailApp in action.

How It Works

Take a look at the all-important activation rule. It is called a complex activation rule, but that doesn't necessarily mean it's complicated to create one. With this rule you simply want your MailApp to activate when the mail item is either a message *or* appointment *and* has any well-known contact *or* URL entity types *or* a regular expression custom pattern match for invoices. To do this you can see that you nest two `Mode="Or"` rule collections inside a `Mode="And"` rule collection node. To simplify how to conceptualize this, see the following structure.

```
<Rule xsi:type="RuleCollection" Mode="And"> (this is the overarching AND)
 <Rule xsi:type="RuleCollection" Mode="Or"> (the OR for Message/Appointment)
 ...
 </Rule>
 <Rule xsi:type="RuleCollection" Mode="Or"> (the OR for well-known Entities/RegEx)
 ...
 </Rule>
</Rule>
```

Additionally, the rule is an example of how to set a filter on a well-known entity to only select contacts that have an address in the state of Idaho. This filter is provided a name so the resulting set can be interrogated directly via code. The syntax for this rule is:

```
<Rule xsi:type="ItemHasKnownEntity" EntityType="Contact" RegExFilter="ID"
FilterName="state" IgnoreCase="false" />
```

Lastly, the complex rule has a custom regular expression to pattern-match for a text-based literal, ignoring letter case, in combination with any six-digit value. This is to simulate how easily you can surface information to the user that might be sourced from back-end LoB or SaaS systems. Consider this: the invoices could actually be links in the MailApp to directly access the LoB system, or you could call out to back-end web services using the invoice numbers, aggregate data from a variety of sources, and construct an information-rich web page for display in the MailApp. Lots of possibilities here!

Nothing is special about the html file; it's just a place to display the goodies available to you in the mail item.

The code in JavaScript is pretty straightforward and shows how to access some of the properties on the user profile and item objects. What's more interesting is how you get the information of interest out of the well-known entities and the matches for the custom regular expression rule.

The pattern first used is to retrieve all the well-known entities that have been processed by calling the `item.getEntities()` method. An important point here is that although you don't have an activation rule based on some of these well-known entities, Outlook is still finding all of them. Therefore, you can use this method to retrieve them, see whether any contain data, and process the data any way you like. In this case you are only interested in checking the well-known URL entity. Once retrieved, the array is traversed and any URL present is constructed as a hyperlink and written to the web page.

The contacts are retrieved directly using the `item.getFilteredEntitiesByName("state")` method by passing in the string value of `"state"` to match the `FilterName` specifically used in the rule. This way you process only the contacts that matched the `RegExFilter="ID"` on the rule.

Finally, you use the `item.getRegExMatches()` method to get all the invoice numbers found in the mail item that matched your custom regular expression.

This Try It Out is not at all exhaustive of the many different ways you can interact with mail and appointment items in a MailApp, but hopefully it pulls together enough of the concepts and code to get you rolling. Mailbox-based apps can provide a convenient vector for engaging a user for interaction with your back-end systems. These can be great companion apps for your SaaS or LoB systems because they render everywhere, whether within Outlook on the rich client, OWA, or Outlook mobile.

App Security

When delivering any technology solution you must give special attention to the types of security measures that have been taken to keep the user's computer safe from malicious attacks. As a developer, you need to have a good sense for what the security framework is and the freedom and constraints with which you have to work.

Figure 11-3 shows the security framework for Apps for Office. Your App for Office actually runs in an Internet Explorer 9 or 10 Web Control out of process from the Office client app itself, in a sandbox host process. This provides a security boundary between your app and the client application and also isolates your app if it should have performance issues. The Office client application hosts the Web Extensibility Framework Runtime, which is the broker that manages communication and monitoring between the two processes, translates the JavaScript calls to native ones, and remotely renders your App for Office in the client application's UI as a TaskPaneApp, ContentApp, or MailApp.

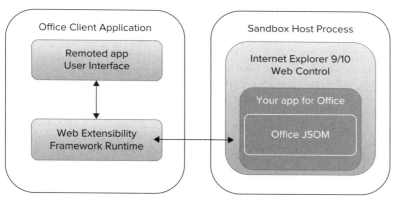

FIGURE 11-3

This security framework cannot be altered. However, as the developer, you can declaratively request what level of security permissions your app for Office needs to carry out its business within the manifest file via the <Permissions> element. You should be familiar enough with the API to set the requested level of permission based on your API use. To use a part of the API that requires more permissions than you've requested in the manifest will result in the Office client blocking the use of that specific part of the API at runtime. This, of course, results in an error being thrown and most likely a frustrated user.

For document-based apps you can request the permission levels shown in Table 11-3. The table intentionally represents gradations from least-privileged permission to most-privileged permission as you move down the table, where Restricted has the least permission on the document and ReadWriteDocument has the most.

TABLE 11-3: Document-based Permissions

PERMISSION	DESCRIPTION
Restricted	Permission that applies to all TaskPaneApps, enables activation, and allows use of the Settings object
ReadDocument	Includes the Restricted permission, and also enables the TaskPaneApp to use the API to read the document, manage bindings, and subscribe to events
ReadAllDocument	Includes the Restricted and ReadDocument permissions, and also enables the TaskPaneApp to use the API to obtain a binary copy of the document
WriteDocument	Includes the Restricted permission, and also enables the TaskPaneApp to use the `setSelectedDataAsync` API to write to the document
ReadWriteDocument	Includes the ReadAllDocument and WriteDocument permissions, and also enables the TaskPaneApp to use all write APIs

*Source: Office manifest's schema reference for apps on MSDN

Table 11-4 shows the MailApp permissions. Note that if your MailApp requires the `ReadWriteMailbox` permission, then an Exchange administrator must install the app. Apps that require this permission level cannot be installed by the user.

TABLE 11-4: Mailbox-based Permissions

PERMISSION	DESCRIPTION
Restricted	Permission that applies to all MailApps, enables the ItemIs and ItemHasKnownEntity activation rules, enables use of the RoamingSettings object, and is a subset of the app JavaScript Object Model
ReadItem	Applies to the selected item, includes the Restricted permission, and enables the MailApp to use all the well-known entities and regular expression activation rules to read all properties and to write custom properties
ReadWriteMailbox	Includes all the ReadItem permission and also enables the MailApp to use the `makeEWSRequestAsync` method to read and write all properties of any item in the user's mailbox

INTEGRATING APPS FOR OFFICE WITH SHAREPOINT

You can integrate Apps for Office with SharePoint in two ways. One method is to configure Office clients to use SharePoint as the central location to browse the available Apps for Office internal to the enterprise. This is an IT/administrator-managed location for manifest files built in to SharePoint. Apps for Office managed this way can be considered standalone Apps for Office. These standalone apps only have SharePoint as the location for their manifest file but they have no other integration or dependency on SharePoint. This is the primary way that IT can centrally approve and manage Apps for Office they want to make available internally across the enterprise, whether the app was internally developed or purchased directly from a vendor.

Another way to integrate these is to incorporate Apps for Office into SharePoint and deploy them with an app for SharePoint. These might be documents or document templates that contain one or more Apps for Office, but they are associated specifically with an app for SharePoint that in turn provides a solution that specifically uses SharePoint artifacts, services, and APIs. The caveat is that Apps for Office deployed inside of an app for SharePoint are not discoverable through the Office client UI because the app for Office manifest file is deployed inside the AppWeb where the app for SharePoint is deployed. You will see an example of this in a later Try It Out.

Standalone Apps for Office

In the case of the standalone app for Office, in the same way you set up the network share as a trusted app catalog in the first Try it Out in this chapter, you can navigate to the Options setting in one of the Office clients and add the URL for your Apps for Office catalog site on SharePoint. After this location is identified to the Office clients, when the user chooses to "See all" when inserting an app for Office, the client application UI shows these apps under the My Organization tab. The following Try It Out shows how a standalone app for Office is made available to enterprise users via SharePoint.

TRY IT OUT   Locating the Apps for Office Catalog in SharePoint Online

IT personnel can centrally manage the Apps for Office they want to make available to the enterprise via a special storage location for manifest files on SharePoint. This exercise shows where to manage these files in Office 365 SharePoint Online and how to configure the Office clients to look to this location for Apps for Office. To do so, follow these steps:

1. Log in to `portal.microsoftonline.com` with your developer tenancy username and password.

2. On the Office 365 Preview admin center page, click the Service Settings link, then the Sites link, and the link under "Don't see what you are looking for?"

3. On the SharePoint Administration Center page, click the Apps link, and then click the App Catalog link on the right side of the page.

4. Click the Apps for Office link to display the manifest storage location.

5. Copy the URL in the browser's address bar.

6. In the center of the Apps for Office page, click the new item link.

7. Browse to the AppManifests folder on your local machine, (the one you created in the first Try It Out), select the `FirstApp.xml` file, click Open, click OK to upload it, and click Save.

8. Open either Word or Excel and log in to the Office client using your Office 365 developer tenancy username and password. The login to the Office client is in the upper-right corner of the client application. When prompted, choose the Organization or School option and enter your Office 365 credentials.

9. Follow the steps 8–10 in the first Try It Out in this chapter to set the Trusted Catalog Locations, except this time, paste in the URL you copied.

10. Before clicking the Add Catalog button, trim back the URL by removing everything from `_layouts/…` forward through the end of the URL. Your final URL should look something like `https://[YourDeveloperTenancyDomain].sharepoint.com/sites/OSPAppCat/`. Click the Add Catalog button.

11. Click the check box beside the newly added item so it will show up in the menu, and then click OK. Close and reopen the Office client so your change takes effect.

12. Return to your browser Apps for Office page. Click the new item icon, click Browse to find the manifest file you created in the first exercise, and upload it.

13. In the Office client you restarted, from the Insert menu, select Apps for Office ➪ See All, and click My Organization. You might need to click the Refresh icon. Choose My First App and Insert it.

How It Works

The Apps for Office location on SharePoint is a custom document library specifically for storing manifest files. After an app for Office is built by either enterprise developers or purchased from a software vendor, the manifest file for the app for Office is given to IT. IT can then upload the manifest file to this SharePoint location and the app is then discoverable by any Office users when they browse the My Organization catalog from the client UI. Also, from this central location, IT can choose to revoke a manifest at any time, giving them complete control over what internally available Apps for Office end users have access to on the desktop.

Apps for Office Integrated with an App for SharePoint

For standalone Apps for Office, SharePoint provides a nice platform for IT to govern these apps within the enterprise. However, integrating Apps for Office into an app for SharePoint solution also makes a lot of sense. From the previous chapters you learned that Apps for SharePoint can be SharePoint-hosted, Provider-hosted, or Autohosted. In all of these cases, irrespective of the hosting platform, one or more Apps for Office can be included within the app for SharePoint. Also, as mentioned earlier, the caveat is that these Apps for Office are not discoverable via the Office client UI as with the Apps for Office that are registered in the SharePoint Apps for Office catalog. These Apps for Office are available and usable only by the users who have access to the SharePoint site where the app for SharePoint was added.

From the developer's perspective, the Apps for Office artifacts are deployed in the app for SharePoint AppWeb infrastructure and the back-end Web application/services are deployed to their appropriate hosting environment. However, as integrated parts of the solution, the Apps for Office are available then to the user where the app for Office can interact directly with the APIs and services exposed by the back-end application. This coupling of one or more Apps for Office with an app for SharePoint opens an opportunity for developers to build a whole new class of point productivity solutions, delivered worldwide as a single unit through the Office Store, to anyone using SharePoint 2013 on-premises and/or Office 365 SharePoint Online. This all speaks to the potential market for the distribution of your app, but in terms of the breadth of opportunity for building composite app solutions, these can be point solutions that target small niche companies to solutions that meet specific needs within any of the broader vertical markets spanning both the private and public sectors. Wow, that's developer opportunity!

Let's examine how to couple an app for Office with an app for SharePoint. In the following example you work an Autohosted exercise.

Integrating an App for Office with an App for SharePoint (CompositeOSPAutoHosted.zip)

An app for SharePoint can be either SharePoint-hosted, provider-hosted or autohosted. In all of these cases, you can incorporate one or more Apps for Office into the app for SharePoint to be delivered as part of a rich composite productivity solution. This exercise shows the basics for how to build such an app; follow these steps:

1. Run Visual Studio 2012 as Administrator. Select New Project.

2. In the New Project dialog, expand the Templates ⇨ Visual C# ⇨ Office/SharePoint ⇨ Apps nodes. Select App for SharePoint 2013 and provide the Name: **CompositeOSPAutoHosted**. Click OK.

3. In the Specify the App for SharePoint settings dialog, provide the URL to your Office 365 developer site and click the Validate button to confirm connectivity to the site.

4. For the question, "How do you want to host your app for SharePoint?" select Autohosted, and click Finish.

5. Open the `Default.aspx` file from the Pages folder and replace everything between the `<body>`...`</body>` elements with the following:

```
<form id="form1" runat="server">
 <div>
     <asp:ScriptManager ID="ScriptManager1" runat="server"
          EnablePartialRendering="true" />
     <asp:UpdatePanel ID="PopulateData" runat="server" UpdateMode="Conditional">
        <ContentTemplate>

        <table border="1" cellpadding="10">
         <tr><th> App for Office in an app for SharePoint</th></tr>
         <tr><td>
        <h2>SharePoint Site Accessed</h2>
        <asp:Label runat="server" ID="WebTitleLabel"/>
        <h2>SharePoint AppWeb, right-click and Open in new tab</h2>
        <asp:HyperLink ID="HyperLink1" runat="server">SPAppURL</asp:HyperLink>
        <h2>Current logged-in User:</h2>
        <asp:Label runat="server" ID="CurrentUserLabel" />
        <h2>Users of the Site</h2>
        <asp:ListView ID="UserList" runat="server">
            <ItemTemplate ><asp:Label ID="UserItem" runat="server"
        Text="<%# Container.DataItem.ToString()  %>"></asp:Label><br />
            </ItemTemplate>
        </asp:ListView>
        <h2>Lists available on the Host Web</h2>
```

```
<asp:ListView ID="ListList" runat="server">
    <ItemTemplate ><asp:Label ID="ListItem" runat="server"
Text="<%# Container.DataItem.ToString()  %>"></asp:Label><br />
    </ItemTemplate>
</asp:ListView>
</td>

</tr>
</table>
</ContentTemplate>
    </asp:UpdatePanel>
</div>
</form>
```

6. Right-click on the `Default.aspx` file from the Pages folder and choose View Code.

7. Add the following variables just before the `Page_ Load` method:

```
string siteName;
string currentUser;
List<string> listOfUsers = new List<string>();
List<string> listOfLists = new List<string>();
```

8. Inside the `Page_ Load` method replace all the code with the following:

```
// The following code gets the client context and site information
// by using TokenHelper.

var contextToken = TokenHelper.GetContextTokenFromRequest(Page.Request);
var hostWeb = Page.Request["SPHostUrl"];
var spAppWeb = Page.Request["SPAppWebUrl"];

using (var clientContext =
TokenHelper.GetClientContextWithContextToken(hostWeb, contextToken,
    Request.Url.Authority))
  {
    //Load the properties for the web object.
    var web = clientContext.Web;
    clientContext.Load(web);
    clientContext.ExecuteQuery();

    //Get the site name.
    siteName = web.Title;

    //Get the current user.
    clientContext.Load(web.CurrentUser);
    clientContext.ExecuteQuery();
    currentUser = clientContext.Web.CurrentUser.LoginName;

    //Load the lists from the Web object.
    ListCollection lists = web.Lists;
    clientContext.Load<ListCollection>(lists);
    clientContext.ExecuteQuery();

    //Load the current users from the Web object.
    UserCollection users = web.SiteUsers;
    clientContext.Load<UserCollection>(users);
```

```
    clientContext.ExecuteQuery();

    foreach (User siteUser in users)
        {
            listOfUsers.Add(siteUser.LoginName);
        }

    foreach (List list in lists)
        {
            listOfLists.Add(list.Title);
        }

    // Display on page
    HyperLink1.Text = spAppWeb.ToString()
+ "/Lists/AppCompositeDocLibrary/";
    HyperLink1.NavigateUrl = spAppWeb.ToString()
+ "/Lists/AppCompositeDocLibrary/";
    WebTitleLabel.Text = siteName;
    CurrentUserLabel.Text = currentUser;
    UserList.DataSource = listOfUsers;
    UserList.DataBind();
    ListList.DataSource = listOfLists;
    ListList.DataBind();

    }
```

9. Right-click `ListCollection` and select Resolve using `Microsoft.SharePoint.Client`. This also fixes the syntax error for `UserCollection`.

10. To set the permissions being requested of SharePoint by the app, double-click the `AppManifest` `.xml` node in the Solution Explorer. In the manifest designer click the Permissions tab. Under Permission requests, click just under Scope to drop down the list, and then select Web. Select Read under Permission.

11. At this point you just have a standard Autohosted app, but press F5 to make sure everything debugs correctly.

12. Provide your credentials at the various prompts, and when prompted for whether or not for SharePoint to trust this app, click Trust It.

13. Close the browser to stop debugging.

14. To add a TaskPaneApp to the solution, right-click the `CompositeOSPAutoHosted` node in the Solution Explorer and select Add ➪ New Item.

15. In the Add New Item dialog, select App for Office and provide the name **AutoHostedTaskPaneApp.**

16. In the Create App for Office dialog, select Excel only as the TaskPaneApp and click Finish.

    Visual Studio has added all the components of the TaskPaneApp that you used earlier when building an app for Office, but has placed them appropriately in either the Web portion of the solution that will be deployed to the Web server or within the part of the app that will be deployed as SharePoint artifacts in your remote site. Notice the `AutoHostedTaskPaneApp` `.html`, `.js`, and `.png` files are all placed nicely in the web structure and the app for Office manifest.xml file is within the SharePoint structure for deployment. Visual Studio also added an OfficeDocuments folder to the SharePoint project that contains a base Excel document that has a TaskPaneApp associated with it.

17. To create a document library for the Excel file, right-click the CompositeOSPAutoHosted node and select Add ⇨ New Item.

18. Select List, name it AppCompositeDocLibrary, and click Add.

19. In the Choose List Settings dialog, click "Create a non-customizable list based on an existing list type of:" and in the drop-down list select Document Library. Click Finish.

20. When the list designer opens, click the ... button under Use this template as the default to browse for a template. In the dialog open the OfficeDocuments folder and select the Excel AutoHostedTaskPaneApp.xlsx file, click Open.

21. Click Content Types, and in the Content Type Settings click to highlight the entire Document row, then right-click and select Delete, and click OK.

22. Press F5, and respond appropriately to all the prompts as the app for SharePoint deploys. After your web page appears, right-click the link to the AppWeb document library and select Open in new tab. Navigate to the newly opened tab in your browser to see the document library.

23. In the AppCompositeDocLibrary, click the Files tab ⇨ New Document ⇨ AppCompositeDocLibraryContentType1.

24. Excel will open with its TaskPaneApp, but the AutoHostedTaskPaneApp.html web page is now being served up from the Pages directory on your remote server!

How It Works

A number of steps in creating an app for SharePoint contain one or more Apps for Office. Here you simply created an out-of-the-box Autohosted app for SharePoint. You then added a standard TaskPaneApp to the solution and its web components, CSS, image, JavaScript and HTML, were added to the web project and the manifest file was added to the SharePoint project by Visual Studio. These, too, are then deployed to the Autohosted website. You set permissions in the Autohosted app's manifest file so it could be trusted to read the Host Web. Your app automatically has full permissions on the AppWeb, but if you want your app to do anything outside the scope of the AppWeb, then permission must be granted to the app when it is installed the first time.

Lastly, you ran the app and navigated from its landing page to the AppWeb document library and opened the Excel document deployed in your AppWeb that contained an app for Office. The app for Office, because it is hosted in your AppWeb context, can reach back into SharePoint and out to the Web to bring together any mixture of content needed for your business solution. This is an example of nesting an app for Office inside an autoprovisioned app for SharePoint. It can also be done coupled with a SharePoint-hosted or Provider-hosted app.

The number of ways to stitch these composite apps together to create innovative solutions for end users is possibly as broad as our collective creativity. Also, the joy in building productivity software is to somehow empower users to do something a bit better, easier, and faster than they could before they had the solution. Building rich integrated Apps for Office and SharePoint can be just such solutions in the hands of end users.

SUMMARY

The new app model for Office opens up opportunities for developers to use standard web technologies to develop a new class of applications called Apps for Office and provides a broader opportunity across devices and hardware platforms to land productivity solutions. These solutions can then be made available to end-users worldwide via the Office.com store or through established direct sales channels that a software provider may already have with customers.

The JavaScript object model that enables the new app model is unlike its predecessors, VBA and VSTO, in that it does not seek to enable any automation of the Office client itself. The JSOM enables you to access the power of the Web in your web application and interact with the document or mail item within an end-user's working context. This is where productivity gains can happen.

Lastly, there are a number of deployment models for Apps for Office. These apps can be discovered within the Office client UI as a user navigates to the Office Store, a corporate network share, or via an enterprise's Apps for Office catalog location on SharePoint. Apps for Office can also be nested within an app for SharePoint where they are accessible only within the AppWeb context, but can be a key part of composite, point productivity solutions. These composite apps can of course be delivered via the Office Store. Visit the MSDN `http://dev.office.com` site for developer guidance to get set up with an Office 365 Developer tenancy and the process for setting up a developer account with the Office Store.

EXERCISES

Answers to Exercises can be found in Appendix A.

1. What technologies can a developer use to create Apps for Office?

2. How does the new JSOM for Office differ from VSTO and VBA?

3. What are the three types of Apps for Office currently available?

4. If you want to programmatically work with a specific section of a document to read/write to it at will, what must you do?

▶ **WHAT YOU LEARNED IN THIS CHAPTER**

ITEM	DESCRIPTION
Manifest	An XML document that describes an app for Office to the Office client.
MailApp	An app for Office that is associated with mail items. It differs from TaskPaneApps and ContentApps in that it renders automatically in the UI based on rules being satisfied by data within the context of the mail item. TaskPaneApps and ContentApps must be inserted by user action.
TaskPaneApp	An app for Office that renders alongside the document. The task pane itself can be undocked and float, but its content is not part of the document itself.
ContentApp	An app for Office that is part of the document in the same way that a chart or image is part of a document. It prints when the document is printed and is saved with the document.
Office.js	The JavaScript library for Office.

RECOMMENDED READING

http://dev.office.com

JavaScript API for Office, http://msdn.microsoft.com/en-us/library/office/apps/
fp142185.aspx

Preparing your app for submission to the Office Store, http://msdn.microsoft.com/en-US/
office/apps/fp179865

12

Remote Event Receivers in SharePoint 2013

WHAT YOU WILL LEARN IN THIS CHAPTER:

➤ Getting to know remote event receivers (RERs)

➤ Understanding how to configure remote event receivers for various authentication methods

➤ Introducing app-level remote event receivers

WROX.COM DOWNLOADS FOR THIS CHAPTER

The wrox.com code downloads for this chapter are found at `http://www.wrox.com/WileyCDA/WroxTitle/productCd-1118495845.html` on the Download Code tab. The code for this chapter is divided into the following major examples:

➤ C12DocLibRERO365.zip

➤ C12RERO365.zip

Because SharePoint continues to play a deeper and more integral role in corporate business systems and processes, getting beyond farm-level custom solutions and sandbox limitations by being able to call Web services as a result of internal events firing became imperative for SharePoint — and the new app model now supports it! SharePoint has had event receivers for some time, but with previous versions of SharePoint your custom code ran either in full trust as a farm solution or in the sandbox with the constraints it imposed. With SharePoint 2013, rather than calling into code running on SharePoint, remote event receivers can now be built as web services and the URL endpoint can be registered with SharePoint. When an event fires on one or more of the numerous events associated with SharePoint components, the Web service is called, SharePoint passes in the item properties for the event, and the Web service carries out its business. Both synchronous and asynchronous calls to your web service are supported, and the Web service can also call back into SharePoint, authenticated via OAuth, to read and write as needed. Synchronous "before" events denoted with "-ing," such as adding, deleting, and so on can perform validation and cancel the event. "After" events denoted with "-ed" — for instance, deleted, added, and so on, can either be synchronous or asynchronous.

Additionally, with the new app model for SharePoint, three new app-level events are provided for app life-cycle management: Installed, Uninstalling, and Upgraded. These app-level events also call out to remote event receiver web services you write and host.

This chapter walks you through some of the nuances in how to construct the remote event receivers based on whether you are in a high-trust server-2-server (S2S) protocol, behind the firewall environment, or are using OAuth. Office 365 SharePoint Online with its Internet-facing endpoints uses OAuth, the authentication method for your app, if you need to call back into SharePoint to perform follow-on actions.

INTRODUCING REMOTE EVENT RECEIVERS

Traditionally, event receivers in SharePoint have been used for a wide range of purposes in business solutions, from sending out email or spawning announcement notifications, to data validation, to canceling a current user action and redirecting him to another action. Event receivers are often used simply for logging or tracking documents in a library for reporting purposes. The new remote event receivers take nothing away from the multiplicity of ways developers can employ them. But more importantly they comply with the objectives of the new app model to move the execution of developer code outside of SharePoint and provide a consistent programming and run-time experience on-premises and across SharePoint Online. Because the remote event receivers run off-box from SharePoint, you do not need to install `.dlls` for event receivers on the SharePoint server. Also, unlike the SharePoint Online sandbox environment, your event receiver is no longer required to complete within 30 seconds and you can now call out to as many external services as needed to support the work required for an event to logically be completed.

However, keep in mind that event receivers were not intended to be depended upon as a mechanism to build a transactional system. These are not wrapped in a transaction framework of, say, a begin and an end commit. So use them wisely and be careful to try not to coerce them into high-value, mission-critical, transactional scenarios they were not meant to be used for.

In the following Try It Out you build a simple RER for Office 365 SharePoint Online to see how event receivers are constructed using Visual Studio and get a sense for how these remote events work.

TRY IT OUT   **Building a Remote Event Receiver for Office 365 SharePoint Online (C12RERO365.zip)**

For this activity you will use your Office 365 tenancy to deploy two lists and exercise a remote event receiver. The remote event receiver web service is autodeployed to Windows Azure, and OAuth is used for the RER to call back into SharePoint Online to log an entry in another list.

1. Run Visual Studio 2012 as Administrator. Select New Project.

2. In the New Project dialog, expand the Templates ➪ Visual C# ➪ Office/SharePoint ➪ Apps nodes. Select App for SharePoint 2013 and provide the name: **C12RERO365**. Click OK.

3. In the Specify the name for your app for SharePoint settings dialog, set the SharePoint site URL you will deploy the app to and choose SharePoint-hosted as the location to host your app for SharePoint. Click Finish.

4. Right-click on the C12RERO365 project node in Solution Explorer and select Add ➪ New item.

5. Select List, provide the name, **ListToFireEvents**, and click Add.

6. In the Choose List Settings dialog, select Create a non-customizable list based on an existing list type of, select Custom List from the drop-down list, and click Finish.

7. Right-click on the C12RERO365 project node in Solution Explorer and select Add ➪ New item.

8. Select List, provide the name, **RemoteEventLog**, and click Add.

9. In the Choose List Settings dialog, select Create a non-customizable list based on an existing list type of, select Custom List from the drop-down list, and click Finish.

10. Right-click on the project node in Solution Explorer and select Add ➪ New item.

11. Select Remote Event Receiver, leave the default name of RemoteEventReceiver1, and click Add.

12. In the Choose Event Receiver Settings dialog, select List Item Events for the type of event receiver you want and Custom List for the event source. Click An item is being added and then click Finish.

13. Visual Studio automatically adds C12RERO365Web, a Web project to host your remote event receiver. In the C12RERO365Web project locate the RemoteEventReceiver1.svc node that was added. This SOAP-based web service is the endpoint for receiving the SharePoint events remotely. Right-click on the RemoteEventReceiver1.svc node and select View Code if the file is not already open in Visual Studio.

14. Delete the following lines from the code:

```
using (ClientContext clientContext =
  TokenHelper.CreateRemoteEventReceiverClientContext(properties))
  {
    if (clientContext != null)
      {
          clientContext.Load(clientContext.Web);
          clientContext.ExecuteQuery();
      }
  }
```

15. In the exact location you deleted the above code, insert the following:

```
// Do not log events written to the remote event log list
string RemoteEventListTitle = "RemoteEventLog";

// Check to see if it is an event on the RemoteEventLog that fired
// and return if so.
```

```
            // You do not want to log these events and an infinite loop would occur
            // as well.
            if (string.Equals(properties.ItemEventProperties.ListTitle,
RemoteEventListTitle, StringComparison.OrdinalIgnoreCase))
                return result;

        // Evaluate the type of event and perform an edit and respond accordingly.
        switch (properties.EventType)
        {
            case SPRemoteEventType.ItemAdding:
                if (string.Equals(properties.ItemEventProperties.AfterProperties
["Title"].ToString(), "TestCancel", StringComparison.OrdinalIgnoreCase))
                {
                    result.ErrorMessage = "Title cannot be 'TestCancel'.";
                    result.Status = SPRemoteEventServiceStatus.CancelWithError;
                }
                else
                {
                    // Retrieve and write the remote events logging list
                    // for the adding event.
                    using (ClientContext clientContext =
TokenHelper.CreateRemoteEventReceiverClientContext(properties))
                    {
                        clientContext.Load(clientContext.Web);
                        clientContext.ExecuteQuery();
                        List myEventLogList =
clientContext.Web.Lists.GetByTitle(RemoteEventListTitle);

                        try
                        {
                            // Add the event entry to the EventLog list.
                            string myItemTitle = "Remote event logged: "
+ DateTime.Now.ToString(" yyyy/MM/dd-HH:mm:ss") + ", Event type: "
+ properties.EventType.ToString() + ", Title: "
+ properties.ItemEventProperties.AfterProperties["Title"].ToString();
                            ListCollection myLists = clientContext.Web.Lists;
                            List myRemoteEventList =
myLists.GetByTitle(RemoteEventListTitle);
                            clientContext.Load<ListCollection>(myLists);
                            clientContext.Load<List>(myRemoteEventList);
                            ListItemCreationInformation listItemCreationInfo = new
ListItemCreationInformation();
                            var listItem =
myRemoteEventList.AddItem(listItemCreationInfo);
                            listItem["Title"] = myItemTitle;
                            listItem.Update();
                            clientContext.ExecuteQuery();
                        }

                        catch (Microsoft.SharePoint.Client.ServerException)
                        {
                            // If a SharePoint server error occurs, return.
```

```
                                    return result;
                                }
                            }
                        }
                        break;
                }
```

16. Right-click on the `AppManifest.xml` file in the `C12RERO365` project in Solution Explorer and select View Code.

17. To make testing the remote event receiver more convenient, you can set the app to start on the list page by changing the `StartPage` element in the manifest to the following:

```
<StartPage>~appWebUrl/Lists/ListToFireEvents</StartPage>
```

18. In the Solution Explorer, right-click on `C12RERO365` and select Deploy. (Not F5. The Autohosted Web service must be fully deployed to Windows Azure.) When the browser launches the trust request page, click Trust It.

19. On the `ListToFireEvents` page, add a new item to the list and click Save.

20. After adding the item, go to the address bar in your browser and click in the bar so the cursor is at the end of the URL. Delete everything back to …/`Lists/`. Following the slash (/), type **RemoteEventLog** and press Enter so the browser navigates to the remote event log list. You'll see the list item that wrote back to SharePoint using CSOM from within the remote event receiver web service.

21. Using the browser's back button, navigate back to the `ListToFireEvents`. Add another new item, but title it **TestCancel**, and click Save. Since there is logic in the remote event to not allow an item with this specific title, an error message is being returned to the user. Go ahead and cancel out of the add, or change the title and choose to save. In either case, you can again navigate to the `RemoteEventLog` list and see that the item with a title of `TestCancel` was not added.

22. Close the browser to stop the debugging session and return to the `RemoteEventReceiver.svc.cs` file to view the code.

How It Works

When you started this Visual Studio project you created two lists to deploy with the app. When adding the remote event receiver to the project, you stepped through the wizard and selected the An item is being added event. Although you didn't select any event sources that fire when an event has completed, the Visual Studio project template automatically provides two methods in the remote event: `ProcessEvent` and `ProcessOneWayEvent`. Both methods pass in a rich `RemoteEventProperties` object from which you can determine everything about the event that just happened. The difference between the two methods is that `ProcessEvent` is for synchronous processing, and the UI in SharePoint will wait until your remote event code completes. Because synchronous events can also be canceled by your code, the `ProcessEvent` returns an `SPRemoteEventResult` object. You can optionally set properties on this object so SharePoint can know how to proceed when the remote event receiver has completed its processing. The `ProcessOneWayEvent` method is for asynchronous processing and returns void.

Synchronous "-ing" actions, adding, deleting, updating, in SharePoint must use the `ProcessEvent` method. The "-ed" events, those that have already added, updated, deleted, can also use the `ProcessEvent` if you want synchronous processing for your code or they can use the `ProcessOneWayEvent` method. Keep in mind, "-ed" events with synchronous processing, by definition, cannot be canceled because the action has already happened in SharePoint. Asynchronous "-ed" events that use the `ProcessOneWayEvent` method can be a fire-and-forget asynchronous action. You can also choose to call back into SharePoint after your code actions complete. What's important to note is that the `ProcessOneWayEvent` method does not hang the UI waiting for your code to complete so you can have long-running processes that are initiated by a SharePoint event if you need to.

In the code example you can observe a few fundamental concepts on how to handle the type of event you're processing, how to cancel an event if a validation check fails, and how to call back into SharePoint to do a follow-on action. Because the `ProcessEvent` method will pass back to SharePoint a `SPRemoteEventResult` object, the `result` object is instantiated and available for use. You might or might not choose to change any properties in this object, but in any case, it will be passed back. A switch statement is used to determine the type of event that was fired on SharePoint. This makes isolating code you want to use based on any specific event easy. Drilling into the `ItemAdding` case, a check exists to see whether a specific value is present in the title. If so, the event loads an error message and cancels with an error. This simple example shows the pattern for how you can insert validation logic in a remote event receiver. Lastly, if the validation completes, then the pattern for how to call back into SharePoint using CSOM is shown. In this simple case, another list is being written to as a log for items being added to the `ListToFireEvents`.

Before you ran the code you made a configuration change to the manifest file to set the start page. By default, the starting page is set to `Default.aspx` but in your case you wanted the starting page to be the `ListToFireEvents` page.

For the code implications, in step 14 in this example, you deleted several project template boilerplate lines of code that indicated how to call back into SharePoint using the client side object model and how to use OAuth to authenticate your remote web service. However, all the code you deleted is actually used within the code you added back in, it's just in its proper location for what you needed to do here. Since the `C12RERO365` part of your solution gets deployed to SharePoint Online and the `C12RERO365Web` part gets automatically deployed to Windows Azure, OAuth is required for the web service to call back into SharePoint. Here too much is managed for you by the `TokenHelper` class incorporated into the project template. This line of code, `ClientContext clientContext = TokenHelper.CreateRemoteEventReceiverClientContext(properties)`, works all kinds of magic on your behalf and is fully discussed in Chapter 10, "OAuth." In this example, using OAuth and CSOM you were able to write a log entry into the `RemoteEventLog` list every time an item was added to the `ListToFireEvents`.

Remote event receivers follow the typical three patterns for authentication that are used for Autohosted and SharePoint-hosted Apps for SharePoint: on-premises only, in the cloud only, and hybrid where part is on-premises and part is in the cloud. Remote event receivers only need to be concerned about authentication if they need to call back into SharePoint to perform some action on SharePoint. If your remote event receiver is of the fire-and-forget model, or if you are simply performing a validation and optionally cancelling an event, you do not need to be concerned with authentication in your code, but the manifest does need to have the correct designation. Figure 12-1 shows the on-premises-only and cloud-only configurations as well as the appropriate authentication used by the remote event receiver if your code needs to call back into SharePoint.

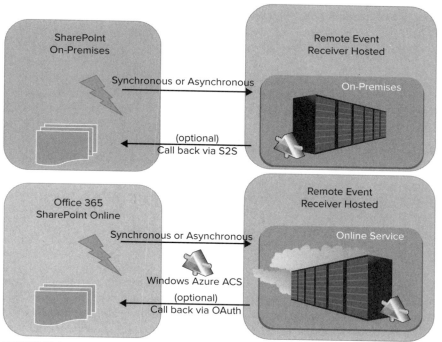

FIGURE 12-1

Some enterprises that have their SharePoint site on-premises will choose to be configured for a hybrid environment where their remote event receivers may reside either on internal servers or in the cloud. In this case the enterprise might want a single authentication method and programming model for its remote event receivers that will work equally well regardless of where the remote event receiver is hosted. To accommodate this, the enterprise must follow the Microsoft-provided guidance to configure SharePoint to use Windows Azure Access Control Services (ACS) as the authorization service and expose the appropriate endpoints for SharePoint and any internally hosted remote event receivers to the public Internet. ACS must be able to access these endpoints to provide the needed authentication via OAuth. Figure 12-2 shows this hybrid pattern.

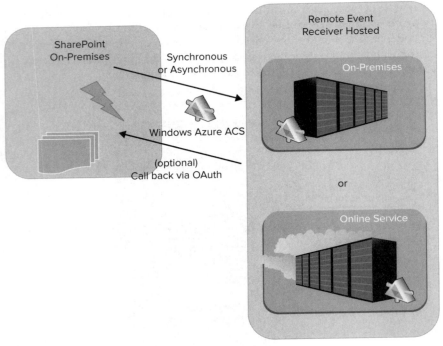

FIGURE 12-2

Although you have the opportunity to call back into SharePoint to do additional work within the app web, host web, or elsewhere depending on your app's permissions, sometimes you might simply want to make some alterations on the list item and its properties that are currently being processed in the `ProcessEvent` method. You can do this by evaluating any value passed in on the `properties` object and then use the `SPRemoteEventResult` object and its `ChangedItemProperties` object to pass your alterations back to SharePoint.

For instance, you can use the `properties.ItemEventProperties.AfterProperties` object in your validation logic to assess whether the incoming values are as you expected them to be. Once you make any changes to your `result` object this will be passed back to SharePoint. SharePoint will update the list columns accordingly.

The following Try It Out walks you through using the `SPRemoteEventResult` object. Additionally, you will see in this example that because your app does not explicitly need to call back into SharePoint to read/write data, there is no need to use the `TokenHelper` class in your code.

TRY IT OUT **Creating a Remote Event Receiver for a Document Library and Content Type (C12DocLibRERO365.zip)**

For this exercise you use your Office 365 tenancy to deploy a document library that contains custom content type, custom columns, and a remote event receiver. The remote event receiver web service is autodeployed to Windows Azure.

1. Run Visual Studio 2012 as Administrator. Select New Project.

2. In the New Project dialog, expand the Templates ⇨ Visual C# ⇨ Office/SharePoint ⇨ Apps nodes. Select App for SharePoint 2013 and provide the name: `C12DocLibRERO365`. Click OK.

3. In the Specify the name for your app for SharePoint settings dialog, set the SharePoint site URL to the app you will deploy to and choose SharePoint-hosted as the location to host your app for SharePoint. Click Finish.

4. Right-click on the `C12DocLibRERO365` project node in Solution Explorer and select Add ⇨ New item.

5. Select Site Column, provide the name, `DocNumber`, and click Add.

6. Right-click on the `C12DocLibRERO365` project node in Solution Explorer and select Add ⇨ New item.

7. Select Content Type, provide the name, `MyC12Document`, and click Add.

8. In the Choose Content Type Settings dialog, select Document from the drop-down list as the content type to inherit from and click Finish.

9. In the content type designer, under the Columns tab, choose Click here to add a column. Using the drop-down list, select and add three columns: Author, Status, and your custom column Doc Number, and save the content type.

10. Right-click on the `C12DocLibRERO365` project node in Solution Explorer and select Add ⇨ New item.

11. Select List, provide the name, `MyDocumentLibrary`, and click Add.

12. In the Choose List Setting dialog, click the Create a customizable list based on radio button and select Document Library from the drop-down list. Click Finish.

13. In the list designer under the Columns tab, scroll down if needed and click the Content Types button.

14. In the Content Type Settings dialog, select Click here to add a content type and select `MyC12Document` from the drop-down list.

15. Select the row of the `MyC12Document` item; click Set as Default and Save.

16. To now remove the extraneous `Document` content type that was previously the default document so it will not show within SharePoint, click Content Types again, select the entire row for `Document`, right-click the selected row, and choose Delete. Click OK.

17. Click on the list designer Views tab. In the Available columns pane, select the Title column and click the right-facing arrow button to move it to the right-hand side.

18. Click on the list designer List tab and copy the List URL. Navigate to the `AppManifest.xml` file, right-click and select View Code.

19. Replace the `StartPage` element contents so the element looks something like this: `<StartPage>~appWebUrl/Lists/MyDocumentLibrary?{StandardTokens} </StartPage>`. Save and close the manifest file. This change directs SharePoint to start at your document library when your app launches.

20. Before going any further, press F5 to validate that the content type and document library are working correctly.

21. When the MyDocumentLibrary page opens, click on the Files tab to open the ribbon. On the ribbon click the New Document drop-down to see your `MyC12Document`. Click it.

22. Word 2013 will open and all the metadata columns associated with your content type will display in the Document Information Panel (DIP) at the top of the document. It's these columns that can be validated or augmented in your remote event receiver code. Go ahead and add some values in the fields and save the document. Word will prompt you to select a location to save the file. Under the Current Folder, click MyDocumentLibrary. Alternatively, you can browse to the document library via the appropriate URL for your site. Close the Word document and refresh the page to see the metadata stored in the columns. Close the browser to stop debugging.

23. Right-click on the `C12DocLibRERO365` project node in Solution Explorer and select Retract. If the retract fails, login to the Office 365 site and remove the app manually from the Site Contents page. Hover over the app tile, click the ellipsis (...) and select Remove.

24. Right-click on the `C12DocLibRERO365` project node in Solution Explorer and select Add ➪ New item.

25. Select Remote Event Receiver, leave the default name of `RemoteEventReceiver1`, and click Add.

26. In the Choose Event Receiver Settings dialog, select List Item Events for the type of event receiver you want. Notice that Visual Studio selects your MyDocumentLibrary by default, so leave this and select An Item is being added. Click Finish.

27. If the code for the remote event receiver does not automatically open, right-click on the `RemoteEventReceiver1.svc` node and select View Code.

28. Delete the following lines from the code:

```
using (ClientContext clientContext =
   TokenHelper.CreateRemoteEventReceiverClientContext(properties))
   {
     if (clientContext != null)
       {
           clientContext.Load(clientContext.Web);
           clientContext.ExecuteQuery();
       }
   }
```

29. In the exact location from which you deleted the above code, insert the following:

```
// Generate a random number to simulate an external system providing
// a reference number for a document.
Random r = new Random();
int myDocNum = r.Next(100) + 1000;

// Evaluate the type of event and perform an edit and adjust
// the result object accordingly.
```

```
switch (properties.EventType)
{
    case SPRemoteEventType.ItemAdding:
        // Set a default title if no Title was input.
        If
(properties.ItemEventProperties.AfterProperties.ContainsKey("vti_title")
                && string.IsNullOrEmpty
(properties.ItemEventProperties.AfterProperties["vti_title"].ToString()))
        {
            result.ChangedItemProperties.Add("vti_title",
properties.ItemEventProperties.AfterProperties["_Author"].ToString()
                + "-" + myDocNum);
        }

        // Set a default status to Draft if no status value was input.
        if
(properties.ItemEventProperties.AfterProperties.ContainsKey("_Status")
                && string.IsNullOrEmpty
(properties.ItemEventProperties.AfterProperties["_Status"].ToString()))
        {
            result.ChangedItemProperties.Add("_Status", "Draft");
        }

        // Always provide a document number.
        result.ChangedItemProperties.Add("DocNumber", myDocNum.ToString());

        break;
}
```

30. In the Solution Explorer, right-click on C12DocLibRERO365 and select Deploy. (Not F5. The Autohosted Web service must be fully deployed to Windows Azure.) Go through the process of adding a new document by clicking on your content type under the FILES tab on the document library landing page. The DIP will be displayed as before; make no changes to the DIP fields, save and close your document.

31. Refresh the browser to see that your file has been added but notice that all the list columns now have information in them due to the processing that happened in the remote event receiver.

How It Works

The biggest difference in this example from the first Try It Out is that you used the SPRemoteEventResult object that is returned to SharePoint. SharePoint honors any modification you made to the object and updates the document list columns appropriately. It's important to note that although you must choose Trust It when your app is installed, when using the SPRemoteEventResult object only, if your code is not explicitly calling back into SharePoint using CSOM or REST to read/write data, then you do not need to write code that uses the TokenHelper class. This example shows the pattern where your remote event receiver can impact data being written to SharePoint by modifying the SPRemoteEventResult object directly.

APP-LEVEL LIFE-CYCLE REMOTE EVENT RECEIVERS

Microsoft has put a significant investment into the life-cycle management for apps in the new cloud app model. One of the investments is to enable you, the developer, to tap into three key events in your app's life cycle: when your app has been installed, when your app is uninstalling, and when your app is upgraded. By writing remote event receivers for when these app-level events fire, you can provide invaluable information back to your own service endpoints. You can track and analyze the install, upgrade, and uninstall your app worldwide from the office.com SharePoint store.

Creating app-level events is just like creating a normal RER. These events are functionally equivalent and coded exactly like the SharePoint-level remote event receivers, including synchronous and asynchronous processing options, and they can use OAuth for authentication or S2S when behind the firewall. However, because the steps to create app-level remote event receivers differ from how to create SharePoint-level remote event receivers, the following Try It Out provides guidance on creating these app-level remote event receivers.

> **TRY IT OUT**   **Wiring Up App-level Life-Cycle Remote Event Receivers**

For this exercise you will use the `C12DocLibRERO365` Visual Studio solution from the previous Try It Out to examine how to include app-level events in your app for SharePoint.

1. Run Visual Studio 2012 as Administrator and open the `C12DocLibRERO365` solution.

2. Click on the `C12DocLibRERO365` project in the Solution Explorer.

3. In the Properties pane for the project, notice the three properties: Handle App Installed, Handle App Uninstalling, and Handle App Upgraded. These are all set to `False` by default.

4. Set Handle App Installed to `True`.

5. If the code page does not automatically open, navigate to the `AppEventReceiver.svc.cs` file to view the code. The code should look really familiar by now because it's identical to what you have been working with — it is just for handling the app-level events.

6. Navigate to the `AppManifest.xml` file. In the `Properties` node an `InstalledEventEndpoint` element has automatically been added. If you change the other two app-level properties to `True`, these events will also be registered in the manifest file.

How It Works

App-level life-cycle events have to fire on the periphery; that is, when your app first touches SharePoint and is installed to when it is upgraded or is uninstalling. Therefore, these events must be registered at the app manifest level; the app life-cycle manager within SharePoint registers these event requests and ensures they happen.

All other SharePoint-level event receivers are registered with the SharePoint artifact inside the app. They get deployed when your app is installed and fire within the context of your app's execution when the appropriate list, library, or other SharePoint artifact is used. Microsoft provides both levels of events so your app can be notified when events are happening during the running of your app as well as when your app is moving through its life cycle.

SUMMARY

This chapter introduced you to the evolution of event receivers on the SharePoint platform: remote event receivers. Rather than relying on full-trust code deployed and running on the SharePoint server, remote event receivers are Web services where the URL is registered with SharePoint and called when an event fires on your specified SharePoint artifact. This provides the way for your app, which is executing remotely from SharePoint, to be called as events are transpiring or have transpired within your installed app on SharePoint.

Remote event receivers support both a server-to-server (behind the firewall) configuration for authentication or OAuth. In either case, appropriate authentication is required for your code to call back into SharePoint to perform a follow-on action. Both synchronous and asynchronous methods are provided for this in the web service.

Lastly, this chapter introduced you to the all-new events that fire during the app's life cycle: when it is installed, upgraded, or uninstalling. These events round out the ability for your remote app to interact with SharePoint from its beginning install, during its execution, through its upgrade, and at the end of life.

EXERCISES

You can find answers to exercises in Appendix A.

1. What is the name of the asynchronous method in the remote event receiver?

2. If you want to cancel an event and provide an error message, what enumeration would you use on `SPRemoteEventServiceStatus`, and what property would you place the text for your message into?

3. What two primary ways can you configure authentication on SharePoint for your app to have the ability to call back into SharePoint to perform follow-on actions?

4. Where would you look in your Visual Studio project to see whether an app-level event has been identified in your app?

▶ WHAT YOU LEARNED IN THIS CHAPTER

ITEM	DESCRIPTION
Remote event receivers	Web services where the URL is registered with SharePoint and called when events you identify on SharePoint artifacts are transpiring or have transpired on SharePoint.
SP remote event result	The `SPRemoteEventResult` object is used only on the synchronous method call and is passed back to SharePoint for processing. You can modify this object prior to its return to SharePoint.
Call back to SharePoint	Both synchronous and asynchronous events can call back into SharePoint using CSOM or REST for follow-on actions but either an S2S or OAuth authentication configuration must be in place.
App-level events	App-level events are identified in the app manifest and registered with SharePoint to fire during the app's lifecycle events of installed, updated, and uninstalling.

RECOMMENDED READING

Creating high-trust Apps for SharePoint 2013 using the server-to-server protocol — http://msdn.microsoft.com/en-us/library/fp179901(v=office.15).aspx

13

Building Line-of-Business Solutions Using Business Connectivity Services

WHAT YOU WILL LEARN IN THIS CHAPTER:

➤ Getting to know Business Connectivity Services in Office 365 SharePoint Online

➤ Understanding how to build app-level external content types using OData

➤ Working with SharePoint and Office integration using Apps for SharePoint and BCS

WROX.COM DOWNLOADS FOR THIS CHAPTER

The wrox.com code downloads for this chapter are found at `http://www.wrox.com/WileyCDA/WroxTitle/productCd-1118495845.html` on the Download Code tab. The code for this chapter is divided into the following major examples:

➤ C13EmployeeBCSApp.zip

➤ C13EmpReferralBCSAppForOffice.zip

➤ Employee.bdcm

Business Connectivity Services (BCS) in SharePoint 2010 made tremendous strides over Microsoft Office SharePoint Server (MOSS) 2007, bringing the capability to conveniently connect line-of-business (LOB) systems to the masses. BCS in SharePoint 2013 continues on this trajectory with new features that make BCS even more compelling to have as a core component when developing solutions for SharePoint users.

Looking back, with MOSS 2007 developers had to fuss around and work directly with the XML to set up connections to LOB systems using the Business Data Catalog. Also, after set up, these ADO .NET- or Web services-based connections were read-only. However, in SharePoint 2010 the tooling was ratcheted up significantly in both SharePoint Designer 2010 and Visual Studio 2010, making it easier for power users, IT professionals, and developers alike to create read-write connections in BCS solutions that ranged from no-code to rich, deeply integrated, code-based solutions spanning SharePoint, Office clients, and LOB systems.

For example, Duet Enterprise is one such solution. It is a product developed and licensed as a joint venture between Microsoft and SAP. Microsoft engineers built all the SharePoint integration components and SAP engineers used the tooling on the SAP platform to expose functional business services from the SAP side. Therefore, Duet Enterprise serves as a reference point in determining the best integration strategy for bringing ERP data into SharePoint because it provides the pattern for the technical architecture and the delineation of business functions surfaced in SharePoint and the LOB system. If your enterprise is looking for deep BCS integration with one of your LOB systems, then you are strongly encouraged to have your architects review the technical documentation for Duet Enterprise on TechNet. It can serve as a framework for discussion as you build your integration and development plan. Some key tenants for deep SharePoint BCS and LOB integration include the following:

➤ SharePoint is not a replacement for the LOB presentation layer.

➤ Do not replicate LOB functionality in SharePoint — augment functionality with SharePoint integration.

➤ The LOB is the system of record, SharePoint is not.

➤ Use the claims-based security infrastructure of SharePoint when connecting to the LOB services, and plan for high availability and reuse of this infrastructure component.

➤ Flow relevant user profile/identity data from the LOB into custom SharePoint profile elements as needed.

➤ Flow relevant LOB permissions data from the LOB into custom SharePoint profile elements as needed.

➤ SharePoint permissions should reflect LOB permissions.

These are some of the principles that you'll see employed in the Duet Enterprise design. So, if you are looking beyond tactical, point solutions for integration to your LOB systems, and if you are considering deep integration with a LOB system, then consider investigating Duet Enterprise as a reference architecture. Additionally, seeing the likes of Microsoft and SAP join together and build an enterprise-scale product on top of BCS should give you a lot of confidence that it's an infrastructure that you can build on too. This chapter offers you a look at some of the new BCS capabilities in SharePoint 2013, most specifically with access to OData endpoints and the new app-level external content types (ECTs) that you can leverage in your business solutions.

BUSINESS CONNECTIVITY SERVICES IN SHAREPOINT 2013

Before looking into what's new in BCS for SharePoint 2013, let's do a quick level-set on the external content type (ECT), a key component in Business Connectivity Services. The ECT is metadata that describes the connection information, methods (`create`, `read`, `update`, `delete`) that can be performed against the connection, data definitions for data elements, and any parameters that might pass between the client and external LOB data source. Security permissions can be set on the ECT to allow access by specific users or groups, and a wide array of authentication methods are supported, including Windows, claims-based, username and password, and certificate. ECTs serve as the basis for external lists. Unlike other lists in SharePoint that have their data stored in the SharePoint content database, external lists retrieve their data from the LOB data source every time the list is accessed by a user or programmatically. Therefore, external lists bring real-time data to SharePoint stakeholders. ECTs can also be made available to SharePoint search for indexing, and the LOB system data is included in a user's search result, trimmed by permissions.

A significant benefit of BCS is that it can provide a central location where IT manages a consistent approach for accessing LOB systems. By investing in building ECTs on a common infrastructure that surfaces LOB information in a usable and reusable form, business users, power users, and developers alike can become consumers of data served up by the ECTs in a variety of contexts. These range from configuring a dashboard of business data Web parts on a page, to configuring document templates for Word to include business data columns, to developers building custom enterprise solutions. Also, the developer's' programming pattern is consistent when building against ECTs because no matter what the LOB system is, they code exactly the same way against the ECT to retrieve or update the data. Because IT also builds the ECTs, it can ensure the efficiency of the ECT by defining the filters and throttling limits on the accesses to the back-end systems.

External content types were broadly welcomed in SharePoint 2010, and Microsoft built on the ECT foundation in SharePoint 2013 by providing new capabilities. Figure 13-1 shows the various BCS components and highlights the primary Microsoft BCS investments in this release.

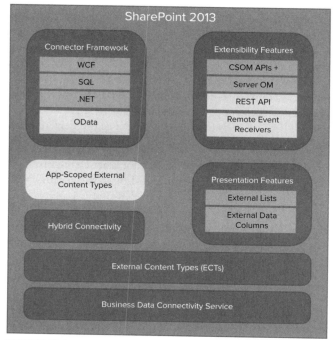

FIGURE 13-1

In the connector framework, alongside the already-popular SQL, WCF, and .NET connectors, the new highly requested OData connector joins the ranks. With the proliferation of OData producers, services that expose their data using the OData protocol, this new class of data services is now available for your BCS solutions.

With the new app model for SharePoint, where apps have a particular scope upon install into SharePoint, BCS now has app-scoped ECTs, too. In other words, an ECT can be created for and deployed within the scope of the app upon install. Typically, where an ECT has a farm-level, on-premises, or tenant-wide scope in Office 365, your app for SharePoint can have ECTs in your solution that run isolated within the app boundaries.

Another much-desired capability for BCS external lists was to have REST support for accessing them. This feature, too, was a significant investment by Microsoft to make the BCS data available via REST, but it has done so while also making meaningful contributions in the CSOM for accessing BCS data.

Microsoft also made significant investments in this release to support alerts and event receivers on external lists; both highly requested features by users and developers. Users can now create alerts in external lists in the same way they do on other SharePoint lists. Event receivers have been available on SharePoint artifacts for some time, but now BCS is a first-class citizen in the event infrastructure. For SharePoint to be notified that data has changed on an external list, configuration both on SharePoint and the external data source is required. The data source needs a way to become aware of underlying data changes; for example, SQL triggers or a service that periodically polls the data source to detect changes. It also needs a way for SharePoint to subscribe to it to receive notification of changes. SharePoint now has the infrastructure to support this interaction and provides a way to register this "notification channel" through an extension to the BDC model schema to include the new `EventSubscriber` and `EventUnsubscriber` stereotypes. At a high level, the communication flow for SharePoint to subscribe to be notified when there is a data change on the external system works like this: when the `Subscribe` method is called on the ECT associated with an external system, the `Subscribe` method passes the event type and delivery address to the external system. The external system records this information in a database and then returns a subscription ID to SharePoint. When the `Subscribe` method completes, notification of a data change can be sent from the external system to the delivery address REST endpoint on SharePoint. Receipt of the notification, in turn, fires an event on the external list and calls into your remote event receiver. Please refer to MSDN for full documentation on this subject.

Of the numerous Microsoft investments for BCS in 2013, let's first take a look at setting up an ECT that connects to an OData service. You will use Office 365 SharePoint Online in this Try It Out since it supports Business Connectivity Services.

TRY IT OUT **Adding a Business Data Connectivity Model to Office 365 SharePoint Online (Employee.bdcm)**

In this exercise you upload a Business Data Connectivity Model (BDCM) file to Office 365 SharePoint Online that defines an OData connection to the OData Northwind service endpoint available on Odata.org. After the external content type is created you then create an external list in a site collection of your choice. This ECT is available tenancy wide. For this exercise you will need an Office 365

Developer Site or an Office 365 Enterprise Preview trial. Visit either `http://on both dev.office .com` to sign up for a Developer Site or `http://on both office.com/preview` for an Office 365 Enterprise Preview trial.

1. Log in to the Office 365 `portal.microsoftonline.com` site using an account with administrative rights on the tenancy.

2. From the Dashboard page, click Service Settings.

3. On the Service Settings page, click Sites.

4. On the Sites page, click the link following the question, "Don't see what you are looking for?"

5. On the SharePoint Administration Center page, click BCS.

6. On the BCS page, click Manage BDC Models and External Content Types. (In an on-premises installation you would use the SharePoint Central Administration portal and navigate to Application Management ⇨ Manage service applications and Business Connectivity Service.)

7. Click the Import icon in the ribbon and browse to the `Employee.bdcm` file found in the code samples for this chapter. Click Open and click Import. The BDCM file will be validated on import; when it has successfully completed, click OK. (If you do not have permissions to import, click Set Metadata Store Permissions and make sure you have administrator-level permissions on the Metadata store.)

8. In the ribbon, click the drop-down list to select different views of the BDC Metadata Store and select BDC Models. Click the `NorthwindModel` check box, and as shown in Figure 13-2, click the Set Object Permissions button in the ribbon.

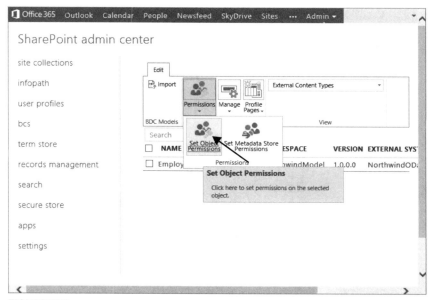

FIGURE 13-2

9. Browse the directory to find and select your user account, and then click the Add button. While your user account is selected in the lower window, click all the check boxes under Permissions to enable the full set of permissions, and then click OK. This gives your account full rights to manage the BDC Model.

10. In the ribbon, click the drop-down list to select different views of the BDC Metadata Store and select External Content Types. Click the Employee check box and click the Set Object Permissions button in the ribbon.

11. Browse the directory to find and select your user account, and then click the Add button. While your user account is selected in the lower window, click all the check boxes under Permissions to enable the full set of permissions for your account to access and manage the ECT. Click the check box to Propagate permissions to all methods and click OK.

12. Navigate to any site collection in your Office 365 tenancy where you want to create an external list for the ECT. When in the site collection, click Site Contents and select Add an app.

13. Scroll through the apps until you can see the External List tile as shown in Figure 13-3. Click it to add an External List.

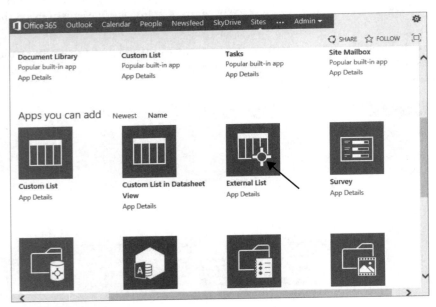

FIGURE 13-3

14. In the Adding External List dialog, enter **Northwind Employees** for the name and click the Select External Content Type icon.

15. In the External Content Type Picker, select the Employee external content type, click OK and the result should look like Figure 13-4. Then click Create.

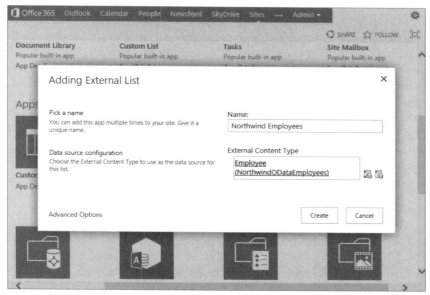

FIGURE 13-4

16. On the Site Contents page scroll until you see the new Northwind Employees app. Click the tile to open the external list. Additionally, a link to the Northwind Employees external list has been added in the left navigation bar under Lists. The completed external list should look something like Figure 13-5.

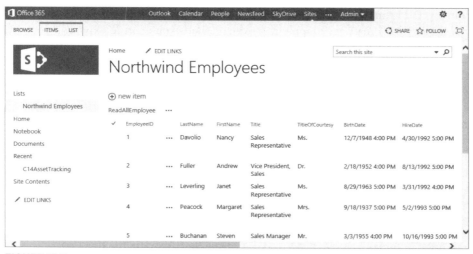

FIGURE 13-5

How It Works

In this example, the `.bdcm` file was already created for you to simply see the pattern for how to wire up the model in the administration portal. This is one pattern you can follow if you already have ECTs in your SharePoint 2010 environment and you want to move them to your 2013 environment. You can export them from 2010 and import them into 2013. For Office 365 SharePoint Online, only BDCMs that are SOAP-based or OData-based connections are supported — no .NET or ADO.NET (SQL direct connections) can be used in SharePoint Online. Also, the SOAP and OData ECTs can only use group-based permissions with authentication managed via the Secure Store Service (SSS).

If you navigate to the `Employee.bdcm` provided in the code sample download for this chapter and open it in Notepad or any XML editor, you can view the XML document structure. Following are a few of the high-level elements with which you should be familiar:

➤ `LobSystem`: This describes the type of connection (DotNetAssembly, Database, Webservice, or OData) to the external data source.

➤ `LobSystemInstance`: This describes the specific implementation of the `LobSystem`; with this element you can see the metadata describing the service URL endpoint and data format.

➤ `Entity`: This describes the business entity or object. It contains both `Methods` and data definitions described in a collection of `Parameters`.

➤ `Method`: This represents the read-write capabilities for the `Entity`. At a minimum a method of the type `SpecificFinder` that will return one item, and a `Finder` that will return all items must exist. These two methods are required for an ECT. Methods of the type `Updater`, `Deleter`, and `Creator` are optional depending on whether your external data source allows them. Or even if the external data source does have methods available beyond `Finder` and `SpecificFinder`, you choose which methods you want to implement in your ECT. Through the ECT creation process using the SharePoint Designer wizard or in Visual Studio, you create the mappings for the methods you want to expose in your ECT to the corresponding methods in the external data source. Lastly, methods can be scoped using a `FilterDescriptor`.

➤ `Parameter`: This describes the data elements that will flow to and from the external system.

BCS IN APPS FOR SHAREPOINT

In the previous exercise you installed a business data connectivity model into SharePoint Online and the external content type you created became available tenancy wide and could be used in any site collection — restricted by permissions, of course. However, the SharePoint 2013 app model provides a new opportunity for you to deliver Apps for SharePoint that have the BDCM deployed at the app-level so it is scoped only to that specific app for SharePoint. This opens up a whole new opportunity to deliver Apps for SharePoint from the Office.com Store that have a self-contained BCS connection to any OData source that you choose to provide. The key point is that app-level solutions must connect to OData sources; that's the only connection type supported in an app for SharePoint. In the following activity you build an app for SharePoint with an OData connection and see how it's defined to SharePoint.

TRY IT OUT Building an App-level BCS Solution for Office 365 SharePoint Online (C13EmployeeBCSApp.zip)

This exercise shows you how to create an app-level scoped BCS connection and then access the external list for the app for SharePoint via a REST call.

1. Run Visual Studio 2012 as Administrator. Select New Project.

2. In the New Project dialog, expand the Templates ⇨ Visual C# Office/SharePoint Apps nodes. Select App for SharePoint 2013 and provide the Name: `C13EmployeeBCSApp`. Click OK.

3. In the New App for SharePoint dialog, set the Office 365 SharePoint Online site URL to use for debugging and choose SharePoint-hosted as the location to host your app for SharePoint. Click Finish.

4. Right-click the `C13EmployeeBCSApp` project node in Solution Explorer and select Add Content Types for an External Data Source.

5. In the Specify OData Source dialog, enter `http://services.odata.org/Northwind/Northwind.svc/`.

6. In the Data Source Name, enter `Northwind OData Producer`. Click Next.

7. In the Select the Data Entities dialog, select `Employees` and confirm that the Create list instances for the selected data entities check box is checked. Click Finish.

8. Visual Studio creates an External Content Types node in the Solution Explorer. Expand the nodes until you see `Employee.ect`, and then double-click the node to open the ECT designer. In the designer you can select individual rows to delete data elements, and you can also add filters in the designer; a filter limit of 100 is set by default.

9. In the Solution Explorer, open the Pages node, right-click `Default.aspx`, and select View Markup.

10. Locate the `<asp:Content...>` element, and replace the entire `<div>...</div>` containing the `id="message"` paragraph with the following elements:

```
<h1>App-level BCS OData Connection</h1>
<div id="showEmployeeInfo"></div>
```

11. In the Solution Explorer expand the Scripts node and click on the `App.js` file to open it.

12. Replace all the code with the following:

```
$(document).ready(function () {
    window.C13EmployeeBCSApp = window.C13EmployeeBCSApp || {};

    C13EmployeeBCSApp.Grid = function (hostElement, spWebURL) {
        this.hostElement = hostElement;
        // Verify proper structure for SharePoint Web URL for REST call.
        if (spWebURL.length > 0 &&
        spWebURL.substring(spWebURL.length - 1, spWebURL.length) != "/")
```

```
            spWebURL += "/";
        this.spWebURL = spWebURL;
    }

    C13EmployeeBCSApp.Grid.prototype = {

        init: function () {
            //Retrieve data from app-level External List via REST
            $.ajax({
                url: this.spWebURL +
                "_api/lists/getbytitle('Employee')/items?" +
                "$select=BdcIdentity,EmployeeID,LastName,FirstName,Title,HomePhone",
                headers: {
                    "accept": "application/json",
                    "X-RequestDigest": $("#__REQUESTDIGEST").val()
                },
                success: this.showEmployees
            });
        },

        showEmployees: function (data) {
            var items = [];
            // Build table for showing Employees
            items.push("<table>");
            items.push("<tr><td>Employee ID</td>" +
                        "<td>Last Name</td>" +
                        "<td>First Name</td>" +
                        "<td>Title</td>" +
                        "<td>Phone Number</td></tr>");

            $.each(data.d.results, function (key, val) {
                items.push('<tr id="' + val.BdcIdentity + '">' +
                    '<td>' + val.EmployeeID + '</td>' +
                    '<td>' + val.LastName + '</td>' +
                    '<td>' + val.FirstName + '</td>' +
                    '<td>' + val.Title + '</td>' +
                    '<td>' + val.HomePhone + '</td></tr>');
            });

            items.push("</table>");

            $("#showEmployeeInfo").html(items.join(''));
        }
    }

    ExecuteOrDelayUntilScriptLoaded(getEmployees, "sp.js");
});

function getEmployees() {
    var gridEmployee = new C13EmployeeBCSApp.Grid($("#showEmployeeInfo"),
        _spPageContextInfo.webServerRelativeUrl);
    gridEmployee.init();
}
```

13. Press F5 to start debugging. When the Site Contents page loads, click the C13EmployeeBCSApp tile.

14. After the app loads, your page should look like Figure 13-6.

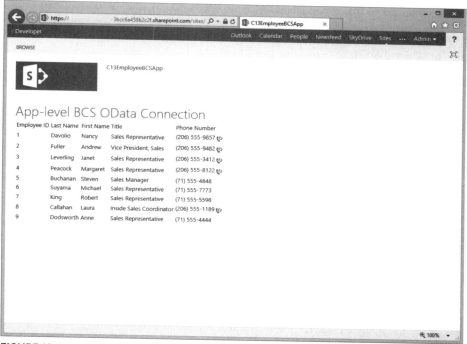

FIGURE 13-6

15. While the app for SharePoint is running you can go back to Visual Studio and set breakpoints in the App.js file and then refresh the browser page to track your way through the code.

16. But just as important, knowing how to find out where SharePoint is putting things and how to access them when at the app-level is always good. To take a look, in the browser trim the URL in the address bar from the tail end back to just after the / following C13EmployeeBCSApp/. This preserves the root appWeb URL where your app for SharePoint is installed. Now you can use the REST _api for SharePoint to look at your appWeb structure in the browser.

17. Following the root appWeb URL, type **_api/web/** to see the base information about your appWeb.

18. Following _api/web/, type **lists/** to see the lists that were deployed to your appWeb. There are several, but the two key lists are the Employee and BusinessDataMetadataCatalog lists.

19. To view the Employee list, you can use the same syntax you used in your App.js file to retrieve the Employee list data, so use _api/lists/getbytitle('Employee')/items in your browser. You can further refine your return payload by appending ?$select=BdcIdentity,EmployeeID, LastName,FirstName,Title,HomePhone to the previous URL.

20. Navigate to the BusinessDataMetadataCatalog via _api/web/lists/ BusinessDataMetadataCatalog/; notice that it's just a document library inside your appWeb.

21. To make this a little more concrete so that your .bdcm file is stored in a standard document library, you can navigate to this list and display it natively within your appWeb, too. Trim your base URL back to the root again as called out in step 16 and append `BusinessDataMetadataCatalog/` `Forms/allitems.aspx` to see your `BDCMetadata` file in its appWeb document library. Since this is a standard document library, you can download the `.bdcm` file if you choose.

22. Navigate to the external list created for your app for SharePoint by appending `Lists/Employee/` to your root appWeb URL.

23. Close the browser and the app for SharePoint will be retracted.

How It Works

In this exercise you worked through how nicely Visual Studio tooling helps you to create an external content type by connecting to an OData producer (data source). Although SharePoint supports a number of connection methods for tenancy-wide BDC Models, Apps for SharePoint only support OData connections. Also, an app for SharePoint can only have one `BDCMetadata.bdcm` file associated with it; however, multiple entities can exist within the external content type for the app for SharePoint. If you download the `BDCMetadata.bdcm` file from its document library location in the appWeb and open it in Notepad, you can map it to the `Property Values` in the external content type `Elements.xml` file. Using the `BDCMetadata.bdcm` file in an app for SharePoint is essentially an extension of the file-based metadata catalog capability introduced in SharePoint 2010. It is just being put to practical use here in a document library inside an app for SharePoint.

The modifications to the HTML were minimal and the JavaScript did all the work. The primary work of the JavaScript was to use the relative URL retrieved from the SharePoint page context, and ensure it was properly formed to serve as the basis for building out the REST URL. Essentially the code just checks to see whether the URL has a trailing slash and if it doesn't, one gets appended. From that point on the process is pretty straightforward: if the REST URL access is successful then an HTML table will be built and the returned data will be added in accordingly as the SharePoint page is displayed. This simple example should get your creative juices flowing when considering the wealth of possibilities in accessing OData data sources in Apps for SharePoint and being able to retrieve any data you want to display via REST!

The last part of the exercise was to mainly show that by simply using the REST-based `_api` against your appWeb you can discover and get eyes on anything that is being deployed in your app for SharePoint. A developer always feels at a disadvantage when he or she can't get visibility into something. The `_api` provides the way for you to interrogate your appWeb just as if it were any other site in SharePoint.

Now that you have the fundamentals of how to build and deploy an app-level ECT, you can take it a step further and build out a business solution. In the following section you combine some of what you learned in Chapter 11, "Developing Integrated Apps for Office and SharePoint Solutions," with what you have now experienced here.

BUILDING A BCS-ENABLED BUSINESS SOLUTION

A common practice in SharePoint is to use document libraries that have prebuilt Office document templates associated with them as the content type. When the user clicks in the SharePoint ribbon to create a new document, the assigned document template can be created by default. The user can quickly fill in the template and save it back to the document library.

Historically, you could have document templates that also included a Visual Studio Tools for Office (VSTO) add-in that loaded into a task pane when the document opened. This add-in could virtually do just about anything that any Windows rich-client applications could do, including call Web services, retrieve data from back-end databases, and more. Data retrieval and the ability to then place the retrieved data into the document was a common pattern.

In the following exercise you create a SharePoint-hosted app that has a number of components: an app-level ECT that retrieves employees from an OData source, a document library that has a custom document template for employee referrals, and a document template content type that is a TaskpaneApp for Office and reads the employees in the app-level external list so users can click an employee and load their data into the Word document template.

TRY IT OUT **Building an Integrated BCS Solution with an App for SharePoint Containing an App for Office (C13EmpReferralBCSAppForOffice.zip)**

This exercise shows you how to build an integrated solution where the app for SharePoint is SharePoint-hosted and contains an app-level ECT for its data source and an app for Office that consumes the external list data using REST.

1. Run Visual Studio 2012 as Administrator. Select New Project.

2. In the New Project dialog, expand the Templates ➪ Visual C# ➪ Office/SharePoint ➪ Apps nodes. Select App for SharePoint 2013 and provide the Name: `C13EmpReferralBCSAppForOffice`. Click OK.

3. In the New App for SharePoint dialog, set your Office 365 SharePoint Online Developer or Enterprise Preview site URL to use for debugging and choose SharePoint-hosted as the location to host your app for SharePoint. Click Finish.

4. Right-click the `C13EmpReferralBCSAppForOffice` project node in Solution Explorer and select Add ➪ Content Types for an External Data Source.

5. In the Specify OData Source dialog, enter `http://services.odata.org/Northwind/Northwind.svc/`.

6. In the Data Source Name, enter `Northwind OData Producer`. Click Next.

7. In the Select the Data Entities dialog, select `Employees` and confirm that the Create list instances for the selected data entities check box is checked. Click Finish.

8. Visual Studio creates an External Content Types node in the Solution Explorer; this should all be familiar to you from the last exercise.

9. Open Word (2013) but before opening a document enter the phrase **employee referral** in the search bar and click the search icon. When the employee referral form is found, click it and then click Create.

10. Click on Your Logo Here, delete it, and change the Company Name to **Company Inc.**

11. If the Develop tab is not showing above your ribbon, click File ➪ Options. Click Customize Ribbon and on the far right click the Developer check box. Click OK to close the dialog.

12. To add a content control to the document so the JavaScript in your app for Office can interact with a named object on the form, click the left side of the line beside the Employee Name. Click the Developer tab and click on the leftmost Aa in the Controls group. This is the Rich Text content control.

13. With the content control highlighted in the document (if it is not then click it), click the Properties button in the Controls group in the ribbon. In the Title text box, enter `ccSPUserTitle` and click OK.

14. Repeat the previous step three more times, placing your cursor in the leftmost position on the line beside E-Mail Address (in the Employee Information section), and Candidate Name and Phone No (in the Referral Information section), and provide these respective Title values for each of the content controls: `ccSPUserEmail`, `ccEmployeeName`, and `ccEmployeePhone`.

15. Select File ➪ Options ➪ Computer and browse to a location of choice to save this file. If prompted to Save, click OK, but you do not want to maintain compatibility. Close Word.

16. Return to Visual Studio, right-click the project, and click Add ➪ New item. Select App for Office, name it `EmployeeReferralForm` and click Add.

17. In the Choose the type of app you want to create and where you want it to appear dialog, uncheck Excel and PowerPoint and click Next.

18. In the Choose a document for your app for Office dialog, select Insert the app into an existing document and click Browse to go to the location where you just saved the Word document. Select the document you saved and click Finish.

19. Right-click the project, and click Add ➪ New item. Select List, name it `EmployeeReferralLibrary`, and click Add.

20. In the Choose List Settings dialog, drop-down the Default (Blank) list, select Document Library and click Next.

21. In the Choose a template for this document library dialog, select Use the following document as the template for this library, and click Browse. The Open file dialog opens with files showing from within your project. Open the `OfficeDocuments` folder, select the Word document, click Open and then click Finish. It's important that you select the file that is within your project and not the original file you saved. The file within your project has been prepared to be an App for Office template.

22. Visual Studio opens the new document library in the list designer. Click on the Columns tab if it is not selected and click the Content Types button.

23. Click the Document row to select the entire row, right-click it and select Del to delete it. Click OK. This allows your content type to be the only one presented to the user of the list.

24. Click the List tab at the top of the list designer and copy the entire List URL.

25. In Solution Explorer, navigate to the `AppManifest.xml` file, right-click, and select View Code. Replace just the `Pages/Default.aspx` portion of the URL with `Lists/EmployeeReferralLibrary`. When you deploy the app for SharePoint, the list will be the default location to which the app opens.

26. The `StartPage` element should look like this:

```
<StartPage>~appWebUrl/Lists/EmployeeReferralLibrary?{StandardTokens}</StartPage>
```

27. For the code, in Solution Explorer, expand the Pages node and open the `EmployeeReferralForm`
`.html` file. Replace all the XML between the body tags with the following:

```
<h2>App for Office using External List Data</h2>
<div id="Content"></div>
<div id="showEmployeeInfo"></div>
```

28. Expand the Scripts node and open the `EmployeeReferralForm.js` file. Replace all the JavaScript
with the following:

```
var user;
var appWebURL; // URL of the appWeb

Office.initialize = function (reason) {
    $(document).ready(function () {

        var $getExternalDataButton = $('<input type="button"
            value="Retrieve Employee BCS Data from
                SharePoint"/>').appendTo($("#Content"));
        $("#Content").append($('<div id="Result"></div>'));

        initializeConnectionToSharePoint(function () {
            $("#Result").append($("<div>SharePoint references loaded,
                click to load data.<div>"));

            // Bind to the named Content Controls in the document
            createContentControlBindings();

            // Automatically load SharePoint user information
            // into the Employee Content Controls in the form
            Office.select("bindings#ccSPUserTitle")
                    .setDataAsync(user.get_title(), function () { });
            Office.select("bindings#ccSPUserEmail")
                    .setDataAsync(user.get_email(), function () { });
        });

        $getExternalDataButton.click(function () {
            getEmployees();
        });


        $(document).on('click','.dataRow', function () {
            //identity
            var id = $(this).attr('id');
            var empFirstName = $('.FirstName[data-identity="' + id + '"]').text();
            var empLastName = $('.LastName[data-identity="' + id + '"]').text();
            var empHomePhone = $('.HomePhone[data-identity="' + id + '"]').text();

            // Get the bound Content Controls for the Employee referral candidate
            // and load with the data from the clicked on row in the table.
```

```
            Office.select("bindings#ccEmployeeName")
                    .setDataAsync(empFirstName + " " + empLastName, function () { });
            Office.select("bindings#ccEmployeePhone")
                    .setDataAsync(empHomePhone, function () { });
        });
    });
};

function createContentControlBindings() {

    Office.context.document.bindings.addFromNamedItemAsync("ccSPUserTitle", "text",
                                { id: "ccSPUserTitle" }, function () { });

    Office.context.document.bindings.addFromNamedItemAsync("ccSPUserEmail", "text",
                                { id: "ccSPUserEmail" }, function () { });

    Office.context.document.bindings.addFromNamedItemAsync("ccEmployeeName", "text",
                                { id: "ccEmployeeName" }, function () { });

    Office.context.document.bindings.addFromNamedItemAsync("ccEmployeePhone", "text",
                                { id: "ccEmployeePhone" }, function () { });

}


function initializeConnectionToSharePoint(functionToExecuteOnReady) {
    // Because calling back into SharePoint,
    // need to dynamically load SP JavaSript references
    var scriptbase = "/_layouts/15/";
    $.getScript(scriptbase + "SP.Runtime.js",
                function () {
                    $.getScript(scriptbase + "SP.js", getAppWebAndUser);
                }
            );

    function getAppWebAndUser() {
        var context = SP.ClientContext.get_current();
        var website = context.get_web();
        context.load(website);
        user = website.get_currentUser();
        context.load(user);
        context.executeQueryAsync(onGetAppWebUserSuccess, onGetURLFail);

        function onGetAppWebUserSuccess() {
            appWebURL = website.get_url();
            functionToExecuteOnReady();
        }
        function onGetURLFail(sender, args) {
            $("#Content").append($("<div>Problems connecting to SharePoint: "
              + args.get_message() + "</div>"));
        }
    }
}
```

```
function getEmployees() {
    $.ajax({
        url: appWebURL +
        "/_api/lists/getbytitle('Employees')/items?" +
        "$select=BdcIdentity,EmployeeID,LastName,FirstName,Title,HomePhone",
        headers: {
            "accept": "application/json;odata=verbose",
            "X-RequestDigest": $("#__REQUESTDIGEST").val()
        },
        success: showEmployees
    });

    function showEmployees(data) {
        var items = [];
        // Build table for showing Employees
        items.push("<table>");
        items.push("<tr><td>Emp ID</td>" +
                "<td>Last Name</td>" +
                "<td>First Name</td>" +
                "<td>Phone Number</td></tr>");
        // Make each row and cell uniquely identifiable
        $.each(data.d.results, function (key, val) {
            items.push('<tr class="dataRow" id="' + val.BdcIdentity + '">' +
                '<td class="employeeId" data-identity="'
                    + val.BdcIdentity + '">' + val.EmployeeID + '</td>' +
                '<td class="LastName" data-identity="'
                    + val.BdcIdentity + '">' + val.LastName + '</td>' +
                '<td class="FirstName" data-identity="'
                    + val.BdcIdentity + '">' + val.FirstName + '</td>' +
                '<td class="HomePhone" data-identity="'
                    + val.BdcIdentity + '">' + val.HomePhone + '</td></tr>');
        });

        items.push("</table>");

        $("#showEmployeeInfo").html(items.join(''));
    }

}
```

29. Press F5 to start debugging.

30. Log in to the site when the browser opens. Above the ribbon, click Files ⇨ New Document and select `EmployeeReferralLibraryContentType`.

31. When Word opens, your document template and TaskpaneApp will load. Notice the document has already filled in your login employee information.

32. Click the Retrieve Employee BCS Data from SharePoint button. When the employee data loads in the task pane, click any employee in the list to see his data load into the template, as shown in Figure 13-7.

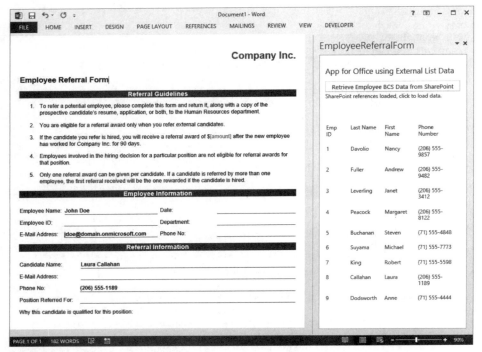

FIGURE 13-7

33. Save the document into the document library if you want to view it in the Word Web app or open it again in Word. Close Word.

34. In the browser, refresh the document library to see your newly saved file. View it if you choose to, and then close the browser to stop debugging.

How It Works

In this exercise you worked a number of components into an integrated solution. Along with knowing how to stitch a solution like this together, the key part is seeing how to write the JavaScript code to retrieve data from SharePoint from an app for Office when its HTML page is also hosted on SharePoint. Because the document template is opened in Word from within the context of a logged-in Office 365 user, you don't need to be concerned about authentication to SharePoint. Therefore, after the TaskpaneApp HTML page is loaded, you can construct the URL for $.getScript() to reach into the /_layouts/15/ directory in your SharePoint site to load and execute the SP.Runtime .js. Upon its success, you load and execute the SP.js. With these loaded, the stage is set for both JavaScript client-side object (CSOM) calls and REST-based calls to retrieve the desired data from SharePoint. First, the Web and user information are retrieved via CSOM and loaded into variables for later use. Then, when the user clicks the button in the TaskpaneApp to load the employee data, a REST call is made to retrieve and display the employee information.

Because the table to display the employee data is being added to the DOM after the DOM has been loaded, you need a way to late-bind a click event to the table so when the users click a row in the table, the appropriate data can be inserted into the desired document content control. To accomplish this you added a class named `datarow` to the `<tr>` element and an `id` attribute with the unique `BdcIdentity` value from the external list data item. Then for each cell in the row, you added a class for the name of the `<td>` element and a custom `data-` attribute so the cell data value can be retrieved directly.

These steps all come together in the `$(document).on()` function. This function essentially late-binds a click event to the data row (identified by the `datarow` class) so when any row is clicked, the data values are retrieved and can be appropriately loaded into the document content controls. To do this, you use the `Office.select()` method passing in the binding name for the content control and then use `.setDataAsync()` passing in the data retrieved from the data row — and that's it. The user has a form automatically populated with data based on her user login retrieved via CSOM and employee data from an OData source retrieved via REST from the SharePoint external list and presented in a clickable table.

Although this exercise focuses on an app for Office reading data from an app-level external list, the pattern for loading the `SP.Runtime.js` and `SP.js` is one you can use extensively when building your SharePoint-hosted apps. By definition, if a user is using your SharePoint-hosted solution, you have an authenticated context and your code has permissions to access any artifacts that you installed into the appWeb, lists, libraries, app-level BCS ECTs, and so on. However, sometimes you want your app to reach up a level and read/write data in the host Web. This, too, is easy enough to do: simply open the `AppManifest.xml` file in the Manifest Designer and under the Permissions tab select a scope of Web and the permission level you desire. On the install of your app, you then receive the "Trust It" prompt to verify that you will allow this app for SharePoint to have the level of access it is requesting. After the app is trusted, your CSOM or REST calls will have access to the SharePoint site within the scope designated.

SUMMARY

The Business Connectivity Services capabilities in SharePoint 2010 on-premises and then in SharePoint (2010) Online remain consistent in SharePoint 2013. At the heart of BCS is the external content type, which has supported connectivity across a variety of external data sources, such as Web services, SQL Server databases, and custom business objects. Some of the gains for developers in this version of SharePoint include the OData connector as the basis for the ECT, REST access to external lists, broader and deeper capabilities in CSOM, and with the advent of the new cloud app model, the ability for app-level ECTs to bring LOB data into your app for SharePoint solutions — whether the app is Provider hosted, Autohosted or SharePoint hosted.

In SharePoint 2013, BCS becomes a first-class citizen in the SharePoint event infrastructure. Alerts on external lists are now available as with any other SharePoint list. Also, events can fire on external lists given that the LOB external system has a mechanism in place to detect underlying data changes and can support the ECT notification infrastructure via the exchange of information between the external system and SharePoint during the subscribe process. Given that external system notifications are in place, you can now write remote event receiver code for these external list events as described in Chapter 12.

EXERCISES

You can find answers to exercises in Appendix A.

1. What is the new connector that has been added to BCS?

2. To interact with data in an external list, what two technologies might you use in your code?

3. What are the new stereotypes added to the BDC Model schema that enable notification of data changes in external LOB systems?

4. With the advent of the cloud app model, what is the new capability for ECTs?

▶ **WHAT YOU LEARNED IN THIS CHAPTER**

ITEM	DESCRIPTION
OData Connector	External content types can now be based off an OData connection to an LOB system.
Data Access	External lists now support REST and the CSOM capabilities have been broadened and deepened.
App-level ECTs	With the advent of the cloud app model, ECTs can be part of an app for SharePoint solutions whether the app is Provider-hosted, Autohosted, or SharePoint-hosted.
External List Events	BCS now participates fully in the SharePoint event infrastructure and can take advantage of alerts and fire events on LOB data changes given that notifications are configured between the ECT and the LOB External System.

RECOMMENDED READING

External events and alerts in SharePoint 2013 — `http://msdn.microsoft.com/en-us/library/`
   `jj164024(v=office.15).aspx`
Business Connectivity Services in 2013 — `http://msdn.microsoft.com/en-us/library/`
   `jj163782.aspx`

14

Developing Applications Using Office Services

WHAT YOU WILL LEARN IN THIS CHAPTER:

➤ Understanding the role of the new Office Web Apps Server

➤ Getting to know what's new in Office 2013 and SharePoint 2013 application services

➤ Creating an app for SharePoint using Access and Access Services 2013

WROX.COM CODE DOWNLOADS FOR THIS CHAPTER

The wrox.com code downloads for this chapter are found at http://www.wrox.com/WileyCDA/WroxTitle/productCd-1118495845.html on the Download Code tab. The code for this chapter is divided into the following major examples:

➤ C14ExcelInteractive.zip

➤ C14ODataAccessSample.zip

➤ C14PPTAutomationSvcs.zip

➤ C14TranslateSPOM.zip

➤ C14WOPI.zip

The Office and SharePoint server-side application services provide a way to have server scale for automating traditional Office client document manipulation and Web scale for sharing, collaborating, and viewing documents with those who might not have the Office rich clients on the desktop. From a developer's perspective, a number of APIs are available for you to leverage to call into these services to further enrich your solutions.

If you are unfamiliar with the application services present in SharePoint 2010, following is a list with a brief description of each one:

> **Excel Services:** Enables viewing of Excel documents in the Excel Web App and Excel Web Access web parts and provides programmatic access to document content via CSOM, REST, and OData.

> **Word Automation Services:** Provides conversion of document files supported by Word into other formats.

> **Visio Services:** Allows viewing of Visio documents in the Visio Web App and Visio Web Access web parts.

> **Access Services:** Provides the ability for Web databases constructed in the Access rich client to be deployed and hosted on SharePoint independent of the Access client.

The new Office 2013 and SharePoint 2013 application services in this release are as follows:

> **PowerPoint Automation Services:** Provides conversion of presentation files into other formats.

> **Machine Translation Service:** Synchronous or asynchronous requests are forwarded on to a cloud-hosted Microsoft service for language translation.

This chapter covers the Office 2013 and SharePoint 2013 application services that are new as well as some new features for the existing services. A deep look into Access and Access Services is provided because these products were significantly transformed in this release, providing the ability to generate an app for SharePoint that has an auto-provisioned Windows Azure SQL Database behind it. When Access generates the web pages for the app that will be hosted on SharePoint, it does so using standard web technologies — HTML, JavaScript, CSS, and so on — to be fully compliant with the new cloud app model. Developers can also submit these apps for SharePoint to the SharePoint Store on Office.com.

WOPI AND THE NEW OFFICE WEB APPS SERVER

With SharePoint 2013 Microsoft took a new architectural approach with the Office Web Apps and decoupled the service from SharePoint. With SharePoint 2010 each SharePoint server in the farm had an instance of the Office Web Apps running to serve up documents for viewing in the browser. But with this release, Microsoft separated the Office Web Apps into its own server product. Now, as a standalone service (server farm capable) the Office Web Apps server can provide the singular function of serving up documents to be viewed in the browser simply by receiving the URL for a specific document. The viewing request, however, can come from any host server: SharePoint, Lync, Exchange or any other server that is designed to use the Office Web Apps' REST-based WOPI (Web application Open Platform Interface) API. What matters to the Office Web Apps server is simply whether or not it can access the document source location that is passed to it; if it can, it renders the document in the viewer. All traffic between the host and the Office Web Apps server is over the standard HTTP/HTTPS ports.

For the developer, your SharePoint on-premises environment will no doubt have been configured to use the Office Web Apps server, and those developing against Office 365 SharePoint Online will have this configuration as a part of their developer site. Because of this, you can take advantage of WOPI in your SharePoint applications, for instance if you want to have an Excel, Word, PowerPoint, or Visio document viewed directly within your Web solution. This allows the user to view the document with the context of your Web application and saves him from having to navigate to the file's location to open it in the Office client application for viewing. The following Try It Out introduces you to the basics for how to do this by embedding an IFrame in your Web app and relying on the SharePoint implementation of WOPI to retrieve the document for display.

TRY IT OUT **Using WOPI in an App for SharePoint (C14WOPI.zip)**

In this exercise you learn the basics for embedding an IFrame in your app for SharePoint to view documents served by the Office Web App server.

1. Run Visual Studio 2012 as Administrator. Select New Project.

2. In the New Project dialog, expand the Templates ⇨ Visual C# ⇨ Office/SharePoint ⇨ Apps nodes. Select App for SharePoint 2013 and provide the name **C14WOPI**. Click OK.

3. In the Specify the app for SharePoint dialog, set the SharePoint site URL you will deploy the app to and choose SharePoint-hosted as the host for your app for SharePoint. Click Finish.

4. In the Solution Explorer, expand the Pages node and double-click the `Default.aspx` file to open it. Add the following HTML immediately after the closing `</div>` tag inside the `PlaceHolderMain <asp:Content...>` element.

```
<div>
<h3>Enter file name you saved to Shared Documents: (.pptx, .docx, etc.)</h3> <br />
<input type="text" value="ExampleName.pptx" id="fileNameTxt"
       style="margin-top: 10px; width: 210px" />
<input type="button" value="Load IFrame" id="loadIFrameBtn"
       style="padding: 0px; width: 100px;" />
<p>
    <iframe id="myFrame" width='600px' height='400px' frameborder='0'></iframe>
</p>
</div>
```

5. In the Solution Explorer, expand the Scripts node, and double-click the `App.js` file to open it. Delete all the code and add the following:

```
var context;
var web;
var user;
var hostweburl;
var WOPIbase;
var actionEmbedParms;
// NOTE: You will need to modify the sourcedoc= with your URL equivalent.
var sourcedocParm = 'sourcedoc=/sites/dev/Shared%20Documents/';
```

```
// This code runs when the DOM is ready and creates a context
// object which is needed to use
// the SharePoint object model
$(document).ready(function () {
    // Parse the URL for the SPHostUrl.
    hostweburl =
        decodeURIComponent(
            getQueryStringParameter("SPHostUrl"));

    // Construct the WOPI URL.
    WOPIbase = hostweburl + "/_layouts/15/WopiFrame.aspx?" + sourcedocParm;
    actionEmbedParms = "&action=embedview&Embed=1"

    context = SP.ClientContext.get_current();
    web = context.get_web();

    getUserName();

    $('#loadIFrameBtn').click(function () { loadIFrame('#fileNameTxt'); });
});

// This function prepares, loads, and then executes a SharePoint query
// to get the current users information
function getUserName() {
    user = web.get_currentUser();
    context.load(user);
    context.executeQueryAsync(onGetUserNameSuccess, onGetUserNameFail);
}

// This function is executed if the above OM call is successful
// It replaces the contents of the 'helloString' element with the user name
function onGetUserNameSuccess() {
    $('#message').text('Hello ' + user.get_title());
}

function loadIFrame(elementId) {
    $('#message').text("WOPIUrl: " + WOPIbase + $(elementId).val()
     + actionEmbedParms);
    $('#myFrame').attr('src', WOPIbase + $(elementId).val()
     + actionEmbedParms);
}

// This function is executed if the above call fails
function onGetUserNameFail(sender, args) {
    alert('Failed to get user name. Error:' + args.get_message());
}

// Boilerplate URL parse code from MSDN
// http://msdn.microsoft.com/en-us/library/office/jj163201.aspx
function getQueryStringParameter(paramToRetrieve) {
    var params =
        document.URL.split("?")[1].split("&");
    var strParams = "";
    for (var i = 0; i < params.length; i = i + 1) {
        var singleParam = params[i].split("=");
```

```
            if (singleParam[0] == paramToRetrieve)
                return singleParam[1];
        }
    }
```

6. Open a browser and navigate to the site where you will be deploying this application. After you're in the site, navigate to the Shared Documents library and upload a PowerPoint presentation or any document that can be viewed in the Office Web Apps.

7. When the document is in the Shared Documents library, click the ellipsis (...) beside the document name so the fly-out menu with the Office Web Apps embedded-viewer loads. On the bottom right of the viewer click the Menu icon and select Embed Information. Select all the HTML text and copy/paste it into Notepad.

8. Examine the pasted URL and copy the parameter `sourcedoc=.` but do not include the filename of your document — you will enter the document name into a text box at runtime. Your URL snippet should look something like the following:

```
sourcedoc=%2Fsites%2Fdev%2FShared%20Documents%2F
```

9. Locate in the code from step 5 the variable definition for `sourcedocParm` and replace the entire literal value with your copied code snippet. Although you are dynamically parsing the URL to get the `SPHostUrl`, this sets the path to your specific document library.

10. Press F5 to run the app. When the page loads, in the text box, type the name of the document you uploaded in step 6 and click the Load IFrame button to view it. Your result should look something like Figure 14-1.

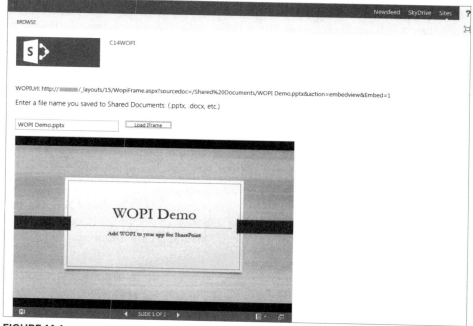

FIGURE 14-1

How It Works

In this exercise you simply added a button, text box, and an IFrame to the `Default.aspx` Web page. You uploaded a document to your site and retrieved the embedded URL. You then worked with the WOPI URL to see how it is constructed and copied out the path to your document library. You wrote code that included a combination of hard-coding URL values and dynamic construction at run-time. Upon execution on the button click, the WOPI URL was fully constructed and passed via the SharePoint `_layouts/15/WopiFrame.aspx` page to the Office Apps Server. The Office Web Apps server rendered the document in the IFrame for viewing.

Certainly the means used for constructing the WOPI URL in this Try It Out can be replaced with a fully dynamic, run-time URL construction scheme of your own. Following is a method you might want to incorporate when writing the code depending on whether your solution is based on .NET, JavaScript or REST.

➤ **.NET:** `Microsoft.SharePoint.Client.ListItem. GetWOPIFrameUrl()`

➤ **JavaScript:** `SP.ListItem.getWOPIFrameUrl()`

➤ **REST:** POST, `http://[YourSiteCollection]/[site]/_api/web/lists([listid])/items([itemid])/getWOPIFrameUrl([action])`

WHAT'S NEW IN EXCEL SERVICES

One of the most interesting outcomes of decoupling the Office Web Apps from the SharePoint server is that now Office documents are being served up in consumer-facing scenarios by both Microsoft, through Hotmail, Outlook and SkyDrive, and by other non-Microsoft websites that have implemented their own Office Web Apps servers. From the Office client and server perspective, the leader in this notion of Office documents being available everywhere is Excel. Excel Services has certainly been one of the innovation leaders over the past two releases of SharePoint and continues to do so with this release. Because of the ability to have public-facing Office Web App servers rendering Excel content, Excel is pressing its end-user, business intelligence (BI) dominance forward to Web endpoints greater than ever before. In doing this, developers can join in by taking advantage of new integration capabilities and the extensibility points that have been provided.

One intriguing new integration capability is Excel Interactive View. This innovative, Excel Services rendered viewer lets you render any HTML table on a Web page within the Excel Interactive View by adding a script element and an HTML anchor tag to the page. Users who do not even have Excel on their device can click the Excel Interactive View icon above the table, and the HTML will be retrieved from the Web page and rendered in the Excel Interactive View. Excel Services auto-matically assesses the best charts to represent the data and determines which Excel slicers to pres-ent for filtering the data. The option to download the HTML table content into Excel for deeper analysis is available as well.

The best way to understand Excel Interactive View is to experience it. In this Try It Out you create an Autohosted app for SharePoint that accesses a public-facing OData endpoint and dynamically builds a table that can be analyzed with Excel Interactive View.

TRY IT OUT **Excel Interactive View in an Autohosted App for SharePoint (C14ExcelInteractive.zip)**

In this exercise, within an Autohosted app for SharePoint, you dynamically create an HTML table in your Web page from an OData source and wire up the Excel Interactive View for end-user analysis.

1. Run Visual Studio 2012 as Administrator. Select New Project.

2. In the New Project dialog, expand the Templates ➪ Visual C# ➪ Office/SharePoint ➪ Apps nodes. Select App for SharePoint 2013 and provide the name `C14ExcelInteractive`. Click OK.

3. In the Specify the app for SharePoint dialog, set the SharePoint site URL you will deploy the app to (this example used Office 365) and choose Autohosted as the host for your app for SharePoint. Click Finish.

4. In the Solution Explorer, expand the Pages node and double-click the `Default.aspx` file to open it. Delete the `<html>...</html>` contents and replace them with the following: (Notice the highlighted lines below are the only lines needed to invoke the Excel Interactive View.)

```
<html xmlns="http://www.w3.org/1999/xhtml">
<head runat="server">
    <title>Excel Interactive Demo</title>

    <script type="text/javascript" src="../Scripts/jquery-1.7.1.min.js"></script>
    <script type="text/javascript" src="../Scripts/App.js"></script>
    <script type="text/javascript"
      src="https://r.office.microsoft.com/r/rlidExcelButton?v=1&kip=1"></script>
</head>
<body>
    <form id="form1" runat="server">
        <div>
            <h2>App for SharePoint using Excel Interactive View</h2>
            <div id="Content"></div>
            <div>
                <a href="#" name="MicrosoftExcelButton"
                    data-xl-buttonstyle="Small"
                    data-xl-tabletitle="Product Sales"></a>
                <table id="showProductCategoryTable">

                </table>
            </div>
        </div>
    </form>
</body> </html>
```

5. In the Solution Explorer, under the `C14ExcelInteractiveWeb` project, right-click the Scripts folder and select Add ➪ New Item.

6. In the Add New Item dialog, select JavaScript File, name it `App.js`, and click Add.

7. In the `App.js` file enter the following code lines:

```
$(document).ready(function () {
    getProducts();
});

function getProducts() {
    //Due to the Web page for the app being HTTPS and the Northwind OData
    //service being HTTP, a proxy page is used to broker the call to
    //keep this code sample simple. You would most likey have your own
    //HTTPS service deployed to broker this call.
    $.ajax({
        url: '/Pages/ProxyHTTPRequest.aspx',
        type: 'GET',
        headers: {
            "accept": "application/json",
        },
        success: showProducts,
        error: function () { alert('Failed!'); }
    });

    function showProducts(data) {
        var items = [];
        // Build table header row for Products
        items.push("<tr><th>Category Name</th>" +
                   "<th>Product Name</th>" +
                   "<th>Product Sales</th></tr>");
        // Load each row with data
        $.each(data.d.results, function (key, val) {
            items.push('<tr>' +
                '<td>' + val.CategoryName + '</td>' +
                '<td>' + val.ProductName + '</td>' +
                '<td>' + parseFloat(val.ProductSales) + '</td></tr>');
        });
        $("#showProductCategoryTable").append(items.join(''));
    }
}
```

8. In the Solution Explorer, under the `C14ExcelInteractiveWeb` project, right-click the Pages folder and select Add ➪ New Item.

9. In the Add New Item dialog, select Web Form File, name it **ProxyHTTPRequest.aspx**, and click Add. This Web page is used to proxy the call to the Northwind OData service which is an HTTP endpoint and your app for SharePoint is HTTPS. It also keeps this code sample simple to implement. You would most likely use your own HTTPS service to make this call in a production setup.

10. Right-click the `ProxyHTTPRequest.aspx` file, select View Code, and enter the following code in the `Page_Load` method:

```
// This is Web page is simply to proxy the HTTP request for the HTTPS page
    var url =
    "http://services.odata.org/Northwind/Northwind.svc/Sales_by_Categories?
$select=CategoryName,ProductName,ProductSales&$format=json";
    string output = new WebClient().DownloadString(url);
    Response.Clear();
```

```
Response.ContentType = "application/json";
Response.Write(output);
Response.End();
```

11. Excel Interactive View cannot interact with your local host so rather than pressing F5, you need to deploy your Autohosted app. In the Solution Explorer, right-click the `C14ExcelInteractive` node and select Deploy.

12. As the app deploys, respond appropriately to the prompts. When your Autohosted app Web page loads, click the Excel Interactive View icon just above your table with its dynamically loaded data. When the Excel Interactive View loads, it should look something like Figure 14-2.

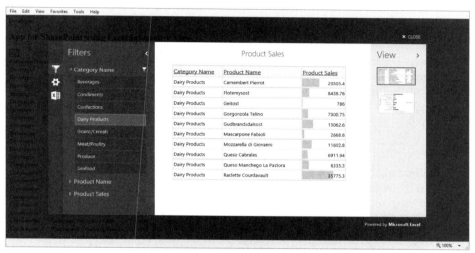

FIGURE 14-2

13. Notice the various sheet formatting and chart options on the right under View. Excel Services automatically assesses (based on the data) and presents the most likely sheet and chart views you would use with this data. On the left side are the data slicers. By single or multi-selecting one or more slicers, you can quickly filter the data, look for trends and so on. Click your way around the UI to experience some of the capabilities this interactive tool brings to what would normally have been a static, flat HTML table on the Web page. And if you want to work with the raw table data directly, click the Excel icon and select whether to open the file in the Excel Web App or download it.

14. Close the Excel Interactive View and close the browser.

How It Works

In this Try It Out you brought together the new cloud app model by retrieving data from an OData source and dynamically building an HTML table in your app for SharePoint. You then coupled the HTML table with the new Excel Interactive View to bring it to life in a quick analysis and data visualization experience for the end user.

Notice in this Try It Out that the `<script>` element `src=` attribute for the Excel Interactive View uses HTTPS because that is the requirement for Apps for SharePoint in Office 365. You can toggle this to HTTP in situations where you do not have an SSL requirement. The `src=` URL can take one additional query string parameter for language localization. For example, add the `&locale=fr-fr` to the end of the URL to specify French or any other language of choice.

Review the `<a>` element for the Excel Interactive View to see the `data-xl-` attributes used. You can also include other `data-xl-` attributes to further customize what the end user will see in the UI. These are `data-xl-fileName="MyBookFileName"` and `data-xl-attribution="Brought to you by CompanyName"`, where `data-xl-fileName` is any arbitrary name you want to set as the default name for the file when downloaded, and `data-xl-attribution` is any arbitrary phrase you want to use to identify the provider of the data. The `data-xl-tableTitle` used in the `<a>` element in the code and the `data-xl-attribution` attributes can be up to 255 characters in length. The `data-xl-attribution` value will be included in the downloaded spreadsheet.

The `data-xl-buttonstyle` attribute used in the `<a>` element in the code can have either the value of `Standard` or `Small`. Lastly, you can use a `data-xl-dataTableID` attribute to uniquely identify your table. However, it's important to note that none of the `<a>` element attributes are required for the Excel Interactive View to render; it will provide an appropriate default value for any `data-xl-` attribute you do not specifically include.

Although the Excel Interactive View is a great tool you can easily integrate into your Web pages, you're going to want to switch gears and leverage the power of Excel Services when it comes time to build out broad and deep solutions. Excel Services made a significant investment to provide Open Data Protocol (OData) access to Excel documents in SharePoint libraries. SharePoint 2010 Excel Services provided REST-based access to these documents, which opened up a host of opportunities for rich clients and Web applications to essentially have any named range or chart in an Excel document as an accessible endpoint for data retrieval. But now the RESTful capability has been extended to include OData access to any Excel table in a document hosted on SharePoint. Therefore your favorite OData client can read from Excel tables like other OData sources.

Because the intent for OData is to be a standards-based protocol, visit OData.org to read the details: The protocol specification is available publicly for anyone to implement and provide OData service endpoints. Microsoft therefore built its OData service for Excel Services using this specification, which also outlines the URL syntax that a calling application must implement to retrieve data from the service. For you to access Excel table data on SharePoint you use a prescribed syntax to construct your URL. You should be aware of the three discrete parts of the URL; these follow the standard OData protocol URI conventions.

➤ **Service root URI:** This includes the host and service endpoint; for example, `https://YourSharePointHost/SiteIfOne/_vti_bin/ExcelRest.aspx/`.

➤ **Resource path:** This includes the name of the document library, name of the Excel file, and the literal value `OData` to define the protocol request; for example, `LibraryName/FileName.xlsx/OData/`.

➤ **System query options:** You can use a number of optional parameters individually or in concert with others to describe specifically what you want to retrieve from a document. For instance, you might just want to know what tables are available in a given document, so you would use the system query option, $metadata.

Using the preceding URL snippets the composed URL would be `https://YourSharePointHost/SiteIfOne/_vti_bin/ExcelRest.aspx/LibraryName/FileName.xlsx/OData/$metadata`. Because a number of system query options are available, working with them and getting a feel for the results they each return is best. In the following Try It Out you exercise several of the system query options available from Excel Services.

TRY IT OUT **Accessing Excel Table Data with OData for Excel Services (C14ODataAccessSample.zip)**

In this Try It Out you exercise a number of system query options using the new OData protocol for Excel Services.

1. Download the code samples for this chapter as described in the introduction. Extract the `ODataAccessSample.xlsx` file to a location on your machine from the `ODataAccessSample.zip` file.

2. Log in to SharePoint, whether on-premises or Office 365, and access the site document library that you can use for this exercise. Upload the `ODataAccessSample.xlsx` document.

3. When the document has uploaded, right-click the link and select Copy shortcut, or click the ellipsis (...) and copy the URL from the fly-out menu.

4. You will be doing a number of copy/paste actions in the browser so first construct the service root and resource path part of the URL you need. For the service root, copy the portion of the URL up through the ending slash (/) just prior to the name of your document library, and then add `_vti_bin/ExcelRest.aspx/` after it. Your URL should match the following pattern (you should use HTTP or HTTPS as appropriate for your service host):

   `https://YourSharePointHost/SiteIfOne/_vti_bin/ExcelRest.aspx/`

5. For the resource path, from your original URL, copy from the beginning of the document library name through the full filename for the Excel document and paste it on the end of your service root. Add `/OData/` following it.

   `https://YourSharePointHost/SiteIfOne/_vti_bin/ExcelRest.aspx/LibraryName/ODataAccessSample.xlsx/OData/`

6. With the service root and resource path fully constructed, now you can exercise OData access using the system query options. But before you do, open the `ODataAccessSample.xlsx` file in Excel. You can see three worksheets, each with a table on it. These tables could all be on one sheet, so that is not important, but what is noteworthy is that the document contains three named ranges, each associated with a table. On the left side of Excel, just under the ribbon, click the drop-down arrow for the Name box. Here you will see three names that begin with `Table_`.

7. Click each of the `Table_` names to navigate to each of the tables and get a sense for the data they contain. Excel Services will expose these three tables to you through its OData service. You can either close Excel at this point or leave it open for reference.

8. Return to your browser that is logged on to your SharePoint site. Copy your fully constructed URL and paste it into the address bar, add `$metadata` to the end, and press Enter. Excel Services returns the entity data model for all the named tables within the document. This includes the property name for each column and its data type.

9. Replace `$metadata` with `Table_Sales_by_Categories` and press Enter. By your just entering the name for the table, Excel Services will return the first 500 rows (0-based count, so from 0–499), which it considers a page. The maximum number of rows to be delivered at a time is 500. Because you do not have enough rows you cannot exercise the `$skiptoken` system query option. However, with this option you can skip to get rows in pages; for example, `$skiptoken=499` starts you at the second page of data and returns the next 500 rows. The `$skiptoken=N` is where Excel Services calculates N+1 for the starting row for the next page. This way you can iteratively retrieve data from the table in your application if needed. However, you can use `$skip` on this example. Add `?$skip=5` after `Table_Sales_by_Categories` and press Enter to skip the first 5 rows.

10. In the browser address bar, remove `?$skip=5`, replace it with `?$orderby=CategoryName`, and press Enter. Now the data is returned sorted by category name.

11. In the address bar, remove `Table_Sales_by_Categories?$orderby=CategoryName` and replace it with `Table_Sales_Totals_by_Amounts?$orderby=SaleAmount desc&$top=5`. Here the sales totals table is sorted in descending order and the top 5 rows are returned.

12. In the address bar, remove `Table_Sales_Totals_by_Amounts?$orderby=SaleAmount desc&$top=5` and replace it with `Table_Alphabetical_list_of_products?$filter=Unit Price gt 200`. Here you apply a filter to the data to only return rows where the unit price for the product is greater than 200.

13. In the address bar, remove `Table_Alphabetical_list_of_products?$filter=UnitPrice gt 200` and replace it with `Table_Alphabetical_list_of_products?$select=ProductName`. Here you requested to only return the product name column. So in cases where you do not want every column in the table, you can request the ones you specifically want with the `$select` system query option. You can string multiple property names together for the selection using a comma as the delimiter.

14. In the address bar, remove `Table_Alphabetical_list_of_products?$select=ProductName` and replace it with `Table_Sales_by_Categories?$inlinecount=allpages`. Here you request a count of the number of rows in the table. This helps when you need to programmatically assess how many iterations you might need in conjunction with `$skiptoken`. You'll see this value returned on the eighth line of XML.

How It Works

In this Try It Out you learned how to construct an appropriate OData URL for accessing SharePoint Excel documents according to the service root, resource path, and system query options pattern. You also exercised all the available system query options currently available for Excel Services except one: `$format`. Although this system query option is available, the Atom XML format is the only supported format that the Excel Services OData service will provide.

As you can see, Excel Services has continued to innovate and provide additional capabilities for developers to build on. In this section you worked with some of the new capabilities, but don't forget that all the great new Excel Services capabilities that came with SharePoint 2010 are still available in this new release. Also, some really exceptional resources came online post-SharePoint 2010 that can help get you bootstrapped so you can tap into the whole of Excel Services when building your solutions. One amazingly such resource is `http://www.excelmashup.com` — it almost writes the code for you.

WORD AUTOMATION SERVICES AND THE NEW POWERPOINT AUTOMATION SERVICES

The all-new PowerPoint Automation Services has brought to SharePoint 2013 for PowerPoint presentations, on-premises, what Word Automation Services brought to Word documents for SharePoint in 2010: the ability to convert documents, at server scale, into other formats.

> **NOTE** *PowerPoint Automation Services runs on-premises only and not in Office 365 SharePoint Online. This was the case for Word Automation Services for SharePoint 2010 and remains the same for SharePoint 2013.*

For Word Automation Services, everything for SharePoint 2010 remains in play for SharePoint 2013. However, the biggest addition is that the architecture for Word Automation Services was reworked to allow for synchronous and asynchronous, on-demand, streamed file conversion to augment the traditional timer job conversions. SharePoint 2010 and 2013 enable you to create a document conversion job that runs on the timed interval of Word Automation Service, which works well to support batch processing of documents. SharePoint administrators can set the time interval for running Word Automation Services to be as often as every one minute, but sometimes that isn't soon enough. With the redesigned architecture, conversion requests can be submitted and processed in real-time. On demand, streamed requests can be made for one file at a time, and whether synchronously or asynchronously requested, the queue manager/scheduler in the new architecture processes the on-demand request as its highest priority.

PowerPoint Automation Services is the newcomer, so you'll take a look at it a little more deeply. Organizations often have thousands of PowerPoint presentations that are in various file formats ranging from the PowerPoint 97–2003 binary formats known as .ppt to the newer file formats based on Open XML known as .pptx. Additionally, sometimes you do not want to provide a presentation in its native format to others so you need to convert it to a fixed format such as .pdf or images such as .jpg or .png. This often is the case for presentations that are used at conferences where you want attendees to receive a .pdf version. For business cases like these PowerPoint Automation Services can now provide the server-side performance and scale to move these file conversions out of being an antiquated, laborious, manual process.

Unlike Word Automation Services though, no timer job option exists for PowerPoint Automation Services. Files are streamed, which you can do in a synchronous or asynchronous pattern. Also, the solutions you build for PowerPoint Automation Services will be farm-level solutions; the APIs are only available on the SharePoint server.

You can develop your solution using the `Microsoft.Office.Server.PowerPoint.Conversion` namespace. Using the namespace you have the classes you need for the types of conversions available. Using the `PresentationRequest` class you can input the binary .ppt file and output a new .pptx file. For fixed format file conversion, the `PdfRequest` and `XpsRequest` classes are used to input either a .ppt or .pptx file and output a .pdf or .xps file, respectively. The `PictureRequest` class can also take as input a .ppt or .pptx file and output either a .jpg or .png depending on your preference. For exposure to the coding involved, the following Try It Out shows you how to build a small console application to exercise PowerPoint Automation Services.

> **TRY IT OUT** Converting PowerPoint Presentation Files to .pdf Files Using the New PowerPoint Automation Services (C14PPTAutomationSvcs.zip)

In this exercise you use a simple console application to see the fundamental code pattern to convert .ppt and .pptx files to .pdf using PowerPoint Automation Services. For this Try It Out you need access to a SharePoint 2013 on-premises server development environment with Visual Studio 2012 installed and PowerPoint Automation Services running on the SharePoint server.

1. Either confirm with your SharePoint Administrator that PowerPoint Automation Services is running in your on-premises environment, or open the SharePoint Administration Console, click Application Management, click Manage Service Applications, and confirm that the PowerPoint Conversion Service Application and Proxy are started. If not, return to Application Management, click Manage Services on Server, locate the PowerPoint Conversion Service, and click the Start link.

2. Run Visual Studio 2012 as Administrator. Select New Project.

3. In the New Project dialog, expand the Templates ⇨ Visual C# ⇨ Windows nodes. Select Console Application and provide the name `C14PPTAutomationSvcs`. Click OK.

4. When the project loads, close the `Program.cs` file.

5. In the Solution Explorer, right-click the project and select Properties. On the Application tab confirm the Target framework is set to .NET Framework 4. If it's not, set it and confirm any prompts and reopen the Properties pane. Click the Build tab, set the Configuration drop-down list to All Configurations, and close the Properties pane.

6. In the Solution Explorer, right-click the project and select Add Reference.

7. In the Reference Manager, under Framework, add `System.Web`, and under Extensions add `Microsoft.SharePoint`. Click Browse and navigate to the following location: `C:\Windows\Microsoft.NET\assembly\GAC_MSIL\Microsoft.Office.Server.PowerPoint\v4.0_15.0.0.0__71e9bce111e9429c`. Click the `Microsoft.Office.Server.PowerPoint.dll`, click Add and then click OK.

8. In the Solution Explorer, double-click the `Program.cs` file to open it. Add the following `using` statements:

```
using System.IO;
using System.Web;
using Microsoft.SharePoint;
using Microsoft.Office.Server.PowerPoint.Conversion;
```

9. In the `Main` method, add the following:

```
try
{
    string mySiteURL = "http://YourServerNameHere/YourSiteHere";
    using (SPSite mySite = new SPSite(mySiteURL))
    {
        using (SPWeb myWeb = mySite.OpenWeb())
        {
            Console.WriteLine("Convert to .pdf Start");
            // Identify document library and input file
            SPFolder myDocs = myWeb.Folders[mySiteURL +
                "/YourDocumentLibrary"];
            SPFile myFile = myDocs.Files[mySiteURL +
                "/YourDocumentLibrary/YourPresentationName.pptx"];
            // Create a stream object for the file
            Stream myFileStream = myFile.OpenBinaryStream();
            SPFileStream myStream = new SPFileStream(myWeb, 0x1000);

            // Rrequest conversion to .pdf format.
            PdfRequest myRequest = new PdfRequest(
                myFileStream,
                ".pptx",
                myStream);

            // Rrequest is sent synchronously, when
            // 'null' value is used for the callback parameter.
            // Response is in the result object.
            IAsyncResult result = myRequest.BeginConvert(
                SPServiceContext.GetContext(mySite),
                null,
                null);

            // Use the EndConvert method to get the result.
            myRequest.EndConvert(result);

            // Add the converted file to the document library.
            SPFile myNewPdfFile = myDocs.Files.Add(
                "newConvertedPresentation.pdf",
                myStream,
                true);
            Console.WriteLine("New file name: {0}", myNewPdfFile.Url);
        }
    }
}
catch (Exception ex)
{
    Console.WriteLine("Error Message: " + ex.Message);
}
finally
{
    Console.WriteLine("Conversion to .pdf completed.
Press <Enter> to quit.");
    Console.ReadLine();
}
```

10. Open a browser, navigate to a site, and upload any .pptx presentation to test conversion from .pptx to .pdf.

11. After the file is uploaded:

➤ Replace the `YourServerNameHere/YourSiteHere` literal in the `mySiteURL` variable with the URL for your SharePoint site that includes the full path to your document library.

➤ Replace the `YourDocumentLibrary` literal in the `myDocs` variable in the code with the name of your document library.

➤ Replace the `YourDocumentLibrary/YourPresentationName` literal in the `myFile` variable with the code to the document library and name of your presentation file.

➤ Optionally, you can replace the `newConvertedPresentation` literal in the `myNewPdfFile` value with the name of your presentation.

12. Press F5 to run the code. Depending on the hardware speed of your test server, this might take a minute or two so be patient. The command window will show the name of the file converted when the operation is completed.

13. When the operation completes, close the command window and look in the document library to review the new file.

How It Works

This Try It Out showed the code pattern for using the `PdfRequest` class for converting a presentation in the .pptx file format to a .pdf format in a synchronous call to PowerPoint Automation Services. Similarly, you can use the `PresentationRequest`, `XpsRequest`, and the `PictureRequest` classes to perform the type of presentation file conversion task unique to each. All the classes inherit from the `Request` class. Three parameters are required to be passed in: an input stream object for the file to be converted, the dot file extension (.ppt, .pptx, and so on) of the file to be converted, and an output `SPFileStream` object that designates the dot extension for the output file where it will be saved on SharePoint. The output file must designate the target dot extension that is consistent with the conversion class you are using. For instance, if you use the `XpsRequest` class, your output dot file extension must be .xps. The exception to this is the `PictureRequest` class. This class requires an additional parameter to designate the format for the picture to be converted to. You use the `PictureFormat` enumeration for this and can choose between `Default`, `Png`, and `Jpg`. Also, when designating the output stream dot file extension, you must use .zip.

PowerPoint Automation Services makes a nice addition to the Office server-side services. In this Try It Out you used a console application to make your conversion request, but in a production enterprise environment, you can drive your conversion requests to PowerPoint Automation Services off a variety of SharePoint interactions, whether it's an end user clicking a button on a web part, an event firing on a list item, or a workflow action calling out to a service endpoint that has access to the SharePoint server. Solutions can also include the use of other technologies such as the Open XML SDK, where you can dynamically augment or generate entire presentations by incorporating data from external data sources, charts or tables from Excel, content from Word, or other PowerPoint presentations for that matter. As with Word Automation Services, PowerPoint Automation Services now joins the ranks for shifting the often manual workload for presentation conversion to other formats into an automated conversion processes on the SharePoint server.

THE NEW MACHINE TRANSLATION SERVICES

Machine Translation Services is also an all-new server-side service with an architecture and runtime patterned after Word Automation Services. Using this service you can request translation of document libraries, folders, and files using a timer job, synchronously or asynchronously. The Machine Translation Service passes your content through to a Microsoft cloud-based translation service and returns the translated results. If you choose to use the Machine Translation Services, for privacy concerns, it is your responsibility to inform your users that their content will be sent to Microsoft and that Microsoft might use the content to improve its translation service. Be sure to see the Microsoft Translator Privacy statement for more detailed information. The reference is provided in the "Recommended Reading" section for this chapter.

Like Word Automation Services, Machine Translation Services is available on-premises only and is configured through the SharePoint Central Administration console. The time interval for the translation service can be set to run as often as every one minute. As a developer you have several ways you might choose to interact with the service. You are not limited to timer jobs only, but on-demand synchronous or asynchronous requests are supported. You can use the SharePoint server object model or you can remotely request translations using the REST API. For the REST API you can asynchronously translate a document library, folder, or file, but synchronously you can only request a single file translation. In the following Try It Out you perform a synchronous file conversion on a document in a document library.

TRY IT OUT Translating a Document Synchronously with Machine Translation Services (C14TranslateSPOM.zip)

In this exercise you use a simple console application to see the fundamental code pattern to synchronously convert a Word document in a document library into French using Machine Translation Services. For this Try It Out you need access to a SharePoint 2013 on-premises server development environment with Visual Studio 2012 installed and Machine Translation Services running on the SharePoint server.

1. Either confirm with your SharePoint Administrator that Machine Translation Services is running in your on-premises environment, or open the SharePoint Administration Console, click Application Management, click Manage Service Applications and confirm that the Machine Translation Service and Proxy are started. If they are not, return to Application Management, click Manage Services on Server, locate the Machine Translation Service and click the Start link.

2. Run Visual Studio 2012 as Administrator. Select New Project.

3. In the New Project dialog, expand the Templates ➪ Visual C# ➪ Windows nodes. Select Console Application and provide the name `C14TranslateSPOM`. Click OK.

4. When the project loads, close the `Program.cs` file.

5. In the Solution Explorer, right-click the project and select Properties. On the Application tab confirm the Target framework is set to .NET Framework 4. If it's not, set it and confirm any prompts and reopen the Properties pane. Click the Build tab, set the Configuration drop-down list to All Configurations, and close the Properties pane.

6. In the Solution Explorer, right-click the project and select Add Reference.

7. In the Reference Manager, under Framework, add `System.Web`, and under Extensions add `Microsoft.SharePoint`. Click Browse and navigate to the following location: `c:\Windows\Microsoft.NET\assembly\GAC_MSIL\Microsoft.Office.TranslationServices\v4.0_15.0.0.0__71e9bce111e9429c`. Click the `Microsoft.Office.TranslationServices.dll`, click Add and click OK.

8. In the Solution Explorer, double-click the `Program.cs` file to open it. Add the following using statements:

```
using System.Globalization;
using System.Web;
using System.IO;
using Microsoft.SharePoint;
using Microsoft.Office.TranslationServices;
```

9. In the `Main` method, add the following:

```
Console.WriteLine("C14TranslateSPOM Started");

string myWebSite = "http://YourServerNameHere";
string myCulture = "fr";
string myInput =
"http://YourServerNameHere/YourDocumentLibrary/YourDocumentName.docx";
string myOutput =
"http://YourServerNameHere/YourDocumentLibrary/YourDocumentName-fr.docx";

serviceContext = SPServiceContext.GetContext(new SPSite(myWebSite));

// Run synchronous conversion on a single file in doc lib.
Console.WriteLine("Synchronous Translation Process Starting");
SyncTranslator job = new SyncTranslator(serviceContext,
    CultureInfo.GetCultureInfo(myCulture));
Console.WriteLine("File names for processing");
Console.WriteLine("File input: " + myInput);
Console.WriteLine("File to be output: " + myOutput);
TranslationItemInfo itemInfo = job.Translate(myInput, myOutput);
Console.WriteLine("Translation Language: {0}",
    job.TargetLanguage.Name);
Console.WriteLine("SaveBehaviorForOutput: {0}",
    job.OutputSaveBehavior.ToString());
displayTranslationItemInfo(itemInfo);

Console.ReadLine();
}

static void displayTranslationItemInfo(TranslationItemInfo itemInfo)
{
```

```
                Console.WriteLine("\nTranslation completed -- Resulting information:");
                Console.WriteLine("File Input: " + itemInfo.InputFile);
                Console.WriteLine("File Output: " + itemInfo.OutputFile);
                Console.WriteLine("Job Start Time: " + itemInfo.StartTime);
                Console.WriteLine("Job Complete Time: " + itemInfo.CompleteTime);
                Console.WriteLine("Error Message: " + itemInfo.ErrorMessage);
                Console.WriteLine("Translation Id: " + itemInfo.TranslationId);
                Console.WriteLine("\nFinal Job Status");
                Console.WriteLine("Succeeded: " + itemInfo.Succeeded);
                Console.WriteLine("Failed: " + itemInfo.Failed);
                Console.WriteLine("Canceled: " + itemInfo.Canceled);
                Console.WriteLine("In Progress: " + itemInfo.InProgress);
                Console.WriteLine("Not Started: " + itemInfo.NotStarted);
                Console.WriteLine("\nTranslation completed. Press <Enter> to quit.");
            }
```

10. Open a browser, navigate to a site, and upload a .docx document to be translated.

11. After the file is uploaded, click the ellipsis (...) by the filename and copy the URL for the document. Use it to do all of the following tasks:

➤ Replace the *YourServerNameHere* literal in the myWebSite variable with the root URL for your SharePoint site.

➤ Replace the *YourServerNameHere/YourDocumentLibrary/YourDocumentName* literal values in the myInput variable, with the full path to your document.

➤ Replace the *YourServerNameHere/YourDocumentLibrary/YourDocumentName* literal values in the myOutput variable with the full path to your document. Be sure to leave the -fr on the filename or some other arbitrary value so the output file does not overwrite the input file when the translation is completed.

12. Press F5 to run the code. Depending on the hardware speed of your test server, this might take several minutes to complete. The command window will show the resulting processing information when the translation is completed. Figure 14-3 provides an example of the output results in the command window.

FIGURE 14-3

13. When the operation completes, close the command window and look in the document library to review the new translated document.

How It Works

For this Try It Out you performed a synchronous translation on a document in a document library, and to do this you used the `SyncTranslator` class. You created an object and passed in the full URL input/output path to a document. It is possible to use `SyncTranslator` to input/output file stream objects and byte arrays, yet in all cases, synchronous interactions with the Machine Translation Service is for a single file translation only. With asynchronous interactions with the service, where you submit timer jobs into the queue, you have more latitude and for this you use the `TranslationJob` class. Using this class you can not only designate a single file on a document library to be translated asynchronously, you can designate `SPFolder` objects for both input and output to translate the contents of an entire folder, or you can translate an entire document library by providing an `SPDocumentLibrary` object for both an input and output location.

Machine Translation Services is a unique asset in the server-side services. It is important to note that it does not translate all Office document types. It's limited primarily to the dot file extensions that Word can read or write such as .docx, .doc, .docm, .rtf, .txt, and some HTML-based files. You can query the server with REST to see which file extensions are supported in your environment using `http://SharePointServer/_api/TranslationJob.EnumerateSupportedFileEXtensions`. To see whether a specific extension is available use `http://serverName/_api/TranslationJob.IsFileExtensionSupported('extension')`. In any case, Machine Translation Services does not translate Excel or PowerPoint files.

Remember to inform the end users of your translation solutions that their document content will be sent to a Microsoft service for translation.

WHAT'S NEW IN ACCESS SERVICES

Access Services has moved forward significantly on its continuous innovation trajectory with this release. Access Services has a redesigned architecture around the new cloud app model so with the Microsoft Access rich client you now create apps for SharePoint. Apps for SharePoint can be deployed to the on-premises SharePoint or Office 365 SharePoint Online corporate catalog for apps and can be published to the SharePoint Store on Office.com for worldwide availability.

In SharePoint 2010 you used the Access client to create and publish Web databases to SharePoint. The publishing process generated native SharePoint artifacts: Access tables became SharePoint lists, forms became .aspx pages, data macros became workflows, UI macros became JavaScript, and so forth. This deployment model benefited end users in that they could create their point, data-centric solutions and make them available to their colleagues via SharePoint. Any colleague, located anywhere in the world with access to SharePoint, could use the Web-based solution without needing the Access client. For updates to the UI and modifications to the database structure, the Web database owner used the Access client to make the changes and then simply republished the Web database to SharePoint and the updates were immediately available.

With Access and Access Services 2013 and the advent of the new cloud app model come two significant changes. One change is that SharePoint is no longer the target as the data store. Where in

SharePoint 2010 the data for the solution was stored in SharePoint lists, now a SQL database is automatically generated for the solution and the data is stored there. For on-premises, this means there is an IT requirement to have a SQL Server environment available for Access Services to use. A reference link for guidance on Access Services administration is provided in the, "Recommended Reading," section at the end of this chapter. However, for Access Apps for SharePoint that target Office 365 SharePoint Online, when the app for SharePoint is installed, SharePoint Online automatically creates a Windows Azure SQL Database instance to store the app's data and content. The data is available for querying and BI reporting by external sources, too, making it an accessible asset for the enterprise — something not easily done with Access data before. Another change is that the generated UI artifacts that targeted SharePoint in the 2010 release have also been decoupled. For consistency with the new app model, all generated artifacts by the Access client for the solution's UI now use standard Web technologies, HTML, JavaScript, CSS, and so on, and these UI content artifacts are now stored within the SQL database, too.

Therefore, the Microsoft Access client continues to provide the tooling and Access Services provides the infrastructure for experts within a specific business domain, independent software vendors (ISVs), or software integrators (SIs) to build a data-centric, Web-based, point solution. But now the result is an app for SharePoint with the enterprise scale of SQL server behind it that's distributable to small and medium businesses and enterprises worldwide through the SharePoint Store. Moreover, the app for SharePoint is deployable both on-premises and in Office 365 — now this is truly taking Microsoft Access from the desktop to the cloud!

To see just how easy building an app for SharePoint with Access and Access Services is, walk through the following example.

TRY IT OUT Creating an App for SharePoint Using Microsoft Access and Access Services

In this exercise you experience installing a Microsoft Access–created app for SharePoint from the SharePoint Store on Office.com and then you build an app for SharePoint using Access and Access Services.

1. Log in to Office 365 Developer Site and navigate to the site collection where you will install an app for SharePoint.

2. Click Site Contents. On the site Contents page click Add an app.

3. On the Your Apps page, in the left navigation bar, click SharePoint Store.

4. On the SharePoint Store page, in the search bar, type **business contact** and click the search icon. When the Business Contact Manager app appears, click the tile.

5. On the Business Contact Manager page, click ADD IT.

6. On the Confirm that you wish to add the app page, click Continue.

7. On the You just got this app for everyone in your organization page, click Return to site.

8. On the Do you trust Business Contact Manager page, click Trust It. SharePoint adds the app to your site and will refresh the tile when the app is fully added.

9. Click the Business Contact Manager tile to open the app.

10. Click your way around the UI to get a sense for what the app does, but then click the About navigation link and watch the 2:25–minute demo of how to use this app for SharePoint.

11. Click the Back to Site link in the top navigation bar to return to the SharePoint site. You can return to the Business Contact Manager app any time by clicking Site Contents.

12. To build an app for SharePoint using Microsoft Access, open Access 2013.

13. Access opens and displays a number of templates that you can use as a quick start foundation for your app. Notice the difference in the graphics used for the template icons. Any graphic that has the globe on it is a Web App for SharePoint. If you choose the Custom web app template, then you start building your app from scratch. For this exercise, select the Asset tracking template.

14. In the Asset tracking dialog, provide `C14AssetTracking` for the App Name, skip the Available Locations, and directly enter the full URL to the Office 365 site collection you want to use to build the app.

15. Before you make any changes, click the File tab and click Info. Here you can see the server and database name for the Windows Azure SQL Database that was created for your app. Notice that you can create a client-only database for reporting that will be a read-only connection to the Azure database. You can also manage a variety of other types of connections from the Info page, too, by clicking the Manage button. Return to the Access design page.

16. In the ribbon, click Launch App. Notice how quickly Access Services renders the app. Return to the Access client.

17. In the ribbon, click Navigation Pane; this provides a handy reference to all the Access objects used in your solution.

18. In the ribbon, click Table to get the Add Tables page. You have an array of options for creating a new table. Notice at the bottom of the page these include options such as other Access databases, Excel tables, SharePoint Lists, and more. A significant feature for this release is the Create a new table using our templates search bar at the top. This is backed by a Microsoft-provided Web service that can continuously be updated with new template table structures. The intent is that you don't need to necessarily do the work of laying out table columns and data types, but you can pull down a table that's "close" to what you need and then augment it with your own custom columns. Type **person** in the search bar and click the search icon.

19. Select Vendors from the list. Notice in the Navigation Pane that a new Table was added for Vendors, as well as a Vendors Datasheet and Vendors List.

20. In the Navigation Pane, right-click the Assets Table and select Design View.

21. In the Field Name column, after Owned by, enter **Vendor**; in the Data Type column enter **Lookup**.

22. In the Lookup Wizard, select "I want the lookup field to get the values from another table or query." Select `Table: Vendors`, select `Company` from "Which value do you want to display in your lookup?", leave the remaining default values, and click OK.

23. In the Assets design view, in the Description column, enter **Lookup to Vendors table**. Close the design view by clicking the "x" on the right side across from the Assets tab. When prompted to save changes, click Yes. Notice on your Assets form that the Vendor lookup field was automatically added.

24. In the ribbon, click Launch App. In the left navigation bar, click Vendors and click the + to add a new vendor. Fill out any data fields you want, but at least enter a Company name because this is the field that you selected to show in the Assets form lookup field. Click the Save icon to save the information and then re-edit it to add an asset to the vendor. (Note that the vendor must be saved before you can associate an asset with it.) At the bottom of the vendor form, click the Add Assets link.

25. In the Assets form you can provide data values, but notice that your Vendor has already been selected. Save the form.

26. You can now explore the UI, and enter Assets using the Assets form or from the Employees form. Return to Access.

27. At this point your solution can only be used by you in the specific site collection where you are building the app. To make this into an app for SharePoint that can be deployed to the corporate app catalog on SharePoint or distributed through the SharePoint Store, click the File tab and click Save As.

28. In the Save As dialog, under File Types, click Save Database As if it is not already selected, and click Save as Package.

29. In the Create New Package from This App dialog, provide a name of `C14AssetTracking` for the Title and do not include data in the package. When prompted, save the file to a location on your disk.

30. Log in to your Office 365 Developer Portal SharePoint Admin center, click the app's link and click the App Catalog link.

31. On the App Catalog page, click the Apps for SharePoint link.

32. On the Apps for SharePoint page, click New app and Browse to the file you just saved. Select it, and click Open. Click OK to add the document.

33. In the Apps for SharePoint `C14AssetTracking.app` dialog, leave all the defaults and click Save. You can now navigate to any other site collection within your Office 365 tenancy, click Site Contents, click Apps from your Organization, and install your `C14AssetTracking` app for SharePoint into that site collection. When you install and run the app it should look something like Figure 14-4.

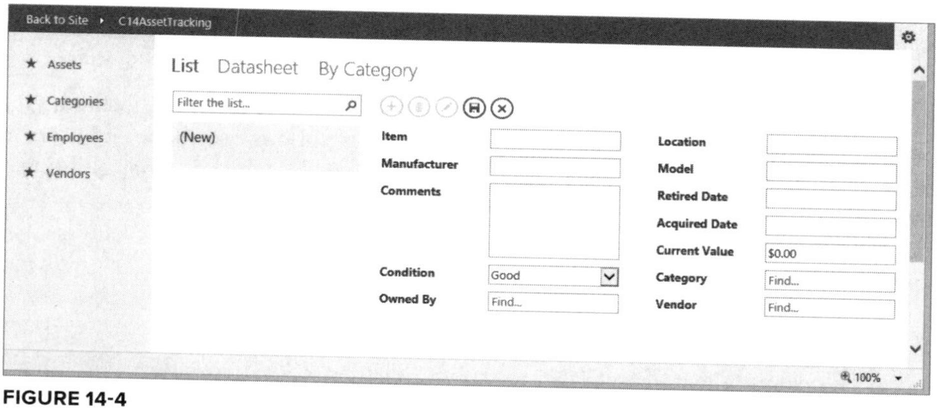

FIGURE 14-4

How It Works

In the first part of this Try It Out you navigated to the SharePoint Store, selected an app, and SharePoint installed it into the site collection. But the installed app for SharePoint is available across all the sites in your Office 365 tenancy. So if you navigate to any other site collection and click Site Contents, you will be able to add this app in this site too. Regarding how it works, at the point you clicked the Trust It button, SharePoint began installing the app and automatically provisioned a Windows Azure SQL Database for the app. When the install completed and you clicked the Business Contact Manager tile to view the app, Access Services was invoked. It then rendered the HTML-based UI elements, executed any business logic, and managed the connection and calls to the back-end SQL database.

You then created an app for SharePoint using an existing template as a base. To the base solution you searched via a Microsoft Web service for a template table that you could simply add in to your solution. After selecting a table you wired it up to an existing form and Access did all the work to adjust the UI elements accordingly. You then tested the app for SharePoint by launching it. When the app was complete you generated an app package for distribution through any number of channels you might choose.

As you can see from this Try It Out, Access and Access Services provide a very quick and powerful way to build data-centric, Web-based business solutions. These solutions can now be broadly distributed and run at Internet scale.

SUMMARY

The new server-side Office application features for SharePoint 2013 include the SharePoint Office Web App Server, PowerPoint Automation Services, and Machine Translation Services.

Excel Services includes new capabilities with the notion of Excel everywhere with the innovative Excel Interactive View that can bring any commonplace HTML table to life with a couple lines of code. Also, the new OData access to Excel tables stored on SharePoint can extend the uses of data with Excel spreadsheet to even greater uses. Lastly, you can easily create data-centric Apps for SharePoint using the redesigned Microsoft Access client tooling and Access Services powered by Microsoft SQL server for on-premises and Windows Azure SQL Database for Office 365.

For a developer, these Office and SharePoint application services provide the APIs, technologies, and infrastructure to build innovative and powerful solutions. Your solutions can shape end users' day-to-day activities and help them to be more productive in what they do, which is what building Apps for SharePoint is about.

EXERCISES

You can find answers to exercises in Appendix A.

1. What are the two all-new services in SharePoint 2013?

2. What service was decoupled from SharePoint to become its own standalone server product?

3. What is the new RESTful protocol added to Excel Services that provides access to Excel tables?

4. Access Services was redesigned for SharePoint 2013 — where are the data and content artifacts stored for the solution?

▶ WHAT YOU LEARNED IN THIS CHAPTER

ITEM	DESCRIPTION
WOPI	Web application Open Platform Interface (WOPI) is the REST-based interface that server applications can use to have documents rendered by the Office Web App Server.
Excel Interactive View	This technology enables any standard HTML table to be viewed in an interactive Excel Services viewer by your adding a couple lines of code to the Web page.
PowerPoint Automation Services	This SharePoint 2013 server-side only (not Office 365) service converts .ppt and .pptx presentation files to .pptx (in the case of .ppt), .pdf, .xpx, and .zip (when the presentation is converted to .jpg and .png).
Machine Translation Services	A new SharePoint 2013 server-side only (not Office 365) service that submits documents to a Microsoft cloud translations service for translation into any supported language. This has privacy concerns to consider for end-user disclosure. See the Microsoft Translator Privacy statement for full details.
Access Services	Access Services was redesigned for SharePoint 2013 where all data and content artifacts for the UI are stored in a SQL Server database for on-premises environments and Window Azure SQL Database in the case of Office 365.

RECOMMENDED READING

The Excel team blog — `http://blogs.office.com/b/microsoft-excel`
`http://www.excelmashup.com`
Microsoft Translator Privacy statement — `http://msdn.microsoft.com/en-us/library/hh464486.aspx`
Machine Translation Services in SharePoint 2013 on MSDN — `http://msdn.microsoft.com/en-us/library/jj163145.aspx`
Machine Translation Services in SharePoint 2013 — `http://msdn.microsoft.com/en-us/library/jj163145.aspx`
Administer Access Services in SharePoint Server 2013 — `http://technet.microsoft.com/en-us/library/ee692394.aspx`
Develop Access 2013 web apps — `http://msdn.microsoft.com/en-us/library/fp179906.aspx`

15

Developing Workflow Applications for SharePoint 2013

WHAT YOU WILL LEARN IN THIS CHAPTER:

➤ Looking at what's new for workflow in SharePoint

➤ Understanding the new decoupled and fully declarative nature of the Workflow Manager Service

➤ Working with the tools to build workflows: Visio Pro, SharePoint Designer, and Visual Studio

WROX.COM CODE DOWNLOADS FOR THIS CHAPTER

The wrox.com code downloads for this chapter are found at: http://www.wrox.com/ WileyCDA/WroxTitle/productCd-1118495845.html on the Download Code tab. The code for this chapter is divided into the following major examples:

➤ C15WFAppForSP.zip

➤ CustomActionGetEmployeeInfoFinal.zip

Workflow in SharePoint is about enabling workplace efficiencies through structured, automated process flows that engage human interaction when needed. SharePoint workflow fundamentally provides the mechanisms to notify people when they need to interact with an automated process via tasks, notifications, e-mail, or any other custom means one might desire to employ. List items, documents, and sites are also valued workflow players because interaction with SharePoint content is central to the beginning, continuation, and ending of many business processes' flows. SharePoint workflow also provides the means for power users and developers to articulate the business logic needed to direct the process flow via declarative logic structures and a runtime engine for workflow execution.

SharePoint 2013 workflow builds on these foundational principles and moves them to a new level. SharePoint 2013 workflow is technically different from previous versions in that it has been completely redesigned to support the scalability and extensibility requirements of the new cloud app model for SharePoint. The new workflow has been built from the ground up to have a purely declarative model and is based on Windows Workflow Foundation 4. Additionally, it is no longer hosted in SharePoint but follows the pattern of the cloud app model and is hosted out of process, in its own server for on-premises deployment or in Windows Azure as a service in cloud deployments. In the cloud the Workflow Service uses the same standard Web technologies of OAuth for service authentication and REST to call into SharePoint via the _API endpoint. The new Workflow Service is an example of the new cloud app model running at cloud scale!

From the business analyst/process consultant, power user, and developer perspective, the tools have become richer and easier to use, and the output is Extensible Application Markup Language (XAML), a declarative markup language. This simply means that your workflows have 100 percent fidelity for execution on-premises and in Office 365 SharePoint Online. For workflows written for SharePoint 2010 against the Windows Workflow Foundation 3 engine, an interoperability bridge is provided so all or part of a workflow from this generation can become a part of a new workflow.

All of this is good stuff so choose your favorite tool, whether Visio Professional, SharePoint Designer 2013, or Visual Studio and begin developing workflows. In this chapter you use each of these tools in one capacity or another and experience this strategic move of the Workflow Service to the cloud.

INTRODUCING WORKFLOW MANAGER

The Workflow Manager is the new workflow engine that runs on the newest workflow technology from Microsoft, the Workflow Framework in .NET 4.5. The Workflow Manager also leverages the Windows Azure Service Bus when running in the cloud or Service Bus for Windows Server when running on-premises to provide workflow state consistency, reliable event delivery, and brokered messaging with the publisher/subscriber (Pub/Sub) messaging pattern. Workflow Manager and Service Bus working in concert provide a workflow service that can work at Internet scale, independent of SharePoint. This independence enables workflow processing to happen in a more predictable and transparent fashion because it is no longer coupled with the SharePoint server, competing for resources. Figure 15-1 shows the high-level architecture for the new workflow.

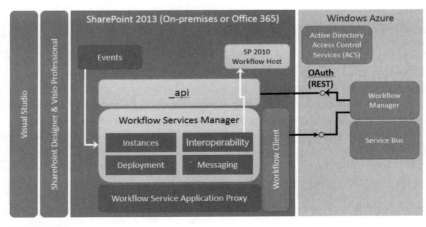

FIGURE 15-1

The integration layer that connects SharePoint to Workflow Manager is through the Workflow Service Application Proxy, and all the new workflow capability is exposed in the object model via the Workflow Services Manager. To make the actual connection from SharePoint to Workflow Manager, a workflow client is required to be installed on the SharePoint machine.

The workflow API has four major components:

➤ **Deployment Service:** This is used to publish workflows and create associations.

➤ **Messaging Service:** Events are piped into the workflow through the Messaging Service. When SharePoint sends an event into the workflow, the event is saved in the Windows Azure Service Bus database before it is delivered to Workflow Manager. The Workflow Manager takes care of keeping the state of the workflow and the state of the message queue in sync. Messaging Services uses another feature of the Service Bus, which is Pub/Sub. With Pub/Sub multiple workflows can subscribe to one event. For instance, suppose you have 10 workflows waiting on a list item. SharePoint will send only one message when an event fires on the list and Service Bus takes care of delivering that message to the 10 workflows that subscribe to that list item. In the classic SharePoint 2010 workflow model, SharePoint would have run 10 event receivers, putting a greater load on the workflow engine.

➤ **Instance Service:** This is used to query an instance to see information about it and control workflow instances; for example, you can terminate them.

➤ **Interoperability Service:** This is used to invoke or start instances of classic SharePoint 2010 workflows.

All workflow callbacks into SharePoint take place over the _API endpoint using the REST/OData protocol. The communication between SharePoint and the Workflow Manager is secured using the OAuth security model, making the new workflow infrastructure a premier implementation of the new cloud app model.

THE BIG NEW FEATURES FOR SHAREPOINT DESIGNER

SharePoint Designer (SPD) has been the mainstay for SharePoint workflow creation. In SharePoint 2013 SPD has advanced its feature set for making workflow design easier, and in some cases, just more enjoyable to work with (as you will experience). Also, although you could stitch together workflows in SharePoint 2010 to do some very powerful things, a number of features, actions, and programming constructs were not available to give you the type of control over the "flow" in workflow that you really wanted and needed. SPD fills these gaps. Following is a list of some of the big new features you'll experience in SPD 2013; these were highly requested features from Microsoft partners and customers alike:

➤ **Visual Designer:** For those who prefer a visual design surface with which to build their workflow, SharePoint Designer has a new Visual Designer. However, you must have Microsoft Visio Professional 2013 installed on your computer to use it.

➤ **Stages:** You no longer need to use just linear workflows that go from top to bottom as with SharePoint 2010. Human business processes are not strictly linear. Typically these processes have a number of tasks to be performed as a *unit of work* and processes generally include one or more units of work. When a unit of work is completed, sometimes there is a pause for a period of time before the next unit of work is triggered. Other times the business process needs to return to a previously completed unit of work to have its steps performed again, or it might proceed on to the next unit of work in a linear fashion. In human processes, business rules and policy guide the transitions between one unit of work being completed and what the next unit of work to be started should be. SharePoint 2013 workflows can now better parallel these human process patterns by representing a unit of work as a specific set of workflow actions within a stage. In your workflow, once a stage, (that is, unit of work), is complete, you can choose the next stage for your workflow to transition to, or whether to pause, return to a stage previously completed for further processing, or continue on to the next stage in a linear flow. Therefore, stages give you the flexibility to logically determine your transition from one stage in your workflow to the next.

➤ **Call Web Services:** You can now extend your workflows to reach data beyond the boundaries of SharePoint. You can reach out to different systems using HTTP/REST and bring the external data you need into the context of your workflow process.

➤ **Copy/Paste:** In SharePoint's Text-based Designer and the new Visual Designer, you can now copy/paste individual lines or complete constructs.

➤ **Looping:** You can loop by using the transition between stages to continue to go to a specific stage unless a specific criterion is met. You can also use the two new loop structures — one describes a determinate loop, the other an indeterminate loop.

➤ **Dictionary Variable:** This new variable data type is suited for storing complex data, such as a JSON object returned from a REST call or an array of data.

➤ **Portability:** Any workflow type can now be packaged as a .wsp file for redeploying from site to site. You can export your SharePoint Designer workflow into a Visio .VSDX file and import it into another site as well.

➤ **App Step:** This contains actions that run with app-level permissions in your workflow. This means that these actions can run outside of the users' permissions if your workflow needs to perform some action on behalf of users where they do not have that level of permission.

➤ **Interoperability:** This provides support for interoperability with classic SharePoint 2010 workflows. Sometimes you might need to use a 2010 action inside of a SharePoint 2013 workflow, but these two workflow engines are inherently incompatible. Two actions are available in SharePoint Designer 2013 — Start a List Workflow, and Start a Site Workflow. With them, you can pass parameters into a SharePoint 2010 workflow, and the 2010 workflow can execute its actions and return data to the 2013 workflow that you can use for its processing.

Hopefully these new feature descriptions have whetted your appetite for wanting to get your hands on the tools, so let's take a look at them.

VISIO PROFESSIONAL, SHAREPOINT DESIGNER, AND WORKFLOW

In SharePoint 2010 the ability to do iterative workflow development was introduced; for example, between a business analyst using Microsoft Visio and a SharePoint power user using SharePoint Designer. Having these two tools (each one more specifically suited to a particular role for a process design participant) enabled a seamless way to divide the labor when creating automated business processes for SharePoint. The business analyst, as the process owner, knowing the organic nature of the process, could use Visio to describe it. The power user, as the SharePoint subject matter expert (SME), could then import the flow, embellish it with the SharePoint-centric nuances and business logic, publish and test it, and return the Visio file for further enhancements by the analyst. This tool support for synergistic process design continues with SharePoint Designer 2013 and Visio Professional 2013, but is enhanced.

As with Visio 2010, Visio Professional 2013 sports a Microsoft SharePoint 2013 Workflow template. This template consists of three stencils: Actions, Conditions, and Components, as shown in Figure 15-2.

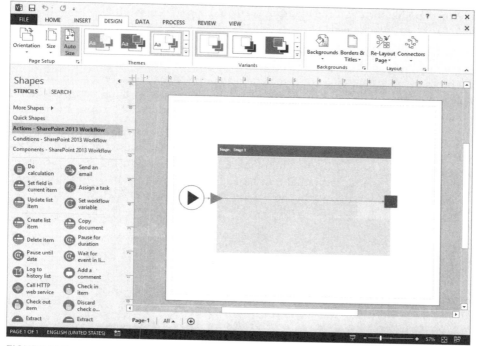

FIGURE 15-2

The Visio shapes in each of these stencils essentially match one-for-one with their counterpart construct in SharePoint Designer 2013. In typical Visio manner you simply drag and drop the shapes you want on the drawing surface and connect them together. What's important to note here is the Stage Outline button under the Process tab on the ribbon in the SharePoint Workflow group. When you click this button, Visio creates an entirely new page and names it Default Stage Outline. You can see this in your page tabs at the bottom of Visio. The purpose of this view is for the business analyst or someone not familiar with the SharePoint Action constructs. Therefore, the Stage Outline lets him model the process flow using this higher-level view. With this view he uses the Simple Stage shape on the Components stencil and any needed shapes from the Conditions stencil to describe the flow. However, the business analyst's design experience is not simply limited to the use of the SharePoint-related shapes. It is possible to actually use any shape from any Visio stencil that helps express the intent and requirements of the process. The business analyst therefore uses Visio as if he were creating any other diagram — selecting and using the shapes that best represent what they want to visually convey.

When the business analyst has completed his work, he can save the file, which is now an XML-based structure with the file extension of .vsdx, to any location where the SharePoint subject matter expert can retrieve it.

The SharePoint subject matter expert has a couple options upon notification of the available Visio file. She can open it using Visio, make her additions, and save it again, or she can import the file directly into SPD. Notice that the business analyst does not need to "export" the file as was the practice in SharePoint 2010. SPD 2013 can read the new .vsdx file format natively so no need exists for the .vwi intermediate file format if the diagram is created with Visio 2013. However, SPD can still import Visio 2010 .vwi when needed.

When the Visio document is imported into SPD, the subject matter expert can first check for errors. SharePoint Designer will review the imported file and list any issues found so the SME can resolve them. These can be anything from a line not being connected to a shape, to a Yes or No label missing from a decision, to a shape being used inside the flow that is not a SharePoint workflow shape. The SME can work through each issue until the workflow contains no errors.

One of the really nice new features in SharePoint Designer is that SMEs can now choose to work within two different designer views to build out their workflows. They can use the Visual Designer view, which is Visio embedded in SPD, as shown in Figure 15-3 (Wow!), or using the Views button in the ribbon, they can toggle to the traditional text-based design view, as shown in Figure 15-4. This provides maximum flexibility in the workflow design-time experience!

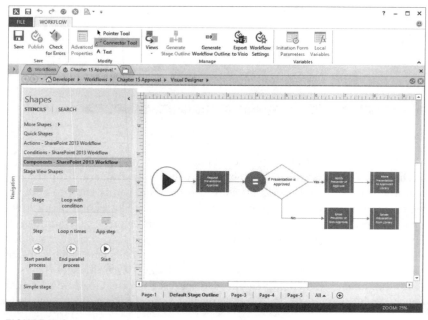

FIGURE 15-3

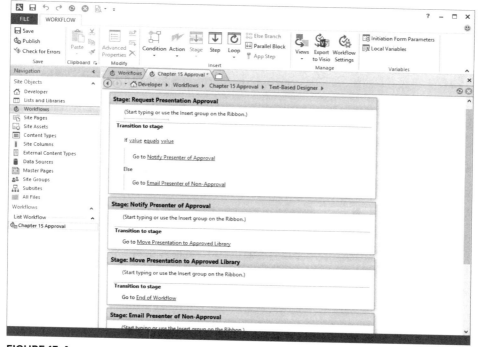

FIGURE 15-4

Visio and SharePoint Designer are certainly first-class tools to use for collaboratively designing and building your SharePoint workflows. The following Try It Out provides you first-hand practice with these tools where you will first assume the role of a business analyst using Visio 2013 to design the workflow from the business perspective, and then you will assume the role of the SharePoint subject matter expert to complete the workflow by adding the SharePoint-specific configuration details and deploying.

TRY IT OUT Employee Time card Approval Workflow with Visio and SharePoint Designer

In this exercise you learn the basics for using Visio Pro and SharePoint Designer by building an employee time card approval process. When an employee submits a time card indicating her total hours worked for the week, the workflow performs a calculation to determine whether the employee worked overtime. When overtime hours are present, these hours are updated to a column in the SharePoint list and must be reviewed by the manager for payment approval. If approved, the hours are paid. If rejected, the employee total hours worked for the week will be reset to 40, but the overtime hours will remain recorded on the list, too, and available for Human Resources review. For this Try It Out you will optionally need Visio Professional 2013 (if you will be using the Visual Designer) and SharePoint Designer 2013. You can complete this exercise with the SharePoint Designer Text-based Designer alone.

1. Log in to your Office 365 SharePoint to a site where you can create lists.

2. Click Site Contents in the left navigation bar and click the Add an app icon.

3. Click the Custom List tile. In the Adding Custom List dialog, type `Employees` and click Create.

4. On the Site Contents page, locate and click the tile for your new `Employees` list. In the ribbon, click the List tab and click List Settings.

5. Under the Columns section, click the Create column link and for:

   ➤ Column name: **EmpID**

   ➤ Require that this column contains information: Yes

   ➤ Enforce unique values: Yes

   ➤ Number of decimal places: 0

   Click OK, and when prompted to create an index, click Yes.

6. Click the Employees link at the top of the page to return to the `Employees` list. To add a new item, click the plus sign (+) and create at least three employees. Use the Title column to enter the employee's first and last name for simplicity and provide each with a unique employee ID number.

7. Click Site Contents in the left navigation bar and click the Add an app icon.

8. Click the Custom List tile. In the Adding Custom List dialog, type `Employee Time Card` and click Create.

9. On the Site Contents page, locate and click the tile for your new `Employee Time Card` list. In the ribbon, click the List tab and click List Settings.

10. Under the Columns section, click the Create column link and complete the following fields as indicated (leave the default value unless directed to change it):

    ➤ Column name: **Employee Name**

    ➤ For the column type: Lookup (information already on this site)

    ➤ Require that this column contains information: Yes

    ➤ Enforce unique values: No

    ➤ Get information from: Employees

    ➤ In this column: Title

    ➤ Add a column to show each of these additional fields: EmpID

    Click OK, and when prompted to create an index, click Yes.

11. Click the Create column link and complete the following fields as indicated:

    ➤ Column name: **Total Hours**

    ➤ For the column type: Number

    ➤ Require that this column contains information: Yes

    Click OK.

12. Click the Create column link and enter the following:

> ➤ Column name: **Overtime Hours**

> ➤ For the column type: Number

Click OK.

13. Click the Employee Time Card link at the top of the page to return to the `Employee Time Card` list. To add a new item, click the plus sign (+) and create at least one employee time card with the following values:

> ➤ Title: **Week of** *mm/dd-dd/20yy*

> ➤ Employee Name: *Select an employee from your list*

> ➤ Total Hours: **42**

> ➤ Overtime Hours: **2**

Click Save.

14. With the lists in place, you will now assume the role of the business analyst who will create the Visio workflow for the employee time card process. Open Visio Professional 2013 and select the Microsoft SharePoint 2013 Workflow template. Click Create.

15. As a business analyst, you do not work with the specific SharePoint shapes that describe Actions; you work at a higher process flow level. Click the Process tab in the ribbon and click the Stage Outline icon. You can zoom in on the size of the design surface if you want the Stage shape to be bigger.

16. Visio has placed a default first stage on the design surface; double-click it and type **Submit time card**.

17. In the Visio Stencils navigation bar, click Components ➪ SharePoint 2013 Workflow. Drag three Simple Stage shapes onto the design surface, double-click each one individually, and type one of the following Text labels for each:

> ➤ **Manager approval**

> ➤ **Reset total hours**

> ➤ **Pay employee**

18. In the Visio Stencils navigation bar, click Conditions ➪ SharePoint 2013 Workflow. Drag two "If any value equals value" shapes onto the design surface, double-click each one individually, and type one of the following Text labels for each:

> ➤ **Is overtime present?**

> ➤ **Is overtime approved?**

19. Using Figure 15-5 as a guide lay out your shapes accordingly. Click the Home tab in the ribbon and select the Connector in the Tools groups. To connect one shape to the next, click and hold inside the shape you want to start with and drag into the shape you want to end with. The connector snaps automatically in place. When you have all the connectors in place for all the shapes, you need to label the Yes/No lines exiting the decision shapes. Right-click each line and select the Yes/No label as appropriate for that line.

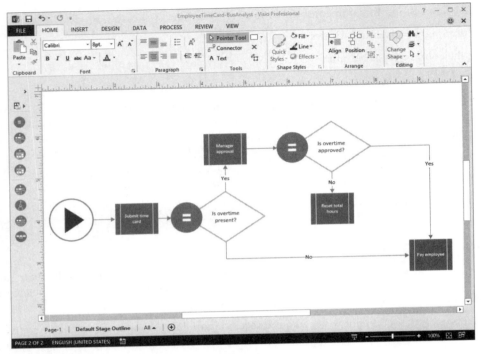

FIGURE 15-5

20. Save the file to disk with the name, `EmployeeTimeCard-BusAnalyst`. You will import it into SharePoint Designer. Close Visio.

21. Open SharePoint Designer 2013 and click the Open Site tile. In the Open Site dialog, enter the full URL path to the site collection where you created the `Employees` and `Employee Time Card` lists. When the site opens, in the left navigation pane, click Workflows under Site Objects.

22. In the ribbon, click Import from Visio and select Import Visio 2013 Diagram. In the file selection dialog, navigate to your `EmployeeTimeCard-BusAnalyst` file, select it, and click Open.

23. In the Create Workflow dialog, type `Timecard Approval` for the Name, and select List Workflow for the Workflow Type and select `Employee Time Card` for the SharePoint list so your configuration looks like Figure 15-6. Click OK.

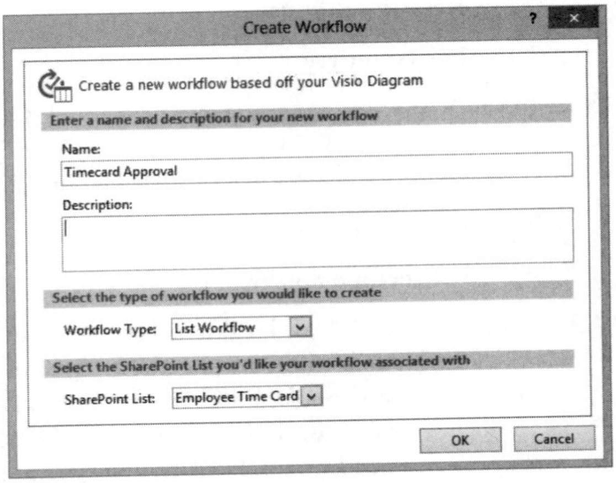

FIGURE 15-6

24. By default, when you import a Visio diagram you will be in the Visual Designer. Also notice that you are still in the high-level view of the business analyst. However, now you are in the role of the power user/SharePoint subject matter expert, so you'll want to work at the lower level of actually adding specific SharePoint Actions and steps. In the Visual Designer ribbon, click the Generate Workflow Outline icon in the Manage group.

25. In the workflow outline, you can now build out, within each of the blue stage containers, all the logic needed to process that stage. This can include any number of actions, steps, loops, conditions, and so forth. In the SPD Visual Designer view, you do this all just as you would in Visio.

26. Before you configure your workflow, you must first create one variable to hold the overtime hours that the workflow will calculate. In the ribbon, click Local Variables and click Add.

27. In the Edit Variable dialog, type `OvertimeHours` for the Name and select Number for the Type.

28. In the left navigation bar, click Actions - SharePoint 2013 Workflows. Locate the Do Calculation shape, and drag and drop it on the Submit time card Stage. Hover over the Do Calculation shape and an icon with a gear and curved arrow appears. Hover over it, click the drop-down arrow, and select LeftOperand. A dialog opens so you can configure the calculation.

29. Click the LeftOperand row in the dialog and click the *fx* button. In the Define Workflow Lookup dialog select the following options:

➤   Data source: Current Item

➤   Field from source: Total Hours

Click OK.

30. Click the Operator row in the dialog, click the list box drop-down on the right, and select Minus.

31. Click the RightOperand row in the dialog, click the white space on the right side under Minus and type **40**.

32. Click the To row in the dialog, click the drop-down arrow on the right side, and select `Variable: OvertimeHours`. Click OK.

33. In the left navigation bar locate the Set field in current item shape, and drag and drop it on the Submit time card Stage following the Do calculation. Here you want to automatically record in the list the number of overtime hours that were worked by the employee. Hover over the Set field in current item shape, click the drop-down arrow, and select Field.

➤   For Field, select Overtime Hours

➤   For Value, click *fx* and select Workflow Variables and Parameters for Data Source

➤   For Field from source select `Variable: OvertimeHours`

Click OK.

34. Hover over the "Is overtime present?" shape, click the drop-down arrow, and select Value. A dialog opens so you can configure the logic for this condition.

35. Click the top Value row in the dialog and click the *fx* button. In the Define Workflow Lookup dialog, complete the following fields as indicated:

➤ Data source: Workflow Variables and Parameters

➤ Field from source: `Variable: OvertimeHours`

Click OK.

36. Click the Operator row in the dialog, click the list box drop-down on the right and select Is greater than.

37. Click the bottom Value row in the dialog, click in the white space on the right side under Is greater than, and type 0. Click OK to close the dialog.

38. In the left navigation panel, click Actions - SharePoint 2013 Workflow. Locate the Start a task process shape and drag and drop it onto the Manager approval Stage.

39. Hover over the Start a task process action and click the down arrow to open the SPD properties. Select Process Settings.

40. In the Start a Task Process dialog perform the following:

a. Click the ellipsis (...) beside Participants. In the Select users dialog, select your login name from the left list. Click the Add>> button to add your name to the left column under Selected User. For simplicity, your login is being made the only approver for this workflow. Click OK.

b. In the Task Title, type: `Overtime Approval`.

c. In the Description, click the Open editor for body button. In the String Builder dialog, type **Please approve the overtime of** and be sure to leave a space following the word of.

d. Click the Add or Change Lookup at the bottom of the dialog, and in the Lookup for String dialog, for Data source, select Workflow Variables and Parameters and for the Field from source, select `OvertimeHours`. Click OK to close the Lookup for String dialog.

e. In the String Builder dialog, following the value just inserted, add a space and type **hours for** (including a space following) and click the Add or Change Lookup button.

f. In the Lookup for String dialog, for the Data source, select Current Item and for the Field from source, select `Employee Name`. Click OK to close the Lookup for String dialog.

g. In the String Builder dialog, following the value just inserted, type a period. The fully constructed body of your task item should look like Figure 15-7.

h. Click OK to close the String Builder dialog.

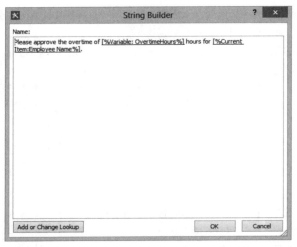

FIGURE 15-7

i. In the Start a Task Process dialog, click to expand the Task Options. For Completion Criteria select Wait for first response.

j. In the Start a Task Process dialog, click to expand the Outcome Options. For Default Outcome, select Rejected. Click OK to close the Start a Task Process dialog.

41. In the Visual Designer, hover over the "Is overtime approved?" shape, and click the drop-down menu on the SPD properties.

42. Click the top Value row in the dialog and click the *fx* button. In the Define Workflow Lookup dialog select the following options:

➤ Data source: Workflow Variables and Parameters

➤ Field from source: `Variable: Outcome`

Click OK.

43. Click the Operator row in the dialog and click the list box drop-down on the right, and select Equals.

44. Click the bottom Value row and select Approved. Click OK to close the dialog.

45. The last part of the business rule to implement is that when the overtime hours are rejected, then the Total Hours submitted need to be automatically set back to 40. In the left navigation bar locate the Set field in current item shape, and drag and drop it on the Reset total hours Stage. Hover over the Set field in current item shape, click the drop-down arrow, and select Field.

➤ For Field: Total Hours

➤ For Value: **40**

Click OK. Notice that you are not resetting the overtime hours, because you still want to record in the list that overtime was worked, even if it was not approved for payment.

46. To show that you could have done all this in the Text-based Designer, too, in the ribbon click Views and select Text-based Designer. You can use the View option to toggle between these designer options and use the one with which you feel the most comfortable.

47. Look at the top of your designer form and you will see your tab labeled Timecard Approval and a number of subtabs. Click the Timecard Approval subtab to return to the page where you can manage the workflow settings. Under Start Options, select the first two for starting manually and automatically when an item is created.

48. To publish your list workflow, click the Publish button. SPD publishes the workflow to the list, where you can check it out.

49. In Office 365 navigate to your `Employee Time Card` list. Create a new item using the following values:

➤ Title: **Week of *mm/dd-dd/20yy***

➤ Employee Name: *Select an employee from your list*

➤ Total Hours: **40**

➤ Overtime Hours: *This value will automatically be calculated*

Click Save.

50. Refresh the browser until you see the Timecard Approval status of Pay Employee. Because there was no overtime, no manager approval was required.

51. Create a new item using the following values:

➤ Title: **Week of *mm/dd-dd/20yy***

➤ Employee Name: *Select an employee from your list*

➤ Total Hours: **44**

➤ Overtime Hours: *This value will automatically be calculated*

Click Save.

52. Refresh the browser until you see the Timecard Approval status of Manager approval. Click the Manager approval link. Because you designated your login to be the approver, you can approve/reject the overtime. On the Workflow Status: Timecard Approval page, click the Overtime Approval link in the middle of the page. On the item page for the approval you can see the description text you configured stating the number of hours of overtime calculated and for which employee.

53. Click the Edit Item button in the ribbon, and click Approved. Return to the Employee Time Card list and see that the Timecard Approval status has updated to Pay employee.

54. Create a new item using the following values:

➤ Title: **Week of *mm/dd-dd/20yy***

➤ Employee Name: *Select an employee from your list*

➤ Total Hours: **48**

➤ Overtime Hours: *This value will automatically be calculated*

Click Save.

55. Refresh the browser until you see the Timecard Approval status of Manager approval. Click the Manager approval link. Click the Overtime Approval link in the middle of the page. On the item page for the approval, click the Edit Item button in the ribbon, and click Rejected. Return to the Employee Time Card list and see that the Timecard Approval status has updated to Reset total hours. Your outcomes should be comparable to Figure 15-8.

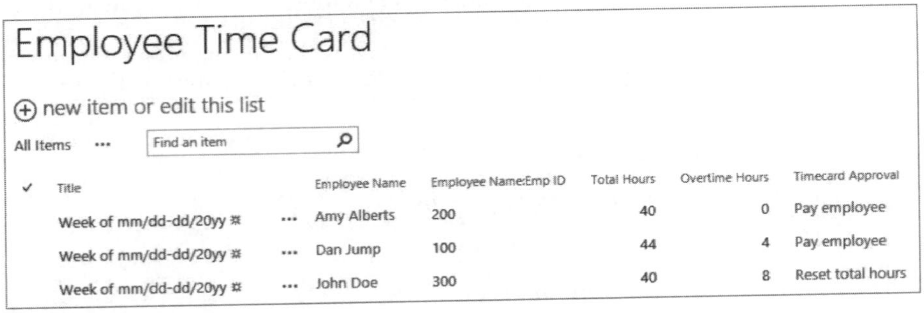

Employee Time Card

⊕ new item or edit this list

All Items ··· | Find an item 🔍

✓	Title	Employee Name	Employee Name:Emp ID	Total Hours	Overtime Hours	Timecard Approval
	Week of mm/dd-dd/20yy ⌘ ···	Amy Alberts	200	40	0	Pay employee
	Week of mm/dd-dd/20yy ⌘ ···	Dan Jump	100	44	4	Pay employee
	Week of mm/dd-dd/20yy ⌘ ···	John Doe	300	40	8	Reset total hours

FIGURE 15-8

How It Works

In this Try It Out you played the role of two different personas, a business analyst and a SharePoint subject matter expert, each with his or her own set of skills and business acumen that they bring to the workflow building processes. Yet in both roles, you experienced the value of having the Visio and SharePoint Designer tools to design the logic for processing. In Visio you constructed the high-level stages and decisions in the business flow. In SharePoint Designer you drilled down deeper into each stage, configuring the Actions to execute in the workflow engine. Your completed workflow included a calculation, setting a couple column values in the SharePoint list (Total Hours and Overtime Hours), and decision logic. You also saw that some tasks, such as the Start a task process, have rich configuration capabilities for constructing dynamic, data-driven content for the user to see when the workflow runs and presenting the UI for the workflow approver to interact with.

At run time, the workflow started automatically upon a new list item being entered. The workflow then sent an e-mail to the approver(s) and the subject and body of the e-mail contained the same information as the workflow approval/rejection form. The e-mail provided a link directly to the workflow task on SharePoint, making it convenient for the approver to follow through and work with it. Alternatively, as you experienced in the exercise, on the `Employee Time Card` list page an approver can simply click the link for manager approval on a list item to navigate to the workflow page to approve or reject the overtime hours.

In your business context, whether you will be in the role of both the business analyst and the SharePoint subject matter expert, or if there is truly a division of labor within your organization and each role is performed separately, Visio Professional and SharePoint Designer are the tools of trade for designing and building your business process workflows for SharePoint 2013. As you explore and use these tools more fully you will quickly get a sense for the broad and deep types of workflows these two greatly enhanced tools provide you in this release.

WORKFLOW AND VISUAL STUDIO

Sometimes there is the need to go beyond the out-of-box capabilities of Visio Professional and SharePoint Designer, and in those cases you can fall back to Visual Studio and create affectively anything you need. With Visual Studio developers can create custom actions that can be made available to SharePoint Designer, workflow templates that can be used from site to site, and deep workflows irrespective of how complex they may get.

New in this release for Visual Studio is that SharePoint workflows are based on Windows Workflow Foundation 4. Therefore, developers use a visual designer to create a XAML-based workflow so no compiled code outputs from the design process. This provides run time consistency for workflows built using either SharePoint Designer or Visual Studio. As with SharePoint Designer, any workflow developed with Visual Studio can execute equally well in the Office 365 environment, which is a huge win and opens up enterprise-grade, workflow solution opportunities to now land in SharePoint Online.

For those new to SharePoint workflow, an *activity* is a Windows Workflow Foundation platform term that describes a fundamental building block of a workflow and is a unit of workflow execution. An *action* is a SharePoint Designer term describing a higher-level, more human-friendly abstraction that is a fundamental unit used in composition with other actions to build SharePoint workflows. Normally, you can assume that one Visual Studio activity maps to one action in SharePoint Designer. However, sometimes for clarity within the SharePoint Designer UI, a single activity might sit behind actions with different names in the UI to avoid end-user confusion in which one to use in a given situation.

With Visual Studio you can create custom activities, and these come in two flavors: *custom declarative activity* and *custom code activity*. Custom code activities can be built and used in on-premises SharePoint environments only because they run on the Workflow Manager server and allow full access to .NET. These code-based activities cannot be deployed to Office 365 because the Workflow Manager activity list is locked down for security purposes. A custom declarative activity, because it is XAML-based, not code-based, can be created using Visual Studio as well but these custom activities can run in both the on-premises and online environments equally well.

In the following Try It Out you build a custom declarative activity that can be used by SharePoint Designer and deployed to either SharePoint on-premises or SharePoint Online.

> **TRY IT OUT**   Create a Custom Declarative Workflow Activity in Visual Studio (CustomActionGetEmployeeInfoFinal.zip)

In this exercise you create a custom activity that will become available in SharePoint Designer. The activity will accept an employee number as input and call a REST-based endpoint to retrieve additional employee information. The retrieved data will be stored in a dictionary object. Note: This Try It Out can only be developed against a test SharePoint 2013 server on-premises setup. Visual Studio 2012 does not support remote development of SharePoint solutions. These sandboxed or farm-level solutions can only be developed against locally installed versions of SharePoint Foundation or SharePoint Server. Remote development is supported only for Apps for SharePoint 2013.

1. Run Visual Studio 2012 as Administrator. Select New Project.

2. In the New Project dialog, expand the Templates ⇨ Visual C# ⇨ Office/SharePoint ⇨ SharePoint Solutions nodes. Select SharePoint 2013 ⇨ Empty Project and provide the name `CustomActionGetEmployeeInfo`. Click OK.

3. In the Specify the site and security level for debugging dialog, set the SharePoint site URL to your local test SharePoint site and select Deploy as a sandboxed solution. Click Finish.

4. In Solution Explorer, right-click the project, and select Add ⇨ New item. In the Add New Item dialog, select Workflow Custom Activity, name it `GetEmployeeInfoActivity`, and click OK.

5. The Workflow Designer opens with the initial status of your workflow and an empty Sequence activity on the page. To design your custom activity to be generic, where it can be hosted in any workflow at run time, take in any employee number passed in by a host workflow, and output a consumable object for the host workflow, you need to define some arguments. At the bottom of the design canvas are three tabs: Variables, Arguments, and Imports. Click the Arguments tab.

6. To create the input parameter, click the Create Argument text box, type `EmployeeID` for the Name and complete the following fields as indicated:

➤ Direction: In

➤ Argument type: Int32

➤ Do not provide a default value.

7. For the output parameter, click the Create Argument text box, type `JsonODataResponse` for the Name and complete the following fields as indicated:

➤ Direction: Out

➤ Argument type: Click the drop-down menu and select Browse for Types. In the Browse and Select a .NET Type dialog, type `DynamicValue`. In the selection list, locate Microsoft.Activities, select `DynamicValue`.

➤ Do not provide a default value.

Click OK.

8. Using the Visual Studio View menu, make sure the Toolbox is open and pinned for convenience. In the Toolbox, expand the Messaging node. Select `HttpSend` in the Toolbox and drag and drop it inside the Sequence.

9. Click on `HttpSend`. In the Properties pane complete the following fields as indicated:

➤ Request Method: `GET`

➤ Request URI: `"http://services.odata.org/Northwind/Northwind.svc/Employees("` `+ EmployeeID + ")?$select=EmployeeID,LastName,FirstName,HomePhone,Report` `sTo&$format=json"` You'll notice that you are dynamically providing your `EmployeeID` argument at run time to retrieve only the information for the employee number that is passed into this activity.

➤ Response: `ResponseContent: JsonODataResponse`

Figure 15-9 shows what your custom action should look like:

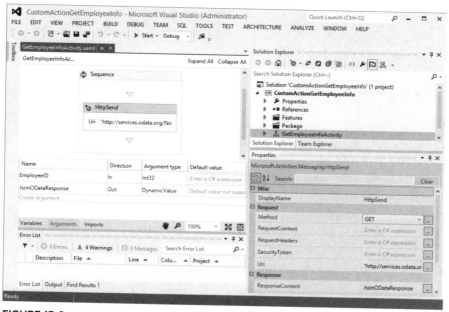

FIGURE 15-9

10. In the Solution Explorer, expand the workflow node and double-click the `.actions4` file. A designer is not available for configuring this file so you need to build it manually by typing in the XML. The `.actions4` file defines the visual appearance of your custom action when deployed to SharePoint. This is what the workflow designers will interact with in the Visual and Text-based Designer views. To construct the action sentence and identify and map the corresponding input and output arguments to it accordingly, delete the `<RuleDesigner>...</RuleDesigner>` elements currently in the file and in their place add the following:

```
<RuleDesigner Sentence="Get employee data for %1 (output to %2)">
   <FieldBind Field="EmployeeID"
              Text="Employee Number"
              Id="1"
              DesignerType="TextArea"
              DisplayName="Get Employee Info"
              />
   <FieldBind Field="JsonODataResponse"
              Text="JsonODataResponse"
              Id="2"
              DesignerType="ParameterNames"
              DisplayName="JsonODataResponse"
              />
</RuleDesigner>
<Parameters>
   <Parameter Name="EmployeeID"
              Type="System.Int32, mscorlib"
              Direction="In"
              DesignerType="TextArea"
              Description="The employee number"
              />
   <Parameter Name="JsonODataResponse"
              Type="Microsoft.Activities.DynamicValue,
Microsoft.Activities,
              Culture=neutral, PublicKeyToken=null"
              Direction="Out"
              DesignerType="ParameterNames"
              Description="Output variable to store the contents
of the HTTP request."
              />
</Parameters>
```

11. Build the project to make sure there are no errors, right-click the project node, and select Deploy to deploy the .WSP file to your test SharePoint site. You will now have a workflow action available in SPD that, when given an employee ID, will make a REST call to the employee data source and return information about the employee that can be used in workflow processing.

12. After the deployment is complete, in SharePoint, navigate to the site collection to which you deployed the file. Select Site Contents, click the Add an app tile, and click the Custom List tile. Name the list `Employee's Manager`.

13. Click the `Employee's Manager` tile, click the List tab, and click List Settings in the ribbon.

14. On the Settings page click Create column link and complete the following fields as indicated:

> ➤ Column name: **EmpID**
> ➤ Type: Number
> ➤ Require: Yes
> ➤ Number of decimal places: 0

Click OK.

15. Click Create column link and complete the following fields as indicated:

> ➤ Column name: **EmpFName**
> ➤ Type: Single line of text

Click OK.

16. Click Create column link and complete the following fields as indicated:

> ➤ Column name: **EmpLName**
> ➤ Type: Single line of text

Click OK.

17. Click Create column link and complete the following fields as indicated:

> ➤ Column name: **ManagerFName**
> ➤ Type: Single line of text

Click OK.

18. Click Create column link and complete the following fields as indicated:

> ➤ Column name: **ManagerLName**
> ➤ Type: Single line of text

Click OK.

19. Return to the `Employee's Manager` list, and click New item. For the Title type **Test 1**, and for the EmpID type **1**. Leave the other columns empty; the workflow will fill those in. Click Save.

20. Start SharePoint Designer 2013 and open the site collection where you deployed the custom action. When the site opens, in the left navigation pane select Workflows.

21. In the ribbon, click the List Workflow drop-down menu and select Employee's Manager.

22. In the Create List Workflow dialog, for the name, type `Get Employee Manager`. Click OK.

23. Here you use the Text-based Designer to build the workflow. Click on Stage 1 and type the name `Get Manager Name`.

24. Click directly under the phrase, "Start typing or use the Insert group on the Ribbon." Type `Get` and press Enter. Your new `GetEmployeeInfoActivity` appears; select it. (This activity is also available in the Actions in the ribbon.)

25. Click the Employee Number link, and click *fx*. In the Lookup for Integer dialog, select Current Item and select EmpID from the field source. Click OK.

You don't need to change the second link in the sentence; SPD automatically creates a dictionary variable `Variable: JsonODataResponse` for you for the returned JSON object from the REST call. SPD makes this default selection based on the JSON object you built into the custom action.

26. Click just under your first sentence, type **Get**, and press Enter. Select Get an Item from a Dictionary. A number of data values were returned from the REST call and you now need to select which ones are important to your processing. It's best to first think about how the data lays out in the returned object. The following is the returned JSON object for the employee with the `EmployeeID` of 1. To identify a specific data element, you use the notation `object/field`, so `d/FirstName` will retrieve the value "Nancy" and so on.

```
{
"d" : {
"__metadata": {
"uri": "http://services.odata.org/Northwind/Northwind.svc/Employees(1)",
"type": "NorthwindModel.Employee"
},
"EmployeeID": 1,
"LastName": "Davolio",
"FirstName": "Nancy",
"HomePhone": "(206) 555-9857",
"ReportsTo": 2
}
}
```

27. To configure the Get an Item from a Directory action, click the `item by name or path` link, type **d/FirstName**, click the `dictionary` link, select `Variable: JsonODataResponse`, click the `item` link, and select `Create a new variable`. In the Edit Variable dialog, type **strEmpFN** for the Name and select `String` for the Type.

28. Hover over the end of the just configured sentence, click the drop-down arrow, and select Copy Action.

29. Click right below the sentence and click Paste in the ribbon. Delete `d/FirstName` and type **d/LastName** and create a new `String` output variable `strEmpLN`, following the pattern you used in step 27 for creating a new variable.

30. Copy and paste the action again, delete `d/LastName` and type **d/ReportsTo**, and create a new output `Integer` variable `intReportsTo`, following the pattern you used in step 27 for creating a new variable.

31. Now retrieve the employee's manager information: Copy the first line of the workflow, which is your custom action line, and paste it following the last line you just completed in step 30. Click the `CurrentItem:EmpID` link. In the Lookup for Integer dialog, select Workflow Variables and Parameters for the Data source and select, `Variable: intReportsTo` for the Field source. Click OK.

32. You can now copy the lines that retrieve the first and last names from the response object and paste them right after the last line from step 31. However, both of these lines should each create a new `String` variable: one for `strManagerFN` and another for `strManagerLN`. Follow the pattern you used in step 27 for creating a new variable for each of these.

33. The last thing to do is use the data values you have collected in the variables to set the values in the columns on your list for this employee. Below the last line from step 32, type `set` and press Enter. Select Set Field in Current Item.

34. Click the `field` link, and select `EmpFName`. Click the `values` link and click *fx*. In the Define Workflow Lookup, select Workflow Variables and Parameters for the Data source and select `Variable: intReportsTo` for the field source.

35. Repeat step 34 for each of the current item columns `EmpLName`, `ManagerFName`, and `ManagerLName`, and configure each of their respective variables as in step 34.

36. To finalize the workflow, click the Transition to stage area, type **Go**, and press Enter. Click a *stage* and select End of Workflow.

37. In the ribbon, click Save to save your workflow. You can also click Check for errors to validate your code. Your completed workflow should look like Figure 15-10.

38. In the ribbon, click Publish.

39. In the browser, navigate to your Employee's Manager site. On the first item you created in step 19, click the ellipsis (...) and select Workflows.

FIGURE 15-10

40. On the Start a New Workflow page, click the Get Employee Manager link to start the workflow. When the workflow starts you will be returned to the `Employee's Manager` list. You can keep refreshing the page until you see the additional columns filled with data via your custom action!

How It Works

In this Try It Out you saw the pattern for how to create a custom activity that can be surfaced in SharePoint Designer and reused across any number of workflows that you choose. In this case you created a reusable activity that, when handed an employee identification number, will retrieve a set of data about that employee. Although the implementation within this example was elementary, you could potentially navigate up the `ReportsTo` hierarchy by adding a looping structure to the workflow until the logical top of the organization structure is reached. You could also use the `ReportTo` to determine an employee's manager to make a manager's approval process more dynamic because any employee's manager can now be retrieved on demand.

In this exercise you also experienced using one of the very useful capabilities within the workflow: the dictionary object. The ability to have a complex data object handled seamlessly for you, so that all you need to do is know the path to the data elements helps you focus on solving the business problem at hand and eliminates the need to write the plumbing code, too.

Lastly, this exercise gave you a glimpse into the `.action4` file. This is the file used to configure the design-time presentation of the Action that will be used in SharePoint Designer. Documentation is still pending at the time of this writing on how exactly a developer can build out the XML for this file to create a compelling user experience for your custom designed actions.

Developing custom declarative activities is a way to provide workflow designers the design-time actions they need to build workflows quickly and efficiently. These actions can consolidate workflow structures into a single action that seems to be repetitively configured across workflows or encapsulates business logic for policy enforcement and compliance that can easily be placed on the design surface and configured. After developing them, you deploy SharePoint declarative activities as a `.wsp` SharePoint solution package. These can be uploaded to a solutions gallery in any site collection for use online or on-premises or managed with other farm-level solutions in on-premises installations.

WORKFLOW IN APPS FOR SHAREPOINT

For developers building Apps for SharePoint, whether SharePoint-hosted, Provider-hosted, or Autohosted, Visual Studio provides the tooling for including SharePoint workflows as a part of your solution. Therefore, you can augment your Apps for SharePoint with the workflow capabilities to encapsulate the business processes you want to deliver with your solutions.

In this Try It Out you learn to include a workflow in your app for SharePoint that shows a pattern for an expense approval workflow structure.

TRY IT OUT App for SharePoint with a Workflow (C15WFAppForSP.zip)

This exercise uses Office 365 but you can use your test on-premises SharePoint setup as well.

1. Run Visual Studio 2012 as Administrator. Select New Project.
2. In the New Project dialog, expand the Templates ➪ Visual C# ➪ Office/SharePoint ➪ Apps nodes. Select App for SharePoint 2013 and provide the name `C15WFAppForSP`. Click OK.
3. In the Specify the app for SharePoint dialog, set the SharePoint site URL to which you will deploy the app, and choose SharePoint-hosted as the host for your App for SharePoint. Click Finish.
4. In the Solution Explorer, right-click the project node, and select Add ➪ New item. In the Add New Item dialog, select Site Column, name it `Manager`, and click Add.
5. In the Solution Explorer, right-click the project node, and select Add ➪ New item. In the Add New Item dialog, select Site Column, name it `Disposition`, and click Add.
6. In the Solution Explorer, right-click the project node, and select Add ➪ New item. In the Add New Item dialog, select Site Column, name it `EmpNum`, and click Add.

7. Open the `Elements.xml` file for `EmpNum` and modify the following two attributes as follows:

```
Type="Integer"

Required="TRUE"
```

8. In the Solution Explorer, right-click the project node, and select Add ⇨ New item. In the Add New Item dialog, select Site Column, name it **ExpenseAmount**, and click Add.

9. Open the `Elements.xml` file for `ExpenseAmount` and modify the following two attributes as follows:

```
Type="Number"

Required="TRUE"
```

10. In the Solution Explorer, right-click the project node, and select Add ⇨ New item. In the Add New Item dialog, select List, name it **ListToHostWorkflow**, and click Add.

11. In the Choose List Settings dialog, leave the defaults, and click Finish.

12. In the List Designer, click Title, and type **Expense Description**. Leave it marked as required.

13. Additionally, in the List Designer, add the columns `Emp Num` and `Expense Amount` (make these required), and add `Disposition` and `Manager` (these two are not marked required; your workflow will populate these with values).

14. In Solution Explorer, expand the Pages node, and double-click the `Default.aspx` to open it. Add the following after the current `<p>...</p>` element on the page and prior to the `</div>` tag:

```
<p>
<a href="../Lists/ListToHostWorkflow"> 1) Create an expense
approval item in the List To Host Workflow</a>
</p>
```

15. Click Start to verify that the SharePoint list structure is all set up correctly and that it works up to this point.

16. In the Solution Explorer, right-click the project node, and select Add ⇨ New item. In the Add New Item dialog, select Workflow, name it **AppListWorkflow**, and click Add.

17. In the Specify the workflow name for debugging dialog, click Next.

18. In the "Select the lists you will use when debugging" make the following selections as indicated:

➤ The library or list to associate your workflow with: `ListToHostWorkflow`

➤ The history and task lists: `<Create New>`

Click Next.

19. In the Specify the conditions for how your workflow is started, select "A user manually starts the workflow" and "The workflow starts automatically when an item is created." Click Finish.

Figure 15-11 provides the high-level structure for this mock expense approval workflow. It shows in an app for SharePoint the pattern for how to get oriented to the context of the current list and item, retrieve data from the current item, and then use this data to bootstrap a lookup into an external system to retrieve additional data for use in the workflow process. The workflow you build here executes end to end, but the location where you would configure either a SingleTask or ComplexTask activity is stubbed in for reference; you will not configure one of these in this exercise.

20. In the Workflow Designer, click the title bar for the initial sequence and for its DisplayName type `Expense Approval`.

21. Click the `Expense Approval` sequence to select it. Click the Variables tab at the bottom of the designer and create the following variables (the scope for all will be `Expense Approval`):

➤ Name: `currentItemGuid` Type: `System.Guid`

➤ Name: `currentListId` Type: `System.Guid`

➤ Name: `EmployeeId` Type: `Int32`

➤ Name: `ManagerName` Type: `String`

➤ Name: `JsonResponse` Type: `DynamicValue`

➤ Name: `ReportsToWF` Type: `Int32`

➤ Name: `ExpenseAmt` Type: `Double`

FIGURE 15-11

22. From the Toolbox, drag a Control Flow, `Sequence` into the `Expense Approval` sequence, click its name and type, **Get current list ID and item**.

23. From the Toolbox, drag an SP - Current Context, `GetCurrentItemGuid` into the `Get current list ID and item` sequence, and for the Result property type **currentItemGuid**.

24. From the Toolbox, drag an SP - Current Context, `GetCurrentListId` into the `Get current list ID and item` sequence and place it under `GetCurrentItemGuid`; and in the Result property type: **currentListId**.

25. From the Toolbox, drag an SP - List Item, `LookupSPListItemProperty` into the `Get current list ID and item` sequence and place it under `GetCurrentListId`; complete the fields for the following properties:

➤ ItemGuid: `currentItemGuid`

➤ ListId: `ListToHostWorkflow`

➤ PropertyName: `Emp Num`

➤ PropertyType: `Int32`

➤ Result: **`EmployeeId`**

➤ DisplayName: **`LookupSP Emp Num`**

26. From the Toolbox, drag an SP - List Item, `LookupSPListItemProperty` into the `Get current list ID and item` sequence and place it under `LookupSP Emp Num`, and complete the fields for the following properties:

➤ ItemGuid: **`currentItemGuid`**

➤ ListId: `ListToHostWorkflow`

➤ PropertyName: `Expense Amount`

➤ PropertyType: `Double`

➤ Result: **`ExpenseAmt`**

➤ DisplayName: **`LookupSP Expense Amt`**

FIGURE 15-12

Your `Get current list ID and item` sequence should look like Figure 15-12 when completed.

27. From the Toolbox, drag a Control Flow, `Sequence` into the `Expense Approval` sequence, below the `Get current list ID and item` sequence, click its name and type, **`Retrieve Employee Info`**.

28. From the Toolbox, drag a Messaging, `HttpSend` into the `Retrieve Employee Info`, and complete the fields for the following properties:

➤ Method: `GET`

➤ URI (include quotes): `"http://services.odata.org/Northwind/Northwind.svc/Employees(" + EmployeeId + ")?$select=EmployeeID,LastName,FirstName,HomePhone,ReportsTo&$format=json"`

➤ ResponseContent: **`JsonResponse`**

➤ DisplayName: **`HttpSend for Emp Info`**

29. From the Toolbox, drag a DynamicValue, `GetDynamicValueProperty<T>` into the `Retrieve Employee Info`, and enter in the fields the following properties (when prompted, select `String`):

➤ PropertyName (include quotes): **`"d/LastName"`**

➤ Result: **`EmployeeName`**

➤ Source: **`JsonResponse`**

➤ DisplayName: **`Get Emp LastName <String>`**

30. From the Toolbox, drag a DynamicValue, `GetDynamicValueProperty<T>` into the `Retrieve Employee Info`, and enter in the fields for the following properties (when prompted, select `Int32`):

> PropertyName (include quotes): `"d/ReportsTo"`

> Result: `ReportsToWF`

> Source: `JsonResponse`

> DisplayName: `Get Emp ReportsTo <Int32>`

Your `Retrieve Employee Info` sequence should look like Figure 15-13 when completed.

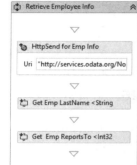

31. From the Toolbox, drag a Control Flow, `If` into the `Expense Approval` sequence, below the `Retrieve Employee Info` sequence, click its name, and type, `If block to determine if approval is needed.` For the Condition property type: `ExpenseAmt > 50`.

FIGURE 15-13

32. Configure the THEN block; from the Toolbox, drag a Control Flow, `Sequence`, click the name and type, `Manager Approval Required`.

33. From the Toolbox, drag a Control Flow, `Sequence` into the `Manager Approval Required` sequence, click its name and type, `Retrieve Manager Info`.

34. From the Toolbox, drag a Messaging, `HttpSend` into the `Retrieve Manager Info`, and complete the fields with the following properties:

> Method: `GET`

> URI (include quotes): `"http://services.odata.org/Northwind/Northwind.svc/Employees(" + ReportsToWF + ")?$select=EmployeeID,LastName,FirstName,HomePhone,ReportsTo&$format=json"`

> ResponseContent: `JsonResponse`

> DisplayName: `HttpSend for Manager Info`

35. From the Toolbox, drag a DynamicValue, `GetDynamicValueProperty<T>` into the `Retrieve Manager Info`, and enter in the fields the following properties (when prompted, select `String`):

> PropertyName (include quotes): `"d/LastName"`

> Result: `ManagerName`

> Source: `JsonResponse`

> DisplayName: `Get Manager LastName <String>`

36. From the Toolbox, drag a Control Flow, `If`, into the `Manager Approval Required` sequence, below the `Retrieve Manager Info` sequence, click its name, and type `Do Full Approval Task Here`. This is just a stub sequence for where you could implement a CompositeTask, SingleTask; simply send an e-mail; or call out to another service. Implementing the logic to meet the needs of your App for SharePoint is up to you.

37. From the Toolbox, drag a Control Flow, `If`, into the `Manager Approval Required` sequence, below the `Do Full Approval Task Here` sequence, click its name and type, **Update List Fields**.

38. From the Toolbox, drag an SP - Current Context, `SetField`, into the `Update List Fields` sequence, and complete the fields with the following properties:

> ➤ FieldName: Manager

> ➤ FieldValue: **ManagerName**

> ➤ DisplayName: **Set Manager Name**

39. From the Toolbox, drag an SP - Current Context, `SetField`, into the `Update List Fields` sequence, place it under the `Update List Fields`, and complete the fields with the following properties:

> ➤ FieldName: Disposition

> ➤ FieldValue, type (include quotes): **"Manager Approved"**

> ➤ DisplayName, type: **Set Manager Approved for Sample**

When completed, your THEN block containing the `Manager Approval Required` sequence should look like Figure 15-14.

40. Configure the ELSE block; from the Toolbox, drag a Control Flow, `Sequence`, click its name and type, **Automated Approval Process.**

41. From the Toolbox, drag a Control Flow, `Sequence`, into the `Automated Approval Process` sequence, click its name and type, **Possibly call a Web Service**. The point is that some expenses might be able to be automatically approved by an external business process. This is a stub for where that action could take place. External systems could be notified at this point to send notifications, transactions logged to meet audit and compliance policy, and so on.

FIGURE 15-14

42. From the Toolbox, drag an SP - Current Context, `SetField`, into the `Automated Approval Process` sequence, and complete the fields for the following properties:

> ➤ FieldName: Disposition

> ➤ FieldValue (include quotes): **"Auto Approved"**

> ➤ DisplayName: **Set Auto Approved**

When completed, your ELSE block containing the `Automated Approval Process` sequence should look like Figure 15-15.

43. If you have any other icon showing in your workflow other than the yellow icon with the exclamation point, right-click the project and select Rebuild. If this doesn't clean them all up, then double-click each one in the Error List pane to troubleshoot.

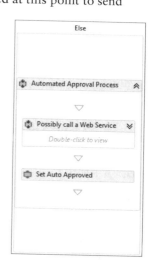

FIGURE 15-15

44. Right-click the project and select Deploy. If you are using Office 365 to develop this solution, then the workflow debugger cannot run against a remote server. If you press F5, you will be prompted to turn off the debugger for this solution, which is your choice. In either case, navigate to the site you developed against, click Site Contents, and click the tile for `C15WFAppForSP`.

45. Your app for SharePoint opens on the `Default.aspx` page with the link to your workflow list. Follow the link.

46. On the ListToHostWorkflow page, click New item and enter the following properties into the fields:

> ➤ Expense Description: **Purchased some office supplies**

> ➤ Emp Num (must be a valid Northwind EmployeeID) : **1**

> ➤ Expense Amount: **10**

Click Save. Keep refreshing the browser until the workflow completes.

47. Click to add another new item and enter the following properties into the fields:

> ➤ Expense Description: **Purchased some software**

> ➤ Emp Num (must be a valid Northwind EmployeeID): **3**

> ➤ Expense Amount: **250**

Click Save. Keep refreshing the browser until the workflow completes. Your result should look similar to Figure 15-16.

FIGURE 15-16

How It Works

This Try It Out showed you how to build in a workflow as an integral component in your App for SharePoint solution. You learned how to get the context of the current list and item being processed from within the Visual Studio design-time environment. This is one of the foundational principles that you will continue to use as your expertise broadens. After you have a context, you can look up any of the properties on the item. You also experienced how to set property values. In building out this workflow, you'll have noticed that in the Visual Studio environment you work at a lower level when building the workflow than you did in SPD. That's because the activities in the Visual Studio toolbox are used to compose the actions exposed in SPD. In Visual Studio you work with the base activities themselves. However, this is the only way to include a workflow in an app for SharePoint. App-level workflows must be built with Visual Studio; SPD cannot build workflows against an AppWeb, only a host Web.

Apps for SharePoint developers have the robust capabilities of the Visual Studio Workflow Designer in their toolkit for building business processes, of almost any scope, into their solutions. Developers can also have confidence that whatever they develop, their workflows can run at scale via the Workflow Manager Service online or the Workflow Manager Server on-premises.

SUMMARY

In SharePoint 2013, workflow has been decoupled from the SharePoint server and runs as the Workflow Manager Server in on-premises installations and as Workflow Manager Service in the cloud. The new workflow engine is written according to the new cloud app model architecture, leveraging the REST _API to call back into SharePoint via the OAuth protocol and employing Windows Azure Service Bus to provide its messaging framework and durable event management.

The tools the business analyst, SharePoint subject matter expert, and developer continue to use are Visio Professional, SharePoint Designer, and Visual Studio, respectively, but these tools sport a host of new features for building workflows. Visual Studio can be used to build custom actions that can be installed into SPD to provide additional productivity gains for those creating workflows.

Lastly, workflows fit very comfortably inside your Apps for SharePoint. Those who are skilled at developing workflows in Visual Studio can build workflows around very common business process scenarios, package them up as an app, and get them into the SharePoint Store on Office.com. Also, because these workflows are XAML-based, they can run equally well both on-premises and on Office 365.

EXERCISES

Answers to Exercises can be found in Appendix A.

1. What role does the Windows Azure Service Bus play in the new Workflow Manager?

2. What action is provided in SharePoint Designer that allows the workflow to do something within SharePoint on behalf of the user, where the user would not have the permissions?

3. What is the new variable type in SPD that allows you to store and process complex data such as a JSON object?

4. In an app for SharePoint workflow, what activity do you use to retrieve the GUID of the current item being processed?

▶ WHAT YOU LEARNED IN THIS CHAPTER

ITEM	DESCRIPTION
Workflow Manager	This is the new workflow engine that hosts workflows and runs as a server on-premises and as a service in Windows Azure.
Visio Professional 2013	Visio has a new `.VSDX` XML-based file structure that SharePoint Designer can natively read. The need no longer exists for the `.VWI` interchange file between these two products. This provides a new portability option for exporting full workflows out of SPD into the `.VSDX` file, and then importing them into any other SPD site or back into Visio for further work by a business analyst.
SharePoint Designer 2013	A new Visual Designer was added to SPD along with many new actions that make workflow design much more person-process oriented rather than a linear top-to-bottom flow.
Apps for SharePoint	Workflows are also first-class participants in Apps for SharePoint and can be delivered as a part of a solution into the SharePoint Store.

RECOMMENDED READING

SharePoint 2013 workflow fundamentals — `http://msdn.microsoft.com/en-us/library/jj163181%28v=office.15%29.aspx`.

Answers To Exercises

CHAPTER 1 ANSWERS TO EXERCISES

Exercise 1 Solution

For the end user and the developer, SharePoint is a Web-based collaboration platform for the enterprise and Web. As an end user, you will natively leverage SharePoint to manage your collaborative tasks. As a developer, you will build apps to enhance the end user's experience to help support different types of scenarios.

Exercise 2 Solution

You can use default SharePoint apps, such as document libraries, lists, and so on. And you can build custom Apps for SharePoint, such as Web parts, event receivers, workflow apps, and so on.

Exercise 3 Solution

Excel Services, Business Connectivity Services, Machine Translation Services, and Access Services are examples.

Exercise 4 Solution

Server-side object model and client-side object model. You use the server-side object model when building applications in SharePoint Server or SharePoint Foundation. You can use the client-side object model for any version of SharePoint.

Exercise 5 Solution

Work through creating a new site collection using the exercises in the chapter to help guide you. Navigate to your SharePoint administration page and click New ⇨ Private Site Collection. Complete the information in the New Site Collection dialog and as you do, ensure you select the Team Site template in the Collaboration tab. Click OK to create, and once created you can click Site Contents to add lists, document libraries, and other apps.

CHAPTER 2 ANSWERS TO EXERCISES

Exercise 1 Solution

SharePoint-hosted, Autohosted, and Provider-hosted.

Exercise 2 Solution

Any Web stack.

Exercise 3 Solution

You can find an example of this in the SharePoint 2013 SDK. See Chapter 2, "Recommended Reading."

CHAPTER 3 ANSWERS TO EXERCISES

Exercise 1 Solution

Visual Studio, SharePoint Designer, and Napa. You can also use tools like Expression Blend for rich design and Fiddler for debugging and tracing.

Exercise 2 Solution

You would use Visual Studio for managed code development and development that requires ALM or source code control. Napa is for rapid development and prototyping — but the code can also be imported into Visual Studio. You use SharePoint Designer for creating, editing and updating Web pages, content types, and so on. You can also use SharePoint Designer for creating rules-based workflow.

Exercise 3 Solution

Open Visual Studio, and click File ⇨ New Project. Select the Empty SharePoint Project template and then add a SharePoint site URL and select Farm-Level trust for your project. Then, Add a web part project to your empty SharePoint project. Add some simple controls to your Web Part, and then add a breakpoint somewhere in your newly added code. Enter F5 to test and debug the code.

CHAPTER 4 ANSWERS TO EXERCISES

Exercise 1 Solution

Using Visual Studio 2012, you can create an Empty SharePoint project. Using the Empty SharePoint project as a shell project, you can then add two items to the project: a Standard Web Part and a Visual Web Part. After you've done this, add the code from this chapter to create the simple Web Parts. You can hit F6 to build the project, and then deploy the project to your SharePoint site. Both of your Web Parts will be deployed to your SharePoint site, and you'll be able to use them separately.

Exercise 2 Solution

You can continue to use the SharePoint project that you used in the first exercise (the project to which you added the two Web Parts), or you can create a new one. Either way, add a new item that is an ASPX Page and then add some simple HTML to the page (for example, `<DIV>Hello World!</DIV>`). After you've completed this, hit F6 to build the project and then deploy to SharePoint.

Exercise 3 Solution

You can create your own Master Page, or you can download a Minimal Master Page or Starter Master Page. The Minimal Master Page is the most basic Master Page that you can use with SharePoint. You can find information about how to create a Minimal Master Page here: `http://msdn.microsoft.com/en-us/library/aa660698(v=office.12).aspx`. A Starter Master Page has some additional elements beyond the Minimal Master Page, and these are typically created by the SharePoint community. One example is here: `http://startermasterpages.codeplex.com/`. Once you've downloaded either of these, use SharePoint Designer to create a new Master page, copy and paste the contents of either the minimal or starter page, and then save to your SharePoint site. You can then set the new Master page as the default Master Page using SharePoint Designer, and your new Master page will take effect.

CHAPTER 5 ANSWERS TO EXERCISES

Exercise 1 Solution

IAAS, PAAS, and SAAS.

Exercise 2 Solution

Cloud Services, Media Services, Data Services, Web Sites, Data Sync, Hadoop on Azure.

Exercise 3 Solution

Autohosted and Provider-hosted.

Exercise 4 Solution

First, create a new SharePoint project (targeting an Office 365 Developer site) and set the project to be Autohosted as you create the project. This provides you with the basic plumbing of an ASP.NET application that you can natively deploy to Office 365 (and of course Windows Azure). After you've created the Autohosted application, you can leverage the REST service project you built at the beginning of Chapter 5 or recreate it within the same solution you just created. Either way, deploy the REST service to Windows Azure. After you've deployed, you now have a REST endpoint that you can call to use the data that is returned from that service endpoint. You can now add a simple Button control and event to call the REST service to show that you can retrieve the data. Keep it simple to understand the data structure that is returned, such that you can build out the application to leverage the data.

CHAPTER 6 ANSWERS TO EXERCISES

Exercise 1 Solution

The new SharePoint application model removes code from running within the core SharePoint processes and moves it externally to another host. The new model provides the APIs for authenticating and calling back to SharePoint for data and responding to events.

Exercise 2 Solution

The SharePoint application model provides the following three areas for integration:

➤ User Interface

➤ Data

➤ Events

Exercise 3 Solution

A Web Part's code is run and rendered by code running in the SharePoint process. An App Part is an iFrame whose contents are rendered on another server.

Exercise 4 Solution

An application's permissions are granted when the application is installed. The user installing the application may accept or decline the invitation to grant the permissions the app is asking for.

Exercise 5 Solution

SharePoint applications can use the provided "Chrome Control" and reference provided style sheets to adopt the same visual styling as SharePoint sites.

CHAPTER 7 ANSWERS TO EXERCISES

Exercise 1 Solution

The four main components of an .app package are the manifest file, the SharePoint solution, the Web deploy package and the database package.

Exercise 2 Solution

In a Provider-hosted application the developer of the application is responsible for running the application code himself. This means the SharePoint application package contains the SharePoint solution and manifest only. The code portion of the solution runs wherever the developer hosts it, such as in Azure.

Exercise 3 Solution

Only two types of components are allowed to be deployed to the host Web during installation of an app: App Parts and Custom UI Actions.

CHAPTER 8 ANSWERS TO EXERCISES

Exercise 1 Solution

Provider-hosted apps need a manually created client ID and secret prior to submission to the store so that the developer can add them to the application's back-end code so that the app is running when it is tested by Microsoft.

Exercise 2 Solution

There are many options for monetizing applications. However, some of the most common are to make the application a paid for product through the store, add ads to the application, and sell in-app purchases in the application.

Exercise 3 Solution

An application can catch any of the following application life-cycle events: App Installed, App Uninstalling, or App Upgraded.

CHAPTER 9 ANSWERS TO EXERCISES

Exercise 1 Solution

The three types of CSOM libraries are: .NET Managed, JavaScript and Windows Phone/Silverlight.

Exercise 2 Solution

OData adds additional filter and query capabilities over and above what is available with the standard REST capabilities.

Exercise 3 Solution

REST and OData support in SharePoint 2013 provides support for Creating, Reading, Updating, and Deleting data.

Exercise 4 Solution

By using the provided CSOM libraries, developers can take advantage of the prebuilt batching capabilities to reduce the number and frequency of calls made to SharePoint.

CHAPTER 10 ANSWERS TO EXERCISES

Exercise 1 Solution

Using either SharePoint Online or SharePoint on premises you can create new application identities using the AppRegNew.aspx page.

Exercise 2 Solution

The three token types used in SharePoint's OAuth flow are the context token, access token and refresh token.

Exercise 3 Solution

When needed, an application may elevate its permissions to those of just the application by using the `GetAppOnlyAccessToken` helper method to generate an app-only access token.

Exercise 4 Solution

The refresh token and access tokens can both be cached. The period for which they can be cached should be determined by looking at the expiry date and time passed back from SharePoint for each.

CHAPTER 11 ANSWERS TO EXERCISES

Exercise 1 Solution

Apps for Office can be written using standard Web technologies hosted on any platform and written in any language.

Exercise 2 Solution

The new JSOM for Office allows the developer's Web application to interact with the document or mail item, but does not provide for automation of the Office client.

Exercise 3 Solution

MailApp, TaskPaneApp, and ContentApp.

Exercise 4 Solution

You can use various strategies enabled by a number of methods on the `Office.context`
`.document.bindings` object such as `.addFromSelectionAsync`, `.AddFromPromptAsync`, and
`.AddFromNamedItemAsync`.

CHAPTER 12 ANSWERS TO EXERCISES

Exercise 1 Solution

`ProcessOneWayEvent`

Exercise 2 Solution

Enumeration, `.CancelWithError` and property, and `.ErrorMessage`.

Exercise 3 Solution

S2S and OAuth.

Exercise 4 Solution

You can actually look in two places. One is in the manifest file, and the other is checking to see whether any one of the app life-cycle properties of the SharePoint project is set to `True`.

CHAPTER 13 ANSWERS TO EXERCISES

Exercise 1 Solution

OData.

Exercise 2 Solution

CSOM or REST.

Exercise 3 Solution

`EventSubscriber` and `EventUnsubscriber`.

Exercise 4 Solution

ECTs can now be deployed as part of an app for SharePoint at the app-level whether the app is Provider-hosted, Autohosted, or SharePoint-hosted.

CHAPTER 14 ANSWERS TO EXERCISES

Exercise 1 Solution

PowerPoint Automation Services and Machine Translation Services.

Exercise 2 Solution

The Office Web App Server.

Exercise 3 Solution

OData.

Exercise 4 Solution

For an on-premises installation of SharePoint, the data and content are stored in a SQL Server database and for Office 365 they are stored in a Windows Azure SQL Database.

CHAPTER 15 ANSWERS TO EXERCISES

Exercise 1 Solution

The Service Bus provides durability for event delivery and for messaging using its Pub/Sub pattern.

Exercise 2 Solution

The App Step action lets the workflow elevate its permissions to perform something on behalf of the user with its own permissions.

Exercise 3 Solution

The Dictionary type variable.

Exercise 4 Solution

GetCurrentItemGuid.

INDEX

P

Q

R

T